The Future of Innovation

The Silicon Valley Way

"Those who dare to fail miserably can achieve greatly."

John F. Kennedy

Henri Swan

Author, Innovator, Entrepreneur, Investor, Speaker, and Lecturer

"The advice, insights, and execution strategies found within may not be suitable for everyone or any situation. This work is sold with the understanding that neither the author nor the publisher be held responsible for the results accrued from the advice in this book "

This book may be purchased for educational, business, or sales promotional use. For more information, please visit or contact us here: wwwTheInnovator.us

New Ventures Press, Silicon Valley

Library of Congress Control Number: 2022900311

Independently published.
ISBN/SKU:9798-3484-8-5917

INTRODUCTION

We face pressing challenges. Eco-degradation, diseases, and new risks brought by the misaligned resources spent on bad innovation that challenged human development.

The solution lies in leveraging breakthroughs in technologies and sciences and a paradigm shift in venture funding, propelled by the fourth industrial revolution, enabling equitable and sustainable innovation models. Moreover, the nature of the innovation-driven development model demands a worldwide assessment and reshaping of leading innovation hubs, urgently of great relevance to ensure a better tomorrow.

We are at the dawn of business management's first century. It is our challenge to capture the opportunity we have been given to ensure that those of us who seek to build the next big thing will have the how-to they need to impact the world positively, across tech, health, and science-based innovation.

This book aligns entrepreneurship, innovation, investment, and exit to a rigorous footing, through emerging and proven practices, perfected by Silicon Valley's pioneers. It is a must-have walkthrough "*blueprint for founders seeking to launch, fund, grow or exit their startup*"; along with investor, engineer, product developer; corporate "innovation, investment or acquisition leader", advisor, and academic lecturer; in need of expanding their horizons, on taking to market innovation with impact.

It is an ideal reference manual, based on first-hand insider scope of thought leadership, packed with research from top tier institutions with actionable insights on startup, corporate innovation, and venture capital ecosystem showcasing a 360-degree cycle of innovation execution "*masterfully crafted in a single volume of 400 pages with over 100 illustrated graphs and charts*".

This volume leverages the experience of prominent innovators by capturing past, current, and projected future innovation, with deep dive into how innovation happens through each stage, and what to do or not to do during its execution. This shall be a prime source for anyone eager to understand or excel in innovation or venture capital.

DEDICATION

To the pioneer of Modern Tech and Scientific Innovation

-------o-o-o-o-o-------

"The scientists of today think deeply instead of clearly. One must be sane to think clearly, but one can think deeply and be quite insane."
Nikola Tesla

-------o-o-o-o-o-------

"One never notices what has been done; one can only see what remains to be done". Two Nobel Laureate ***Marie Curie***

-------o-o-o-o-o-------

"If I had asked the public what they wanted, they would have said a faster horse". ***Henry Ford***

-------o-o-o-o-o-------

"Imagination is more important than knowledge". ***Albert Einstein***

-------o-o-o-o-o-------

"If I have a thousand ideas and only one turns out to be good, I am satisfied". ***Alfred Nobel***

-------o-o-o-o-o-------

"A pile of rocks ceases to be a rock pile when somebody contemplates it with the idea of a cathedral in mind". ***Antoine Saint-Exupéry***

-------o-o-o-o-o-------

"Innovation distinguishes between a leader and a follower." ***Steve Jobs***

-------o-o-o-o-o-------

"Instead of thinking outside the box, get rid of the box."
Deepak Chopra

-------o-o-o-o-o-------

"Women In Science Can Also Have Impact":
Nobel Laureate ***Emmanuelle Charpentier***

CONTENTS 1 - 3

CONTENTS 2 - 3

CONTENTS 3 - 3

An eBook version is available globally at major bookstores and recommended with this print edition to enable the zooming of color graphs.

PREFACE

Our media perpetuate a myth that entrepreneurs are born not made, by glorifying prominent innovators like Gates, Jobs, and Bezos; because they possess a superior sense of predicting the future, visualize a product then build it "like a master chef" performing masterful skill in front of your eyes.

This book will replace the entrepreneur myth with practical key steps from converting ideas into product vision and then iterating through sustainable startups with revenues and growth till exit. Enabling anyone to be an entrepreneur, as long you are driven, flexible, and a fast learner located anywhere in this world.

We will exclude the business school elaborate theories that had no relevance outside academia or large organization designed for the industrial era and focus on execution based on collective intelligence learned in Silicon Valley through years of execution by dealing, investing, and advising 1000's startup, along top venture capital investors, Fortune 500 acquirers and Unicorn Exit.

To innovate, you do not need an MBA, Ph.D., or 10 years in R&D labs; rather a curious mind, a thirst to impact the world positively "not changing it" and the drive to make it happen no matter what.

Start by assessing your ***passion*** and desire to improve one product or service by 3X or more, that you happen to use or consume, then connect your vision to your skills, ability, and how you can disrupt a whole industry that becomes your ***purpose***.

Innovation is not about a Startup that is worth billions through financial engineering but fails to sustain itself without new investments, monopolistic acquisition by market dominant players, or the false narrative of "changing the world" spread by certain business schools "since the world cannot improve without their elite's technocrat analyst and must depend on them to do so".

Instead, the world as we know it today is made of collective innovation accumulated through millions of years and copied, improved, and scaled by successive civilizations and dynasties which will be discussed further.

This book is about bringing clarity and transparency into the knowledge economy and helping accelerate its evolution further, by *democratizing innovation execution* and thought leadership, accessing actionable insights to level the playing field and help shape the current and future generation of innovators from across the world on how to execute incremental improvement to the human lives and solve pressing global challenges of our times.

Each chapter will take a deep dive into past, current, and future state projection and how to contribute or capitalize on each stage of future human evolution through disruptive innovation that solves pressing challenges "instead of creating new ones".

And help avoid the repeat of the Covid-19 disaster that affected and impacted the human species in every aspect, and proven in a very harsh way, how vulnerable and unprotected we are against a virus iteration known to us for centuries as "seasonal flu"; even with perceived access to information "i.e., unfiltered web" that's causing more harm than good.

CHAPTER I
INNOVATION TIMELINE

Innovation through "*Necessity as a mother of innovation*" started million years ago by first humans and evolved with civilizations, courage, sacrifice, and the need to improve and safeguard human beings, making our modern life possible.

Ancient to Middle Ages Era: helped shape the foundation of modern life from ancient times through the Middle age.

Prehistoric Era: 10m years to 10,000 years BC

- Tools: hand made of stones, and bones to hint and self-protect
- Fire: discovered and integrated into food and materials making
- Boat: built using tools, fire, and wood to sail, ship, and discover

Ancient Time Era: 9,999 to 3,200 years BC.

- Agriculture: settlement of large groups within the tribes to farm
- Iron and Glass: invented and incorporated into a daily lifestyle.
- Wheel: invented by perfecting tools and materials to haul things

Egyptian Era: 3150 to 332 years BC

- Building: cut large stones, with a water channel as a transporter
- Paper: papyrus which is the early version of our modern paper
- Language: Africans created a first dialect through hieroglyphics

Greek Empire: 800 to 146 years BC.

- Bridge: first arch bridge and the foundation of modern bridges
- Algebra: first books solving equations with the Greek numbers
- Computing: invented analog prediction of lunar-solar eclipses

Roman Empire: 600 BC to 400 years AD.

- Concrete: mixed material used to build road and sewer systems
- Turbine: first vertical water wheel for clean energy propulsion
- Books: handwritten manuscripts used as newspapers or books

African Civilization: 200 BC to 100 years AD.

- Commerce: first import of goods from tropical areas to Africa
- Textile: craft gradually evolved from East Asia to the West
- Navy Fleet: First developed by a Carthaginian in North Africa.

Indian Civilization: 500 BC to 100 years AD.

- Number: Indian ancestor to the Arabic number used globally
- Cotton: cultivation and incorporation into clothing and house

- Weighting: created & used first scale to weigh gem and gold

Arab Civilization: 200 BC to 1200 years AD.

- Robot: invented early automation with feedback mechanisms
- Surgery: crafted a first science-based medical-surgical practice
- Flying: invented the first working prototype to gravitate and fly

Chinese Civilization: 1050 BC to 1280 AD

- Eyeglass: developed the first magnifying eye lens for reading
- Money: led the first conversion from gold coin to paper money
- Compass: first used for a building layout and ships navigation

Native American Civilization: 1800 BC to 1492 years AD.

- Rubber: first developed and used to sustain various daily needs
- Syringes: made of sharp animal bones to inject herbal medicine
- Binaries Digit: Maya Civilization where the first to use a 0 & 1

Persian Civilization: 10 BC to 1500 years AD.

- Calendar: first used solar number of days per year calculation
- Canal: built the water irrigation with its management system
- Battery: the chemical discovery was initially used for medicine

Jewish Civilization: 2000 BC to 1500 years AD.

- Astronomy: Defined Science leading to Exploratory Discovery
- Medicine: Crafted autopsy, diseases discovery including cholera
- Education: gradually advanced secular domain and its methods

Christian Civilization: 100 to 1500 years AD.

- Military: Led advance in the defense and offense technologies
- Patents: created foundation method to protect inventors' right
- Trade: Enabled progress in Agriculture, Shipping, and Banking

Islamic Civilization: 800 to 1500 years AD.

- University: the first university was in Morocco, see (Guinness)
- Sciences: led a major discovery in mathematics and sciences
- Arts: Led Advance in architecture, literature, poetry, and music

The widespread use of Latin in Europe offered an integrated market for ideas, a network of educated innovators, in which new ideas were distributed and circulated. The structure of the medieval Christian Church also became an enabler throughout the continent which was called 'Christendom'. In early modern Europe, national boundaries mattered little for the active and mobile community of intellectuals. Despite slow and uncomfortable travel between kingdoms.

Modern Age Revolutions: helped shape the foundation of innovation during the last 500 years.

Agriculture Revolution: 16th to mid 17th Century

- Crop Rotation: the use of the same soil for a multi-harvesting.
- Ownership: landowners evolved from solo to group with scale
- Farming: scaled from manual labor to horses and big machines

  Featured Contributing Countries:
  1. Refrigeration (Perishable Food): US, Fertilizers: Germany
  2. Perfection of horse-drawn seed press across the world
  3. New Crops growth: potato, maize in Europe, chocolate in Mexico, coffee in Yemen, and clementine in Algeria.

Industrial Revolution: 17th Century to mid-19th Century.

- Propulsion: Traction generated by the water and steam energy
- Machine: handmade production transition into manufacturing
- Steel: by converting the iron through a scaled chemicals process

  Featured Contributing Countries:
  1. Electricity: Nikola Tesla (Serbia), Generation (Edison), US
  2. Microwave: Bangladesh, made by France, Germany, UK
  3. Combustion Engine: first by French & German Inventor

Technical Revolution: 1940 to 1970s

- Automation: manufacturing & shipping across large industries
- Electronics: the incorporation of sensors into various hardware
- Communication: human to human, and machine to machine

  Featured Contributing Countries:
  1. Assembly Line: Large scale at low cost first by Ford, USA
  2. GPS: Global Positioning Satellite, Developed by NASA
  3. Telephone: The First long distance calls made in Belgium

Digital Revolution: 1980s to 2000s

- The Computing: Foundation of all modern software languages
- Server: evolved from mainframe by IBM to portable storage
- The Web: first human-to-machine interaction as read/write.

  Featured Contributing Countries:
  1. Computer: The Universal Computing Machine 1936, UK
  2. Internet: Minitel by Telecom France 1980, CSN, US 1981
  3. Mobile Phone: First East / West call - Motorola 1984, US

Twenty-Century Tech Innovation: the most impactful technology innovation that helped shape the foundation of modern tech by Industry, innovators, and country are:

- Data:
  - Open Sources: computing languages/storage servers
  - Real-Time Processing: For Video, Audio, and Text
  - Human Languages Processing: ML AI and QC
- Software:
  - Live data processing: ERP, Transaction, eCommerce
  - Cloud Computing: Open Nebula NASA, Edge, USA
  - VoIP: Replaced a long-distance call, first by "Skype"
- Hardware:
  - Storage drives: Flash Drive: 800X the 1.44 MB Disk
  - Mobile Computing: Blackberry, Canada, iPhone USA
  - Robotics: First Human-like Robot "Android – Japan"
- Network:
  - Authentication: IP, ID, Directory, SSO, Blockchain
  - Connection: Hi-Speed Internet, Wi-Fi, and Hotspot
  - Bluetooth: connecting hardware, software & devices.

Notable Innovators by Country:

- Mac: Apple inc, by Steve Job, US with (Syrian Father)
- C# Language: EU, Anders Hejlsberg from Denmark
- 3G Mobile Network: Asia, was first by NTT in Japan

Notable Companies by Country:

- IBM, Microsoft, America Online, Yahoo, HP, USA
- Blackberry, Canada
- Nokia, Finland - Olivetti, Italy, Philips, Netherlands
- Panasonic, Sony, Japan

Demographic Adoption of Portable Technology:

Internet: 147 million in 1998 (Top Countries: US, Japan, UK)
Computer Users in 1999: (US: 50%, Europe-Japan: 25%)
Mobile Users in 99 (300m: US: 86m, Europe: 55m, Japan 45m)

2021: Total users with access to all three are 7 billion +.

Silicon Valley Emergence: Its name is driven from the "silicon" used in transistors and computer chips, pioneered in the region during the semiconductor startup era in the 1950s, while "valley" was the precursor of its geography as the orchard farming capital of the world in the 19th century.

A powerful sense of regional solidarity accompanied the rise of Silicon Valley to build a self-sustained economy away from the perceived exploitation of the West at the hands of Eastern interests, which began with the industrialist named Leland Stanford donation of today's equivalent of $1 Billion to launch a university in the 1890s called Stanford University. This enabled Silicon Valley to evolve from farmlands to a science research base housed in the area by subsequent universities, along with generous U.S. Department of Defense spending on innovation sustained with seed investments from angel investors and early founders who become wealthy, of the semiconductor startup era exits.

In 1951, Stanford University's dean of engineering school, Frederick Terman, enabled the creation of its Industrial Park (now called Stanford Research Park) located next to the campus and encouraged faculty and student to launch their startup, some became today's titans such as Hewlett-Packard (HP), and later Google (Alphabet). Propelling Silicon Valley growth to an area over 50 miles of industrial and office park (including San Francisco), which host the most valuable global Fortune 500 companies, including Apple, Salesforce, Uber, Robinhood, Tesla, and many more.

Silicon Valley is in Northern California in the southern part of the San Francisco Bay Area, roughly the geographical Santa Clara Valley, it starts from San Jose and extends north to Redwood City, and includes these counties (Santa Clara, San Mateo), which include these cities, San Jose, Sunnyvale, Santa Clara, Cupertino, Los Altos, Los Altos Hills, Mountain View, Palo Alto, East Palo Alto, Menlo Park, Portola Valley, Woodside, and Redwood City.

According to Brookings Institution, the San Jose Metro Area has the third-highest GDP per capita in the world (after Zurich, Switzerland, and Oslo, Norway) and has the highest percentage in the US of homes valued at $1 million +.

Area: San Jose - Redwood City: 24 miles (1900 Square Miles
Population: 3 million - Jobs: 1.5 million - Avg. Salary: $150k
GDP Global Rank: $1 Trillion, #3 after Zurich and Oslo

Residents by Birthplace and Education

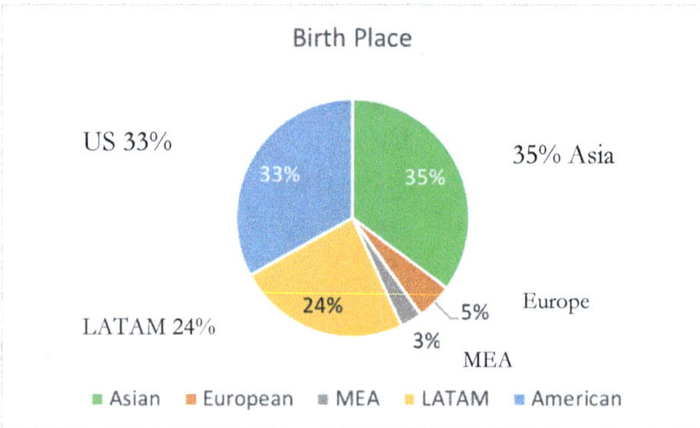

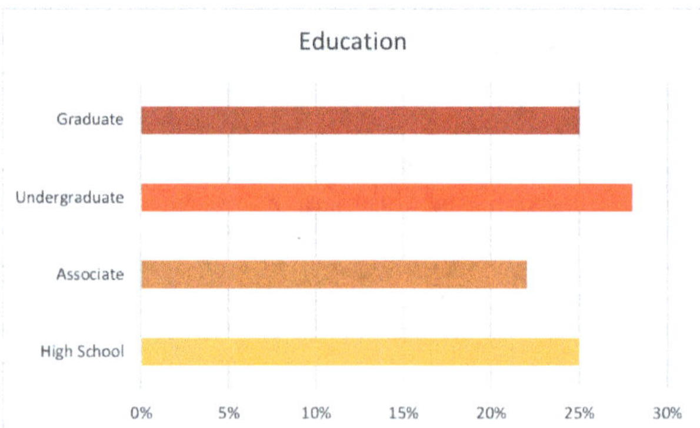

Source: US Census Bureau

Innovation Timeline

Residents by Age Group

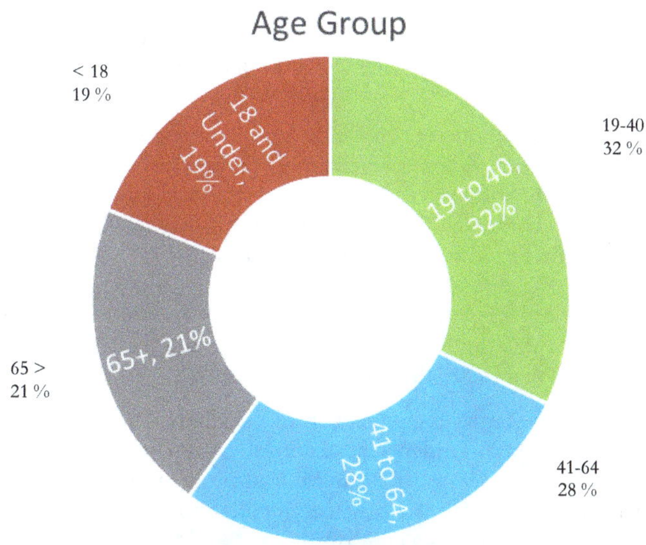

Data Source: United States Census Bureau, American Community Survey

Notable Events:

1909 FTC launched a first global radio-transmitted communication.
1953 William Shokley 1 developed a first semiconductor transistor.
1957 Mohamed Atella 2 miniaturized the transistor for mass usage.
1963 Licklider 3, enabled the foundation of Computer Science field.
1968 Doug Engelbart 4, developed a first Computer Mouse at SRI
1971 Intel developed first commercial single-chip microprocessor.
1972 Kleiner Perkins and Sequoia 5, launch of the first V.C Funds

1 William Shockley and Co-founder Frederick Terman are called "the father of Silicon Valley". Eight engineers left him to form Fairchild Semiconductor; Two of them founded later Intel Corporation.

2 Mohamed Atella of Egypt started the Silicon Revolution, by enabling the integration of transistors into microprocessors and portable computer CPUs (Central Processing Unit).

3 Licklider launched a computer science department at local universities. In 1969, Stanford Research Institute (now SRI International), operated one of the four ARPANET, a predecessor to the Internet.

4 First computer mouse demo was shared in 1968, becoming known as The Mother of All Demos.

5 Funded from the early exit by Fairchild's eight co-founders. The venture capital investments become a profession after the $1.3 billion IPO Exit of Apple in 1980. Leading Silicon Valley to become a home for the largest concentration of venture capital firms in the world.

Although semiconductors are still a major component of the area's economy, Silicon Valley has been most famous in recent years for innovations in software and Internet services and has significantly influenced computer operating systems, software, and user interfaces that produced top industry leaders such as:

1977 Oracle: Larry Ellison founded Oracle Corporation with Bob Miner and Ed Oates to sell business software and hardware, which grew to a global leader through acquisitions.

1996 Google: Started as a research project by Larry Page and Sergey Brin (both Ph.D. students at Stanford University) with "third founder", Scott Hassan, the original lead programmer who wrote much of the code for the original Google Search engine but left before it was formed as a company.

2011 Zoom: Founded by Eric Yuan, a former vice president for Cisco Webex. In 2012, the company signed Stanford University as its first customer due to its ease of use. The company had trouble finding investors because many thought the video conferencing market was already saturated, still, the service was publicly launched in January 2013 and reached 400,000 users in its first month, by May 2013 it had 1 million users. In April 2020, daily users ballooned to more than 200 million (filling the gaps among difficult-to-use peers' services and remote workers' urgent needs during the global confinement caused by Covid-19).

Key Metrics from Local Tech Companies with Global Reach: Users: 5 billion +, Customers: 2 billion +, Revenues: $1 Trillion +, Valuation: $4 Trillion +, Cash in Bank: $500 Billion +, Employees: 500,000.

Housing Cost

Nearly 30% of Silicon Valley households cannot afford it without assistance.

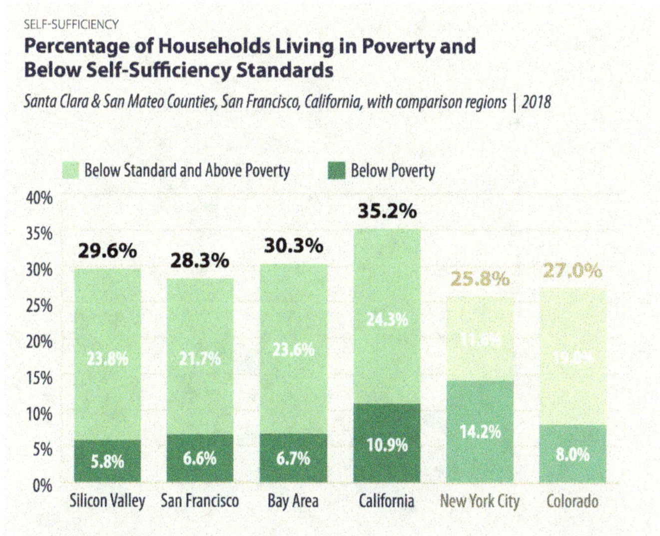

Poor Air Quality: EPA, Outdoor Air Quality Data | Institute for Regional Studies

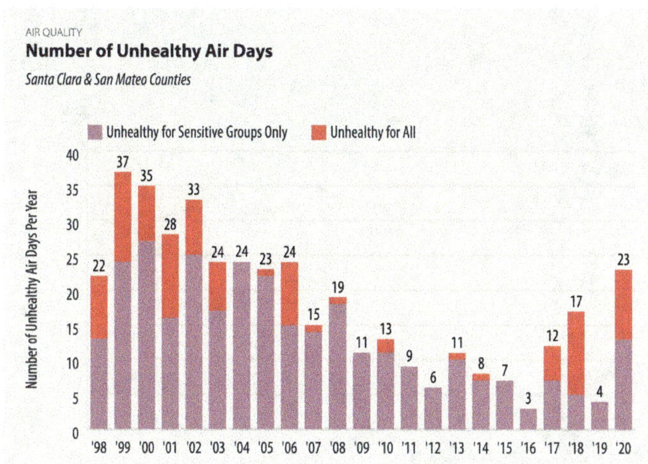

Talent Area: CBRE 2020 Scoring Tech Talent | Institute for Regional Studies

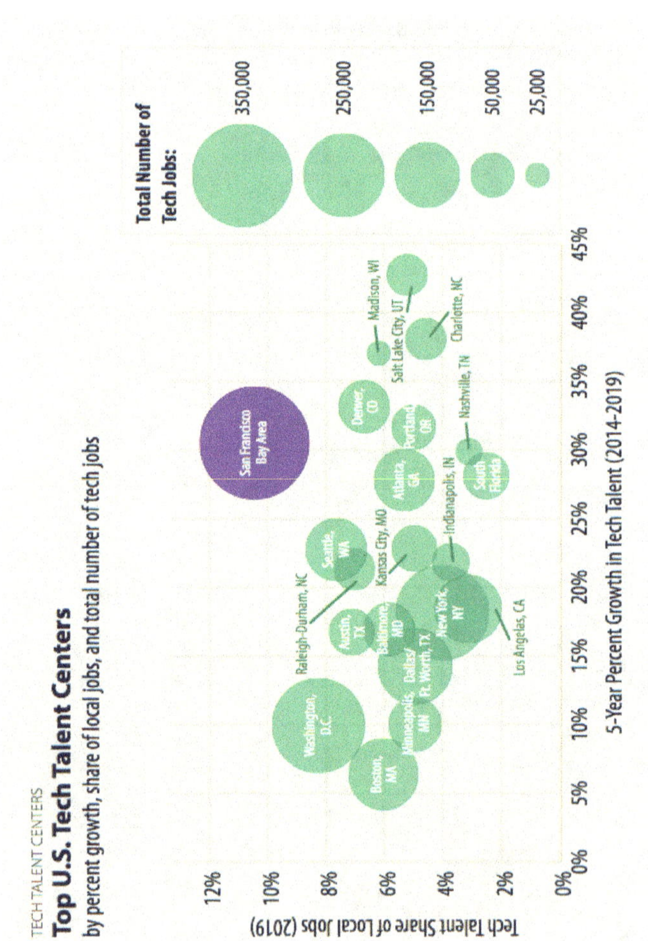

Jobs by Sector: BW Research; U.S. Bureau of Labor Statistics; LinkedIn

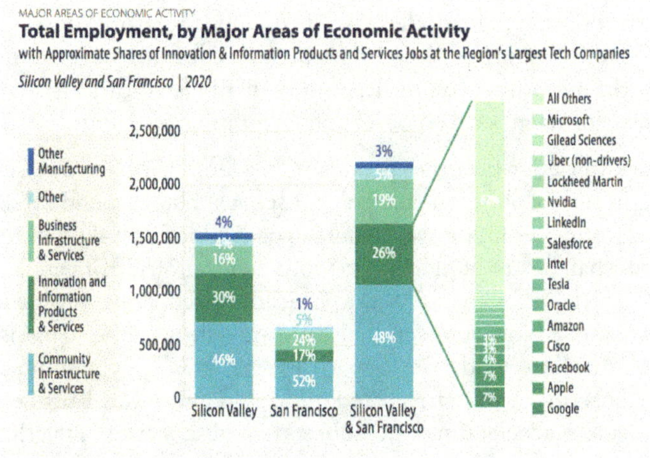

New Startup Growth: Crunchbase | SV Institute for Regional Studies

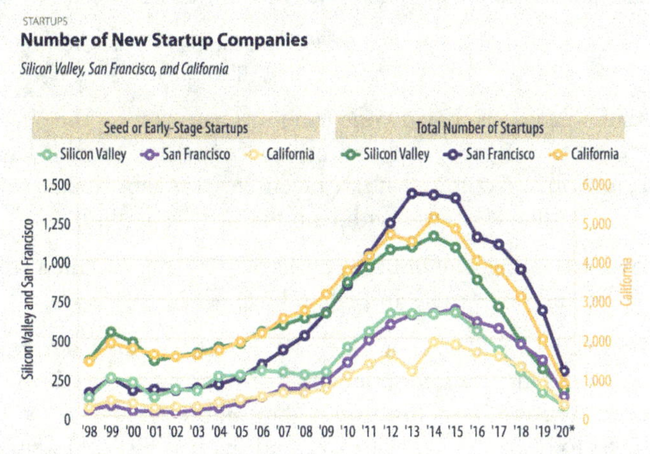

Takeaways: Historians took for granted a notion, that revolutionary changes in astronomy and physics occurred during the 16th and 17th centuries Renaissance in Europe, leading to the scientific revolution that enabled all future development of modern science and therefore leap the Western countries' development ahead of the rest of the world, reinforced by misleading media believe of gifted and superior talents based purely on geographic affiliation.

As knowledge becomes prevalent, modern historians not only expressed doubt on such a consensus but argue that the scientific revolution was a mere expansion of past discoveries that shall be credited to all previous civilizations, from ancient to medieval, especially the Muslim discoveries given its proximity and impact on Europe during the Spanish colonization from the 9th to 14th centuries, where many manuscripts where translated into Latin and other European language accelerating the subsequent discoveries, including Christopher Columbus trip to the new world "America" which was planned based on translated previous work of scientist and astrologist from the Muslim world.

"There is no such thing as the scientific revolution" By Steven Shapin
Harvard Professor and Historian

A tangible proof that anyone can innovate, as long they have access to decent infrastructure compelled with legal protection and commensurate incentives, is simply baked into Silicon Valley's success, with its two third immigrants.

For Innovator: The bubble era (1996 – 2002) was called "the biggest and fastest rise and fall in business history.

The Failure of Marketing Fueled Innovation: Most dot-com companies incurred net operating losses as they spent heavily on advertising and promotions to harness viral network effects to build market share or mind share as fast as possible, using the twisted venture capital mottos "get big fast or go home".

These companies offered their services or products for free or at a discount with the expectation that they could build enough brand awareness to charge a profitable sales price for their services in the future. But most were forced to adjust their valuation accounting and ads spending.

Featured Innovators Ahead of their time:

- 1995: theGlobe.com a social network that reached the largest first-day gain of any IPO to date.
- 2001: Webvan promised delivery in 30 minutes went bankrupt after $396 million of VC funding and an IPO of $375 million and was folded into Amazon
- The first to sign agreements with major music publishers and the predecessor of iTunes was Ritmotech.

For Investors: During the height of dotcom, 90% of startups that launched, got funded, or completed their IPO went bankrupt within 3 to 24 months, sinking the NASDAQ from 1,000, down 75% from its peak, and whipping 5$ Trillion of investor money (Venture Capital and Public)!

CMGI was worth $41 Billion in the 1990s which provides supply chain management services to software companies. Between 1995 and 1999, its stock was the best-performing stock in the US, returning 4,921% then declined 99% when the bubble burst and is worth less than $0.25% today.

For Acquirer: America Online announced a merger with Time Warner in 2000, as the largest in history, questioned by many analysts, for the combined value of $360 billion (today's dollars: $500 Billion), sold later to apollo private equity in 2021 for $5 Billion (combined with Yahoo was acquired for $10 Billion then sold for $5 Billion in 2021)

Yahoo!: A predecessor of Google and the largest search engine of the 1990s, acquired several startups for billions of dollars, only to shut them down a few years later. In 2008, Microsoft made an offer to acquire it for $44 billion, which was rejected but was acquired later for $4.83 Billion (Internet Business), then got resold in 2021 for much less

Human Innovation and Disruption Evolution

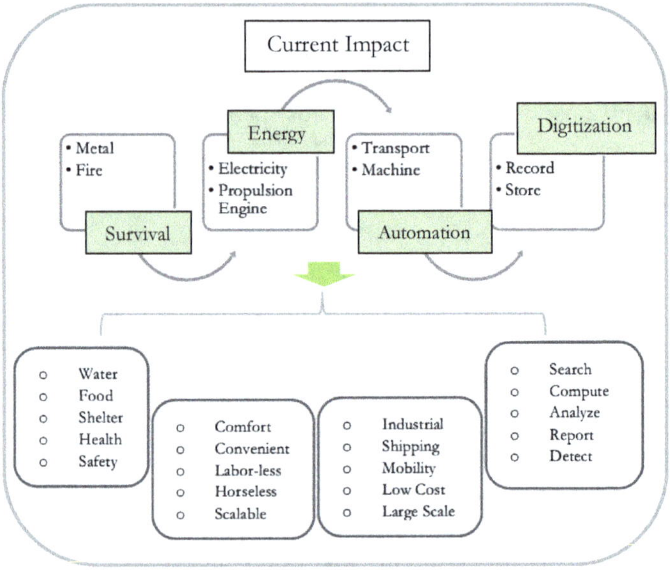

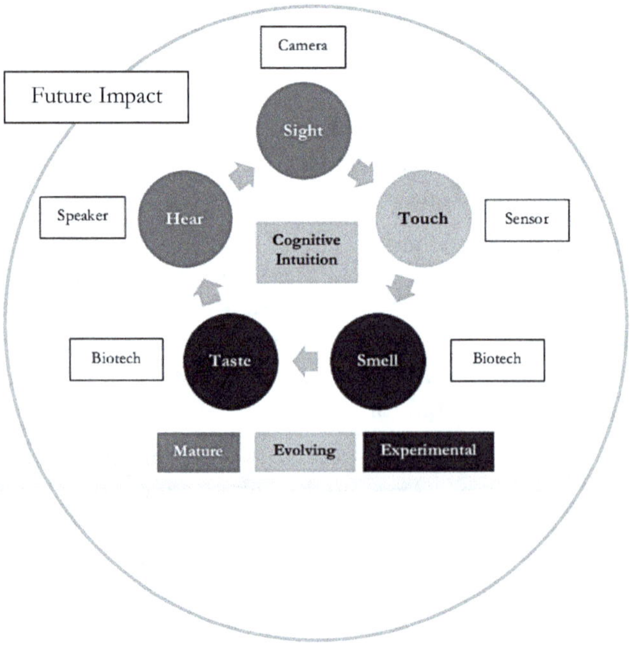

CHAPTER II
WHAT'S INNOVATION

Innovative Culture: America emerged from a British colony with 2.4 million habitants in the 18th century to become the strongest military power in the world, made possible through innovation that still powers and sustains major economic and social progress. It has increased per capita income more than sevenfold since the 19th century, has added three decades to the average lifespan, and has revolutionized the way we live and share information.

Innovation tends to take place in an ecosystem where the entrepreneurial spirit is prevalent, with access to good research institutions and ample funding, enabling a vibrant collaboration between individuals that foster innovation.

The university system in America is unusual among industrialized countries to have a long history of interaction with the commercial corporation "The Industry", where many of the innovative activities within universities rely on the input of both ideas and people along with generous financial support. As an example, work done at UC Berkeley on the Unix operating system relied on people from Bell Laboratories (acquired by NOKIA) spending time on the campus. Such interactions are very rare in Europe, Japan, or most developing countries, but are becoming common gradually.

A key aspect of an ecosystem's success in Silicon Valley is its venture capital sector, which grew from invisible privately financed to an engine that fed a larger part of the economy through stock market exit and recycled funding of both, post IPO startup and large V.C funds from public money through Limited Partners.

Physical proximity between venture capitalists, academia, and entrepreneurs is often critical for early-stage startups to access immediate advice as needed (located within the same metro area) but becomes less needed for later-stage startups.

Ecosystems that support the commercialization of innovations solving pressing human challenges in areas such as the life sciences, energy, mobility, health, and agriculture are the future, as the major tech pioneer of the first digital platform wave become entangled with consumer groups and government regulators to remediate their negative impact.

Silicon Valley entrepreneurs have been learning how to build high-growth companies for over half a century. They have had experience not only with university research but with research and development in companies, from which many innovative ideas emerged on a global scale.

An entrepreneur knows how to start and run a startup, which is a very different experience from being part of a large company. Many have connections with both universities and with commercial corporations, these dual accesses are a prominent part of the Silicon Valley culture that can be difficult to replicate elsewhere, as many are willing to move among institutions and sectors, thereby bringing their experience to new endeavors.

University faculty may be smart and creative, but many have no idea of what it means to go to market, how to launch a startup, how to handle sales and growth, and so on. Technical entrepreneurs tend to see the glass as half full, but often they need to help convince potential investors that the glass is not half empty, Yi Cui, Associate Professor in the Department of Materials Science and Engineering at Stanford University, agreed.

They need to learn lean and execution-driven management skills or partner with founders with those skills to be successful. In such cases, a startup may need to learn how to work with a large company, especially in areas that require large investments.

The transfer of technology from universities often takes place through the creation of new companies (Startup), that attract talented and experienced executioners to turn the invention into a prototype, gather customer interest, and take a technology to market or be acquired by a larger company that can do so, they are the bridge between academia and public impact.

Technologies generally are not transferred from university, but rather people, to help bring the ability to innovate if provided with the opportunity to do so. Some of the success stories involving the transfer of people from Stanford include Larry Page and Sergey Brin (the founders of Google), along with others from the University of California, Berkeley, UC San Francisco, and many local companies.

The direct transfer of technology to a large corporation tends to be difficult. Even when a new product or service is generating profits, it may change a little to the bottom line.

Additionally, a disruptive technology may threaten an existing business or sector, where a large corporation may acquire a startup to shut it down, like in the early days of electric car deployed in Los Angeles, only to see that business or industry undermined by small startup company anyway later on, and in this case the emergence of Tesla.

Managerial talent may be less mobile geographically than capital or labor. "Part of what you develop as a venture capitalist is a good network of people within 50 miles, and that talent is a very important part of what VCs are bringing to these new startups, especially the one founded by inexperienced entrepreneurs in their first spinouts." Startups may even move from other countries to take advantage of the managerial expertise in the United States.

The culture that thrives the most, is fueled by the willingness to accept failure. In many countries, acceptance of failure is limited, which constrains the ability to invest in risky ideas. Compounded by both the legal liability of investment as debt vs equity and personal shame stigma by seed investors to the first-time founders.

Innovation vs Invention vs Patent:

Innovation: is the practical implementation of an invention that may or may not be protected by one or more patents. Implemented innovation makes a meaningful impact on a market and society, which does not require new inventions but can be powered by one or more inventions, when the problem being solved is driven by real-world needs.

An example of Innovation is a smartphone's use of several inventions that existed years before, which package them efficiently into a better user-friendly experience and build around it an ecosystem that protects it. The ecosystem expanded into several industries including Media, Music, Telecom, Hardware, Software "developer apps", Books "and eBooks" and many sub-segments, creating a multi-trillion new industry. There are three types of Innovation:

- Sustaining innovation: which consists of improving products or services based on current customer needs.
- Core Innovation: an incremental evolution of products or services based on emerging technologies (e.g., faster microprocessors, flat-screen televisions).
- Transformative: the creation of new capabilities and new business to take advantage of or respond to disruptive opportunities or to counter disruption.

An invention is a unique method, composition, or process. It can be an improvement of a system or product or a process for creating a result that may be a radical breakthrough.

The invention is normally patentable and must be both a first in the market and unique in its application to a new or improved product, process, or automation that can be tangible or intangible. It is the creation of what did not exist before, usually done by a Research and Development team within a large commercial or academic organization that takes years and is driven by market research, customer insights, and expertise within the same industry.

Patent: is an intellectual property asset that gives the legal owner a right to exclude others from making, using, or selling an invention, in exchange for publishing the invention's technical spec or how it works. Patent law is governed by international treaties and falls under private law in most countries. In case of infringement, the patent holder must sue the infringing party to protect their asset.

Patents are an essential competitive advantage in certain industries "i.e., Biotech, Hardware.", but they are irrelevant in most digital tech that is consumer-facing. Publishing your invention makes it easy for your competitors to create a similar product or service and submit their patent, therefore opting for trade secret protection is best.

Technological progress has a direct impact on living standards, for example, Argentina and Austria have roughly the same level of per capita inputs (labor and capital), but the economic output of Austria is more than double Argentina's. High national living standards—are due to the various ways that economies use their resources, and not just to the quantities of resources available.

Total Patents Grant by US Metro for Top Universities Brookings Institute

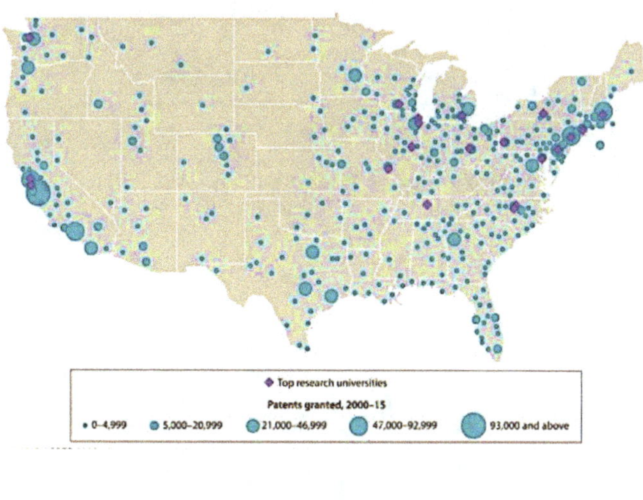

Total R&D Expenditure and Patents filed by Country by Brookings Institute

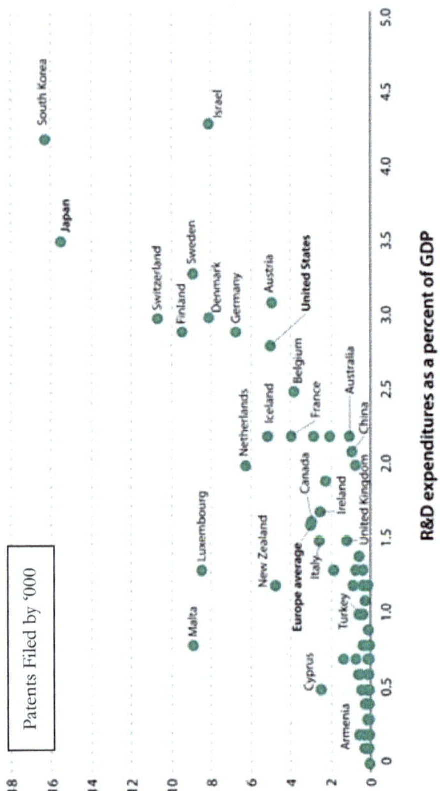

Patents Lawsuits by owners that go to market "Operating" vs non-operating speculators "troll" by Brookings Institute

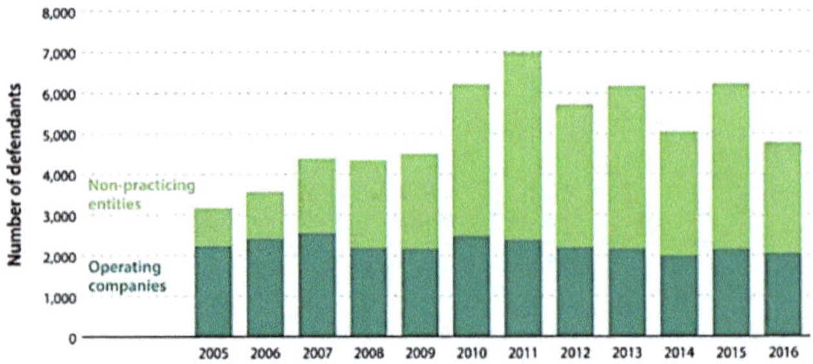

First Wave of Tech Innovation: this caused a massive shift in the industrial revolution by accelerating its growth at an exponential rate for the U.S. economy.

The Auto Industry: The combined efforts of innovation and industrialization allowed the automotive industry to take off during a nationwide highway buildup period and become the backbone of American transportation and shipping.

The Internet: A network of networks composed of private, public, academic, business, and government local networks connected globally, using fiber-optic cables and wireless technologies. Commissioned by the U.S., Government in the 1960s to enable multi-users sharing of computer data. Which evolved to connect regional academics, then grew to link commercial and enterprises.

Portable Computer (PC): The evolution of mainframe and mid-size computers, into a movable display and keyboard station. Introduced by IBM in the 1970s, paving the way for mobile laptops.

Operating System: MS-DOS (Microsoft Disk Operating System) was the first operating system for IBM PC-compatible personal computers during the 1980s, which was followed by a graphical user interface (GUI) of the MS Windows operating system.

The World Wide Web: First successful online e-commerce "Minitel" was released in France in the 1980s by the Postal Service using a telephone lines connection, users could make online purchases, make train reservations, check stock prices, search the telephone directory, have a mailbox, and chat, which was the precursor of the modern web. Then Timothy Berners-Lee developed the first web browser in 1989 that bypassed "Minitel" to access the web, while employed at CERN in Switzerland and released it to academia in January 1991, and then to the public in August 1991.

Commercial Web Browser: The first was Mosaic released in 1993 and subsequent web browsers during the following years gave computer users access to the World Wide Web, popularizing the use of the Internet, which was increased because of advances in data networking connectivity.

Second Wave of Tech Innovation: The significant technological advancements and societal shifts that occurred during the 2010s. Yet many of these developments became so quickly ingrained in our daily lives that they often went relatively unnoticed, and their impact was all but forgotten. Moore's law suggests that over a ten-year period, semiconductors will advance by 32 times, bringing about mesmerizing innovation in the digital age that should not only change technology but society, as well.

The 3G networks: introduced a new age of calling, texting, and internet connectivity for mobile devices. 4G offered 10x faster speed than 3G networks, increasing download speeds from 1.5 Mbit/s to 15 Mbit/s. For perspective, this reduced the download time for an 800MB movie from 5 hours to 43 seconds. This improvement made 4G a foundational technology for a range of mobile applications that pried users away from desktops and let them stream music and videos, shop on e-commerce, and use social media, all on the go.

Sectors that benefited are Mobile manufacturers, telecom, social media, e-commerce, and media. Daily time spent online on mobile grew from 32 min in 2011 to 132 min in 2019.

Social Media: In the age of desktop computers, social media was a log of what happened in the past – a collection of experiences uploaded after the fact. As social media shifted to the smartphone, it became an instantaneous broadcast of life experiences. Businesses, news organizations, and governments leveraged them to communicate in real-time. Social media became one-stop-shops for information, capturing users' attention and occupying significant amounts of their time. Advertisers took notice and continued to pour spending across platforms and search engines: in 2019, digital advertising spending surpassed that of traditional advertising mediums like TV and radio.

Social media users' growth: 970m in 2010 to 2.96 billion in 2020.

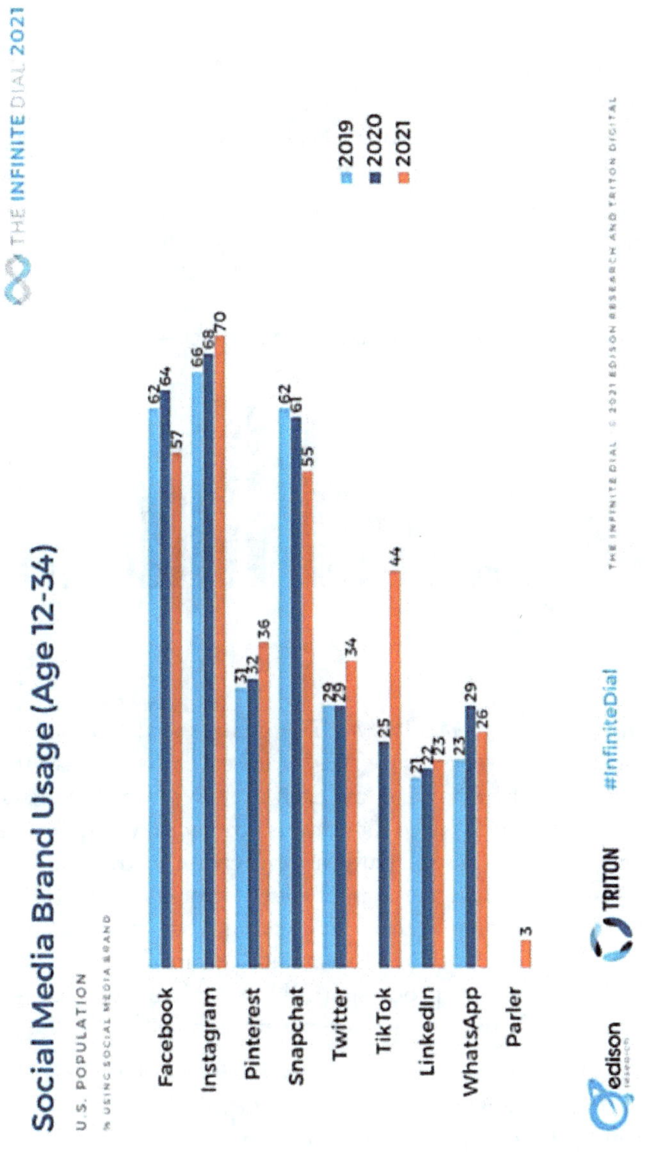

Electric vehicles (EVs): started to pose a legitimate threat to internal combustion engine (ICE)vehicles, as improvements aided performance and falling battery costs broadened the potential market. Bloomberg estimates that lithium-ion battery prices fell by approximately 90% over the course of the decade. Traditionally, batteries represented over 50% of an EV's total cost, enabling EVs to be sold at lower prices that are conducive to mass adoption.

Sectors that benefited are Lithium miners, battery manufacturers, and EV Original Equipment Manufacturers (OEMs). There were barely any EVs on US roads in 2010. By the end of the decade, there were over 1 million.

ELECTRIC VEHICLES ON THE ROAD IN THE US & BATTERY PACK PRICE
Source: Global X Research, Benchmark Mineral Intelligence, Edison Electric Institute, BloombergNEF

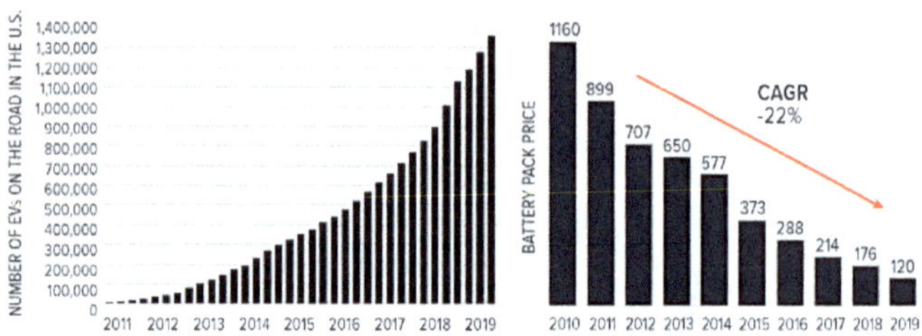

CAGR (Compounded Annual Growth Rate)
Note: From 2010 to 2018 numbers reflect real $/kwh per BloombergNEF estimates and 2019 reflects Benchmark Mineral Intelligence estimates.

AI, ML and Big Data Analytics: Payments, social media, online searches, and app usage leave an extensive digital trail, creating gigabytes of data for each user. With the emergence of artificial intelligence algorithms, these large datasets are sifted through to spot patterns and create instructions that optimize search engines, target advertisements to individuals, or offer real-time directions. As data has become more prolific, AI has continued to learn and advance its capabilities. In 2018, language processing AI outperformed humans at Stanford on a reading and comprehension test.

In 2010, 2 zettabytes of data were created globally, with 9% available in a structured format (i.e., data that has been organized or indexed for easier referencing). By 2019, it reached 41 zettabytes with 13% structured.

Third Wave of Tech Innovation: Already in full steam since 2020, even with the covid-19 global setback.

New wireless standard: 5G means more than just a faster internet. It proliferates the mass adoption of connected devices in homes, cities, and enterprises, including those involved in agriculture, health care, manufacturing, and infrastructure. Increasingly, these industries rely on connected devices to gather and analyze data, making processes more efficient, reducing downtime, and freeing up time to focus on new products and initiatives.

GLOBAL NUMBER OF CONNECTED DEVICES BY 2030 (IN BILLIONS)
Source: Global X Research, Ericsson Mobility Report, Cisco

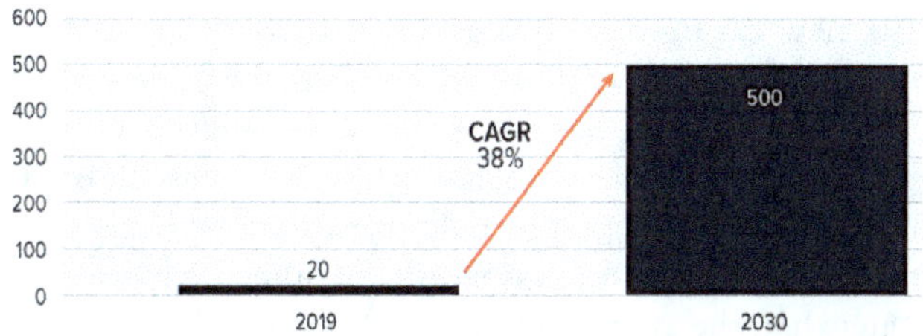

The cloud moves to the edge: The continued decline of computing costs and improvements in network infrastructure and artificial intelligence are key drivers of the emergence of edge computing conducted locally without transmission across a large network. Some technologies require instantaneous data interpretation and can't rely on networks with higher latency. Autonomous vehicles, robotic surgery, gaming, and smart factories, for example, can require near-simultaneous data transmission. Edge computing reduces latency to 5-10 milliseconds from 25-35 milliseconds for early deployed 5G devices. A recent study estimates the economic impact of edge computing to reach $4.1 trillion by 2030.

Sectors that will benefit are Cloud infrastructure companies, IoT device makers, AI developers, smart factories, streaming, autonomous vehicle, surgical robots

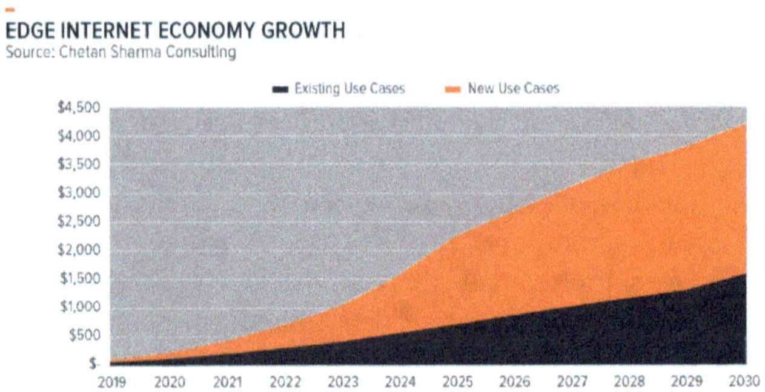

Transportation and Shipping: Shared autonomous and electric vehicles are expected to cost $0.35 per mile by 2030, less than half the cost of owning a personal sedan ($0.88 per mile). By 2030, new car models equipped with self-driving technology are expected to be commonplace. This transition will allow drivers to take their hands off the wheel while their vehicles drive autonomously, or to hail driverless shared robot axis using last-mile shipping delivery vehicles. The average American spends 18 days' worth of time driving each year, greater than the average number of vacation days per year (10 days), the productivity and leisure impact of autonomous vehicles is enormous.

Sectors that will benefit: Lithium miners and battery producers, radar and lidar manufacturers, ride-hailing platforms, 5G, and AI hardware.

Autonomous Mobility VS Human Driven in 2030

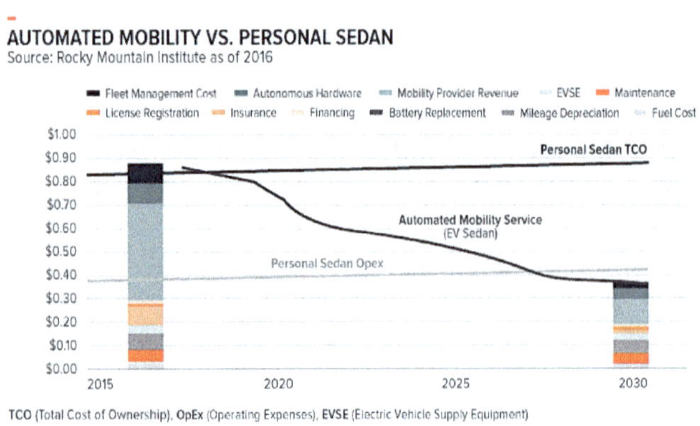

Robotics enters new industries: Improvements in artificial intelligence and dexterity are the result of advanced 3D vision capabilities and end-of-arm tooling for precise movements. While the auto manufacturing segment remains robotics' largest end-market, emerging segments like healthcare and hospitality can benefit from smarter, more capable robots that can conduct surgery, check on patients, cook food, or deliver items to hotel rooms. Agriculture will also see a robotics-driven revolution with automated spraying, monitoring, and picking likely resulting in reduced costs and improved crop yields. The global stock of industrial robots is expected to reach 20 million by 2030, representing a 24% CAGR as robots enter more industries.

Sectors that will benefit are Robotics and AI, chip developers.

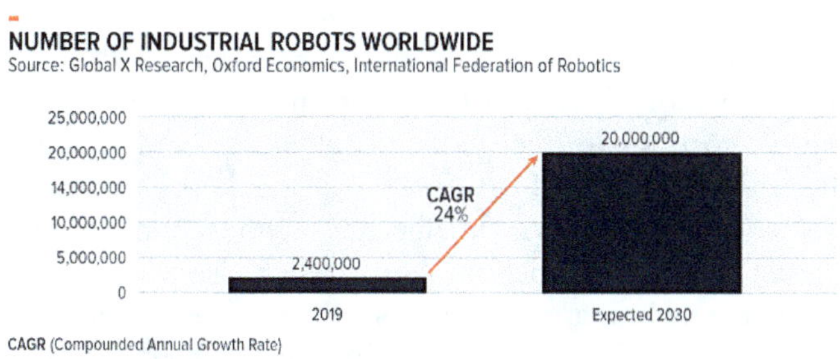

Omnichannel-commerce: The separation between e-commerce and brick-and-mortar retail will blur as digital and physical shopping experiences become the same. Augmented reality will give consumers the ability to try on and order clothes from the comfort of their homes, but physical stores with reduced footprints will feature unique consumer experiences, immediate purchases, and try-before-you-buy optionality. Coupled with IoT technologies that track consumer behavior and build datasets around it, and advances in AI, retailers could be able to predict consumer behavior at almost 100% accuracy.

We also expect to see e-commerce as a value add for small and mid-sized businesses, providing a medium for them to sell products outside of their locality and giving them a means of accessing global consumer bases.

Sectors that will benefit are E-commerce platforms, FinTech, and augmented reality.

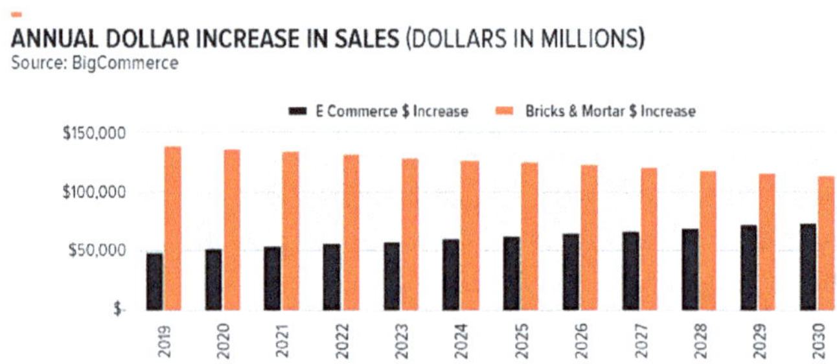

Healthcare: goes digital with AI diagnoses and telemedicine; as the population ages, there will be increasing pressure to reduce costs, improve patient outcomes, and optimize physicians' time. All of this is possible by leveraging telemedicine and artificial intelligence – two technologies that are set to disrupt health care. Telemedicine offers an alternative solution to in-person doctor visits, providing diagnostic and clinical services to patients around-the-clock, from the convenience of one's home or workplace.

Currently, telemedicine utilization rates remain below 10% in the U.S., but penetration is likely to grow as technology reduces costs and adds convenience. Further digitalization of healthcare will enable new use cases for AI.

Recent developments like AI-driven, real-time MRI interpretation could mean enhanced diagnoses and treatments across other verticals, in addition to its use in telemedicine as an AI chatbot for triage or basic medical advice.

Sectors that will benefit: Cloud computing, big data & AI

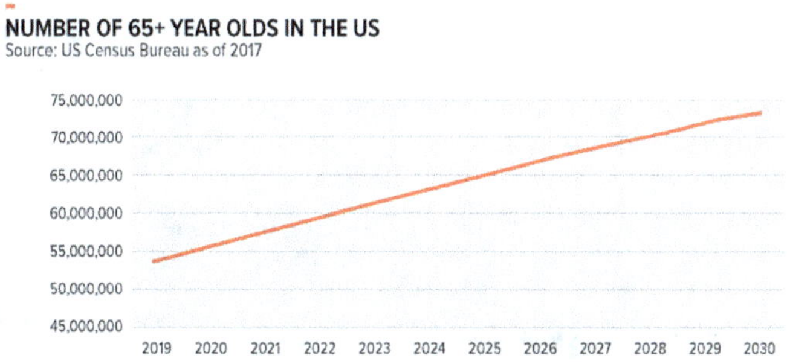

Genomics and Precision Medicine: commonly referred to as personalized medicine, uses patients' genetic information to determine the most suitable treatment option for illness and to proactively identify health risks. As genomic sequencing costs rapidly fell, computing power increased, and biotech research advanced, precision medicine became a reality.

Developments like the CRISPR-Cas9 approach to gene editing introduced new efficient and reliable ways to make precise, targeted changes to the genome of living cells. In practice, this means editing or removing portions of DNA that present health issues. In 2019, such technology showed promise in treating blood disorders like sickle cell and other genetic conditions like muscular dystrophy.

CRISPR technology could correct up to 89% of disease-causing genetic variations in the future.

Sectors that will benefit are Biotechnology, gene editing, and genetic diagnostics.

Genomics has the potential to cure the previously incurable. Advances in genomics could offer the first realistic opportunity to cure certain illnesses previously deemed fatal.

Scientists have identified more than 50,000 genetic diseases caused by a single gene mutation in humans, known as Mendelian diseases. These are likely to be the first diseases treated through gene editing techniques.

As the medical and scientific communities' understanding of gene expression and protein pathways improves and genomic sequencing costs continue to fall, we expect a vast increase in the number of tested and proven genomic therapies.

Sectors that will benefit: Gene therapy, gene sequencing, gene editing, and biotechnology.

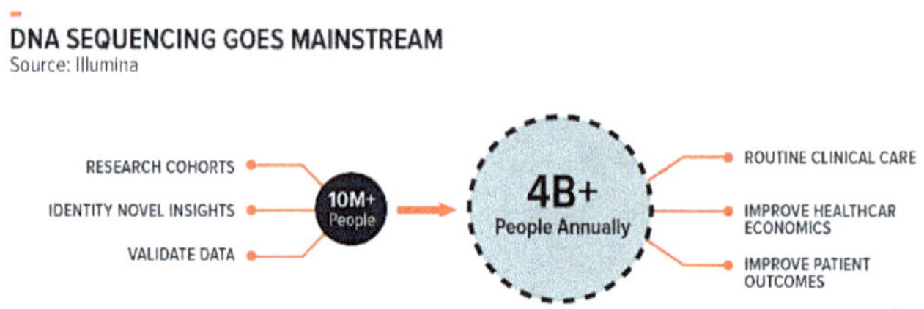

Taste and Smell Tech: A new Intel chip uses machine intelligence to identify different odors without the need for a nose. This is the latest breakthrough to arrive, further highlighting how fast research in artificial intelligence (AI) is advancing.

Intel Labs is designing a computer chip capable of smelling and identifying hazardous gasses, which is notable. The test chip, named Loihi, is a neuromorphic (replicates human function) computer chip that has been developed jointly by researchers from Intel Labs and Cornell University, especially for application in chemical sensing processes.

This chip can be a smart, reliable, and fast tool for detecting and identifying chemicals, especially those that are hazardous, and could greatly help in quality control in factories, security checkpoints in airports, and even in the diagnosis of some diseases that give out a certain odor.

What's not Innovation: There are many misconceptions out there, among which these are not innovation:

Ideas: Can be a result of brainstorming in corporate, a deep know-how, professional experiences, or simply a user-driven insight by customers; regardless of its origin it is simply creative thinking and not an innovation; unless fully developed and successfully reached the target market with both revenue and profit growth.

Technologies: Regardless of its origin or form, it is an enabler "i.e., Raw Material Commodities" and not an end by itself and therefore cannot be innovation. Many examples can be summed up in the invented wheel that took centuries to become a self-propelled vehicle, sands before its evolution to cement and software coding languages which are mostly "free" open sources and although protected by IP, they are not innovation.

Successful Industry Short of Innovation but Evolution

Software		Hardware	
Digital Tech	Replaced	Hardware Tech	Replaced
Social Media	White Page	Rideshare	Private Limo / Taxi
Big Data	CRM	3D Printing	Paper Print
Search	Yellow Page	EV Cars	Fuel with Electric
Ads	Paper	Mobile	Telephone / Laptop
eCommerce	Mall	Cloud	Co-host Data Center

Conclusion:

- Innovation is not technology.
- Innovation is not a new Product.
- Innovation is not Inspiration.
- Innovation is not Incremental.
- Innovation is not an end in itself.
- Innovation is more than evolution.

Takeaways: The following will encompass the most insightful past events that can help navigate the future:

For Innovator: The 2010s were a decade of phenomenal innovation, led largely by the transition to mobile and the rise of data, which accelerated the growth of AI, e-commerce, social media, and biotechnology.

In the 2020s, additional foundational changes will take place as data latency shortens and AI algorithms improve. Such progress should enable new technologies to flourish, including autonomous vehicles, conversational AI, the massive Internet of Things, and augmented and virtual reality.

As new technologies are introduced to the marketplace, they will have a profound impact on our lives, workplaces, and even investments as they reshape the economy.

The tremendous success of general management over the last century has provided unprecedented material abundance, but those management principles are ill-suited to handle the chaos and uncertainty that startups must face.

Entrepreneurship requires a distinct managerial discipline to harness the entrepreneurial opportunity we have today, such as Entrepreneurship Management.

Building a startup involves management. Entrepreneurs are rightly wary of implementing traditional management practices early on in a startup, afraid that they will invite bureaucracy or stifle creativity.

As a result, many entrepreneurs take a "just do it" attitude, avoiding all forms of management or discipline.

We are living through an unprecedented worldwide entrepreneurial renaissance, and there are more entrepreneurs today than at any time in history. This was made possible by dramatic changes in the global economy.

But this opportunity is laced with peril. Because we lack a coherent management paradigm for new innovative ventures, we're throwing our excess capacity around with wild abandon.

Despite this lack of rigor, we are finding some ways to make money, but for every success, there are far too many failures: products pulled from shelves mere weeks after being launched, high-profile startups lauded in the press, and forgotten a few months later.

What makes these failures particularly painful is not just the economic damage done to individual employees, companies, and investors; they are also a colossal waste of our civilization*.

For Investors: Like previous innovation revolutions, the negative impact on end users, the environment, and society will become a key focus that drives strict governance that will restrict key market players' growth and therefore bring to rest the astronomical growth and valuation of both tech giants and emerging startups.

For Acquirer: Enactment of strict governance both locally and globally to regulate all types of acquisitions.

Given the prevalent abuse of market leaders in terms of acquiring small but potential disruptors to only let them fail or shut them down "as a cost to protect their own business" and protect monopolistic dominance.

*To put in perspective here is where we stand:

- 4,500 years later, Egyptian handmade Pyramids still standing.
- 2,500 years later, Greek structures still stand with no care.
- 2,300 years later, the Great Wall of China 13k miles is standing.
- 2,000 years later, the Romain building, "Pantheon" still stands.
- 100 year is what our civilization structure can stand with no maintenance, and after that, it will be erased with no evidence of our existence.

CHAPTER III
WHAT'S DISRUPTION

Disruptive innovation: is the process by which a new product or service creates a new market (e.g., Uber for Taxi, Wikipedia free crowdsourcing contributors for Encyclopedia.), often enabled by new technology and eventually displacing established competitors. Disruption tends to transform old business models into emerging new ones over many years, or upon new players gaining market shares. Mainly due to social segments and institutions that tend to gain adoption more slowly.

The following are examples of the most disruptive innovation that shaped the market and society:

- 20th Century: Ford, Assembly Line; Ries and Horhey candies, McDonald, and Fridge by Frigidaire
- 21st Century: Microsoft (Software), Google (Ads), Apple (Computer), and Amazon (Shopping)
- Internet Search (Google): Expanded the advertising market into an online segment and reversed its business model by having a target audience embedded in its free products "i.e., email, video, Android OS for mobile".

Technology (Apple): Integrated several emerging consumer hardware and software products into one Smartphone "i.e., Mobile Phone, Camera, Music Player, and PC" as iPhone; built under a sleek and user-friendly "user interface", along with expanding its ecosystem into proximate segments "i.e., Media Distribution by Unit and usage not Album for Music". In addition to having the most efficient production (made possible by Foxconn) and distribution in the industry by focusing on design with retail showroom and delegating the rest to its on-demand global supplies partners.

Commerce (Amazon and Alibaba): Two giants that captured, integrated, and streamlined several large industries primarily by connecting the offline (Supply Chain Management) to the digital (Shopping and Payment) with nearly real-time delivery. Enabling global consumers and businesses to trade at the most efficient rate ever existed in human history, by providing three values "access to the largest selection at the lowest prices with the fastest delivery".

Energy (Tesla): among the first in the industry to connect cars to home energy "through its subsidiary SolarCity" and integrate the entire value chain of producing, storing, and consuming clean energy at the most efficient cycle that reduces the two sources of pollution "Cars / Building" driving 75% of global air pollution.

Healthcare (Moderna and Pfizer): Helped shape the post-Covid-19 era, by leading the entire industry into the 21st-century Vaccine development and distribution cycle, which was reduced by 10X from an average of 10 years for previous pandemics to less than 12 months.

The Followings are Notable Founder or Co-Founder of the above Companies by Continent (Ethnic Background):

- Africa (Tesla): Elon Musk
- America (Amazon): Jeff Bezos
- Asia (Alibaba): Jack Ma
- Europe (Google): Sergey Brin; (Pfizer) Charles Pfizer
- Middle East (Apple): Steve Jobs "Father"; (Moderna) Noubar Afeyan "Born in Lebanon".

The Theory of Disruption: was introduced in 1995 and proved to be a powerful way of thinking about innovation-driven growth. Many leaders of entrepreneurial companies praise it as their guiding star, including many executives of large organizations, including Intel, and Salesforce.

The problem with conflating a disruptive innovation with any breakthrough that changes an industry's competitive patterns is that different types of innovation require different strategic approaches. To put it another way, the lessons we've learned about succeeding as a disruptive innovator (or defending against a disruptive challenger) will not apply to every company in a shifting market.

If we get sloppy with our labels or fail to integrate insights from subsequent research and experience into the original theory, then managers may end up using the wrong tools for their context, reducing their chances of success. Over time, the theory's usefulness will be undermined.

First, a quick recap of the idea: "Disruption" describes a process whereby a smaller company with fewer resources, can successfully challenge established incumbent businesses. Specifically, as incumbents focus on improving their products and services for their most demanding (and usually most profitable) customers, they exceed the needs of some segments and ignore the needs of others.

Entrants that prove disruptive begin by successfully targeting those overlooked segments, gaining a foothold by delivering more-suitable functionality—frequently at a lower price. Incumbents, chasing higher profitability in more-demanding segments, tend not to respond vigorously.

Entrants then move upmarket, delivering the performance that incumbents' mainstream customers require, while preserving the advantages that drove their early success. When mainstream customers start adopting the entrants' offerings in volume, disruption has occurred.

Is Uber a Disruptive Innovation? Let's consider Uber, the transportation company whose mobile application connects consumers who need rides with drivers who are willing to provide them. Founded in 2009, the company has enjoyed fantastic growth (it operates in hundreds of cities in 60 countries and is still expanding).

It has reported tremendous financial success (the most recent valuation implies an enterprise value in the vicinity of $90 billion). And it has spawned a slew of imitators (other start-ups are trying to emulate its "market-making" business model). Uber clearly transformed the taxi business in the United States and the world almost at the same time. But is it about *disrupting* the taxi business?

According to the theory, the answer is no. Uber's financial and strategic achievements do not qualify the company as genuinely disruptive—although the company is almost always described that way. Here are two reasons why the label doesn't fit. Disruptive innovations originate in low-end or new-market footholds.

Disruptive innovations are made possible because they get started in two types of markets that incumbents overlook. *Low-end footholds* exist because incumbents typically try to provide their most profitable and demanding customers with ever-improving products and services, and they pay less attention to less-demanding customers.

In fact, incumbents' offerings often overshoot the performance requirements of the latter. This opens the door to a disrupter focused (at first) on providing those low-end customers with a "good enough" product.

In the case of *new-market footholds,* disrupters create a market where none existed. Put simply, they find a way to turn non-consumers into consumers. For example, in the early days of photocopying technology, Xerox targeted large corporations and charged high prices to provide the performance that those customers required.

School librarians, bowling-league operators, and other small customers, priced out of the market, made do with carbon paper or mimeograph machines. Then in the late 1970s, new challengers introduced personal copiers, offering an affordable solution to individuals and small organizations—and a new market was created.

From this relatively modest beginning, personal photocopier makers gradually built a major position in the mainstream photocopier market that Xerox valued.

A disruptive innovation, by definition, starts from one of those two footholds. But Uber did not originate in either one. It is difficult to claim that the company found a low-end opportunity: That would have meant taxi service providers had overshot the needs of a material number of customers by making cabs too plentiful, too easy to use, and too clean.

Neither did Uber primarily target non-consumers—people who found the existing alternatives so expensive or inconvenient that they took public transit or drove themselves instead: Uber was launched in San Francisco (a well-served taxi market), and Uber's customers were generally people already in the habit of hiring rides.

Uber has quite arguably been increasing total demand—that's what happens when you develop a better, less-expensive solution to a widespread customer need. But disrupters *start* by appealing to low-end or unserved consumers and then migrate to the mainstream market. Uber has gone in exactly the opposite direction: building a position in the mainstream market first and subsequently appealing to historically overlooked segments. Disruptive innovations don't catch on with mainstream customers until quality catches up to their standards.

Disruption theory differentiates disruptive innovations from what are called "sustaining innovations." The latter make good products better in the eyes of an incumbent's existing customers: the fifth blade in a razor, the clearer TV picture, and better mobile phone reception. These improvements can be incremental advances or breakthroughs, but they all enable firms to sell more products to their most profitable customers.

Disruptive innovations, on the other hand, are initially considered inferior by most of an incumbent's customers. Typically, customers are not willing to switch to the new offering merely because it is less expensive. Instead, they wait until its quality rises enough to satisfy them. Once that's happened, they adopt the new product and happily accept its lower price. (This is how disruption drives prices down).

Most of the elements of Uber's strategy seem to be sustaining innovations. Uber's service has rarely been described as inferior to existing taxis; in fact, many would say it is *better*. Booking a ride requires just a few taps on a smartphone; payment is cashless and convenient; and passengers can rate their rides afterward, which helps ensure high standards. Furthermore,

Uber delivers service reliably and punctually, and its pricing is usually competitive with (or lower than) that of established taxi services. And as is typical when incumbents face threats from sustaining innovations, many of the taxi companies are motivated to respond. They are deploying competitive technologies, such as hailing apps, and contesting the legality of Uber services.

Uber has certainly thrown the taxi industry into disarray: Isn't that "disruptive" enough? No. Applying the theory correctly is essential to realizing its benefits. For example, small competitors that nibble away at the periphery of your business very likely should be ignored—unless they are on a disruptive trajectory, in which case they are a potentially mortal threat. And both challenges are fundamentally different from efforts by competitors to woo your bread-and-butter customers.

As the example of Uber shows, identifying true disruptive innovation is tricky. Yet even executives with a good understanding of disruption theory tend to forget some of its subtler aspects when making strategic decisions.

We've observed four important points that get overlooked or misunderstood:

Disruption is a process, the term "disruptive innovation" is misleading when it is used to refer to a product or service at one fixed point, rather than to the evolution of that product or service over time. The first minicomputers were disruptive not merely because they were low-end upstarts when they appeared on the scene, nor because they were later heralded as superior to mainframes in many markets; they were disruptive by virtue of the path they followed from the fringe to the mainstream.

Most innovation—disruptive or not—begins life as a small-scale experiment. Disrupters tend to focus on getting the business model, rather than merely the product, just right.

When they succeed, their movement from the fringe (the low end of the market or a new market) to the mainstream erodes first the incumbents' market share and then their profitability. This process can take time, and incumbents can get quite creative in the defense of their established franchises.

For example, more than 50 years after the first discount department store was opened, mainstream retail companies still operate their traditional department-store formats. Complete substitution, if it comes at all, may take decades, because the incremental profit from staying with the old model for one more year trumps the proposal to write off the assets in one stroke.

The fact that disruption can take time helps to explain why incumbents frequently overlook disruptors. For example, when Netflix launched in 1997, its initial service wasn't appealing to most of Blockbuster's customers, who rented movies (typically new releases) on impulse.

Netflix had an exclusively online interface and a large inventory of movies, but delivery through the U.S. mail meant selections took several days to arrive.

The service appealed to only a few customer groups—movie buffs who didn't care about new releases, early adopters of DVD players, and online shoppers. If Netflix had not eventually begun to serve a broader segment of the market, Blockbuster's decision to ignore this competitor would not have been a strategic blunder:

The two companies filled very different needs for their (different) customers.

However, as new technologies allowed Netflix to shift to streaming video over the internet, the company did eventually become appealing to Blockbuster's core customers, offering a wider selection of content with an all-you-can-watch, on-demand, low-price, high-quality, highly convenient approach. And it got there via a classically disruptive path.

If Netflix (like Uber) had begun by launching a service targeted at a larger competitor's core market, Blockbuster's response would very likely have been a vigorous and perhaps successful counterattack. But failing to respond effectively to the trajectory that Netflix was on led Blockbuster to collapse.

Disrupters often build business models that are very different from those of incumbents. Consider the healthcare industry. General practitioners operating out of their offices often rely on their years of experience and on test results to interpret patients' symptoms, make diagnoses, and prescribe treatment.

We call this a "solution shop" business model. In contrast, several convenient care clinics are taking a disruptive path by using what we call a "process" business model: They follow standardized protocols to diagnose and treat a small but increasing number of disorders.

One high-profile example of using an innovative business model to effect a disruption is Apple's iPhone. The product that Apple debuted in 2007 was a sustaining innovation in the smartphone market: It targeted the same customers coveted by incumbents, and its initial success is likely explained by product superiority.

The iPhone's subsequent growth is better explained by disruption—not of other smartphones but of the laptop as the primary access point to the internet. This was achieved not merely through product improvements but also through the introduction of a new business model.

By building a facilitated network connecting application developers with phone users, Apple changed the game. The iPhone created a new market for internet access and eventually was able to challenge laptops as mainstream users' devices of choice for going online.

Some disruptive innovations succeed; some don't. A third common mistake is to focus on the results achieved—to claim that a company is disruptive by its success. But success is not built into the definition of disruption: Not every disruptive path leads to a triumph, and not every triumphant newcomer follows a disruptive path.

For example, any number of internet-based retailers pursued disruptive paths in the late 1990s, but only a small number prospered. The failures are not evidence of the deficiencies of disruption theory; they are simply boundary markers for the theory's application.

The theory says very little about how to win in the foothold market, other than to play the odds and avoid head-on competition with better-resourced incumbents.

The mantra "Disrupt or be disrupted" can misguide us. Incumbent companies do need to respond to disruption if it's occurring, but they should not overreact by dismantling a still-profitable business. Instead, they should continue to strengthen relationships with core customers by investing in sustaining innovations.

In addition, they can create a new division focused solely on the growth opportunities that arise from the disruption "i.e., Innovation Centers and Corporate Ventures".

Our research suggests that the success of this new enterprise depends in large part on keeping it separate from the core business. That means that for some time, incumbents will find themselves managing two very different operations. Of course, as the disruptive stand-alone business grows, it may eventually steal customers from the core. But corporate leaders should not try to solve this problem before it *is* a problem.

What a Disruptive Innovation Lens Can Reveal? The theory of disruption predicts that when an entrant tackles incumbent competitors head-on, offering better products or services, the incumbents will accelerate their innovations to defend their business. Either they will beat back the entrant by offering even better services or products at comparable prices, or one of them will acquire the entrant.

The data supports the theory's prediction that entrants pursuing a sustaining strategy for a stand-alone business will face steep odds, i.e., within the disk drive industry, only 6% of sustaining entrants managed to succeed.

In Uber's case, we believe that the regulated nature of the taxi business is a large part of the answer. Market entry and prices are closely controlled in many jurisdictions. Consequently, taxi companies have rarely innovated. Individual drivers have few ways to innovate, except to defect to Uber. So, Uber is in a unique situation relative to taxis: It can offer better quality and the competition will find it hard to respond, at least in the short term.

To this point, we've addressed only whether Uber is disruptive to the taxi business. The limousine or "black car" business is a different story, and here Uber is far more likely to be on a disruptive path.

The company's Uber Premium option provides more-luxurious cars and is typically more expensive than its standard service—but typically less expensive than hiring a traditional limousine.

This lower price imposes some compromises, as Uber currently does not include one defining feature of the leading incumbents in this market: acceptance of advance reservations. Consequently, this offering from Uber appeals to the low end of the limousine service market: customers willing to sacrifice a measure of convenience for monetary savings.

Should Uber find ways to match or exceed incumbents' performance levels without compromising its cost and price advantage, the company appears to be well-positioned to move into the mainstream of the limo business—and it will have done so in a classically disruptive fashion.

How Our Thinking About Disruption Has Developed. Initially, the theory of disruptive innovation was simply a statement about correlation. Empirical findings showed that incumbents outperformed entrants in a sustaining innovation context but underperformed in a disruptive innovation context.

The reason for this correlation was not immediately evident, but one by one, the elements of the theory fell into place.

Smart disruptors improve their products and drive upmarket. First, researchers realized that a company's propensity for strategic change is profoundly affected by the interests of customers who provide the resources the firm needs to survive.

In other words, incumbents (sensibly) listen to their existing customers and concentrate on sustaining innovations as a result.

Researchers then arrived at a second insight: Incumbents' focus on their existing customers becomes institutionalized in internal processes that make it difficult for even senior managers to shift investment to disruptive innovations.

For example, interviews with managers of established companies in the disk drive industry revealed that resource allocation processes prioritized sustaining innovations (which had high margins and targeted large markets with well-known customers).

While inadvertently starving disruptive innovations (meant for smaller markets with poorly defined customers).

Those two insights helped explain why incumbents rarely responded effectively (if at all) to disruptive innovations, but not why entrants eventually moved upmarket to challenge incumbents, repeatedly.

It turns out, however, that the same forces leading incumbents to ignore early-stage disruptions also compel disrupters ultimately to disrupt.

What we've realized is that, very often, low-end, and new-market footholds are populated not by a lone would-be disrupter, but by several comparable entrant firms whose products are simpler, more convenient, or less costly than those sold by incumbents.

The incumbents provide a de facto price umbrella, allowing many of the entrants to enjoy profitable growth within the foothold market. But that lasts only for a time: As incumbents (rationally, but mistakenly) cede the foothold market, they effectively remove the price umbrella and price-based competition among the entrant's reigns.

Some entrants will founder, but the smart ones—the true disrupters will improve their products and drive upmarket, where, once again, they can compete at the margin against higher-cost established competitors. The disruptive effect drives every competitor—incumbent and entrant upmarket.

With those explanations in hand, the theory of disruptive innovation went beyond simple correlation to a theory of causation as well.

The key elements of that theory have been tested and validated through studies of many industries, including retail, computers, printing, motorcycles, cars, semiconductors, cardiovascular surgery, management education, financial services, management consulting, cameras, communications, and computer-aided design software.

Making sense of anomalies: Additional refinements to the theory have been made to address certain anomalies or unexpected scenarios, that the theory could not explain.

For example, we originally assumed that any disruptive innovation took root in the lowest tiers of an established market yet sometimes new entrants seemed to be competing in entirely new markets. This led to the distinction we discussed earlier between low-end and new-market footholds.

Low-end disrupters (think mini-mills and discount retailers) come in at the bottom of the market and take hold within an existing value network before moving upmarket and attacking that stratum (think integrated steel mills and traditional retailers).

By contrast, new-market disruptions take hold in a completely new value network and appeal to customers who have previously gone without the product.

Consider the transistor pocket radio and the PC: They were largely ignored by manufacturers of tabletop radios and minicomputers, respectively, because they were aimed at non-consumers of those goods. By postulating that there are two flavors of foothold markets in which disruptive innovation can begin, the theory has become more powerful and practicable.

Another intriguing anomaly was the identification of industries that have resisted the forces of disruption, at least until very recently.

Higher education in the United States is one of these. Over the years indeed, over more than 100 years new kinds of institutions with different initial charters have been created to address the needs of various population segments, including non-consumers.

Land-grant universities, teachers' colleges, two-year colleges, and so on were initially launched to serve those for whom a traditional four-year liberal arts education was out of reach or unnecessary.

Many of these new entrants strived to improve over time, compelled by analogs of the pursuit of profitability: a desire for growth, prestige, and the capacity to do the greater good.

Thus, they made costly investments in research, dormitories, athletic facilities, faculty, and so on, seeking to emulate more-elite institutions.

Doing so has increased their level of performance in some ways—they can provide richer learning and living environments for students, for example. Yet the *relative* standing of higher-education institutions remains largely unchanged: With few exceptions, the top 20 are still the top 20, and the next 50 are still in that second tier, decade after decade.

Because both incumbents and newcomers are seemingly following the same game plan, it is perhaps no surprise that incumbents can maintain their positions. What has been missing until recently is experimentation with new models that successfully appeal to today's non-consumers of higher education.

The question now is whether there is a novel technology or business model that allows new entrants to move upmarket without emulating the incumbents' high costs that is, to follow a disruptive path. The answer seems to be yes, and the enabling innovation is online learning, which is becoming broadly available.

Real tuition for online courses is falling, and accessibility and quality are improving. Innovators are making inroads into the mainstream market at a stunning pace.

Will online education disrupt the incumbents' model? And if so, when? In other words, will online education's trajectory of improvement intersect with the needs of the mainstream market?

We've come to realize that the steepness of any disruptive trajectory is a function of how quickly the enabling technology improves.

In the steel industry, continuous-casting technology improved quite slowly, and it took more than 40 years before the mini-mill Nucor matched the revenue of the largest integrated steelmakers.

In contrast, the digital technologies that allowed personal computers to disrupt minicomputers improved much more quickly; Compaq was able to increase revenue more than tenfold and reach parity with the industry leader, DEC, in only 12 years.

Understanding what drives the rate of disruption helps predict outcomes, but it doesn't alter the way disruptions should be managed. Rapid disruptions are not fundamentally different from any others; they don't have different causal mechanisms and don't require conceptually different responses.

Disruption theory does not, and never will, explain everything about innovation specifically or business success generally. Far too many other forces are in play, each of which will reward further study. Integrating them all into a comprehensive theory of business success is an ambitious goal, one we are unlikely to attain anytime soon.

But there is cause for hope: Empirical tests show that using disruptive theory makes us measurably and significantly more accurate in our predictions of which fledgling businesses will succeed.

As an ever-growing community of researchers and practitioners continues to build on disruption theory and integrate it with other perspectives, we will come to an even better understanding of what helps firms innovate successfully.

Disruptive Innovation from Foundation to Paradigm

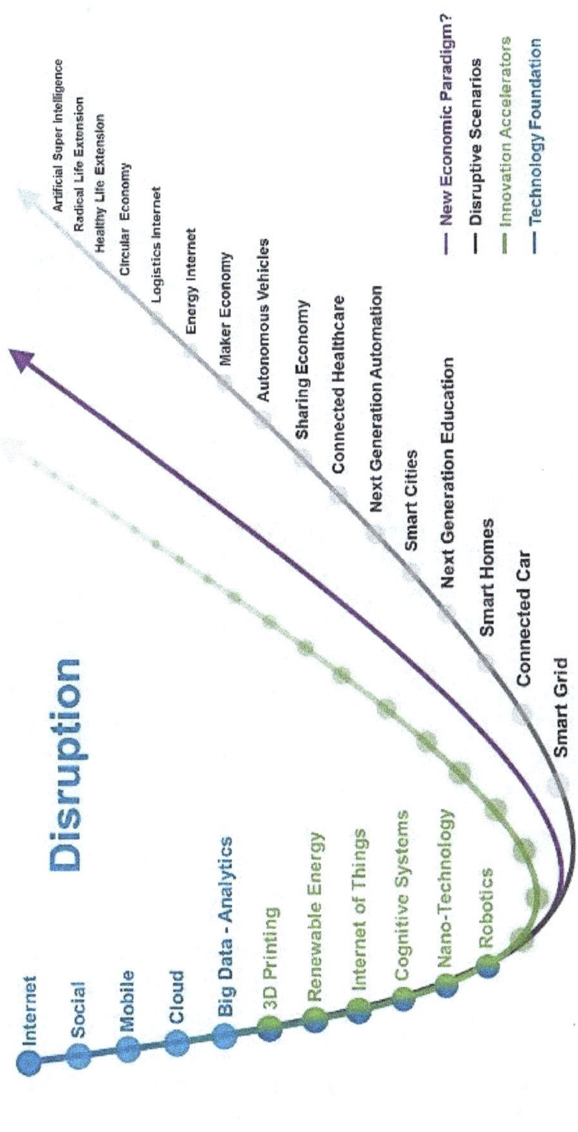

Takeaways: Disruptive innovation refers to the innovation that transforms expensive or highly sophisticated products or services previously accessible to a high-end or more-skilled segment of consumers to those that are more affordable and accessible to a broader population.

This transformation disrupts the market by displacing long-standing, established competitors.

- Disruptive innovation refers to innovations and technologies that make expensive or sophisticated products and services accessible and more affordable to a broader market, like Blackberry which was targeting business users, that become sidelined by Apple iPhone with its far superior design and larger mass market.
- Disruptive innovation refers to the use of technology that upsets a structure, as opposed to "disruptive technology", which refers to the technology itself.
- Amazon, launched as an online bookstore in the mid-1990s, is an example of disruptive innovation.
- Disruptive innovation requires enabling technology, an innovative business model, and a coherent value network.
- Sustaining innovation is the process of innovating to improve products and services for existing customers.

Disruptive innovation is not the process of improving or enhancing products for the same target group; rather, it involves the technologies used to make them easy to use and available to the larger, non-targeted market.

An example of disruptive innovation is the introduction of digital music downloads, which have, by far, replaced compact discs.

These technologies and the way they were incorporated into the business were primarily designed to allow companies to remain competitive, or at least maintain a status quo.

Disruptive technologies and the way they are integrated—the disruptive innovations were less easy to plan for and potentially more devastating to companies that did not pay enough attention to them.

Investing in a disruptive innovation can be complicated. It requires an investor to focus on how companies will adapt to disruptive technology, instead of focusing on the development of the technology itself. Companies such as Amazon, Google (GOOGL/ALPHABET), and Facebook (FB/META) are examples of companies that have heavily focused on the internet as a disruptive technology.

The internet has become so ingrained in the modern world that the companies that failed to integrate disruptive innovation into their business models have been pushed aside. Artificial intelligence (AI) and it's potential to learn from employees and perform their jobs may be a disruptive innovation for the job market as a whole soon.

What makes a technology or innovation "disruptive" is a point of contention. The term may be used to describe technologies that are not truly disruptive. The internet was disruptive because it was not an iteration of previous technology.

It was something new that created unique models for making money that never existed before. Of course, that created losses for other business models.

People using smartphones instead of laptops and desktops for their computing needs, including web browsing and streaming, is another example of disruptive innovation.

Technological enhancements have enabled cell phones to be equipped with small processors, chips, and software applications that support these functions.

Smartphone developers targeted the broad market of mobile consumers who have cellular devices and find it inconvenient to carry and access laptops when wanting to surf the net (not to mention an impossible task for desktops).
Smartphones are small, easily storable, accessible, and relatively affordable as compared to laptops and desktops.

In contrast, the Model T car is not considered a classic example of disruptive innovation because it was an improvement on existing technology and wasn't widely adopted upon its release.

The auto industry didn't take off until mass production brought prices down, moving the entire transportation system from hooves to wheels. In that sense, the mass production system meets the criteria for disruptive innovation.

Requirements for Disruptive Innovation: Disruptive innovation requires access to ignored or overlooked markets and technology that can transform a product into a more accessible and affordable one.

To be disruptive, the network of partners—suppliers, contractors, and distributors—must also benefit from the new, disruptive business model. Certain core requirements include:

- *Enabling Technology*: In business, enabling technology is defined as the technologies and innovations that substantially change or improve processes or how people do things. Specific to disruptive innovation, enabling technology is the technology that makes possible a product's affordability and availability to a broader market. Basically, the speed with which a market can be disrupted depends on how quickly the technology is developed and subsequently improved upon.
- *Innovative Business Model*: The innovative business model is a business model that uses innovations to target new or bottom-tier customers. These segments generally don't drive profits for established companies, nor do they buy their offerings because they either could not afford them, or the products were too sophisticated for use. This business model—a model not adopted by incumbents because of the disruptor's initial low-profit margins—seeks to present easy-to-use, economical solutions.

- *Coherent Value Network*: The coherent value network includes the upstream and downstream business partners that benefit from a successful disruption. The distributors, suppliers, and vendors may require process changes or reorganization to adapt or conform to the new business model. Members of the network must subscribe to the new business model to prevent failure.
- Disruptive Innovation Vs. Sustaining Innovation: Disruptive innovation is an innovation that simplifies and makes more affordable products and services to undesirable or ignored markets. Established companies typically strive to improve their products and services for their profitable customer base, largely ignoring the needs and desires of untapped segments.

On the other hand, sustaining innovation is the process of innovating to improve existing products and services for the existing customer base, either based on customer or market demands. Sustaining innovation does not target untapped or ignored markets; it's innovating to remain relevant and competitive.

Disruptive innovation requires technology that can transform the product or service into something more affordable and easier-to-use, and a network of partners who support and will benefit from the success of the disruption.

CHAPTER IV
INNOVATION HUBS

Purpose: Around the world, in places like Paris, Buenos Aires, or New York, there's a new concept spurring innovation in multi-sector hubs that span a range of business models, ownership structures, and physical layouts.

The goal is to create an incentivized ecosystem called a hub where businesses of all sizes can learn from each other, connect with peers, develop new skills, and get inspired to innovate faster.

Many of these hubs occupy repurposed iconic buildings from the industrial era, including warehouses, train stations, or navy yards, giving new life to underutilized parts of cities that had lost their vibrancy.

The ability to generate innovative solutions is mandatory for large companies to survive and grow in a very competitive environment full of changes and challenges. As a result, there is an increasing number of companies combining their resources with those offered by peers and external partners using an open innovation framework, a trend that has been gaining momentum among large organizations.

The word "hub" refers in technological language to a central piece, which receives the signals transmitted by the stations and relays them to all the others. Innovation ecosystems refer to an interconnected network of companies and other entities, which jointly develop a set of technologies, knowledge, or skills, working cooperatively to develop new products and services.

Innovation hubs exist, to drive and sustain initiatives aimed at generating business between universities, large companies, and startups. Enabling people to interact, create, undertake, work, and innovate together, to ultimately develop technology-based innovation with high growth potential.

The operation of innovation hubs enables organizations with similar objectives: to innovate and generate new business. Today, hubs have become quite popular in the business world.

The participation of companies and educational institutions, for example, has intensified, which contributes to the formulation of increasingly strategic and specialized hubs. As a result, hubs emerge as highly effective sources of innovation, whether creating new products and services or improving existing ideas on the market.

In this scenario of high demand for new and accelerated dynamics, many companies have found it difficult to innovate and remain competitive in the market. It is not difficult to find examples of highly profitable businesses in the past that have become outdated and, today, are little sought after by the public.

Going against all that, the innovation hub offers a modern alternative to evolutionary stagnation. In these environments, what we find are different brains working together, people looking for solutions to existing problems and the one that still arises.

As a result, hubs provide innovation in a much more agile and broader way, since they provide the connection of a large ecosystem, in which companies, startups, universities, and development institutions are inserted.

In other words, there is the continuous and strategic interaction of different minds engaged, prepared, and willing to innovate in projects.

In addition, if a company participates directly in an Innovation hub, it may have access to several others, expanding its opportunities and connecting with startups.

Major Global Hubs:

Are pivotal connections between leading businesses, entrepreneurs, investors, academic institutions, and services provider partners; designed to sustain, grow, and perpetuate the innovation cycle within the region and compete globally by enabling entrepreneurs to fund, launch and scale innovation. Characteristics of successful Hubs are:

1. Major STEM Research University
2. Cultural Metro with Outdoor Attraction
3. Young Professional Tailored Attraction
4. Weather and Hospitality Infrastructure
5. Moderate Rent, Fast Internet, and Safety
6. Angel Investments of (Past Startup Exit)
7. Local Pool of Skilled Knowledge Workers
8. Foreign Friendly with Protective Regulation
9. Generous Taxes and Health Care Quality
10. Global Banks, Accounting, and Law Firms
11. Local Incubators, Accelerators, and VCs
12. Satellite of Corporate Innovation Centers
13. Acclaimed Innovation Network Mentors

Must have to attract Global Corporate, including when looking to build a new HQ, launch an innovation center, acquire a company, or enter a joint venture.

1. Political stability with environmental safety
2. Affordable housing, Labor, road, and transit
3. Fast internet and good health care facility
4. Green spaces with mixed-use development
5. Population Growth and Quality of life index
6. Location attraction to Millennials and Gen Z
7. Universities' pipeline of tech-savvy workers
8. Local market consumption of emerging tech-driven by demographic growth and tech jobs
9. Global investments access from both private and public sources, with scalable funding
10. Local culture adaptability to global multinationals

Featured global innovation hubs:

Largest Facilities: Open Innovation Hubs

Barcelona Tech City, Spain: In June 2016, Barcelona Tech City opened in Pier 01, a converted building that was a shipping warehouse, next to the Historical Museum of Catalonia. It overlooks a marina on the Mediterranean and couldn't be a more inspiring place to work. Barcelona Tech City is a private non-profit membership association led by Miguel Vicente (Chairman) and Miquel Martí (CEO) that represents the tech and digital ecosystems of the city.

Approximately 100 of the total 500 members are located at Pier 01. Rents are reasonable and there's room for about 1000 individuals. Tenants are a mix of:

- Startups, accelerators, and incubators, mostly in the tech
- The Volkswagen Group's SEAT Metropolis Lab spinoff
- A payments innovation center with La Caixa Bank, Global Payments, Visa, Arval, and Samsung working together.

The City of Barcelona is also a member and hopes to integrate the energy and business opportunities created at Barcelona Tech City with companies throughout the region.

The goals of the unique cluster are to help attract local and international investment, create a more international outlook for the start-ups, help them get to the next level with legal and financial advising, connect their talent with firms needing their expertise, and provide activities and networking events so all can learn from and inspire each other. Barcelona Tech City plans to expand to more buildings in the area. The excitement and pride of working there are palpable.

Station F in Paris, France: In July 2017, Station F opened in Paris, financed by Xavier Niel, a tech billionaire who wanted to give the diffused Paris startup scene a central hub. Housed in a refurbished train depot, Station F's goal is to be the biggest startup hub in the world and break even by charging low rates for startups to rent its open-air desks. Phase one is home to 3,000 individuals working in tech, including incubators for large multinationals like Facebook with their first startup incubator, Microsoft with an Artificial Intelligence program, video game publisher Ubisoft, Airbnb, The Japanese/Korean messaging app Line, and L'Oréal, who is running an accelerator program.

Startups at Station F span across sectors from medicine, to food, fashion, software, beauty, and e-commerce. Last year France surpassed Germany in the level of venture capital funding deals, behind the UK. President Macron and Xavier Niel expect Station F to further energize the economy, providing new opportunities for the engineering and design talent France has had throughout its history.

At Station F, graffiti railway cars have been turned into cafes. There are areas for meetings, relaxation, and events, and housing for entrepreneurs is planned down the road.

Buenos Aires, Technological District, Argentina: Over the past decade, Argentina has created 4 of South America's 6 unicorns (sales of over $1 billion annually). In 2007 and 2008, when Mauricio Macri, now Argentina's President, was mayor of Buenos Aires, he started a movement to improve neighborhoods in the city's poorer south side and simultaneously jump-start a technology and design revolution.

One of the hottest new tech neighborhoods in Buenos Aires is Parque Patricos, bordering on lively San Telmo. Macri sought to bring business, investment, infrastructure, security, and transportation to areas of the city that had been industrial but isolated in part due to a lack of nearby subways. A new subway stop and city bike share stations have been added there.

A Norman Foster-designed building with an undulating roof in Parque Patricios is the first building in South America to be LEED Certified. Banco Ciudad has extended bank loans to new tenants. The city offered tax breaks, and charming cafes and restaurants moved in little by little. Today, companies like Telefónica, the massive telco from Spain, Deloitte, Accenture from the US, Huawei from China, Nokia from Finland, Tata consulting from India, and two Argentine unicorns, Despegar.com (like Kyak) Mercadolibre.com (like eBay) are based there.

The nearby Metropolitan Design Center and Institute of Technology of Buenos Aires have both been catalysts for design, tech, and social media-based startups coming to the area. Private/public sector collaboration has greatly impacted developing Argentina's tech industry.

The Brooklyn Navy Yard, NY. US: For more than 150 years, The Brooklyn Navy Yard built and launched America's most famous warships. During WWII there were 70,000 workers there. In 1966 the US Federal Government decommissioned the shipyard and expected a major auto manufacturer would take its place.

None did and for decades the property was underutilized. In 2003 Steiner Studios, the largest movie and TV production studio in the Northeastern U.S. began development. Little by little, a mix of hard goods manufacturing, craft studios, food production, start-up incubators, and rooftop agriculture have been moving in, adding back thousands of jobs and a highly creative vibe. The interesting mix includes:

- New Lab for advanced technology, growth-stage startups in robotics, artificial intelligence, connected devices, nanotech, med tech, and indoor agriculture.
- Metal fabrication firm Situ Studio, started by grads from Cooper Union, is a part craft-making shop, part art studio.
- CUNY's Fierstein Graduate School of Cinema is considered to be second only to USCs in Los Angeles
- Brooklyn Grange, the largest urban rooftop farm in the world

Greenpoint & Williamsburg, Brooklyn, NY. US: A 10-block radius including Greenpoint, Brooklyn, known for decades as Little Poland, and Williamsburg, has transformed into an innovation neighborhood, in contrast to other planned, contained hubs. Over a short time, span, a mix of global brand innovation studios have opened there, to be near the creative sensibility and energy of nearby Williamsburg.

- Adidas located one of its 3 global innovation studios there. It is known as Brooklyn Creative Farm, and its MakerLab is called a "Disneyland for Designers".
- BMW launched an accelerator for urban living ideas with a creative workspace for residents called A/D/O. The environment is light and airy, and the café is run by Claus Meyer, a former partner in NOMA of Copenhagen, ranked #1 Restaurant in the World by San Pellegrino several times in the past decade. Events that celebrate different types of creativity are open to the public. The goal is to support an exchange of ideas across fields.
- The Richemont Group (Cartier & Van Cleef & Arpels) has a small creative studio, tucked away in a newly renovated office building.
- Wylie Dufresne, considered the molecular gastronomy king of New York, opened an inventive donut shop.

Government Funded Largest Programs: doing the most to innovate in science and technologies:

1. CEA, France (16,000 Technician, 115 Spinoff Startup)
2. Fraunhofer Society, Germany (24,000 Staff Members)
3. Science and Technology Agency, Japan
4. Department of Health and Human Services, US

Source: Ranking by Thomson Reuters

Corporate Innovation Centers: Today, the need to be digitally innovative is obvious: The top 5 of the most valuable tech companies in the world are former digital startups.

Many previously globally leading companies such as Kodak and Nokia, missed the digital revolution and lost their leading position or went bankrupt. In fact, 52% of Fortune 500 companies have merged, acquired, or gone bankrupt since 2001. The message that companies need to be innovative and disruptive in their products and services, culture, and processes should have reached every manager today.

Corporate R&D and innovation organizations "Including academia and government-funded" spend billions to keep their edge ahead in the market. For 2022, forecasts predict around $5 Trillion ($2.9 trillion of global corporate R&D spending, plus another $2.1 trillion from academia and government funding).

Despite these significant investments, companies fear that the results are falling short. While R&D costs increase and respective returns decrease, the constant rise of successful startups continues, even though they leverage comparably small investments.

Recent research indicates that more than 85% of new products fail for consumer goods. After further investigation, of emerging trends of startup innovation, it was apparent that most companies grew independently, while famous spin-offs with innovative businesses from large organizations are quite very rare.

Corporations begin to question how many startups with such small investments can rock the boat of traditional business models, taking significant market share away from large companies. The promising advantages and specific qualities of innovation centers have proven effective in supporting the setup of an environment to innovate separately from company constraints and create an openness for external ideas and/ or people.

Corporations embed innovation centers as an instrument to support their innovation strategy, establishing their own corporate VCs, accelerators, incubators, and labs.

There are also similar models with additional names like campuses or hubs for very similar innovation centers. These are the leading pioneers:

Google x: the lab where a team of scientists, engineers, and entrepreneurs attempt to take moonshots from concept to reality. The guiding philosophy is to radically reimagine what's possible, especially when it comes to intractable issues like clean energy and connectivity.

Amazon Lab126: Amazon founded this lab with a simple directive: reinvent the book. Lab126 devoted years to the project, releasing the first Kindle in 2007. It sold out in 5.5 hours. Since then, the lab's hardware, software, and operations teams have further streamlined the device.

"We really didn't want any bezel or bling," Chris Green, Lab 126's VP of Design, told TechCrunch. "Everything we've done over 15 generations has been to reduce [the Kindle] to basically a piece of paper."

They've gotten impressively close. Modern Kindles weigh less than their clunkier predecessors and have no keypads or buttons. Lab126 does more than just Kindles, though they conceptualize and finesse all Amazon hardware, which includes Fire TVs and tablets, and Echo, which houses the smart and widely known personal assistant Alexa.

The team strives to make these gadgets powerful, easy to use, and genuinely fun.

Volkswagen Automotive Innovation Lab: Led by three Stanford professors, the Volkswagen Automotive Innovation Lab, or VAIL, is located on campus at the Center for Automotive Research at Stanford (a.k.a. CARS). Its teams comprised of academics and Volkswagen partners from Silicon Valley, among others, work to invent cars of the future.

And, yes, that includes driverless cars. In fact, Volkswagen's team has been working on autonomous vehicles since the early aughts; in 2005, a Volkswagen Touareg SUV drove itself more than 100 miles in the Mojave Desert.

It was a first for the auto industry, and Volkswagen has been building on that success.

Xerox Parc: (Palo Alto Research Center: formerly Xerox PARC) is a research and development company in Palo Alto, California, Founded in 1969.

It has been at the heart of numerous revolutionary computer developments such as laser printing, Ethernet, the modern personal computer, graphical user interface (GUI) and desktop paradigm, object-oriented programming, ubiquitous computing, electronic paper, amorphous silicon (a-Si) applications, the computer mouse, and advancing very-large-scale integration (VLSI) for semiconductors.

After three decades as a division of Xerox, PARC was transformed in 2002 into an independent, wholly owned subsidiary company dedicated to developing and maturing advances in science and business concepts leading to its merger with SRI.

SRI International (SRI): The trustees of Stanford University established it in 1946 as a center of innovation to support economic development in the region.

SRI performs client-sponsored research and development for government agencies, commercial businesses, and private foundations. It also licenses its technologies, forms strategic partnerships, sells products, and creates spin-off companies.

Top 10 Global Fortune 500 Rank in 2000 and 2021 by Revenues

2000 Rank	Company	HQ	2021 Rank	Company	HQ
1	GM	US	1	**Walmart**	US
2	**Walmart**	US	2	State Grid	China
3	Exxon	US	3	Amazon	US
4	Ford	US	4	China NP	China
5	GE	US	5	Sinopec	China
6	IBM	US	6	Apple	US
7	Citigroup	US	7	CVS	US
8	AT&T	US	8	UnitedHealth	US
9	Altria	US	9	Toyota	Japan
10	Boeing	US	10	Volkswagen	Germany

Top 10 Global Fortune 500 Rank in 2021 by Revenues vs Valuation

Revenue	Company	HQ	Valued	Company	HQ
1	Walmart	US	1	**Apple**	US
2	State Grid	US	2	Microsoft	US
3	**Amazon**	US	3	**Amazon**	US
4	China NP	US	4	Alphabet	US
5	Sinopec	US	5	Facebook	US
6	**Apple**	US	6	Tencent	China
7	CVS	US	7	Tesla	US
8	UnitedHealth	US	8	Alibaba	China
9	Toyota	US	9	TSMC	Taiwan
10	Volkswagen	US	10	Berkshire	US

Top 10 Global Fortune 500 Rank in 2021 by R&D vs Profit

R&D	Company	HQ	Profit	Company	HQ
1	Amazon	US	1	**Apple**	US
2	**Alphabet**	US	2	Aramco	Saudi A
3	Volkswagen	US	3	Softbank	US
4	Samsung	US	4	ICBA	China
5	**Microsoft**	US	5	**Microsoft**	US
6	Huawei	US	6	Berkshire	US
7	Intel	US	7	**Alphabet**	US
8	**Apple**	US	8	CCB	China
9	Roche	US	9	ABOC	China
10	Johnson & J	US	10	Facebook	US

Incubators and Accelerators:

Commercial Startup Incubators: begin with companies (or even single entrepreneurs) that may be earlier in the process and do not operate on a set schedule. An incubator will not necessarily expect you to be ready to go to the mass market. Instead, as the name suggests, this support 'incubates' an idea or innovation from inspiration to launch.

That doesn't mean you won't be expected to do the hard work, but it can mean that the work is made easier for you. For example, a startup incubator might facilitate networking opportunities or put you in contact with investors who are a good match for your idea.

Like a medical incubator, the business equivalent creates the best conditions for survival and growth. In the first instance, it's about making sure your business lives. Beyond that, it becomes more about helping your venture to thrive. Different startup incubators receive their funding from different sources. Some examples of these include:

VC firms, angel investors, government entities, and major corporations, among others. Some incubators have an application process, but others only work with companies and ideas that they come in contact with through trusted partners.

Commercial Startup Accelerators: A prerequisite for acceptance is the fact that you should already have a commercially viable idea that is ready to take to market and scale up massively. Startup accelerator programs often put in place a fairly strict schedule, which can be over as little as a few weeks or months, during which time frame the accelerator will work with you to build your business and iron out any problems you may encounter.

Accelerator programs usually have a set timeframe in which individual companies spend anywhere from a few weeks to a few months working with a group of mentors to build out their business and avoid problems along the way. Accelerators start with an application process, but the top programs are typically very selective. They accept about 2% of the applications they receive.

Non-Profit Startup Incubators:

Stanford University: StartX has the Student-in-Residence (SIR) program for current Stanford students, which is a six-month program offering up to $8,000 in financial aid per founder as well as dedicated office space, customized coaching and mentorship, an Investor Day Demo, and a conversion path into StartX full-time. Full-time StartX companies raise an average of $7.2 million in funding.

University of California, Berkeley: The Berkeley SkyDeck fund offers up to $100,000 for companies accepted to their six-month cohort program. Recipients get $50,000 upon acceptance and $50,000 at the 3-month mark offered via a SAFE note with no discount.

The incubator also offers to invest up to 10% in the first funding round, with a $2 million cap. Companies can use the financing for a range of business activities, such as hiring, product development, and marketing.

Harvard University: For current Harvard students, the Venture Incubation Program (VIP) within Harvard's Innovation Lab fund is a 12-week program with mentoring and resources. Harvard's Innovation Lab also hosts the President's Innovation Challenge, where students can win funding money of up to $75,000 for a great idea. Judging criteria includes viability, empathy, rigor, ingenuity, traction, economics, and impact.

Massachusetts Institute of Technology: Massachusetts Institute of Technology (MIT)'s delta v is an educational startup accelerator for student entrepreneurs to build viable, sustainable businesses.

MIT students get customized, intensive coaching and mentoring, networking opportunities, and funding through summer programming in NYC and at MIT. Delta-v provides up to $20,000 equity-free additional funding for each venture (achievement-based), $2,000 per month for living expenses, and the chance to pitch to investors at MIT Demo Days. This program is especially geared toward early-stage startups.

Top 3 Incubators and Accelerators in Silicon Valley by Startup Stage,

Rank	Pre-Seed	Rank	Launch	Rank	Revenues
1	Angel Pad	1	Y Combinator	1	OneTraction
2	OneTraction	2	Techstars	2	Mach49
3	Founder Institute	3	500 Startup	3	Alchemist

The Four Institutions That Support Startups

	INCUBATORS	ANGEL INVESTORS	ACCELERATORS	HYBRID
Duration	1 to 5 years	Ongoing	3 to 6 months	3 months to 2 years
Cohorts	No	No	Yes	No
Business model	Rent; nonprofit	Investment	Investment; can also be nonprofit	Investment; can also be nonprofit
Selection	Noncompetitive	Competitive, ongoing	Competitive, cyclical	Competitive, ongoing
Venture stage	Early or late	Early	Early	Early
Education	Ad hoc, human resources, legal	None	Seminars	Various incubator and accelerator practices
Mentorship	Minimal, tactical	As needed by investor	Intense, by self and others	Staff expert support, some mentoring
Venture location	On-site	Off-site	On-site	On-site

SOURCE "WHAT DO ACCELERATORS DO? INSIGHTS FROM INCUBATORS AND ANGELS" BY SUSAN COHEN, 2013; ADAPTATIONS BY IAN HATHAWAY

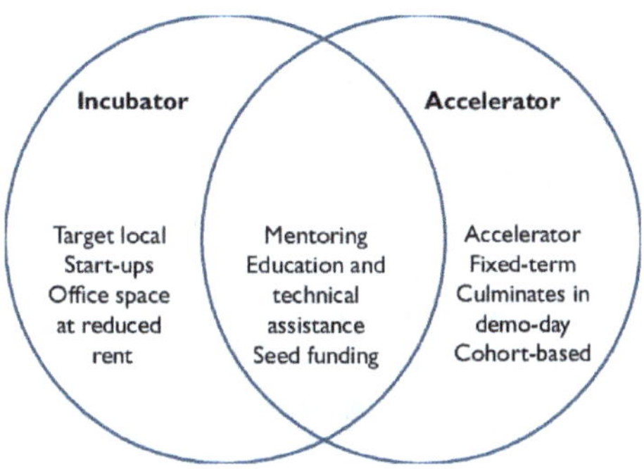

Co-Tenant Innovation Open Space: or coworking is when people assemble in a neutral space to work independently on different projects, or in groups on the same projects. It's different from a typical office workspace because the people in a coworking environment generally aren't working for the same company.

Coworking spaces offer the same amenities you would find in a traditional office, along with a lot more.

A major differentiator is flexibility since you don't need to sign a long-term lease in a coworking space. Every coworking space will always have basics like WIFI, printers, and usually, some type of conference room, some will have tea, coffee, and snacks. Some will have startup resources ranging from digital assets, and even coaches to advisors.

Some may have 3D printers and other tech that you may not always have access to. Some budget-conscious coworking spaces are more barebones, offering little more than a desk and WIFI. Coworking spaces come in all shapes and sizes.

There are many things to consider when searching locations, community, amenities, and workspace environment are all factors that vary from space to space. The main types are:

- Open Workspaces: different companies share hot and dedicated desks in an office-less space.
- Private Workspaces: One Company uses the entire space.
- Industry-Specific: designed for one or more industries.
- Venture/Incubators: Vetted or Portfolio Startups only.

As young people continue to realize that they don't necessarily have to fall in line and follow a more traditional path in their careers, we'll likely see an increase in the number of freelancers and entrepreneurs who will make the leap. This will be led by technology, awareness, and opportunity. Coworking will be the new norm for people who enter the workforce today.

It's unlikely that coworking will replace office buildings in general, or that everyone will one day become a freelancer. Large organizations will continue to thrive, and new ones will be built from the ground up, but they may focus less on having centralized locations and more on offering perks like remote working.

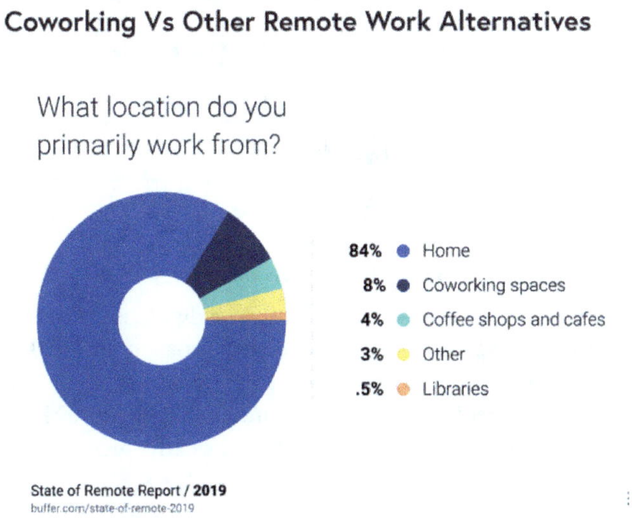

There were roughly 57.3 million freelancers in the United States alone in 2017, and by 2027, they estimate that most of the U.S. workforce will do some type of freelance work, in some capacity, including people who have a side gig as a freelancer and do it part-time.

Top 3 Innovation Space vs Coworking Space vs Global Access in Silicon Valley

Rank	Innovation Space	Rank	Coworking	Rank	Global Access
1	Plug and Play	1	Galvanize	1	WeWork
2	GSV Labs	2	Bespoke	2	Regis
3	Hanahaus	3	NextSpace	3	CIC

It is estimated that almost **5 million people** will be working from coworking spaces by 2024, an increase of 158% compared to 2020.

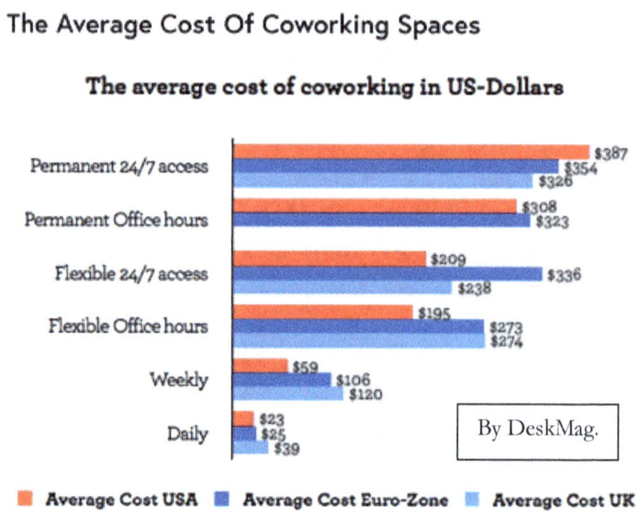

The number of coworking spaces worldwide is **projected to reach almost 20,000** this year and **cross over 40,000 by 2024**. While the industry is set to grow at a slower pace in 2020, we expect growth to rebound and develop even more rapidly from 2021 onwards, with a yearly growth rate of 21.3%.

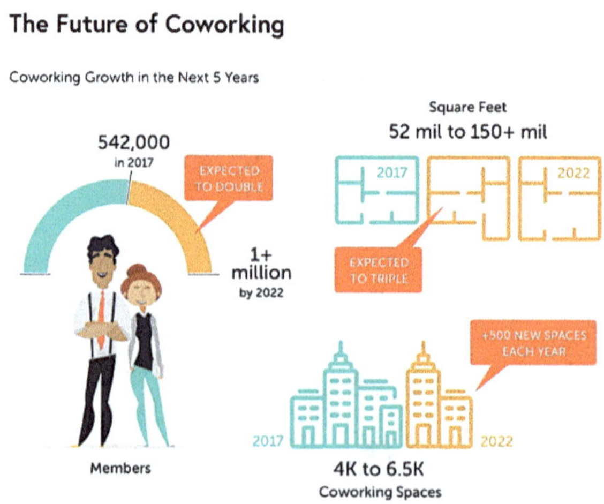

Coworking Growth (Source: DeskMag)

Universities Education vs Innovation:

The rising cost of attending a college or university has caused the public to question the worth of a college education. There have been several studies regarding this issue and the data conclude that those with college educations will experience higher earnings throughout their lives, will be less likely to experience layoffs, will contribute more to their communities, and are more likely to be physically healthy.

Yet, the financial outlay for many students causes families with already strained resources to question if it is worth it.

Added emphasis by the federal government on "gainful employment" statistics and loan repayment rates immediately after graduation as a measure of the quality of education from each institution can enhance this rising skepticism about college education.

Higher education institutions will need to demonstrate value to the public and potential students if they are to remain viable.

The U.S. economy is becoming more reliant on colleges and universities to prepare students for "middle-skill" jobs. These jobs often require post-secondary education but, perhaps, not a bachelor's degree. It is estimated that nearly half of all job openings within the next five years will be "middle-skill" jobs.

While this may be good news for community colleges, it may be bad news for the rest of the higher education industry. Focusing on developing students for work in "middle-skill" jobs means focusing on more practical skills and less on theoretical knowledge.

Again, this has been a large market for community colleges. However, over the past decade, private for-profit colleges have pursued this market vigorously and grown their enrollments at a much faster rate than community colleges.

The traditional business model for colleges and universities is in jeopardy. Several factors are disrupting the higher education business model that will likely force college leaders to rethink their models to survive.

As these challenges continue to face higher education, leaders of colleges and universities will need to be more innovative. They will need to examine their business models, their consumer markets, their infrastructures, and their processes to create a value proposition that positions their institution for a sustainable financial future. But true innovation in higher education is not easy.

Higher education is filled with highly educated people who hold advanced degrees; many of whom are seen as national experts in their fields of study. Additionally, through research at colleges and universities, many of the innovations that we see in thousands of products that are used around the world were made possible by creative faculty in research labs.

These individuals are innovative. It would stand to reason that with so many creative and highly educated people, colleges and universities would be institutions of innovation.

They would have cultures of creativity and disruptive innovation that would establish new standards for education around the world. However, largely, institutions are not innovative. While college and university presidents across the country tout the advancements of their institutions, give presentations at conferences, write papers, etc. it appears that much of this innovation on campuses is sustaining innovation at best (small improvements).

Like shared governance, the faculty of any institution can propel it forward or hold it back. As stated above, the overall process of higher education has not changed in hundreds of years. It is well recognized that without the faculty of an institution firmly committed to innovation at a college or university, any efforts to significantly change the institutions are likely to fail.

Sometimes getting faculty buy-in to innovate can be difficult due to resistance to change.

While much of the current criticism about higher education would reflect the teaching role of faculty, most of the current higher education reward systems (particularly big-name universities) are based on research. A nationwide study of faculty salaries conducted by James Fairweather, of the Pennsylvania State University, in which this is very clearly exemplified.

He found that those who spent more time on research and published the most received higher salaries than their colleagues who were focused on teaching - regardless of the program area.

Top 50 Metro Areas for College Grads

Share of residents 25 and older who have completed a bachelor's degree and above, as of 2019.

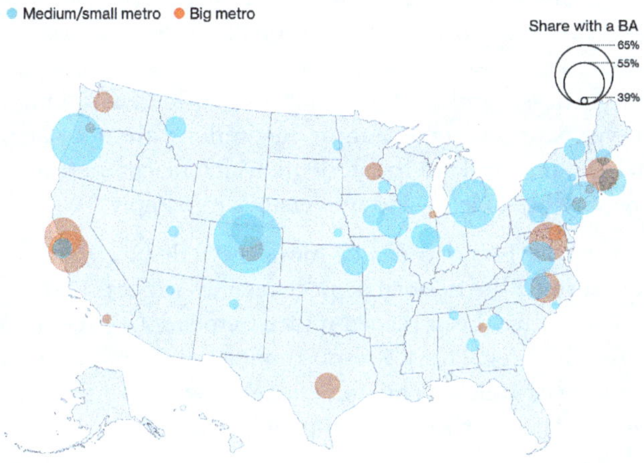

Source: U.S. Census Bureau
Note: Big metros have over 1 million residents

The big takeaway: Despite the continued dominance of a few coastal metro areas, many more affordable places have made considerable strides in attracting talent in the nation's heartland,

It is no wonder that faculty attitudes reflect the perception that research is much more valued in higher education, even at institutions with strong teaching histories.

Faculty have and value their autonomy within the structure of the college and university environment. The Fairweather study also found that faculty believe that they are "safer" if they keep to themselves and maintain the status quo.

He found that faculty believe that assistant professors who devote time to teaching and curricular reform are much more at risk. Department chairs consistently warned assistant professors to stay out of coalition activities despite the commitment by deans to improve curriculum and pedagogy.

This suggests that faculty have a stronger affiliation with their discipline and department than with the college or university (a finding in numerous studies of faculty life) which keeps them from participating in college-wide innovations.

In the United States, institutions of higher education are accredited by regional (or occasionally sector) accrediting agencies. The process of accreditation is essentially a peer review process and accreditation is considered voluntary. However, without accreditation, institutions are not eligible for federal financial aid for students which places a great deal of pressure on colleges and universities to comply.

Over the past two decades or more the federal government has questioned the rigor of a "peer review" process and thus, accreditation has been placed under tremendous pressure to increase its regulatory responsibility and improve its monitoring of colleges and universities. Some even argue that the accreditation process is completely broken.

Senator Marco Rubio (R-FL) stated that "We have a broken accreditation system that favors established institutions while blocking out new, innovative, and more affordable competitors." Nonetheless, there is a sentiment that accrediting bodies focus on processes and traditional structures, rather than outcomes and impact.

They suggest that this focus keeps institutions from being innovative in their approaches to education and learning to remain in compliance with accreditation standards.

Stanford University has developed a reputation for excellence in innovation, liberal arts, and research. Looking more deeply, one can see that Stanford University has developed a culture of innovation and entrepreneurship that is not likely to be matched by any other university. Stanford's ability to help graduates launch new businesses is unparalleled.

In a time when governments are looking to higher education to spark and advance the economy, Stanford seems to be an institution that embodies that spirit of innovation.

Unlike institutions that conceal themselves from the "outside world" to protect an academic environment, Stanford welcomes interaction with the business world. In fact, Stanford offers faculty members opportunities to take a two-year leave to work in the industry or start a venture company. The belief is that those faculty will bring.

Most organizations are not necessarily doing anything groundbreaking, or new, they still call it 'innovation.' Just because it just sounds grander." "These are not innovations - rather they are simply improvements. Innovation is a skill that can be taught and, if managed well, become the culture of an organization. Through a process called Innovation by Design or Design Thinking (often used interchangeably).

Any organization can develop breakthrough ideas and products that provide sustaining or disruptive innovation in the market. Design Thinking is "...a human-centered, prototype-driven process for innovation that can be applied to a product, service, and business design."

Human-centered means that from the very start, the innovation team needs to understand what the customer wants at a very core level. The team may develop an understanding of the customers' wants better than the customers, themselves, know them. This understanding doesn't come from surveys and interviews; rather, it comes from observations and research. It is a very empathetic approach - and not very linear.

A prototype-driven approach can be uncomfortable. It means that the team will brainstorm many ideas that could solve the "problem" (the problem being the issue that sparked a need for a new product or service).

Brainstorming identifies numerous approaches to potential solutions, no matter how far-fetched they may seem. Then, the team develops inexpensive prototypes of the product, or service, to explore what works and what doesn't work. The motto for this process is "Fail often, fail early, and learn from failure." If there are no failures in the process, the team is not truly innovating.

STEM Education: fewer than 40 percent of students who enter college intending to major in a STEM field complete a STEM "Science, Technology, Engineering and Math" degree, and the greatest loss of those students occurs during the first two years of college, while the US has many jobs in technical fields for which U.S. workers do not have the needed skills.

Community colleges do much of the training for technical jobs in the United States and are extensively involved with the first two years of STEM education in college. They are urged by universities to think in a very different way about how they teach science courses to students so that students are more engaged in what they are learning and less likely to leave STEM fields for other majors.

Given the difficulty of attracting sufficient U.S. students to STEM fields, the United States will depend on the inflow of foreign graduate students in these fields for the foreseeable future. Many students who earn a Ph.D. in a STEM field from a U.S. university should automatically qualify for permanent resident status in the United States.

People are mobile globally, and many scientists, engineers, and innovators still want to come to the United States or stay in the country once they earn degrees from U.S. colleges and universities. More rational immigration and naturalization policies would benefit the United States, specifically highly educated individuals, whether they have degrees from U.S. institutions or universities in other countries.

The French 42 Model: which is a tuition-free computer programming school created and funded by French billionaire Xavier Niel with several partners including Nicolas Sadirac (previous leader of the Epitech school in France), out of more than 80,000 candidates in France, 3,000 were selected to complete a four-week intensive computer programming boot camp called piscine (swimming-pool).

Any person older than 18 can register for the piscine after completing the logical reasoning tests on the website. The school does not have any professors and is open 24/7 and entirely free. The training is inspired by peer-to-peer, pedagogy, and project-based learning. All the intellectual property belongs to the students.

42 Silicon Valley is the US campus and has been created and funded by the same team from France, its name is a reference to the science fiction book The Hitchhiker's Guide to the Galaxy written by British author Douglas Adams: in the book 42 is the Answer to the Ultimate Question of Life, the Universe, and Everything.

In addition to the two official campuses in Paris, France, and Fremont, California, the school model was adopted across France, as well as in Europe, and other parts of the world, including South Africa, Morocco, Indonesia, Canada, and the UAE with the help and support of 42.

The higher education Business Model is under more scrutiny than ever in its history. Pressure to keep costs low, minimize tuition increases, demonstrate a positive value proposition, and operate efficiently is mounting from elected officials and the public.

At the same time, for public institutions, state financial support has withered and is not likely to return in abundance in the predictable future.

This will require colleges and universities to think and act more like a business. Some nurtured ideas are:

- Link degree performance to jobs upon graduation
- Pay for education through a fixed percentage of paid jobs.
- Hire professors from outside academia as "dowers."
- Allow lecturer access based on operational execution experience, not wealth or media-fueled prominent managers "Doers not Talkers".
- Limit professor tenure to 5 years and retirement at 60
- Match students with professors by age group, gender
- Rotate professors with students of various backgrounds.
- Link Research to industry sponsors that commit to taking it to market.
- Open doors for non-university incubators and startups, by offering free events space and academia-student access.
- Restrict major venture capital and tech companies' financial support that excludes small and under-funded peers, by enabling equal and transparent access.

2021 Top 10 US Startup valued $10B+ by Founder Education:

Startup	Industry	Founder	Education	Alumni	Born
Stripe	Finance	Patrick Collison	Undergrade	Ireland	Ireland
SpaceX	Space	Elon Musk	Undergrade	U of Penn	S/Africa
Instacart	Delivery	Apoorva Mehta	Undergrade	Canada	India
Databricks	Software	Ali Ghodsi	PhD	Sweden	Iran
Chime	Banking	Chris Britt	Undergrade	Tulane U	US
Fanatics	Retail	Michael Rubin	Drop out	Villanova	US
GoPuff	Shopping	Yakir Gola	Drop out	Drexel	US
Grammarly	Utility	Max Lytvyn	MBA	Vanderbilt	Ukraine
Brex	Finance	Henrique Dubugras	Drop out	Stanford	Brazil
Biosplice	Health	Osman Kibar	Undergrade	Caltech	Turkey

Entrepreneurship: How many successful entrepreneurs would recommend a bachelor's degree followed by a graduate degree in entrepreneurship? No survey has been conducted to my knowledge, but it probably wouldn't be an overwhelming majority. After all, entrepreneurs are time-driven risk-takers and might not see the best ROI in taking such a costly and relatively time-consuming approach. This doesn't mean a college degree is useless for entrepreneurs, but it might mean that it shouldn't be the sole foundation for your dreams. One way to bridge industrial-era education to the knowledge economy is as follows:

- College/University Degree must be two years.
- Degrees must be tied to open jobs and role-based skills.
- Education must be based on successful experience in the field, not scientific or academic theory "Excluding Ph.D.".
- Students must get inputs from the industry along with external innovators.

Universities Research Park:

Research parks enable the flow of ideas between innovation generators such as universities, federal labs, and non-profit R&D institutions and companies located in both the research park and the surrounding region.

They are physical environments that can generate, attract, and retain science and technology companies and talent in alignment with sponsoring research institutions that include universities, as well as public, private, and federal research laboratories.

Universities are important sources of many of the new ideas in science and technology that contribute to innovation in the US. Students, graduates, and faculty members sometimes play a direct role by consulting with existing companies or even starting their own companies.

By producing new knowledge and exposing students to that knowledge, Universities not only generate new ideas but prepare knowledgeable, innovative, and motivated graduates who can carry those ideas into the market through commercial businesses across industries, NGOs, and governments.

The Role of Universities: The culture of a university influences its success in producing innovation and can influence the culture of the whole region where it is based. A university does not merely prepare young people for a wide variety of roles in an innovative economy; its higher mission is to "discover and invent the future."

Universities might benefit from examining the rules governing the amount of time faculty can devote to outside activities. Faculty members and students can have conflicts of interest and conflicts of commitment that need to be understood and properly managed.

The technology transfer policies of universities may be in need of rigorous review and assessment.

University Research Parks Facts:

- They are a major economic driver in many universities.
- Corporate Innovation centers are major key sponsors.
- A key focus is the Incubation of emerging tech startups.
- Part of key regional economic development policies
- Attract and grow high-skilled paying jobs in a region.

Universities exist to produce educated students. These students include not just the founders of new companies but the employees and customers of those companies. The first few hires for a startup are critical, but the next one hundred or one thousand people are also important for its success.

Universities should not be farming teams for industry; they should not be engaged in designing the next product for a company's line. Instead, they should seek the continuous innovations that create or transform a positive impact industry while teaching their students how to execute within.

The mission of the university is to "discover and invent the future," as quoted by John Hennessy, "Ex-President of Stanford University and Google Board member". Investments by governments are essential if universities are to fulfill them.

Technology Transfer Offices: They can establish beneficial relationships with individuals and organizations outside universities, many universities have created these offices to foster the transfer and licensing of technologies developed by faculty members and students to commercial companies' "industry" but they often have competing mandates:

- The university president sets one set of goals.
- Licensing officers are evaluated on a different goal
- State legislators mandate yet another set of objectives.

This reflects the fact that universities have multiple objectives that they want to achieve through technology licensing, including regional development, revenue generation, and recruiting and retaining faculty (for example, by supporting faculty spinoff companies), and these objectives are rarely prioritized.

At the same time, technology licensing offices often are evaluated solely by the amount of revenue they generate, which creates the wrong incentives and can disrupt the academic environment and culture, thus suppressing interactions with industry rather than fostering them.

The revenue generated from technology licensing tends to be featured in publications from universities and talks by administrators, but nearly all available data on licensing revenues consist of gross revenues. The net returns are much smaller after operating expenses and other liabilities are subtracted.

With a few exceptions, such as Stanford, the net licensing revenues are much smaller than the amount of industry-sponsored research at a university, this creates a tension between using licensing policy to maximize revenue vs using licensing policy to develop broader relationships with industry.

There is "an astonishing lack of experimentation" by universities of different ways of organizing their relationships with industry. An example of such experimentation is the University of California system, where faculty members have the option of not working with the technology licensing office.

Instead of patenting an invention, they can put it in the public domain and seek benefits from exchanges with people who want to discuss innovation and make a product based on that idea.

This does not work in all fields of technology, and administrators may lament potential losses of revenue, but in some areas, it is a valuable alternative to technology licensing. Many universities have tried to emulate the licensing successes of Stanford when in fact they are very different kinds of institutions.

The heterogeneity of U.S. higher education has always been one of its strengths and creates opportunities for experimentation. In addition, collaboration among different types of colleges and universities offers the potential to increase benefits and reduce costs.

Even at universities that have had great successes with technology licensing, the returns can be deceptive.

The current chairman of COSEPUP, Richard Zare, the Marguerite Blake Wilbur Professor in Natural Science at Stanford, said that he had looked at the greatest returns to Stanford from licensing. The greatest single return came from patents that Stanley Cohen and Herbert Boyer were granted on the recombinant DNA techniques they pioneered.

The second biggest return came from the School of Music for the invention of technologies used in the Yamaha synthesizer. The third largest return was for licensing the Stanford logo. Zare insisted that Stanford graduates return much more to the university than its licensing. "It's not Hewlett-Packard but Hewlett and Packard individually and their families who have given money back to Stanford."

As Hennessy said, the philanthropy from Hewlett and Packard to Stanford dwarfed any licensing fee that could have been charged for the discoveries they used to start their company.

Technology licensing offices can be counterproductive if they cause negotiations to be so complex that agreements are scuttled. They also pointed to the negative consequences of a widespread belief among state legislators that licensing offices could produce abundant resources for universities, which then could displace government funding.

Even senior university officials and technology licensing officers sometimes have a "somewhat naïve view" that all areas of technology have the potential to create successes, but in the past, it occurred in just a few circumstances. The objectives of technology licensing offices are much broader.

These offices can forge connections with industry, help faculty members move their ideas beyond the walls of the university, and support regional and national economies

Hennessy described one approach Stanford has pursued to support student-driven incubated innovations for three to six months to see if they can be developed to the point where they would attract commercial interest or the interest of a venture capital firm or angel investor.

It remains an interesting educational experience for the students with very minimal investment, Hennessy observed. For example, he mentioned a group of students who were working on a way for students to pay each other money using their phones.

The students got money to spend three months working on the project, and they lived in a house together and spent 12 hours a day working to see what the technology could do. It cost $5,000 to support the students, and they had an educational experience that resulted in a potential business opportunity.

The biggest problem with university incubators, according to Hennessy, is that they need to be shut down if they are not producing results, and shutting them down can be difficult. "You give them a hard deadline and say, go out and get funding by this deadline or you are out."

The history of incubators at universities is not promising, because they often require that university staff members shut down projects led by faculty members. "You could do it and make it work, but it would take tough love," said Hennessy. One possibility suggested by Zare would be to have the industrial part of an incubator report directly to the administration of a university and be judged over a five-year time frame rather than on a year-to-year basis.

Another possibility would be for the Universities Research Park to be part of a university-government entity that could take equity in early start-up companies or let privately owned incubators co-host rent-free on the university research park contingent on reaching pre-agreed annual goals.

Research Parks Role: It is important to consider regional and institutional cultures. universities and private companies have very different cultures, and a major challenge is to understand and deal with the differences. One way to bridge the gap is to create a hybrid (Research Park - Corporate Innovation Center – Startup Incubators) housed under one roof.

Research parks are important institutions for filling in some of the gaps between research institutions and industry. They help regions turn their investment in education into good jobs and economic productivity. Significant variety and scale exist among research parks, but they still need external support. The formation of research parks has continued at a rapid pace and has spread quickly internationally.

Research parks are not necessary to develop research capacity. However, they can stimulate the economy by enhancing research capacity enough to support higher-value activities and attract business investment. They also benefit from evolving and responding to both regional and global competition.

Types of Research Park: The oldest parks are Stanford Research Park (Stanford University in California, 1951) and Cornell Business and Technology Park (Cornell University in New York, 1952). Even though by the 1970s there was general acceptance of the concept of a park benefiting both research organizations and universities, park creation slowed at this time because several park ventures failed, and an uncertain economic climate led to a decline in total R&D activity.

The founding of new parks increased in the 1980s in response to public policy initiatives that encouraged additional private R&D investment and more aggressive university technology transfer activities. Economic expansion in the 1990s spurred another wave of new parks.

Cornell Tech is building a diverse environment of academics and practitioners who excel at imagining, researching, and building digitally enabled products and services to directly address societal and commercial needs, particularly in areas that both draw on and contribute to the vibrancy of New York City.

Cornell Tech arose from an economic development initiative of Michael Bloomberg's mayoral administration in 2008. The initiative sought to attract another engineering school to the city in the hope that it would produce entrepreneurial engineers who would in turn start job-creating companies.

Seven bids were submitted for the competition, with the administration ultimately selecting Cornell/Technion's bid. As proposed, Cornell Tech would create 28,000 jobs, including 8,000 for academic staff. It would also be able to create 600 companies, leading to $23 billion in economic benefits and an additional $1.4 billion in taxes, during its first three decades of operation.

Research Triangle Park (RTP): founded in 1959, was among the first and is perhaps the world's best-known research park. It was a "highly ambitious 'big bet' that catalyzed assembling and aligning the knowledge resources and business climate attributes to create opportunities for the people of North Carolina."

Cited as one of the best gambles taken by a state, it was intended to link Duke University in Durham, North Carolina State University in Raleigh, and the University of North Carolina at Chapel Hill, and utilize a local airport in an originally low-population, primarily farmland region.

While RTP might not be known for cutting-edge innovations, its regional economic impact cannot be overstated. Known primarily for its success in attracting large companies such as IBM, RTP has drawn a much more diverse clientele. Over 60 percent of RTP's 170 companies have fewer than 25 employees.

Most companies (about 82 percent) are involved in scientific industries, with the preponderance of those in the life sciences. Research parks in general work primarily with established companies, but some also include incubator programs designed to help entrepreneurs launch new companies. RTP, for example, has six start-up incubators, but this is a relatively small part of the operation.

There are also SBIR and STTR matching grant programs across the state of North Carolina, as well as other, sector-specific networking and mentoring programs. Even with all of these supports in place, for small new companies, "it is easier to fail than to succeed." Indeed, in the past decade, RTP has seen a slowdown in employment growth. As a state, North Carolina has seen a fall in per capita income as compared to the U.S. average.

Sandia Science and Technology Park (SS&TP): In 1998, Sandia National Laboratory turned to the National Academy of Sciences to help it plan a new research park, the original vision was to create "a place that would serve as a partnership tool for Sandia by providing direct access to industry science and technology to further the labs' mission." by bringing new ideas to the lab and marketing products developed by researchers at the lab, as well as providing individuals access to some otherwise inaccessible parts of lab.

It is now an internationally recognized, master-planned system, and while Sandia does not own any of the lands on which the park is housed, it oversees the daily management, executive overview, and vision.

The park has received many awards over the years, including the Outstanding Research Park of the Year from the Association of University Research Parks, the Outstanding State and Local Economic Development from the Federal Laboratory Consortium, the Technology-Led Economic Development Award from the U.S. Department of Commerce Economic Development Administration, and the

Partnership Award from the International Economic Development Council.

Most recently Sandia is looking into creating an "incubator-like space" or a proof-of-concept program. Originally, this was not part of the design of the park because the need was not seen as pressing. The University of New Mexico (UNM) already had an incubator. But UNM had very little land, whereas SS&TP had plenty. The two institutions started to work collaboratively to foster new companies.

Other Parks: NASA's Research Park at NASA Ames, Oak Ridge Science & Technology Park at Oak Ridge National Laboratory, and the Livermore Valley Open Campus, which is associated with Lawrence Livermore National Laboratory and the Sandia National Laboratories California

Globally, the research park model has spread quickly in Asia and Europe, though the university role is smaller in those areas. In many regions, governments are funding research parks that are then "poaching" U.S. companies to move in by offering cheap land and labor.

The Fraunhofer Institute: is the best-known European park. Based in Germany with funding from the federal government, state government, and industry, the institutes conduct application-oriented research of use to industry, the service sector, and public administration. They also operate several Fraunhofer Academies that provide sophisticated vocational training. This model is now migrating to the United States.

Since there is no single model for a research park. Each park must be designed to suit its region, available resources, and economic needs. Parks require active interaction with a focus on research such as a university or national lab, a long-term perspective, competent leadership, and a willingness to adapt to evolving conditions.

Startup Focus: Research parks generally focus on working with existing companies rather than nurturing startups.

However, some parks have begun to add incubators that cater to the needs of entrepreneurs.

This is consistent with the original impetus to create parks that fill in gaps that exist in the local economy and innovation ecosystem. Park must have "a self-supporting business model in balance; even with all the other player[s], it needs to be able to take care of itself." It was generally agreed that scale matters and that some research parks are simply not big enough to make a difference.

However, research parks do not have to re-create every aspect of Silicon Valley to be successful. They can stimulate the economy by enhancing capacity enough to support higher-value activities and attract innovation investment.

Park Key Performance Metrics: Most parks are related to a single university and are located within a few miles of its campus but are not owned or operated by the university. About one-half of the parks were initially established with public funds. As parks have grown, the technologies represented at parks have expanded, and incubator facilities have been established.

Park size varies considerably. Research Triangle Park (Duke University, North Carolina State University, and the University of North Carolina; 1959) has 37,000 employees on a 6,800-acre site. Research and Development Park (Florida Atlantic University, 1985) has 50 employees on a 52-acre site.

Park directors associate employment growth with park success, and the following tables compare key characteristics, and growth rates of key performance against peers. Parks with single dominant technology, based close to campus and managed by private-sector, are the faster-growing.

The fastest-growing newer park is the University of Arizona Science and Technology Park (1995), which has been adding an average of more than 1,100 employees per year. The fastest growing of the older parks in Research Triangle Park, which has been adding an average of almost 950 employees per year since its founding in 1959.

Parks key characteristics against total peers

Parks formally affiliated with multiple universities	6%
Parks owned and operated by a university	35.4%
Parks on or adjacent to a university campus	24.6%
Park distances to a university campus.: 0 - 26 miles	Mean: 5.7
Parks located in distressed urban areas	11%
Parks initially funded with public money	50.4%
Parks with a single dominant technology	37.7%
Parks with a dominant technology: Bioscience	48.5%
Parks with a dominant technology: IT	42.4%
Parks with a mix of technology: all	9.1%
Percentage of parks with an incubator facility	62.3%
Mean Size: employees: 2,740. acres: 552 (Range: 6—6,800). Employees Range:	30 - 37,000

Source: National Science Foundation

Parks growth rates performance against peers

Annual growth averaged over the population of university-related research parks	13.0% per year
Parks with a single dominant technology Grow	3.2% faster than the average, per year
Off-campus parks (evaluated at the mean distance from the university)	Grow 3.7% slower than the average, per year
Parks that are university-owned and -operated	Grow 6.7% slower than the average, per year
An incubator facility	Has no effect on park growth (but this will change in the future as was proven by Stanford alumni Founders)

Source: National Science Foundation

The Top 10 global universities by impact innovation research

The Impact Rankings highlight actions taken by the world's higher education institutions to realize the United Nations 17 Sustainable Development Goals (SDGs); thereby contributing to the planet's economic and social well-being.

Rank	University name	Country/Region
1	University of Auckland	New Zealand
2	University of Sydney	Australia
3	Western Sydney University	Australia
4	La Trobe University	Australia
5	Arizona State University (Tempe)	United States
6	University of Bologna	Italy
7	University of British Columbia	Canada
8	University of Manchester	United Kingdom
9	King's College London	United Kingdom
10	RMIT University	Australia

Source: World Economic Forum

The University of Auckland, New Zealand, tops the rankings for the second consecutive year, ahead of three universities in Australia. Universities from developed economies dominate the top 20, punctuated by two newcomers: China's Tongji University, in 13th place, just ahead of Brazil's University of São Paulo.

Universal goals: The SDGs are the UN's Road map for building a better world – both for people and the planet – by 2030. Adopted by all UN member states in 2015, the goals are a call to action for all nations to work together to end poverty and hunger, while meeting a range of social needs, including universal access to education, healthcare, and clean water.

Government Support and Regulation: The United States does not have an innovation problem, given the "massive amounts" of innovation occurring at research universities. Rather, the United States has a problem benefitting from the innovations that occur in its universities.

In a global economy, capital, technology, and increasingly people flow across national boundaries quickly. Private capital markets in the United States also are reluctant to finance the scale-up of a first new facility in a fundamentally new area, as a result, innovators often must go outside the United States to find the capital for such a facility.

Otherwise, "you close the company, or you sell the intellectual property and whatever assets have been developed." The Department of Energy hoped to solve this problem in the energy area through a large loan guarantee program, but the program encountered strong political headwinds after the bankruptcy of the Solyndra solar cell company.

And even before that, the program was operated so conservatively that it did not do what it was intended to do.

It would only fund proven technologies, much as a commercial bank would do. In exploring ways to retain the benefits of innovation in the United States, there must be a dedicated startup agency at the federal level to hear and sustain young researchers, innovators, and entrepreneurs. at the same speed or better than Silicon Valley seed investors

People in their 20s and 30s have grown up in a world radically different than the world experienced by older people, "People younger than 25 are thinking in a completely different way than we might think, and that set of perspectives would be very useful for The Committee on Science, Engineering, Medicine, and Public Policy "COSEPUP."

Overly cautious or burdensome regulations can be another reason why innovations originating in the US are commercialized elsewhere.

For example, it can be easier to do the clinical trials of a new cancer drug in China than in the US because of access to a large population, lower costs, and a cooperative regulator, the fact that the regulation of medical devices poses many barriers to their commercialization in the United States, which means that these devices often are developed elsewhere and subsequently imported into the United States, even if they are based on ideas that originated in U.S. universities.

The Food and Drug Administration (FDA) is charged with protecting the safety of the American public, and drug companies sometimes have broken the rules established to protect public safety. But the FDA has responded by setting up barriers that can make it very difficult for small companies to get products to the marketplace.

Perhaps the FDA could establish separate categories for companies with stellar safety records and those with less-than-stellar records. Another possibility would be to prioritize the review of important drugs with the potential to produce great benefits ahead of drugs intended to produce incremental improvements.

A mix of outdated regulation and the ignorance of basic knowledge on how startup vs small business and corporate labor relation works, usually result in suffocating early-stage startup through non-revenues taxation, and even levy of bank account for as little as a few hundred dollars in the past due taxes, resulting in shattered dreams and lost innovation.

There must be new rules geared toward early-stage startups, especially during the pre-funding critical stage.

By prudently lowering the costs of doing business, the United States could create an environment that is much more attractive to investors. Edward Penhoet mentioned one particular approach to reducing the burden of regulations.

As a member of the President's Council of Advisors on Science and Technology (PCAST), he has been involved in a review of the National Nanotechnology Initiative undertaken every two years in response to a request from Congress.

The most recent nanotechnology report called on the nation to invest in regulatory science, which Penhoet defined as "the science that needs to be done to make an informed regulatory decision.

In nanoscience, for example, federal agencies fund studies of the effects of nanoparticles on cell cultures, but they do not support work, either individually or collaboratively, on the problem of how to move nanoparticles toward approval by the Environmental Protection Agency or the FDA.

Penhoet said. Today, the FDA simply counts the number of drugs it has approved as a measure of its impact, but many of these drugs have only incremental effects on the lives of patients. A much better measure is the impact of the new products the FDA approves.

In particular, PCAST recommended a more facile way of dealing with breakthrough drugs. PCAST has also recommended reforms in the way clinical trials are done in the United States.

For example, clinical trials are currently hampered by the need to gain approval from the institutional review boards at each institution participating in a trial. A more consolidated and streamlined review process could speed up drug development. Finally, the pharmaceutical industry could benefit from much more collaboration on precompetitive research that takes place before companies can compete in the marketplace.

"There is an effort now to open up much more transparency in the drug development process," he said.

The government has many ways of spurring investments in innovation beyond direct support for research and development, including modification in its tax, regulatory, and trade policies.

For example, the capital gains tax could be restructured in a way that further incentivizes investors to focus on a company's long-term vision of its future rather than on short-term fluctuations in the company's value, which tends to be the case today.

Another possibility would be to allow copyrighting of scientific research for a long period and allow the holder of the copyright to charge a very small royalty for the use of the results. Such an action would funnel money back into research while simultaneously allowing the uses of research to be tracked.

Recognizing that the availability of venture capital for particular fields goes through cycles, one role of government might be to invest against the cycles.

Intellectual property: considerations vary widely across technological fields and even within fields. Some companies want patents to trade them or to cross-license with other companies. Others may seek to amass a large portfolio of patents in a field with very short product life cycles to control the evolution of that field.

In some fields, such as pharmaceuticals, it takes a long time for innovations to reach the market, and patents are crucial to protect an idea until the innovator can profit from that idea.

In other industries, patents are rare and are easy to work around when they do exist. There is a growing emphasis on the importance of innovation for sustained economic growth and competitiveness in today's global, fast-paced, knowledge-based economy.

Not only is innovation critical for industry development, but it also directly impacts the standard of living found in a nation and its regions.

US SBA: as a main agency to finance small businesses shall be replicated to create a startup financing agency (SFA) by offering a 100% guarantee loan of up to \$1m for impact innovation (based on founder experience as 5X of last salary).

Global Hubs and Universities Ranking:

Living in a global economy means that Americans should not be overly concerned about, whether an American-owned company or a foreign-owned company commercializes a product in the United States. Foxconn, a Taiwanese company, is building a large plant in Texas to build products for Apple, with financial incentives from the state, just as many large foreign pharmaceutical and automobile companies have invested in U.S. production Trends in the Innovation Ecosystem

Reflecting, on the race to reach a vaccine for the Covid-19 pandemic that paralyzed the global economy and brought innovation to the forefront as a matter of life or death, from government efforts to contain the pandemic to the digital infrastructure gaps that catch most countries unprepared but allowed few leading economies to work through it.

"In the year of Covid-19 and facing the urgency of climate change, the importance of innovation fundamentals only increases," said Catherine Mann, global chief economist at Citigroup Inc. "Innovation is often measured by new ideas, new products, and new services," she said, but it's their "diffusion and adoption" that is the real metric of success.

Below is a list of countries that shows the most promise for developing globally impactful disruptive technologies:

1. US (Silicon Valley): With $120,000 per capita in GDP, it would be the second wealthiest behind Qatar if it was a country. It is home to major tech leaders above $1 Trillion valuation (Apple, Alphabet), where top Tech Companies employed 400k workers and generated over $400 Billion in revenues in 2020, along with top Venture Capital that invested over $50 Billion in local startups. There are over 10,000 VC-backed startups based in the SF Bay Area (Including Silicon Valley) with over $200 Billion in Funding and half of the world's tech billionaires call it home with a $1,000 Billions (Trillion) net worth.

2. Singapore: Offers advanced infrastructure, strong government support "Smart Nation" with IP protection, and a deep pool of talent from top universities. Switzerland: a leader in FinTech and BioTech, with strong research capabilities. South Korea: Mainly driven by the rise in its IP Patents and R&D output. Germany: Although the country lacked skilled workers and a proper strategy for next-generation technology, it is catching up very fast.
3. China: As the second biggest economy after the U.S., China accounts for much of the world's innovation, Its appetite for innovation has helped its ascent to economic prominence over the past 30 years through ongoing urbanization and a shift from basic manufacturing to robotics, smart cities, electric vehicles, and artificial intelligence.

Global Map of Top 60 Innovative Countries by Bloomberg

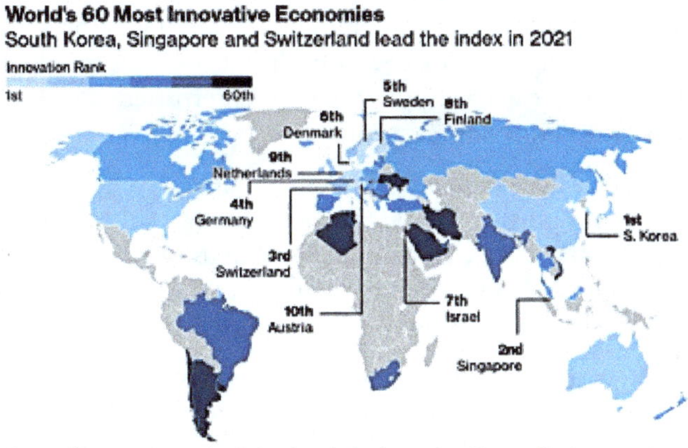

Global innovation hubs are defined as cities or metropolitan areas that can lead the flow of global innovation elements and influence the efficiency of resource allocation, drawing on their unique advantages in science and technology innovation.

The Global Innovation Hubs Index (GIHI) developed by the Center for Industrial Development and Environmental Governance at Tsinghua University in China, with support from Nature Research, aims to set up an index system, based on scientific methods and objective data, to evaluate the innovation capacities and development potentials of global science and technology innovation hubs, providing a reference for policymakers and practitioners.

The GIHI primarily assesses global innovation hubs in three dimensions: research innovation, innovation economy, and innovation ecosystem.

First, an innovation hub is a center with extensive research activities and research networks. In the GIHI, the dimension of research innovation examines the scientific and technological resources of its people, research institutions, research infrastructure, and knowledge creation of the city or metropolitan area.

Second, a global innovation hub, with vibrant innovation activities, typically has a booming innovation economy. This dimension includes metrics on the region's technological innovation capacity, high-tech enterprises, emerging industries, and economic growth.

Third, the development of a global innovation hub benefits from a supportive innovation ecosystem. This dimension focuses on the openness and collaboration networks of a region, its support for entrepreneurship, public service infrastructure, and the innovation culture.

Seeking to be scientific, objective, independent, and impartial, the GIHI system has distinct features compared with other index systems in the world for innovation evaluation. It makes use of metrics, such as network centrality to measure the relative potential and influence of a city in a global network.

It uses micro-level data with fine granularity to measure a city's research output, patents, foreign investment, high-tech companies, as well as the international flight network. It also adopts metrics constructed by international organizations based on large surveys to measure system or culture-related factors, like business environment, talent attraction, and entrepreneurship, to add a subjective perspective.

Lastly, it focuses on cutting-edge technologies and emerging economic sectors, such as artificial intelligence, information, communication technologies, and biomedicine, to demonstrate the development potential of a city.

Given the tight timeline and limitations for data collection, this is just a beta version, and the ranking provided by this report is preliminary. The indicators and data analysis in the report will be updated and improved in the future.

The report assessed 30 cities or metro areas, as follows:

The top ten overall are: San Francisco-San Jose, New York, Boston-Cambridge-Newton, Tokyo, Beijing, London, Seattle-Tacoma-Bellevue, Los Angeles-Long Beach-Anaheim, Baltimore-Washington, and Chapel Hill-Durham-Raleigh.

The top 10 in research innovation are: New York, Boston-Cambridge-Newton, San Francisco-San Jose, London, Baltimore-Washington, Paris, Chapel Hill-Durham-Raleigh, Beijing, Los Angeles-Long Beach-Anaheim, and Tokyo.

The top 10 in the innovation economy are: San Francisco-San Jose, Tokyo, Beijing, Shenzhen, Shanghai, Tel Aviv, Seoul, Kyoto-Osaka-Kobe, Seattle-Tacoma-Bellevue, and Boston-Cambridge-Newton.

The top 10 in the innovation ecosystem are: San Francisco-San Jose, New York, London, Boston-Cambridge-Newton, Chicago-Naperville-Elgin, Los Angeles-Long Beach-Anaheim, Amsterdam, Singapore, Seattle-Tacoma-Bellevue and Philadelphia.

Further analyses show that:

Global innovation cities have varied development paths and positioning. While few cities, like San Francisco-San Jose and Boston-Cambridge-Newton, have balanced performance in all dimensions, most follow divergent paths in the development of research innovation, innovation economy, and ecosystem. It suggests that cities/metropolitan areas have distinct advantages, and their development may be unbalanced.

Big international metropolises and smaller cities with their distinctive features are complementary to each other in the progress of innovation. Big international metropolises, like New York, Tokyo, Beijing, and London, enjoy inherent advantages in bringing together innovation resources, creating scientific knowledge, and incubating high-tech start-ups, given the clustering effects they have.

Yet, some cities/metropolitan areas with smaller populations, like Seattle-Tacoma-Bellevue, and Chapel Hill-Durham-Raleigh, have their distinctive features in innovation-driven development, with specialties in certain technological fields. Each city plays a significant role in its own field and is exploring its unique path toward innovation development.

Basic research and technological innovation capacities remain important elements that determine a city or metropolitan area's position in the global innovation network. More than half of cities/metropolitan areas in the overall top 10 list, like San Francisco-San Jose, Boston-Cambridge-Newton, New York, Beijing, and London, have a concentration of renowned universities and research institutions, with solid bases in scientific research, and therefore, have an edge in innovation capacities, and their positions are difficult to challenge.

Digitalization has accelerated technological innovation and research translation.

The rapid progress of the digital economy has highlighted Asian cities' advantages in the innovation economy. Asian cities are gaining development momentum in emerging new economies, which are exerting an increasingly significant impact. Seven Asian cities are ranked among the global top 10 list in the innovation economy.

Chinese cities like Beijing, Shenzhen, and Shanghai are establishing their unique strengths by stimulating the innovative potentials of digital technology companies; cities/metropolitan areas such as Tokyo, Seoul, Kyoto-Osaka-Kobe, and Tel Aviv have also shown the world their distinct culture, tradition, and innovation.

In its September 16, 2015, issue of U.S. News and World Report, Delece Smith-Barrow cites the "Top 10 Most Innovative National Universities." Each of these universities demonstrated terrific achievements. However, none of these achievements were related to student learning, effective operations, or improvements in approaches to higher education. These achievements were primarily research related. They are as follows:

1 - Drexel University (PA): "Live Note" application that provides concertgoers with historical and musical data
2 - Harvard (MA): new study on cell phone data that can use information to track the transmission of infectious diseases
3 - University of Ann Arbor (MI): technology that allows cars to "talk" to each other as machine to machine.
4 - Duke University (NC): conducted an algae study that will drive down the cost of extracting oil from plants
5 - Northeastern University (MA): national security research
6 - Georgia State University (GA): developed a new survey to better follow the prevalence of sexual assaults on campus
7 - University of Maryland - Baltimore (MD): developed a virtual reality system for research in biology, math, engineering, visual arts, and digital humanities
8 - Massachusetts Institute of Technology (MA): developed a more user-friendly 3-D printer for various purpose
9 - Stanford University: created objects for everyday use
10 - Arizona State - Tempe (AZ): a study on how refugee camps,

military camps, and neighborhoods form; a study of domestic violence, and research that affects our daily lives

In its summer 2021 issue of U.S. News and World Report listed the "Top 10 Most Innovative National Universities." that are making the most innovative improvements in terms of curriculum, faculty, students, campus life, technology, or facilities, which dramatically shifted the 2015 ranking as following:

1. Arizona State University
2. Georgia State University
3. Massachusetts Institute of Technology
4. Georgia Institute of Technology
5. Carnegie Mellon University
6. University of Baltimore Maryland
7. Stanford University
8. Purdue University West Lafayette
9. Elon University
10. The University of Michigan Ann-Arbor

Takeaways: Creative hubs, whatever the form, from neighborhoods to planned, contained communities, are stimulating environments to work in for both large corporations and startups. Success and energy breed success and energy. Exposure to creativity of all kinds stimulates creativity of all kinds.

My favorite quote from Thomas Edison, who was a methodical inventor, is that "to invent you need a good imagination and a pile of junk", aka stimuli. Many of the best inventions have resulted from cross-pollination of ideas from one industry to another.

Learning from what others are doing can spark the kind of random associations new ideas and better processes are built upon.

If you're a large corporation and have not already launched a creative office away from the day-to-day of your own business, you might consider it. If you're a startup looking for an uplifting, positive, and supportive, cross-sector work environment that can provide the mental nutrition to spur you on and valuable connections, you should investigate innovation hubs in the works.

Since they often have reasonable rents or financial incentives to attract startups, sometimes in collaboration with local governments, they may not be as costly as you think.

Universities: since most are funded by the government or through a tax-deductible grant, to stay relevant they must adapt to a borderless knowledge economy, by abolishing the barrier between their elitist graduates' alumni groups, and end users "i.e., end users from the broad economy who are sustaining this institution as paying customers", as follow:

- Grant brand office licensing use at no cost to startup as long they are affiliates through research park space, alumni advice, or as a partner, user, or customers of the university "i.e., renting events space at no cost".

- Mandate that all faculty must allocate 10% of their time to advise startups outside their alumni and students' network at no cost but can get equity up to 0.5% per 4 years.
- Forbid all investments, innovation, or events groups that are exclusive to alumni, and must be open to the public.
- Open licensing office to have special programs for local startups only, and outside the students or alumni network as free IP licensing for 18 months, then gradual licensing fee tied to a percentage of net profit.
- Open lecturer program to entrepreneurs with proven positive impact innovation that want to market and serve at least 10,000 customers. Exclusion must be enforced to venture capital and investors who simply monopolize the channel of innovation through student lecturing.
- Open innovation seed funding for students through an auction-based demo pitch open to the public with a low subscription "i.e., $100 per investor" and must exclude venture capital.

- **Engineers as a Percentage of all occupations**

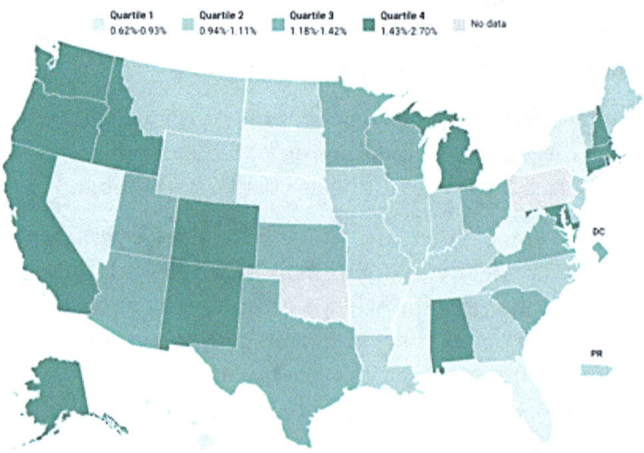

SOURCE: Bureau of Labor Statistics, special tabulations of the Occupational Employment and Wage Statistics Survey (various years), data available as of May 2020

Singapore has clinched the top spot in KPMG's global ranking of leading technology innovation hubs outside of Silicon Valley/San Francisco this year. This puts the nation ahead of other cities like New York, Tel Aviv, Beijing, and London for the second year running.

The 2021 KPMG Technology Industry Survey surveyed more than 800 global leaders from various sub-sectors in the technology industry on the cities they see as leading technology innovation hubs over the next four years. Among the top factors seen as important in the ranking were an urban locale that attracts young professionals, a pipeline of skilled talent, and modern infrastructure (including high-speed bandwidth).

People believe knowledge is power and that success depends on how much a person knows. Knowledge is power but knowledge without action can be useless. Professors and academics of the world, despite possessing a great deal of education and knowledge, are not the millionaires of today's world.

You also see people like Steve Jobs who despite dropping out of college make it big in life. Henry Ford, the inventor of the automobile and the founder of the Ford Motor Company had only but a few years of schooling. How did these men become successful and do better than other educated men of their time?

Imagine you had a bucket. If every time you tried to fill this bucket, 90% of the water leaked out, you probably would not fill this bucket until the leak is fixed. All the reading that you do, is like filling a bucket which leaks 90% of the water.

You only retain 10% of what you read after 24 hours. Knowledge is power but you are wasting time acquiring it if you retain very little of it. This is the key finding behind the study that produced the learning pyramid seen in the picture below.

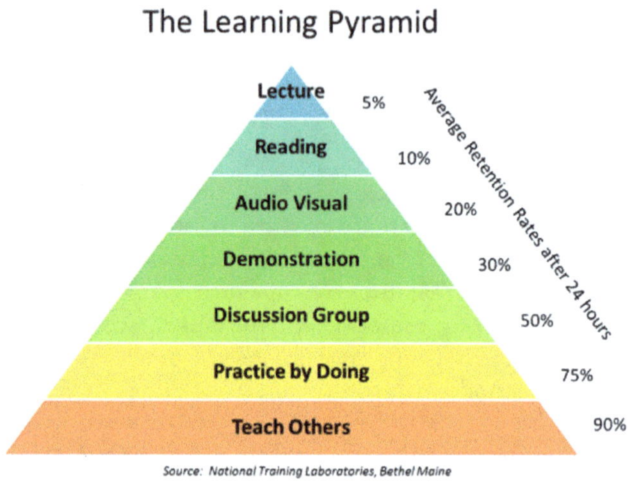

The National Training Laboratories in Bethel Maine measured the retention rate after 24 hours for different types of learning. People retained 90% when they taught someone because when they teach, they instantly make mistakes and see gaps in what they know. By teaching they began to understand.

The National Training Laboratories in Maine measured the retention rate after 24 hours for different types of learning, people retained 90% when they taught someone because when they teach, they instantly make mistakes and see gaps in what they know. By teaching they began to understand.

If you had to extend this beyond 24 hours, you will have to apply what you learn. By applying you will run into difficulty, make mistakes, and see gaps in what you know the same way you would if you taught someone.

No matter how good the original explanation is in the book or lecture, you will retain very little of it, if you do not understand it through application. Your interpretation of the concept will always be different from that of the speaker/author because there is a very big difference between knowing something and understanding it. Knowledge is power only when you truly understand it. Understanding something involves internalizing a concept.

CHAPTER V
BAD INNOVATION

The two sides of Innovation: Since the Industrial Revolution, which is fueled by energy-driven consumption of fossil fuels has led to a rapid increase in CO_2 emissions, disrupting the global carbon cycle and leading to global warming.

In addition to the sides effect of a polluted environment from manufacturing, and an unhealthy obese society caused by the convenience of overconsumption and a sedentary lifestyle compounded by digital computing.

A recent report published by Nesta, the UK agency for innovation titled, Good and Bad Innovation: What kind of theory and practice do we need to distinguish the two sides?

Some excerpts capture the ambivalence of acceptable innovations that we came to use. For example, pesticides kill parasites but also pollute the water supply. Another is the application of new surveillance technologies to increase workplace productivity and safety.

If it can be helpful and effective on one hand, it can cause huge amounts of stress and unhappiness in the workforce and might deprive citizens of their privacy.

The report expands to the controversial field of financial innovation, which as we all know, has destroyed more value than they created, at the cost of the enrichment of their providers. Unfortunately, regulators and policymakers failed to distinguish the good from the bad, with very costly results.

Thinking about ethics and innovation, one must come to terms with how blind innovation tends to be in tune with the traditional approach to a mainstream capitalist market economy, and the belief that innovation *"creates more winners than losers", and that markets are better able to pick and manage "technologies adaption with its impact than regulators."*

Leading Government agencies have committed themselves to better distinguishing good from bad innovation. The European Commission, for example, recently promised to back 'responsible innovation'. They define responsible innovation as an *'approach that anticipates and assesses potential implications and societal expectations… with the aim to foster the design of inclusive and sustainable research and innovation.*"

The past has shown us how traditional disciplines that could have provided a more rigorous and useful approach to assessing innovation have largely failed to do so. That is the case of Economists, who are unable to find a few coherent or comprehensive methods for analyzing which kinds of innovation are good and which are bad.

They do let us know though, when consumers do or don't want to buy something new, which can show in retrospect which innovations generate bad results (like pollution) as well as benefits (for example, cheaper products).

The Hidden Impact of Technology: What's happening in the world, in challenging this point of view? Technological progress makes the world better but also brings new challenges, say Erik Brynjolfsson and Andrew McAfee, faculty members at the MIT Sloan School of Management, who have studied the impact of technology on economies for years.

Here is an excerpt of their interview with Harvard Business Review editor Amy Bernstein and editor at large Anand Raman, Brynjolfsson and McAfee explain that while digital technologies will help economies grow faster, not everyone will benefit equally as the latest data already shows.

Compared with the Industrial Revolution, digital technologies are more likely to create winner-take-all markets. Brynjolfsson and McAfee also believe that despite the heady pace of technological development, business dynamism has dipped, and they worry that the policy response has been inadequate.

They conclude that though no one knows what the future holds, the time to start tackling the economic downside of new technologies is now.

The Pop-Up Online Ads by Ethan Zuckerman: Among the top web browsing frustration is yet another pop-up ad that blocks your view, obscures the content behind it, and freezes your computer,

Zuckerman was head of the Center for Civic Media at the Massachusetts Institute of Technology, wrote an essay for The Atlantic in 2014 entitled "The Internet's Original Sin," in which he took full responsibility for the pesky blighters. Working as an employee of web host Tripod at the time, Zuckerman explained that the company, which provided free web pages for consumers, had spent five years looking for a way to generate revenue.

"At the end of the day, the business model that got us funded was advertising. The model that got us acquired was analyzing users' personal homepages so we could better target ads to them. Along the way, we ended up creating one of the most hated tools for advertisers: the pop-up ad."

Explaining that the intention had been to allow advertising to appear when users visited a page without necessarily associating the advert with the content of the page, Zuckerman explained, "We came up with it when a major car company freaked out when they'd bought a banner ad on a page that celebrated porn. I wrote the code to launch the window and run an ad in it. I'm sorry. our intentions were good."

The Office Cubicle by Bob Propst: Bob Propst introduced America to the open plan office and with it, the office cubicle during his work as a consultant for Herman Miller in the 1960s, It was, he told the New York Times in 1997, designed to "give knowledge workers a more flexible, fluid environment than the rat-maze boxes of offices."

The corporate world leveraged his invention as a driver to save on rent, by replacing individual offices with open plans and cubicles. Propst came to lament his invention. "The cubitization of people in modern corporations is monolithic insanity," he said.

When Corporate Innovation Goes Bad

More than 25% of total revenue and profits come from the launch of new products

Revenue and Profit from new Products in the last 3 years

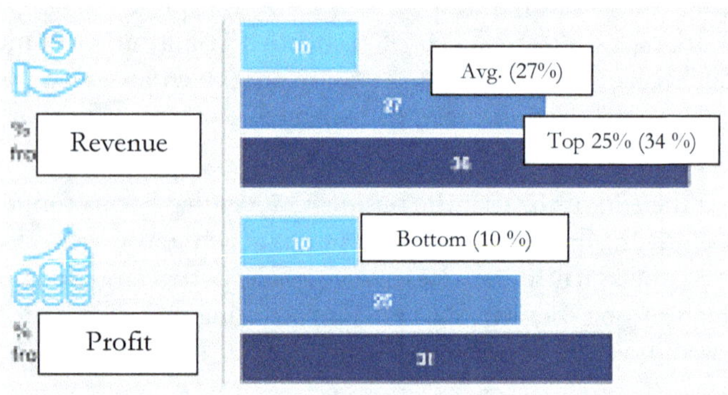

Source: American Productivity & Quality Center (APQC)

DeLorean DMC-12, DeLorean Motor Company (1981): This stainless-steel sports car is most famous for its appearance in the "Back to the Future" movies. Notable for its gull-wing doors and unique body styling, the DMC-12 (usually just referred to as "the DeLorean," as it was the company's only model) was plagued by performance and safety issues.

Its fate was sealed when the auto industry faced a dramatic downturn in the early 80s and only about 9,000 cars were built before production ceased in 1983. This flop has a happy ending, albeit 30+ years later: DMC Texas has received federal approval to produce about 50 new DeLoreans a year, starting possibly as soon as 2017.

Airboard, Sony (2004): The Sony Airboard was, unwittingly, another pre-iPad attempt at building a tablet. Launched in 2004, the Airboard boasted wireless streaming TV and internet access, but at $1,300 the price was far too high for what was likely seen as an expensive portable TV. Sony abandoned the product completely in 2008.

Blackberry Storm, Blackberry (2008): In 2008, Verizon looked to Blackberry to develop an "iPhone killer." The result was the Storm, a touchscreen-enabled smartphone with a "clickable" screen. Users could navigate with touch, then click the entire screen down like a button to make choices.

But faulty tech and bugs in the software doomed the phone from the start. Most Storms that did sell were quickly returned, and the phone was shelved later the same year.

Google Glass, Google (2013): Google Glass might have come too soon. Between a sky-high price, issues around privacy, and cultural backlash, this wearable product just didn't connect.

Micah Altman, director of the Center for Research in Equitable and Open Scholarship at MIT, commented, "A 19th-century French critic famously quipped: 'The more things change, the more they stay the same.' And there are many regularities in human preferences; limits on individual human physical, emotional, and cognitive performance; and entrenched societal interests that create substantial inertia in human social and civic institutions. However, in the last decade and a half, we've witnessed social-media-powered revolutions, crowd-sourced surveillance and counter surveillance, do-it-yourself redistricting, and even a public-participation draft of a national constitution. This decade will see many more experiments, some will have an impact, and a few will stick.

Douglas Rushkoff, a media theorist, author, and professor of media at City University of New York, said, "Interesting that you didn't have an answer that was more like, 'Technology will hamper but not prevent our ability to enact social and civic innovation.' Tech will make it harder, but it won't prevent us from doing so. As inequality increases, eventually people will need to turn to one another for mutual aid. Communities will have to form for basic survival. The wealthy may move into augmented realities to shield themselves from the realities of the 99%, but most others will begin to find rapport and then solidarity by looking up from tech at one another, instead."

Paola Ricaurte, a fellow at Harvard's Berkman Klein Center for Internet and Society, wrote, "As technologies evolve with new functionalities, awareness about their risks and harms will increase. People will demand the improvement of their quality of life, the respect for human rights, and the environment. However, there will be greater difficulties for those who are excluded from the digital economy to participate actively in the generation of new knowledge and to resist the power of big tech."

While technologies are being used to surveil, control, and attack them, such groups are also innovatively repurposing technologies to respond, resist and fight back. *Axel Bruns*

James Mickens, associate professor of computer science at Harvard University, formerly with Microsoft, commented, "Technology will obviously result in 'civic innovation.' The real question is whether 'innovation' will result in better societal outcomes. For example, the gig economy is enabled by technology that finds buyers for workers and their services. However, given the choice between an economy with many gig workers and an economy with an equivalent number of traditional middle-class jobs, most people would prefer the latter."

A large share of these experts say among the leading concerns about today's technology platforms are how they are exploited by bad actors who spread misinformation, and the privacy issues arising out of the business model behind the systems.

The Hidden Impact of Knowledge: We spend a lot of our time acquiring knowledge and information that we don't need. When I wanted to build an online business, I spent two years consuming information on making a website and running a business online. I was an expert in everything from social media to copywriting. Guess how much money I made by becoming an expert over the course of two years?

Not even a single penny. I didn't make any money because I never created anything. How much I knew did not matter because I never applied what I learned. Knowledge is power only when you act. All the knowledge without action only left me overwhelmed. I had been accumulating information without applying and when I wanted to apply there was so much information that I did not know where to begin.

We spend so much time, money, and energy acquiring knowledge that we will not use and that will leave us paralyzed from taking any action. We do it through our reading and online consumption. Knowledge is power but time is money. I later discovered something about how successful people acquire knowledge that changed my mind set about learning.

Have you ever felt the constant need to consume more information because it feels like you don't know enough yet to act? Successful people start before they are ready, with incomplete information. They succeed despite lacking advanced degrees and skills by using the knowledge of other men and directing it to a definite purpose.

Knowledge is power but by itself, it cannot help anybody become successful. It is only potential power that must be organized and directed to a definite result, using practical plans of action. A person doing this doesn't have to possess this knowledge in his mind. He just has to acquire this knowledge when he needs it or intelligently organize the knowledge of others. We will see how to do this.

Digital age potent problems: Numerous experts described misinformation and fake news as serious issue in digital spaces. They expressed concern over how users will sort through fact and fiction in the coming decade.

Oscar Gandy, a professor emeritus of communication at the University of Pennsylvania, said, "Corporate actors will make use of technology to *weaken* the possibility for improvements in social and civic relationships. I am particularly concerned about the use of technology in the communications realm to increase the power of strategic or manipulative communications to shape the engagement of members of the public with key actors within a variety of governance relationships."

Jonathan Grudin, principal researcher at Microsoft, commented, "Social and civic activity will continue to change in response to technology use, but will it change its trajectory? Realignments following the Industrial Revolution resulted from the formation of new face-to-face communities, including union chapters, community service groups such as the Rotary Club and League of Women Voters, church groups, bridge clubs, bowling leagues, and so on.

Our species is designed to thrive in modest-sized collocated communities, where everyone plays a valued part. Most primates become vulnerable and anxious when not surrounded by their band or troop. Digital media are eroding a sense of community everywhere we look.

Can our fundamental human need for close community be restored or will we become more isolated, anxious, and susceptible to manipulation?"

Rebecca Theobald, an assistant research professor at the University of Colorado, Colorado Springs, said, "Technology seems to be driving people apart, which would lead to fewer connections in society."

Many of the experts in this canvassing said power dynamics play a key role in technology development and social and civic innovation and have a substantial impact on broad societal issues. These experts highlighted the discrepancies they see regarding who has access to power and who controls the instruments of power. Some said well-meaning individuals in positions of power do not understand the issues faced by the public that relies upon digital platforms and systems.

While some experts are greatly concerned about how tech companies' capitalist interests may affect social and civic innovation in the next decade, others expect that tech and social evolution will allow the public more opportunities to advocate for change.

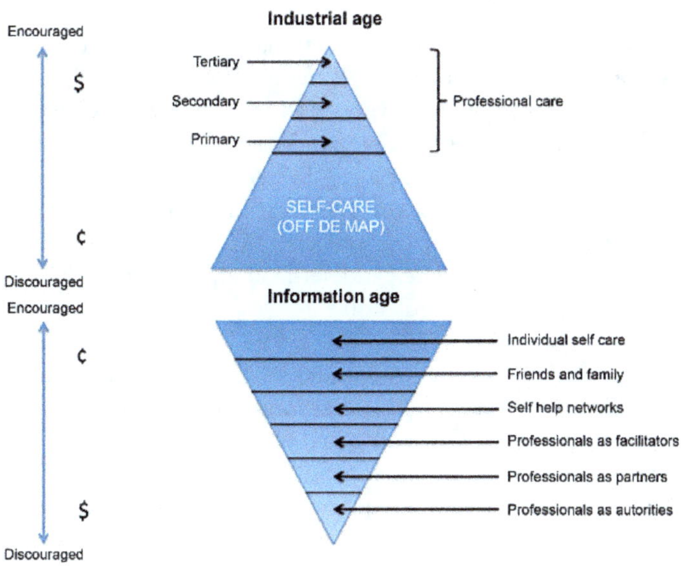

Impact of Technology on Innovation by 2030: Those in power seek to maintain it; those in power have no incentive to change; government regulation could address these problems; surveillance capitalism is coming to a head; and technology can be a catalyst for advocacy against abuses of power.

Today's digital form of market capitalism has created an environment that is proving to be problematic on many levels. Money equals power. Those in control of digital systems and platforms are highly motivated to remove or subsume any threats to their dominance.

Market capitalism in today's digital realm has led to a small number of large players who are driven by driving up profit. These companies hold all the cards. And governments don't have the expertise they need to regulate them.

Jonathan Morgan, a senior design researcher for the Wikimedia Foundation, said, "I'm mostly concerned with the role of digital platform owners and technology providers as stiflers of innovation. People are locked into the tools they use to live, work, and socialize. Increasingly, these activities are mediated by a small number of economically and politically powerful companies that actively squash competition, undermine, and jettison open standards and protocols and resist regulation.

These are anti-competitive practices that stifle innovation; they are anti-social practices that inhibit the development of new social norms. Our continued use of dependence on the technologies they provide props up these organizations, allowing them to continue to engage in activities that undermine the fabric of our society in a variety of subtle and not-so-subtle ways."

Mark Surman, executive director of Mozilla Foundation and co-founder of Commons Group, wrote, "Right now, the big U.S. tech companies write the rules of the road. If governments and citizens can take back some of that power and build up the talent and vision to create civic innovation, we'll see the kind of social innovation we need. That said, current trends don't bode well. The companies hold all the cards. And governments don't have the expertise they need to regulate in ways that will be effective or work out well."

Jeff Johnson, a professor of computer science at the University of San Francisco, who previously worked at Xerox, HP Labs, and Sun Microsystems, responded, "Although the question considers 'social and civic innovation' as a positive force, it can also be negative.

Gaming the system for corporate or personal benefit is a negative form of social and civic innovation. Internet worms, viruses, hackers, and bots that gather people's information, target ads and messages or wreak havoc are another form of social and civic innovation.

Not all innovations are positive. In the 1990s, Richard Sclove hosted a series of citizen panels on democracy in the (still young) digital age (see the book "Governance.com: Democracy in the Digital Age").

His prognosis was positive, but at that time the main 'social' media consisted of email lists, electronic bulletin boards, and Usenet newsgroups. The rise of Facebook, YouTube, Snapchat, and the like has unfortunately turned the tide toward the negative."

Bernie Hogan, a senior research fellow at Oxford Internet Institute, said, "Technology warps scales in favor of those who can wield the technology. It has always been the case, from the gun, the stirrup, the telephone, and now the internet. This time, however, technology is operating on scales that we simply do not comprehend and cannot meaningfully do so.

Google and Facebook can only make inferences about the rankings of their search results and news feeds, respectively; they cannot give a clear answer about why precisely one element showed up before another. High-frequency trading algorithms are similarly abstract and opaque. … The notion that we are either going to have 'no change' or substantial improvement is remarkably rosy. We are much more likely to have increased inequality, greater more effective propaganda, and dissent codified and monitored.

Ann Adams, a retired technology worker, commented, "Once the profit model changes, mitigation will follow. Unfortunately, governments must intervene, as business currently has no incentive to change."

Ioana Marinescu, an assistant professor of economics at the University of Pennsylvania School of Social Policy and Practice, and an expert in labor policy responded, "I think new tools will likely be created to strengthen the voices of workers and the disadvantaged". These tools' emergence would be strengthened by regulations that empower people."

Melissa Michelson, a professor of political science at Menlo College and author of "Mobilizing Inclusion: Redefining Citizenship Through Get-Out-the-Vote Campaigns," wrote, "Despite the many shortcomings and negative impacts of the digital age, I remain optimistic that innovators and leaders will find ways to overcome those negatives to use digital tools to allow for overall positive impacts on our social and civic lives.

Every generation is threatened by the perceived drawbacks of new communication technologies, including television and telephones. Change is scary, and it can be easier to see the threats than the promise, but I believe that civic-minded people will find ways to control those negatives and allow for the benefits of the digital world to enhance and strengthen our democracy, whether that is through regulation, market competition or other new technologies that we cannot yet imagine."

Ethan Zuckerman, director of MIT's Center for Civic Media and co-founder of Global Voices, said, "Development of social media technologies over the past 20 years has suffered from the false assumption that technology is and can be neutral. The assumption was that platforms like Facebook could be used for good or for ill, and that platform designers should work to keep their tools as open to as many uses as possible. We're now realizing that no technologies are neutral. Build a technology around the idea of increasing engagement and you're likely to create incentives for clickbait and disinformation.

Over the next 10 years, I hope to see a wave of new platforms consciously "designed to evoke different civic behaviors". We need mass innovation in the design of social tools that help us bridge fragmentation and polarization, bring diversity into our media landscapes, and help find common ground between disparate groups.

With these as conscious design goals, technology could be a powerful positive force for civic change. If we don't take this challenge seriously and assume that we're stuck with mass-market tools, we won't see positive civic outcomes from technological tools." Surveillance capitalism is a term used to describe the market-driven business practice of digital platform providers and others of offering a "free" or reduced-rate service while collecting data about users to sell to third parties, often for marketing purposes.

Many of the experts in this canvassing see this as a major underlying flaw in the design of today's digital information platforms – the primary cause of many digital threats to democracy.

Takeaways: Technology could be used as a tool for the betterment of humanity, from improving education to enhancing people's social lives. Some experts emphasized the need to do a better job of harnessing technology for good, expressing concern that the alternative is unthinkable.

Mike Roberts, Internet Hall of Fame member and pioneer CEO of ICANN, confidently predicted, "We are in a technology-fueled Age of Innovation. 'Technology got us into this mess and technology will get us out of it.'"

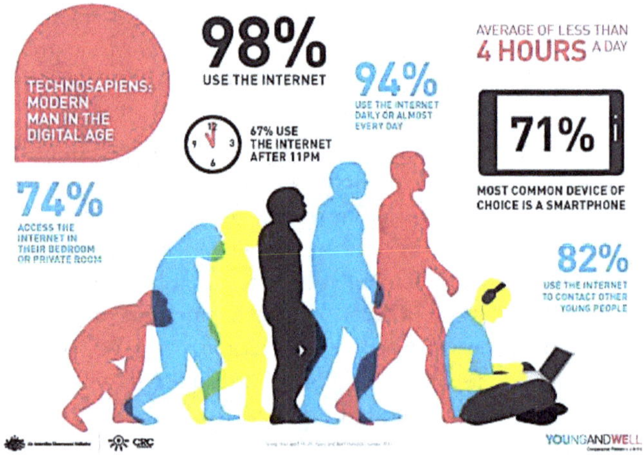

Global Internet Users with the Impact of Tech
by Young and Well, CRC

Positive Ecological effects	Negative Ecological effects
➢ Improved quality of life ➢ Greater economic growth ➢ Rapid and bulk production of goods ➢ Better transportation ➢ Faster communication ➢ Comfortable housing ➢ Enjoyable recreation	➢ Pollution of life support systems ➢ Degradation of natural habitats ➢ Global warming and climate changes ➢ Depletion of natural resources ➢ Impact of industrial agriculture ➢ Toxic contamination ➢ Depletion of ozone layer

The root cause of bad innovation and potential remediation:

Technology: The largest software companies that sell 100% of their product or services to the Global Fortune 500 conglomerate who themselves control 75% of global GDP are the biggest drivers of the following:

- Intentional lack of industry-standard in both coding and servicing, which lock both customers and end users in endless legacy technology, worst "engineers spend 75% of their time integrating vs innovating" and making their skills nontransferable; to sustain monopoly and inflated trillion dollars valuation at the expense of society.
- Monopolized Operating System: Mobile phone manufacturers must create their own OS which shall be enforced by their distributors "Telecom to have 12 OS per carrier" vs currently two OS "iOS and Android", additional OS cannot be free or open source as it masks the hidden cost of its monopoly. This shall be the same for car companies since tech companies will soon be doing to cars what they did to phones: Tying their exclusive operating systems to specific products to force out competitors and dominate a huge swath of the global economy.
- Ideal Solution: Enforce interchangeable industry standards like the car industry where a part "i.e., tire" fits any car and can be installed anywhere by anyone "In tech API is a start" and tech companies shall be run like OEM "original equipment manufacturers".

Patents: two third of patents are intended to either prevent others from entering their market or used as a subversive troll to make money on infringement. These must be stopped and replaced with, 1- Software based patents must be eliminated, 2-process and services based patents must be also eliminated, 3-tangible product based innovation especially new material and biotech must be restricted to commercialized protection only (meaning the first ten companies to commercialize will gain protection for 5 years max and within their headquarters location not the globe), Universities and other non-profit must be excluded from patents but allowed to opt for open sources or make money on commercialized technology granted to new startup only within first three years as a percent of revenues.

Communication: start with the monopoly of telecom companies that must be eliminated to enable real innovation, while enforcing industry standards 'i.e., OEM" that govern it to reach the following ideal solutions:

- Infrastructure: we need to go back to when phone and internet hardware are provided free to subscribers to enforce industry standards, while telecom companies must open their network to peers to enable the best connection any time anywhere by peer's subscriber.
- Data Privacy: as an extension to the above, telecom must enable users to have their contents stored within a single account as an industry standard, instead of within their phone or by third-party hardware or software "i.e., app or social media providers", and shall not share access with anyone other than the subscriber or judiciary channel.

Cybersecurity: The whole business model of the tech and contents industry must change to remediate most of the common breach as follow:

- Access: UOD "use own devices must be standard to access any online services, which replace the email and password with machine-to-machine authentication like POS payment enabled by Apple Wallet or Apple Pay. Except, the credential must be at each app level pushed to the user's devices and changed randomly on a weekly basis.
- Availability: Starting with data centers and cloud providers, they must have an industry standard SLA "service level acceptance", which credits paying and free users with a percent of the down or slow time out of

100% being the full 24 hours day.

- Backup: must be standard and included in services provided by all data centers and cloud vendors, across segments from business to end consumers.
- Security Upgrade: must be embedded into software to automatically upgrade during scheduled standard downtime "i.e., 12 am to 3 am", and exclude all nice to have as a package in the next purchase. The upgrade must provide 7 days' notice.
- Network: providers must be accountable for those who use their services to breach someone else and pay for each breach using SLA above
- Contents: providers must be accountable for those who use their services to breach someone else and pay for each breach using SLA above
- Stolen Devices and Data: must be tracked at the global level through one entity "i.e., Interpol and made available to the public so anyone can check the authenticity of assets or data breach", supported by harsh extradition and criminal code. That penalizes anyone that facilitates such an act, including platforms, networks, and any entity not just individuals.

Media and Marketing: since these two sectors accumulate over 80% of user's data it is past time to have them both regulated as utilities with strict governance as follows:

- Addictive Media: Social, Audio, and Visual Media, all rely on advertiser's payment, they have no incentive to provide end users value, other than maximizing their payment from their advertisers through manipulative content that hooks users into spending a third of their day if not more on non-value addictive contents. End users are part of the product "Real customers are advertisers paying when users watch their ads embedded into contents mostly created by other users". Negative impacts on society are well documented and urgently in need of a permanent solution.

- Privacy: Marketing: digital campaign and online ads rely on NII "Non-Identifiable Information" for promotional purpose, it is naïve to still think NII exist, the truth is any platform can identify the end users by mapping their mobile location, IP address, and email address, browsers history to physical location and therefore their full name, home, and work address, etc.
- Ideal Solution: no need to reinvent the wheel, this industry must be regulated like the car industry and OEM, by enforcing three rules:
    - Service offered cannot be free and must be charged to end users "i.e., email, social media account, etc.", with a strict limit of 1 hour per day from all devices to access entertainment content").
    - Platform providers cannot share access to user data with third parties and must delete it each week with 30 days gaps; Ads campaigns must be run using NII at the demographic and metro area level, not at the individual user level, where advertisers pay only when users transact, not just by clicking.
    - The budget to deduct ads and marketing expenses must be regulated and maximized to 10% of the net profit using updated accounting standards and cannot be passed on to customers as a hidden cost of products and services, additionally, sales cost shall be governed in the same way as ads and marketing.
    - Media Companies cannot categorize themselves as technology companies or use the tech term in their branding, this shall be regulated as exclusive for truly technology companies that generate 70% of their revenues from technology sold as products or services, "i.e., Apple, Microsoft, IBM, Oracle".

Banking and Investment: these two sectors are not working for mass and need an equalizer regulation that enables innovation not monopoly as follows:

Financing: providing a loan must be an industry standard that is based on the ability to pay not a credit report "which shall be illegal as it infringes on a large swath of the globe's privacy laws. Ideal Rules:

1. The loan must be based on assets and exclude intangible brand valuation or accrued sales based on non-cash payment or inter-entities deals.
2. The special clause must be for a startup that allows during the first three years to base its asset on the founder's experience within the target industry i.e., "$1m year."
3. The loan must be allocated by industry, size; location, and demographic, i.e., 10% + must be for a startup with less than three years and $0 investments.
4. The loan cannot be secured by private assets, including startup investments shares vested or not.
5. Government Grant: must be offered as a bid competition per startup stage and based solely on deep tech innovation needs, through quarterly marketplace and one platform access at the federal and state level.

Investments: Venture capitalists play a decisive role in shaping the future of technology and with it the future of our economies, politics, and societies. As VC firms provide critical early-stage funding for new and emerging initiatives, they have a unique opportunity to support projects that contribute to advancing the UN Sustainable Development Goals, human rights, and a healthy environment, and fund diverse entrepreneurial teams, while minimizing funding projects that result in harm to society. By increasing diversity in VC firm staffing and management, firms will also be more likely to support startups that consider how new technologies will impact women as well as minority and marginalized communities.

Venture capital must be regulated with standard to enable fair and accelerated impact innovation as follow:

- Fund Origin: personal name of the end beneficiary must be listed on each firm website with origin and subscription amount, including LP's FO, GP's, and Partners. An exception to list entities instead of personal names for large LPs like government pension funds and publicly listed companies.

- Fund Performance: quarterly statements must be posted on the firm's website, including the last four quarters' investment performance, and the amount invested by startup, industry, stage, location, and demographic. Portfolio performance must be based on startup with 20%+ gross profit and profitable exit per each investment, not valuation.
- Portfolio Valuation: this must be standardized and allow valuation on gross profit generated per startup per quarter, not masked by free user traction.
- Venture Capital Compensation: must be based on quarterly profit generated by its portfolio, i.e., 20% with a direct positive impact on society. The 2% management fee must be replaced with standard salary and expenses per $1m of funds, i.e., 15%.
- Investments: each investment round must include 20% for small investors to join from the local area and posted on the firm's website, along with criteria that a startup must have to get funded, along with a quarterly report for funded startup backed with met criteria and how the startup reached the firm. Additionally, each fund must allocate equally a percent per stage, industry, and round, i.e. Seed is $1m to $5m with 35% of the fund, Series A is $7m to $10m with 25% of the fund, Series BC is $11m to $30m with 40% of the fund, V.C shall be forbidden from investing in pre-exit unicorn which usually performs at loss after IPO, and all startup at series D stage or later must exit through IPO or Acquisition not subsidized funding at loss from the V.C to mask their AUM "asset undervaluation" growth.
- Support: each firm must list and enables customer services phone line and email and answer each investment request within 10 days "similar bank industry"
- Board Seat: V.C. employees, partners, and founders

cannot be on any publicly listed company.

- Backroom deal: V.C. cannot reply on the private intro, or top universities and exclusive events to monopolize fundraising, investments, and acquisition and must compete through the open market, therefore these practices must be forbidden. One possible solution is to have local partners ``i.e., Accelerator, Universities, etc.", invite equally all local V.C. to particular events or deals.
- All quarterly reports must be audited by major providers and aligned to current accounting best practices.

Control & Exit: This stage is where most benefit or damage is done to innovators and must be regulated further to spread the benefit to the society as a whole as follow:

- Founders cannot be pushed to relinquish their control by key investors unless crime or gross negligence occurred and is confirmed through the court of law. Preferred shares, liquidation preference, and double dipping must be eliminated.
- Investors cannot control collectively over 10% during each stage of funding, Seed, Series A, and Series B for a total of 30% when a startup raises $30m.
- Founders shall have automatically a 10X vote per share on all shares issued before the first $1m investments, while all investors cannot have more than 1X vote per share.
- Each round of future investments must allocate 5% for previous investors to invest as a requirement.
- A startup must have a target profit of 20% after the first $1m investment, and this is where their valuation will be based on and not the number of users. Debt cannot be claimed against a startup with less than $1m profit.
- Startup exit decisions must be done by the founders' and employees' total consensus vote and exclude the investor's vote for any sales less than $100m.
- An acquirer of a Startup must be capped to a $10 billion valuation, beyond which they can only acquire publicly

- listed startup, additionally no more than three acquisitions by the same entities can be done within 12 months or up to $1 billion amount.
- Global Fortune 500 with tech-based offerings must be restricted to 3 acquisitions a year and up to $1 billion to reduce the monopolistic effect.
- The acquirer must commit to sustaining the acquired startup for up to 5 years and cannot buy it to shut it down to protect their monopoly

Leading Bad Innovation with Negative Impact on Consumer

Media Sector (Marketed as Free)

Services	**Product**	**Owner**	**Paid By**	**Full Cost**	**Impact**
Search Eng.	Links	Public	B2B Ads	Time+Power	Unvetted
Messaging	Email	Public	B2B Ads	Time+Power	Privacy
Social Media	Content	Public	B2B Ads	Time+Power	Addict
Television	Program	Studio	B2B Ads	Time+Power	Bias
Television	Show	Studio	B2B Ads	Time+Power	Addict
Television	News	Studio	B2B Ads	Time+Power	Bias
Movie	Films	Studio	Users	Time+Power	Unvetted

Food and Beverage Sector

Services	**Product**	**Owner**	Paid By	UserCost	**Hidden Impact**
Fast Food	Meals	Business	Users	Pre-Paid	Unhealthy Effects
Processed	Grocery	Business	Users	Pre-Paid	Unhealthy Effects
Processed	Snacks	Business	Users	Pre-Paid	Unhealthy Effects
Processed	Desserts	Business	Users	Pre-Paid	Unhealthy Effects
Processed	Candy	Business	Users	Pre-Paid	Unhealthy Effects
Processed	Beverage	Business	Users	Pre-Paid	Unhealthy Effects
Frozen	Grocery	Business	Users	Pre-Paid	Unhealthy Effects

Travel and Transportation Sector

Services	**Product**	**Owner**	**Paid** by	**User Cost**	**Impact**
Mobility	Cars	Users	Loan	Congestion	Unhealthy
Mobility	Van/SUV	Users	Loan	Pollution	Unhealthy
Shipping	Truck	Business	Users	Pollution	Unhealthy
Ride-Share	Private Taxi	Business	Users	Congestion	Unhealthy
Travel	Flight	Business	Users	Pollution	Unhealthy
Travel	Cruise	Business	Users	Pollution	Unhealthy
Travel	Resorts	Business	Users	Pollution	Unhealthy

Peter Lunenfeld, a professor of media at UC, Los Angeles, and author of "Tales of the Computer as Culture Machine," predicted, "We will use technology to solve the problems the use of technology creates, but the new fixes will bring new issues. Every design solution creates a new design problem, and so it is with the ways we have built our global networks. Highly technological societies must be iterative if they hope to compete, and I think that societies that have experienced democracy will move to curb the slide to authoritarianism that social media has accelerated. According to a national survey by the University of Pittsburgh Center for Research on Media, Technology, and Health, young adults who use seven to 11 social media platforms had more than three times the risk of depression and anxiety than those who use two or fewer platforms. "This association is strong enough that clinicians could consider asking their patients with depression and anxiety about multiple platforms use and counseling them that this use may be related to their symptoms," said Brian A. Primack, director of the research center.

Top 10% Wealthiest pollute as much as 50% of poor population!

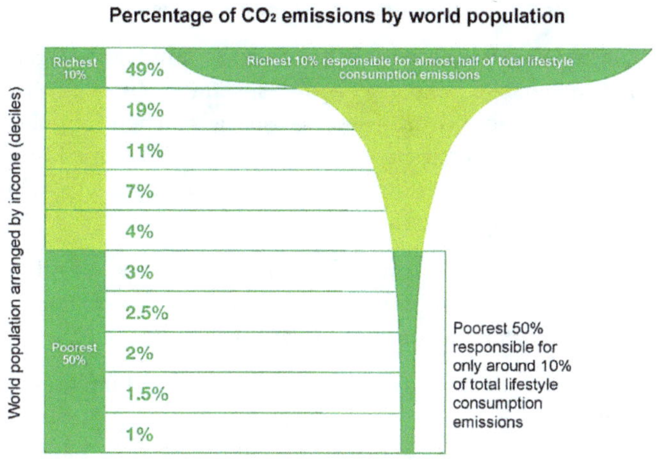

CHAPTER VI
GOOD INNOVATION

Good Innovation Urgently Needed: Over three third of corporate executives say that their future success depends on innovation, according to the latest survey conducted by McKinsey. If a corporation isn't making any progress, it simply cannot stay relevant. Innovation is the introduction of something new.

"Without innovation, there isn't anything new, and without anything new, there will be no progress".

Besides the fact that innovation allows corporations to stay relevant in the highly competitive market, it also drives economic growth. Where the ability to resolve critical problems depends on innovations, especially in developing countries that need it more than ever.

Because corporations often work with other startups and industry partners, it is challenging to understand the impacts of innovation on our society at large. There is a lot more to innovation than just achieving competitive advantage, innovation is the core reason for modern existence.

Change is inevitable and, in most cases, innovation creates positive change, but in some instances, it may have some undesirable consequences, especially when innovation is the way to combat critical social risks and threats. Human society revolves around continuous economic growth, which is driven by population growth.

When populations shrink due to aging in the developed world, innovation solves these kinds of social problems and enhances society's capacity to act.

Good Innovation is responsible for solving human social problems sustainably and efficiently, mostly with new technologies, enabling products and services that meet simultaneously a social need "i.e., Health, Food, Safety" and drive improved capabilities for better use of resources "i.e.,

Finance, Farming, Manufacturing, Shipping, Transportation"; primary led by private "Corporate, Startup", public "Research and Investment" and non-profit sectors in conjunction.

The impact of innovation should always be continuous improvement. From the human society's perspective, the fundamental expected outcomes should be increased wealth through economic growth, healthy, safer well-being, fast and transparent communication, low barrier to education access, and a sustainable environment as follow:

Economic growth: is the increase in the inflation-adjusted market value of the goods and services produced by an economy over time. It is conventionally measured as the percent rate of increase in real gross domestic product, or real GDP, and there are two ways to achieve it by either increasing the number of inputs or creating new ways to get more output from the same number of inputs.

If we look at the transformation of the US, which advanced from emerging nation status "once a largely agrarian economy" in the mid-19th century to an industrial economy by the beginning of the 20th century, we can see that agricultural innovations and inventions were the key factors that helped the transition to the Industrial Revolution.

In Europe a shift from hand-made to machine-made products increased productivity, directly affecting living standards and growth. Driven by a vast improvement in agricultural productivity which transformed the way farmers work, releasing and allowing them to move to cities for industrial work.

The positive impact on human society is the transition from one worker previously able to feed a fraction of their family, to one person producing more in less time and providing for the entire family.

Human well-being: Since innovation powers economic growth, it does increase well-being through higher living standards, which is supported by prominent research including the

Brookings Institution that average life satisfaction is higher in countries with greater GDP per capita. However, Often, a rise in real GDP mostly leads to greater wealth inequality.

Although there isn't a threshold for how much inequality is too much, greater gaps drive negative social well-being, especially when purchasing power decreases.

Most developing countries depend on new digital technologies Innovation creates huge opportunities to fight sickness, nutrition, poverty, and hunger, along with developing countries also rely on innovation to solve their problems related to these areas.

Food and Agro-Tech: Reducing hunger, "i.e., agricultural productivity, weather, and irrigation monitoring" is critical in the developing world, where a population boom is taking place. And small farms play an important role by producing up to 80% of the food locally, which eventually helps alleviate poverty and hunger.

Information Access: We've already seen in the last thirty years since the World Wide Web's inception, a huge technological revolution and continue to do so in the future. According to the World Bank's recent finding, two third of the poorest 20 percent of the world population have a mobile phone. This means that more people now have mobile phones than sanitation or clean water.

Innovation can also help rural areas thrive and become more sustainable, and educated with better communication, even where there are adoption barriers, such as low income or user capability.

Innovation Positive Impact: The current Silicon Valley trends defining success, is always about users spending more and more time on their mobile apps or browsing the web content. But the near future of good innovation would reverse these trends to showcase tangible value beyond tools and contents and focus on end-user positive impact "i.e., would the maker of a hammer boast about how long his customers spent using it?".

Although consumerism is the impact of innovation on economic growth, it is at the heart of the modern economy. The rising consumption of innovative products and services is often considered the main reason for the environmental deterioration of our planet.

Political or financial incentives are often not enough to make a change – at least not quickly enough. Policy changes take time to take effect, which is why the long-term survival of our society and nature depends on new, responsible innovative technologies with positive impact.

Global Governance: The UN Global Compact is a principle-based framework for businesses, stating ten principles in the areas of human rights, labor, the environment, and anti-corruption. Under the Global Compact, companies are brought together with UN agencies, labor groups, and civil society. Cities can join the Global Compact through the Cities Program.

The UN Global Compact is the world's largest corporate sustainability (a.k.a. corporate social responsibility) initiative with 13000 corporate participants and other stakeholders over 170 countries with two objectives: "Mainstream the ten principles in business activities around the world" and "Catalyze actions in support of broader UN goals, such as the Millennium Development Goals (MDGs) and Sustainable Development Goals (SDGs)".

Moving forward, the UN Global Compact and its signatories are deeply invested and enthusiastic about supporting work towards the SDGs.

The UN Global Compact was initially launched with nine Principles. On 24 June 2004, during the first Global Compact Leaders' Summit, Kofi Annan announced the addition of the tenth principle against corruption by the UN Convention Against Corruption adopted in 2003.

Human Rights:
1 Business should support and respect the protection of internationally proclaimed human rights: and
2 Make sure that they are not complicit in human rights abuses.

Labor:
3 Businesses should uphold the freedom of association and the effective recognition of the right to collective bargaining.
4 The elimination of all forms of forced and compulsory labor.
5 The effective abolition of child labor; and
6 The elimination of discrimination in respect of employment and occupation.

Environment:
7 Businesses should support a precautionary approach to environmental challenges.
8 Undertake initiatives to promote greater environmental responsibility; and
9 Encourage the development and diffusion of environmentally friendly technologies.

Anti-Corruption:

10 Businesses should work against corruption in all its forms, including extortion and bribery.

The Global Compact also will periodically create resources and guides that business and nonprofit organizations may use in their efforts to support the Compact's overall mission.

One such example is the SDG Compass, developed in collaboration with the Global Reporting Initiative (GRI) and World Business Council for Sustainable Development (WBCSD), which is a collection of resources (analysis of the goals, indicators for businesses, tools for stakeholders) that companies can utilize in finding out their role in helping to achieve the SDGs.

Some critics believe that without any effective monitoring and enforcement provisions, the Global Compact fails to hold corporations accountable. Moreover, these critics argue that companies could potentially misuse the Global Compact as a public relations instrument for "bluewash".

Bluewashing refers to the alleged practice of companies claiming their membership or participation in philanthropic and charity-based activity as an excuse, and perhaps as an entry door to increase corporate influence upon international organizations.

An informal network previously known as Global Compact Critics leveled a variety of criticisms at the Global Compact, citing a lack of mechanisms for sanctioning non-compliance or lack of progress.

The Global Compact critics formally disbanded in February 2015, recommending that interested parties consult the Centre for Research on Multinational Corporations website. Similarly, the Alliance for a Corporate-Free UN, which also no longer exists, was a campaigning organization of several international NGOs, led by Corpwatch, which highlighted weaknesses in the principles underlying the Global Compact.

The Global Compact was criticized by Maude Barlow, senior adviser on water issues to the President of the United Nations General Assembly in December 2008, who accused the Global Compact of bluewashing.

David Andrews, senior adviser on Food Policy and Sustainable Development, and Peter Utting, deputy director of UNRISD. Leaders of the tribe Ayoreo Indians in Paraguay wrote to the UN Global Compact saying they are "concerned and frustrated" by the inclusion in it of a controversial Brazilian ranching company.

The company, Yaguarete Porá, was charged and fined for illegally clearing the Ayoreo's forests and concealing evidence of uncontacted Ayoreo living there. The Ayoreo asked that it be expelled from the Global Compact.

The Global Compact provides a list of its 12,000+ participant organizations, composed of roughly 8,000 businesses and 4,000 non-business entities on its website.

The site provides a brief overview of each participant, and a link to their Letter of Commitment (if new), Financial Overview and Contributions (if applicable), and Communication on Progress (COP).

Notable companies who have signed on the Global Compact include but are not limited to, Starbucks, L'Oréal, Bayer AG, Coca-Cola, 3M, and Deloitte.

In addition to its signatories, the Global Compact has been repeatedly supported by the UN General Assembly, honoring its 15th anniversary in June 2015 alongside the Secretary-General, Ban Ki-Moon, himself who claims that "Business can be a global force for good" and that "advocacy and example can drive action to achieve a life of dignity for all people".

Creating Social Impact: Innovation Plus Scaling

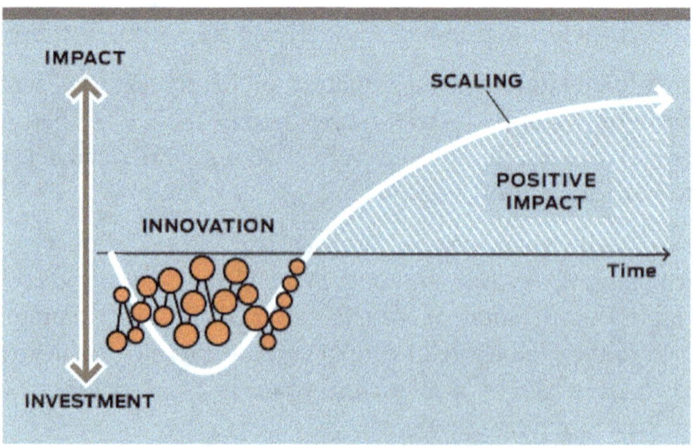

Source: Stanford Social Innovation Review

Impact Innovation for Organization: We've looked at the role of innovation from society's perspective, and now we can take a closer look at the importance of innovation for organizations. Rarely are industries where innovation wouldn't be important. Although certain digital industries depend on innovation more than non-digital, innovation and the ability to improve impact, everyone.

Even highly regulated industries, such as telecom and finance aren't immune to change. Look what iPhone or Robinhood has done to these traditional industries. In general, transformational innovation can deliver significant benefits and is one of the critical skills for achieving success in any business. Some examples are:

Competitive advantage: These are capabilities that provide an edge in comparison to competitors in the industry. Successful, innovative businesses can keep their operations, services, and products relevant to their customer's needs and changing market conditions.

According to Deloitte, only 12% of the Fortune 500 companies listed in 1955 are still in business, and half of the S&P 500 companies will be replaced in the next ten years, which is why it's important to be able to quickly respond to external challenges. Maximize profit: Continuous innovation often has a direct impact on performance and profitability.

Increased productivity: is driven by innovation and technological improvements, which reduce the costs of production and enable higher output. If we look at this from the perspective of an organization, different automation solutions decrease manual, repetitive work and release time for more important, value-creating tasks.

Positive impact on culture: Innovation also has a positive impact on company culture as it increases the ability to acquire, create and make the best use of competencies, skills, and knowledge. Innovation doesn't come just from giving people incentives; it comes from enabling environments where ideas can blossom.

Impact Innovation on Business Profit

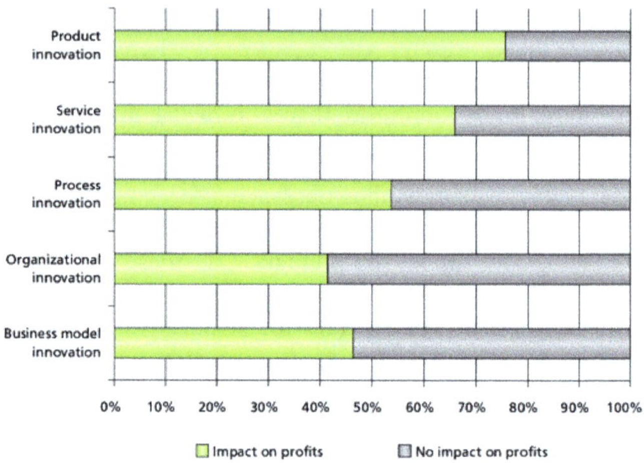

Impact Innovation on Business Performance

Patents Protection vs Monopoly:

A patent is a type of intellectual property that gives its owner the legal right to exclude others from making, using, or selling an invention for a limited period of years in exchange for publishing and enabling public disclosure of the invention.

In most countries, patent rights fall under private law, and the patent holder must sue someone infringing the patent to enforce their rights. In some industries patents are an essential form of competitive advantage; in others they are irrelevant.

Under the World Trade Organization's (WTO) TRIPS Agreement, patents should be available in WTO member states for any invention, in all fields of technology, provided they are new, involve an inventive step, and are capable of industrial application.

Nevertheless, there are variations on what is patentable subject matter from country to country, also among WTO member states. TRIPS also provides that the term of protection available should be a minimum of twenty years.

A patent, being an exclusionary right, does not necessarily give the patent owner the right to exploit the invention subject to the patent. For example, many inventions are improvements of prior inventions that may still be covered by someone else's patent.

If an inventor obtains a patent on improvements to an existing invention that is still under patent, they can only legally use the improved invention if the patent holder of the original invention gives permission, which they may refuse.

Alternatives: A defensive publication is the act of publishing a detailed description of a new invention without patenting it, to establish prior art and public identification as the creator/originator of an invention, although a defensive publication can also be anonymous. A defensive publication prevents others from later being able to patent the invention.

A trade secret is an information that is intentionally kept confidential and that provides a competitive advantage to its possessor. Trade secrets are protected by non-disclosure agreements and labor laws, each of which prevents information leaks such as breaches of confidentiality and industrial espionage.

Compared to patents, the advantages of trade secrets are that the value of a trade secret continues until it is made public, whereas a patent is only in force for a specified time, after which others may freely copy the invention; does not require payment of fees to governmental agencies or filing paperwork; has an immediate effect; and does not require any disclosure of information to the public.

The key disadvantage of a trade secret is its vulnerability to reverse engineering.

Criticism: Legal scholars, economists, activists, policymakers, industries, and trade organizations have held differing views on patents and engaged in contentious debates on the subject. Critical perspectives emerged in the nineteenth century that were especially based on the principles of free trade.

Contemporary criticisms have echoed those arguments, claiming that patents block innovation and waste resources (e.g., with patent-related overheads) that could otherwise be used productively to improve technology.

These and other research findings that patents decreased innovation because of the following mechanisms:

- Low-quality, known, or obvious patents hamper innovation and commercialization and weaken the public domain.
- Blocking the use of fundamental knowledge with patents creates a "tragedy of the anti-commons, where future innovations cannot take place outside of a single firm in an entire field".
- Patent thickets, or "an overlapping set of patent rights", in particular slow innovation.
- Broad patents prevent companies from commercializing products and hurt innovation. In the worst case, such broad patents are held by non-practicing entities (patent trolls), which do not contribute to innovation. Enforcement by patent trolls

of poor-quality patents has led to criticism of the patent office as well as the system itself. Lawsuits brought by "patent assertion companies" made up 61% of all patent cases in 2012, according to the Santa Clara University School of Law.

- Patents apply a "one size fits all" model to industries with differing needs, as is unproductive for the tech industry.
- Rent-seeking by owners of pharmaceutical patents has also been a particular focus of criticism, as the high prices they enable puts life-saving drugs out of reach of many people.

Digital technologies have enabled the emergence of an "*intangible economy*," based on soft assets like algorithms and lines of code, rather than physical assets like buildings and machinery. In this environment, intellectual-property rules can now make or break business models and reshape societies, as they determine how economic gains are shared.

Yet the main features of today's IP regime were established for a very different economy "Industrial Era". Patent rules, for example, reflect the long-held assumption that strong protection provides an essential incentive for businesses to pursue innovation.

Recent studies by Petra Moser and Heidi Williams, among others, find little evidence that patents boost innovation. On the contrary, because they lock in incumbents' advantages and drive up the costs of new technology, such protections are associated with less new or follow-on innovation, weaker diffusion, and increased market concentration. This has contributed to growing monopoly power, slowing productivity growth, and rising inequality in many economies over the past couple of decades.

Patents also invite considerable lobbying and rent-seeking. Most patents are used not to produce commercial value, but to create defensive legal thickets that can keep potential competitors at bay. As the system expands, patent trolling and litigation soar. Lawsuits by patent trolls "*comprise more than three-fifths of all lawsuits for IP infringement in the U.S. and cost the economy an estimated $500 billion in 1990-2010*".

Corporate Social Responsibility (**CSR and ESG)**: is a form of international private business self-regulation which aims to contribute to societal goals of a philanthropic, activist, or charitable nature by engaging in or supporting volunteering or ethically oriented practices.

While once it was possible to describe CSR as an internal organizational policy or a corporate ethic strategy, that time has passed as various national and international laws have been developed and various organizations have used their authority to push it beyond individual or even industry-wide initiatives.

While it has been considered a form of corporate self-regulation for some time, over the last decade or so it has moved considerably from voluntary decisions at the level of individual organizations to mandatory schemes at regional, national, and international levels.

Considered at the organizational level, CSR is generally understood as a strategic initiative that contributes to a brand's reputation. As such, social responsibility initiatives must coherently align with and be integrated into a business model to be successful.

With some models, a firm's implementation of CSR goes beyond compliance with regulatory requirements and engages in "actions that appear to further some social good, beyond the interests of the firm and that which is required by law".

Proponents argue that corporations increase long-term profits by operating with a CSR perspective, while critics argue that CSR distracts from businesses' economic role. A 2000 study compared existing econometric studies of the relationship between social and financial performance, concluding that the contradictory results of previous studies reporting positive, negative, and neutral financial impact, were due to flawed empirical analysis and claimed when the study is properly specified, CSR has a neutral impact on financial outcomes.

Critics questioned the "lofty" and sometimes "unrealistic expectations" in CSR. or that CSR is merely window-dressing, or an attempt to pre-empt the role of governments as a watchdog over powerful multinational corporations. In line with this critical perspective, political and sociological institutionalists became interested in CSR in the context of theories of globalization, neoliberalism, and late capitalism.

Some institutionalists viewed CSR as a form of capitalist legitimacy and in particular point out that what began as a social movement against uninhibited corporate power was transformed by corporations into a "business model" and a "risk management" device, often with questionable results.

The concept and ambit of Corporate Social Responsibility (CSR) has exponentially increased in the recent past, particularly during the outbreak of the novel coronavirus disease (COVID-19) which was declared as a pandemic by the World Health Organization (WHO) on 11.03.2020.

The number of people affected due to the virus and its resulting impact on CSR has transformed the outlook of businesses toward society all over the world.

Corporate social initiatives: Corporate social responsibility includes six types of corporate social initiatives:

- Corporate philanthropy: company donations to charity, including cash, goods, and services, sometimes via a corporate foundation
- Community volunteering: company-organized volunteer activities, sometimes while an employee receives pay for pro-bono work on behalf of a non-profit organization
- Socially responsible business practices: ethically produced products that appeal to a customer segment
- Cause promotions and activism: company-funded advocacy campaigns
- Cause-related marketing: donations to charity based on product sales
- Corporate social marketing: company-funded behavior-change campaigns

All six of the corporate initiatives are forms of corporate citizenship. However, only some of these CSR activities rise to the level of cause marketing, defined as "a type of corporate social responsibility (CSR) in which a company's promotional campaign has the dual purpose of increasing profitability while bettering society."

Companies generally do not have a profit motive when participating in corporate philanthropy and community volunteering. On the other hand, the remaining corporate social initiatives can be examples of cause marketing, in which there is both a societal interest and a profit motive.

Environmental, Social, and Corporate Governance (ESG) is an evaluation of a firm's collective conscientiousness for social and environmental factors. It is typically a score that is compiled from data collected surrounding specific metrics related to intangible assets within the enterprise. It could be considered a form of corporate social credit score.

Research shows that such intangible assets comprise an increasing percentage of future enterprise value. While there are many ways to think of intangible asset metrics, these three central factors together, ESG, comprise a label that has been adopted throughout the United States financial industry.

They are used for a myriad of specific purposes with the ultimate objective of measuring elements related to sustainability and the societal impact of a company or business. In less than 20 years, the ESG movement has grown from a corporate social responsibility initiative launched by the United Nations into a global phenomenon representing more than US$30 trillion in assets under management.

In the year 2019 alone, a surge of capital totaling US$17.67 billion flowed into ESG-linked products, an almost 525 percent increase from 2015, according to Morningstar.

Banks and asset managers representing 40% of the world's financial assets have now pledged to meet the goals set out in the Paris climate agreement, as an alliance championed by former central banker Mark Carney swells under the gaze of a world increasingly alarmed by planetary warming.

More than 450 firms representing $130 trillion of assets now belong to the Glasgow Financial Alliance for Net Zero, almost double the roughly $70 trillion when GFANZ was launched in April, according to a progress report published by the coalition on Wednesday.

Signatories must commit to using science-based guidelines to reach net zero carbon emissions by mid-century and to provide 2030 interim goals.

The threat of climate change and the depletion of resources has grown, so investors may choose to factor sustainability issues into their investment choices. The issues often represent externalities, such as influences on the functioning and revenues of the company that is not exclusively affected by market mechanisms.

As with all areas of ESG, the breadth of possible concerns is vast (e.g., greenhouse gas emissions, biodiversity, waste management, water management) but some of the chief areas are listed below:

Climate crisis: The body of research providing evidence of global trends in climate change has led investors—pension funds, and holders of insurance reserves—to begin to screen investments in terms of their impact on the perceived factors of climate change.

Fossil fuel-reliant industries are less attractive. In the UK, investment policies were particularly affected by the conclusions of the *Stern Review* in 2006, a report commissioned by the British government to provide an economic analysis of the issues associated with climate change.

Its conclusions pointed towards the necessity of including considerations of climate change and environmental issues in all financial calculations and that the benefits of early action on climate change would outweigh its costs.

Sustainability: In every area of the debate from the depletion of resources to the future of industries dependent upon diminishing raw materials the question of the obsolescence of a company's product or service is becoming central to the value ascribed to that company. The long-term view is becoming prevalent amongst investors.

Diversity: There is a growing belief that the broader the pool of talent opens to an employer the greater the chance of finding the optimum person for the job. Innovation and agility are seen as the great benefits of diversity, and there is an increasing awareness of what has come to be known as 'the power of difference'.

Human rights: In 2006 the US Courts of Appeals ruled that there was a case to answer bringing the area of a company's social responsibilities squarely into the financial arena. This area of concern is widening to include such considerations as the impact on local communities, the health and welfare of employees, and a more thorough examination of a company's supply chain.

Consumer protection: Until recently, caveat emptor ("buyer beware") was the governing principle of commerce and trading. In recent times however, there has been an increased assumption that the consumer has a right to a degree of protection, and the vast growth in damages litigation has meant that consumer protection is a central consideration for those seeking to limit a company's risk and those examining a company's credentials with an eye to investing.

The collapse of the US subprime mortgage market initiated a growing movement against predatory lending has also become an important area of concern.

Animal welfare: From the testing of products on animals to the welfare of animals bred for the food market, concern about the welfare of animals is a large consideration for those investors seeking a thorough understanding of the company or industry being analyzed.

Corporate governance concerns: Corporate governance covers the area of investigation into the rights and responsibilities of the management of a company—its board, shareholders, and the various stakeholders in that company.

ESG Corporate Governance from the Board of Directors' view, Governance Lens watching over the Corporate Behavior of the CEO, C-Suite, and employees at large includes measuring Business ethics, anti-competitive practices, corruption, tax, and providing accounting transparency for stakeholders.

MSCI puts in the Governance side of the bucket corporate behavior practices and governance of board diversity, executive pay, ownership, control, and accounting that the board of directors must oversee on behalf of stakeholders.

Management structure: The system of internal procedures and controls that makes up the management structure of a company is in the valuation of that company's equity.

Attention has been focused in recent years on the balance of power between the CEO and the Board of Directors and specifically the differences between the European model and the US model—in the US studies have found that 80% of companies have a CEO who is also the Chairman of the Board, in the UK and the European model it was found that 90% of the largest companies split the roles of CEO and Chairman.

Employee relations: In the United States Moskowitz's list of the *Fortune 100 Best Companies to Work For* has become not only an important tool for employees but companies are beginning to compete keenly for a place on the list, as not only does it help to recruit the best workforce, but it also appears to have a noticeable impact on company values.

Employee relations relate also to the representation of co-workers in the decision-making of companies, and the ability to participate in a union.

Executive compensation: Companies are now being asked to list the percentage levels of bonus payments and the levels of remuneration of the highest-paid executives are coming under scrutiny from stockholders and equity investors alike.

Employee compensation: Besides executive compensation, equitable pay of other employees is a consideration in the governance of an organization. This includes pay equity for employees of all genders.

Pay equity audits and the results of those audits may be required by various regulations and, in some cases, made available to the public for review. Hermann J. Stern differentiates four methods to include ESG performance in employee compensation:

1. ESG Targets (Objectives for activities, projects, and ESG results set by the company as a goal)
2. ESG Relative Performance Measurement (compared to peers, based on key figures the company considers relevant)
3. ESG Ratings Agencies (Refinitiv, S&P Trucost and Robeco Sam, Sustainalytics, ISS ESG, MSCI ESG, Vigeo Eiris, EcoVadis, Minerva Analytics, etc.)
4. ESG Performance Evaluations (internal or independent performance assessment through expert opinions, based on internally and externally available objective and subjective facts)

Responsible investment: The three domains of social, environmental, and corporate governance are intimately linked to the concept of responsible investment. RI began as a niche investment area, serving the needs of those who wished to invest but wanted to do so within ethically defined parameters. In recent years it has become a much larger proportion of the investment market.

By June 2020, flows into U.S. sustainable funds reached $20.9 billion, nearly matching 2019's flows of $21.4 billion. By the end of 2020, flows into U.S. sustainable funds surpassed $51 billion. Globally, sustainable funds held $1.65 trillion in assets at the end of 2020.

Investment strategies: RI seeks to control the placing of its investments via several methods:

- Positive selection: where the investor actively selects the companies in which to invest; this can be done either by following a defined set of ESG criteria or by the best-in-class method where a subset of high-performing ESG-compliant companies is chosen for inclusion in an investment portfolio.
- Activism: strategic voting by shareholders in support of a particular issue, or to bring about change in the governance of the company.
- Engagement: investment funds monitor the ESG performance of all portfolio companies and lead constructive shareholder engagement dialogues with each company to ensure progress.
- Consulting role: the larger institutional investors and shareholders tend to be able to engage in what is known as 'quiet diplomacy', with regular meetings with top management to exchange information and act as early warning systems for risk and strategic or governance issues.
- Exclusion: the removal of certain sectors or companies from consideration for investment, based on ESG-specific criteria.
- Integration: the inclusion of ESG risks and opportunities into traditional financial analysis of equity value.
- *Institutional investors:* One of the defining marks of the modern investment market is the divergence in the relationship between the firm and its equity investors. Institutional investors have become the key owners of stock—rising from 35% in 1981 to 58% in 2002 in the US and from 42% in 1963 to 84.7% in 2004 in the UK and institutions tend to work on a long-term investment strategy. Insurance companies, Mutual Funds, and Pension Funds with long-term payout obligations are much more interested in the long-term sustainability of their investments than the individual investor looking for short-term gain. Where a Pension Fund is subject to ERISA, there are legal limitations on the extent to which investment decisions can be based on factors other than maximizing plan participants' economic returns.

Based on the belief that addressing ESG issues will protect and enhance portfolio returns, responsible investment is rapidly becoming a mainstream concern within the institutional industry. By late 2016, over a third of institutional investors (commonly referred to as LPs) based in Europe and Asia-Pacific said that ESG considerations played a major or primary role in refusing to commit to a private equity fund, while the same is true for a fifth of North American LPs.

In reaction to investor interest in ESG, private equity, and other industry trade associations have developed many ESG best practices, including a due diligence questionnaire for private fund managers and other asset managers to use before investing in a portfolio company.

There was a clear acceleration of the institutional shift towards ESG-informed investments in the second semester of 2019. The notion of "SDG Driven Investment" gained further ground amongst pension funds, SWFs, and asset managers in the second semester of 2019, notably at the World Pensions Council G7 Pensions Roundtable held in Biarritz, on 26 August 2019, and the Business Roundtable held in Washington, DC, on 19 August 2019.

Principles for Responsible Investment: The Principles for Responsible Investment Initiative (PRI) was established in 2005 by the United Nations Environment Program Finance Initiative and the UN Global Compact as a framework for improving the analysis of ESG issues in the investment process and to aid companies in the exercise of responsible ownership practices. As of April 2019, there are over 2,350 PRI Signatories.

Equator Principles: framework, adopted by financial institutions, for determining, assessing, and managing environmental and social risk in project finance. It is primarily intended to provide a minimum standard for due diligence to support responsible risk decision-making. As of October 2019, 97 adopting financial institutions in 37 countries had officially adopted the Equator Principles, most of the international Project Finance debt in emerging and developed markets. Equator Principles Financial Institutions (EPFIs) commit to not provide loans to projects where the borrower will not or is unable to comply with their respective social and environmental policies and procedures.

The Equator Principles, formally launched in Washington DC on 4 June 2003, were based on existing environmental and social policy frameworks established by the International Finance Corporation.

These standards have subsequently been periodically updated into what is commonly known as the International Finance Corporation Performance Standards on Social and environmental sustainability and the World Bank Group Environmental, Health, and Safety Guidelines.

ESG rating agencies: Asset managers and other financial institutions increasingly rely on ESG rating agencies to assess, measure, and compare companies' ESG performance. More recently, data providers have applied artificial intelligence to rate companies and their commitment to ESG.

Each rating agency uses its own set of metrics to measure the level of ESG compliance and there is, at present, no industry-wide set of common standards.

A strong ESG movement exists in Brazil and all of Latin America. More and more companies are aware of the importance of the best practices in environmental, social, and governance issues. In Latin America, it is the Latin American Quality Institute with headquarters in Panama and operations in 19 countries that leads the movement with more than 10,000 certifications issued.

Disclosure and regulation: The first ten years of the 21st century have seen growth in the ESG-defined investment market. Not only do most of the world's big banks have departments and divisions exclusively addressing Responsible Investment but boutique firms specializing in advising and consulting on environmental, social, and governance-related investments are proliferating.

One of the major aspects of the ESG side of the insurance market which leads to this tendency to proliferation is the essentially subjective nature of the information on which investment selection can be made. By definition ESG data is qualitative; it is non-financial and not readily quantifiable in monetary terms.

The investment market has long dealt with these intangibles—such variables as goodwill have been widely accepted as contributing to a company's value. But the ESG intangibles are not only highly subjective they are also particularly difficult to quantify and more importantly verify.

A lack of clear standards and transparent monitoring has led to fears that ESG avowals mainly serve purposes of greenwashing and other company public relations objectives while distracting from more substantive initiatives to improve the environment and society.

One of the major issues in the ESG area is disclosure. Environmental risks created by business activities have an actual or potential negative impact on air, land, water, ecosystems, and human health.

The information on which an investor makes their decisions on a financial level is fairly simply gathered. The company's accounts can be examined, and although the accounting practices of corporate business are coming increasingly into disrepute after a spate of recent financial scandals, the figures are for the most part externally verifiable.

With ESG considerations, the practice has been for the company under examination to provide its figures and disclosures. These have seldom been externally verified and the lack of universal standards and regulation in the areas of environmental and social practice means that the measurement of such statistics is subjective, to say the least. As integrating ESG considerations into investment analysis and the calculation of a company's value become more prevalent it will become more crucial to provide units of measurement for investment decisions on subjective issues such as, for example, degrees of harm to workers, or how far down the supply chain for the production of a cluster bomb do you go.

One of the solutions put forward to the inherent subjectivity of ESG data is the provision of universally accepted standards for the measurement of ESG factors. Such organizations as the ISO (International Organization for Standardization) provide highly researched and widely accepted standards for many of the areas covered.

Some investment consultancies, such as Probus-Sigma have created methodologies for calculating the ratings for an ESG-based Ratings Index that is both based on ISO standards and externally verified, but the formalization of the acceptance of such standards as the basis for calculating and verifying ESG disclosures is by no means universal.

The corporate governance side of the matter has received rather more in the way of regulation and standardization as there is a long history of regulation in this area. In 1992 the London Stock Exchange and the Financial Reporting Commission set up the Cadbury Commission to investigate the series of governance failures that had plagued the City of London such as the bankruptcies of BCCI, Polly Peck, and Robert Maxwell's Mirror Group.

The conclusions that the commission reached were compiled in 2003 into the *Combined Code on Corporate Governance* which has been widely accepted (if patchily applied) by the financial world as a benchmark for good governance practices.

In the interview for Yahoo! Finance Francis Menassa (JAR Capital) says that "the EU's 2014 Non-Financial Reporting Directive will apply to every country on a national level to implement and requires large companies to disclose non-financial and diversity information. This also includes

providing information on how they operate and manage social and environmental challenges.
The aim is to help investors, consumers, policy makers, and other stakeholders to evaluate the non-financial performance of large companies. Ultimately, the Directive encourages European companies to develop a responsible approach to business".

One of the key areas of concern in the discussion as to the reliability of ESG disclosures is the establishment of credible ratings for companies as to ESG performance.

The world's financial markets have all leaped to provide ESG-relevant rating indexes, the Dow Jones Sustainability Index, the FTSE4Good Index (which is co-owned by the London Stock Exchange and Financial Times, Bloomberg ESG data, the MSCI ESG Indices, and the GRESB benchmarks.

There is some movement in the insurance market to find a reliable index of ratings for ESG issues, with some suggesting that the future lies in the construction of algorithms for calculating ESG ratings based on ISO standards and third-party verification. European regulators have introduced concrete rules to deal with the problem of greenwashing.

A growing focus on impact

Most respondents take into consideration the creation of positive impact

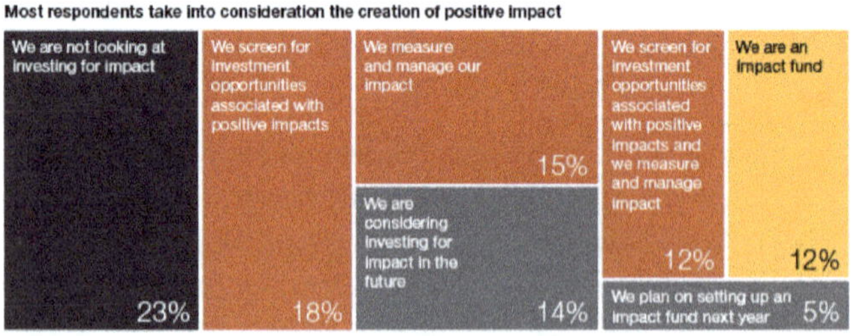

■ We consider impact because we're an impact fund ■ We consider impact, but we're not an impact fund
■ We don't yet consider impact ■ We don't consider impact

Note: Percentages shown do not total 100 due to rounding. **Source:** PwC Private Equity Responsible Investment Survey 2021 **Base:** 180 (excluding Venture Capital-only respondents)

Example of ESG Criteria used by Impact Investors by FSRI

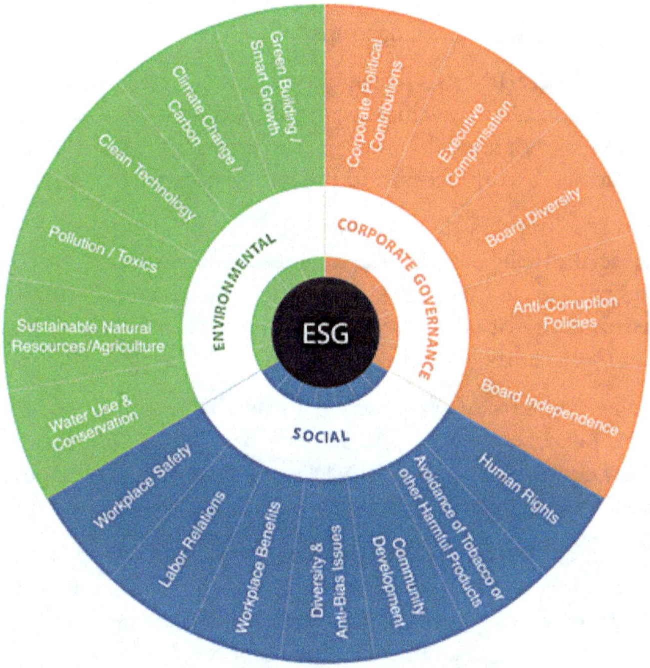

"Impact innovation harnesses emerging technologies to create solutions to urgent, sometimes life-threatening, problems".

UN Sustainability - Compact Goals (Business Driven)

The Future of Work: The world of work is changing. Artificial intelligence and automation will make this shift as significant as the mechanization in prior generations of agriculture and manufacturing. While some jobs will be lost, and many others created, almost all will change.

The COVID-19 crisis accelerated existing trends and caused organizations to reevaluate many aspects of work. The future of work is defined by two major trends that are changing workplaces, workforces, and the nature of work in the 2020s.

The first trend is the growing adoption of technologies like artificial intelligence (AI), machine learning, and robotics in the workplace. And the second is the changing physical distribution of the workforce and the rise in remote employees and gig workers.

Many elements of what was considered the future of work have been accelerated and have become today's reality for many companies, as COVID-19 made it necessary to undergo rapid workplace restructuring.

But changes in the working world were already well underway long before the pandemic was upon us. In the past 10 years, the number of employees working remotely increased by 91% according to a 2019 FlexJobs report.

The number of gig workers has also been steadily on the rise, expanding by over 15% since 2010 according to a 2020 ADP report. The adoption of AI in the workplace has been another growing trend, according to the most recent Deloitte survey reporting that 71% of executives plan to spend more on AI in the coming year.

In 2020, Gartner reports that 41% of workers will continue to work remotely on an indefinite basis, versus fewer than 30% who were doing so before COVID-19.

The world economy is projected to double in size by 2050 due to continued technology-driven innovation. Today, technological innovation is increasing workers' productivity, driving major changes in professional careers.

According to the World Economic Forum, nearly two new jobs are created for every job being displaced by the emerging tech “i.e., AI, autonomous, and robotics”. There will be more demand for experts, whereas "white- and blue-collar workers" with roles prone to automation “i.e., Accountant, Lawyer, Customer Service” are the most at risk of being eliminated. The workplaces and workforces of the future focus on:

How and where we work: Until recently, a mobile device was simply a phone – but today, smartphones are used by workers as portals for increasingly sophisticated software and data management tools, where 87% of companies were dependent upon employees having access to mobile business apps from their devices. When portable devices such as laptops and mobiles are augmented with AI and connected to advanced systems, employees become untethered from the cubicle. They are freed up to work wherever they are and focus on solutions and innovation, not repetitive tasks.

Changing roles in the workforce: As the use of AI in the workplace increases, so does the demand for roles that are primarily knowledge-based and cognitive. And despite concerns about humans being pushed out of the workforce by AI and robots, the forecast is much rosier than many may think. The digitalization of the workforce is on track to create up to 133 million new roles by 2022.

New skills in the workplace of the future: As the digital workplace reduces the need for an on-site workforce, it also increases the need for knowledge-intensive tasks. From 2000 to 2019, the proportion of employees with graduate-level qualifications rose from 24% to 42%, also showing a nearly 20% rise in the past 10 years in jobs calling for evidence of complex problem-solving and innovative thinking. with a sophisticated level of computer and software literacy which is essential for the workforce of the future.

Takeaways: Generally speaking, the main purpose of good innovation is to improve people's lives and not drive revenues while impacting people's lives negatively. When it comes to managing a business, innovation is the key to making any kind of progress.

The Venture Capital Exclusion: Most VCs don'ts seek to fund innovation that solves immediate and large human challenges, but rather a new monopoly that usually creates new side effects, i.e., ridesharing congestion, pollution, and labor exploitation. John Hennessy, the previous President of Stanford University, pointed out that the technology industry has become more bimodal in its success rates, with a smaller percentage of companies succeeding.

About 70 percent of the spinoffs from Stanford in the information technology sector got to the breakeven point, he said. Today the percentage is much smaller -- perhaps 30 percent. Investors seem to be searching for the occasional company that produces very large returns, even if small investments are lost in most startups. "If you get Google or Facebook, you pay off the last four funds with one company," Hennessy said.

Emerging Standard: Led by Tech for Life as a movement, which champions the responsible creation and use of technology, and provides leaders with a framework based on established guiding principles. Tech for Life asks those that create and use technology to take steps to put people back at the center of tech. The Tech for Life initiative wants businesses to optimize their organizations for profit and purpose, by adding sustainability and trust to the financial bottom line.

And it calls for technology leaders to commit to the five Tech for Life principles. They aspire to do more; to solve problems that are relevant to people in their daily lives; to change the world; to make a positive and sustainable difference. The Innovation Impact Exchange (IIE) or Social Exchange (SE): Beyond simple research, our goal should be to change the entire ecosystem of entrepreneurship. Too much of our startup industry has devolved into a feeder system for tech-media companies and investment banks with little impact.

Part of the reason established companies struggle to invest consistently in innovation is intense pressure from public markets to hit short-term profitability and growth targets. Mostly, this is a consequence of the accounting methods we have developed for evaluating managers, which focus on the kinds of gross "vanity" metrics.

What is needed is a new kind of stock exchange, designed to trade in the stocks of companies that are organized to sustain long-term thinking. We must create Innovation Impact Exchange (IIE) or Social Exchange (SE). In addition to quarterly reports on profits and margins, companies on the IIE would report using innovation positive impact (to all stakeholders) accounting for their internal entrepreneurship efforts. Like Intuit, they would report on the revenue they were generating from products that did not exist a few years earlier.

Executive compensation in IIE companies would be tied to the company's long-term performance. Trading on the IIE would have much higher transaction costs and fees to minimize day trading and massive price swings. In exchange, IIE companies would be allowed to structure their corporate governance to facilitate greater freedom for management to pursue long-term investments.

In addition, to support long-term thinking, the transparency of the IIE will provide valuable data about how to nurture innovation in the real world. Something like the IIE would accelerate the creation of the next generation of great companies, built from the ground up for continuous innovation that drives sustainable living over consumption.

As a movement, Startup Innovation must avoid doctrines and rigid ideology. We must avoid the caricature that science means formula or a lack of humanity in work. Science is one of humanity's most creative pursuits. I believe that applying it to entrepreneurship will unlock a vast storehouse of human potential. We would look to eliminate waste not to build immersive castles in the sky but rather to stir our resources to service agility and breakthrough business results with positive impact.

Venture Capital - Environmental Sustainability and Social Equity

ENVIRONMENTAL SUSTAINABILITY			
Built Environment	**Energy Systems**	**Food Systems**	**Land & Water**
Energy Efficiency	Battery Storage	Agriculture	Land Conservation
Sustainable Infrastructure	Mobility Infrastructure	Food Processing & Transport	Sustainable Timber
Water Efficiency	Renewable Energy	Technology & Safety	Water Technologies
	Sustainable Transport	Vertical Farming	

SOCIAL EQUITY			
Civic Practices	**Education**	**Heath & Wellness**	**Social Justice**
Anti-Corruption	Early Childhood & K-12	Access to Healthcare	Community Development
Arts & Culture	Lifelong Learning	Diagnostics & Detection	Economic Access
Civic Engagement	Student Loan Financing	Drug Discovery	Quality Employment
Technology	Technology	Health IT & Infrastructure	Workforce Development
		Prevention	

We would dedicate ourselves to the creation of new institutions with a long-term mission to build sustainable value and change the world for the better. Most of all, we would stop wasting people's time feeding wasteful ads.

CHAPTER VII
HOW TO INNOVATE

Converting Idea to Product or Service: How to capture transformational and avoid core innovation, by aligning your execution into a new market with a product or service that stands out of the dominant players' segment "i.e., Uber vs Taxi, Google Ads vs print ads, iPad news feed vs printed newspaper", which render current products or services absolute and create new and untapped revenues stream.

The golden rule in innovation is to start by solving old problems with a large base of paying customers and very complaisant market leaders with monopolistic tendencies. Some examples of space are Education, Health, Transportation, Food, Energy, and Entertainment.

Your offering should be at least three times better than the closest competitors, and build on a digital platform "i.e., Software" that can scale fast to billions of users while keeping your fixed cost the same or lower. The three foundations are:

Ideation: Generating new ideas is the first stage of successful capabilities, mapped to proven methods discussed further.

Incubation: Validating the New Idea where companies usually do not lack new ideas. But how does a leader separate the good ones that are worth investing in from the bad? The answer is through incubation or validation—a process to determine whether the idea meets a market test.

Execution: You have reached the point where a well-designed and executed incubation proved its success, that pivot from a successful experiment to a fully operational business creating its challenges, including when customers behave and spend money as indicated by the experiment.

The following approaches emphasize intensive interaction with customers, rapid prototyping, and fast iteration, which are incorporated within many accelerator programs including Y Combinator. Design Thinking is one proven method, among many others, including Open Innovation, Launch Pad, and Lean Startup, Business Model Canvas discussed further.

Design Thinking Innovation:

The identified steps in Design Thinking are, *EXPLORE* - identifying and investigating an issue, *FOCUS* - Narrowing the field and choosing the most effective site for intervention, *IMAGINE* - Brainstorming possible solutions, no matter how far-fetched, *DISTILL* - Analyzing ideas and choosing the most promising solutions to pursue, *EVOLVE* - Prototyping solutions and refining them based on feedback, *SHARE* - Reflecting on those experiments with experts and end-users, *BUILD* - Implementing the final idea and making it real.

While there are numerous innovative organizations, three are identified below that stand out as organizations that embraced innovation from their very beginnings.

Perhaps because of the personality of the CEO or perhaps because of the work that they chose to do, innovation became a culture that defined the organization and how it approached development. The businesses identified will immediately invoke a recognition of innovation in their industries.

IDEO: is a global design company. They are well known for their innovative approaches to problems and have been recognized as leaders in innovation. Working with companies and organizations to make significant improvements to products and services, IDEO uses a team approach to every design.

They have been highlighted on CBS 60 Minutes and have been very willing to share their process with anyone interested. IDEO's design teams are not a cadre of engineers.

They include engineers, but also sociologists, designers, business analysts, psychologists, etc. Teams start by "diving deep" into an understanding of the end-user of a product or service before beginning to design anything. Tim Brown, the president, and CEO states that "Design Thinking is Innovation by Design".

A human-centered approach to innovation that draws from the designer's toolkit to integrate the needs of people, the possibilities of technology, and the requirements for business success."

This approach brings together: what is desirable from a human perspective; what is technologically feasible; and what is economically viable to craft an innovative yet practical solution.

IDEO summarizes these in a simple graph. Further, IDEO states that for their company, Design Thinking is best thought of as overlapping spaces rather than orderly steps. These spaces, as they call them, are inspiration, ideation, and implementation. *Inspiration is the problem or opportunity that brought out the need for a solution.* It is what motivates the team to innovate.

Ideation is the process of creating potential solutions, developing, and testing ideas, and creating prototypes to see how these ideas might work. Finally, implementation is bringing the prototype from a project to a product in people's lives.

Apple: is known by computer users around the world as an innovative company that has created products that bring computing into homes and lives. While not possessing the largest market share for personal computers, Apple is known for its designs, its user-friendly and intuitive interface, its creativity, and for developing an almost emotional bond between consumer and product that has inspired unprecedented brand loyalty.

When Apple launches a new product, consumers wait in lines or sit by their computers until the second that they can purchase the product.

For Apple, innovation means developing products that are simple to use and beautiful in every detail. This dedication came from Apple's former CEO Steve Jobs.

Mr. Jobs believed in the following six design principles and instilled them in his company:

1. Craft Above All - attention to details matters, even those details that many may never notice; 2. Empathy - an intimate connection with the feelings of their customer and understanding them better than any other company can; 3. Focus - perform well on the things that you decide to do and eliminate all of the unimportant opportunities that you didn't decide to do; 4. Impute - people form an opinion about a company based on the signals it provides - even the best products will look bad if not presented well - people do judge a book by its cover; 5. Friendliness - high-tech products should look friendly, not off-putting; 6. Finding Simplicity for the Future in Metaphors from the Past - make things intuitively obvious, the user interface should remind them of things they already know.

By having this six-pillar philosophy to design and innovate, Steve Jobs parlayed Apple into the most recognized brands in the world, he created a culture of innovation and passion that is dedicated to designing products and services that impress and inspire customer loyalty.

IDEO summarizes these in a simple graph.

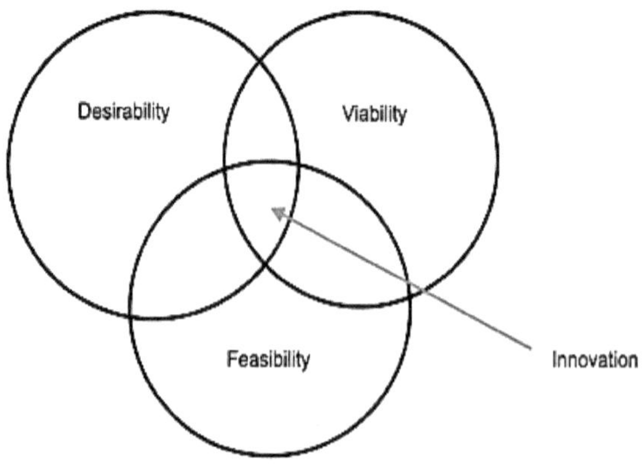

Open Innovation and Launch Pad:

Open Innovation: innovations tend to be produced by outsiders and startups, rather than large organizations, the foundation behind open innovation is that, in a world of widely distributed knowledge, companies cannot afford to rely entirely on their research but should instead buy or license processes or inventions (i.e., patents) from other companies.

This is termed inbound open innovation. In addition, internal inventions not being used in a firm's business should be taken outside the company (e.g., through licensing, joint ventures, or spin-offs). This is called outbound open innovation.

These include sharing intellectual property so others can develop products with it (e.g., Apple, Google, Amazon, and Intuit), inviting customers to suggest ideas for new products and services (e.g., Lego, P&G), and offering contests for participants who can provide solutions for company problems (e.g., NASA, and Kaggle), or fostering networks or communities of interest (e.g., IBM, Wikipedia, and Facebook).

Launch Pad: a Stanford Design School class for entrepreneurs that has generated more than 100 new companies over the past several years, 60% of which are still operating. Over the course, participants are required to talk to a minimum of 100 potential customers.

Combining elements of design thinking, the lean startup, and the business canvas, the emphasis is on listening to the customer, rapid prototyping, and fast iteration.

The class begins with an idea for a product or service and addresses three questions: Who is the hyper-specific target user? What is their specific pain point? and What single function have you performed to reduce this pain?

Lean Startup and Business Model Canvas:

Start by incorporating lean in each step from the idea through the commercialization stage. Lean comes from proven execution initiated in manufacturing by Toyota, then was gradually adopted in product and software development by startup and tech giant as an evolution called "Lean Startup". It is about optimizing efficiency within the full cycle of innovation and minimizing or eliminating all non-value-added activities.

Startups must be laser-focused on value-added activities that directly serve their customers and create products that customers want to be driven by any of these advantages ``i.e., Pricing, Quality, Selection, Reliability, Support", with a built-in to capture continuous feedback and iterate improvement to that value.

Since a startup is driven by uncertainty and the unknown, you should skip traditional management techniques that are based on time-consuming research, analysis, and forecasting that lead to analysis paralysis; and rather focus on fast iteration to convert the Idea into Prototype "MVP" and sustain it by early adopters "target users or customers" feedback to test target segment at a very early-stage vs full-blown product launch by large R&D group within Fortune 500.

Although your innovation activities aren't necessarily powerful enough to change the world, you should focus on improving the things you can affect within your immediate market. The sheer volume of technological breakthroughs promising to make things simpler, keep us more connected, and improve our daily lives, often deliver the opposite, where additional complexity, feelings of disconnection, and small erosion of our freedoms are becoming the norms. And more it feels like we're the ones adapting to these rapid advances instead of seeing technology adapt to us.

That's why it's important to focus on people, organizations, and companies who use science and technology to fulfill that promise and make a lasting positive impact on the world.

Lean Startup: is nothing more than adhering to the most efficient way to take your idea to market and does omit the most challenging questions of how to build, what, when, and why "which are covered throughout this book". It is about product development, not innovation, engineering, or marketing. The Lean Principles are:

- Startup: a venture designed to create new products or services under extreme uncertainty.
- That Lean: approach can work in any size, even a large enterprise, in any sector or industry.
- Entrepreneurship: is a management style geared to extreme uncertainty for small businesses or startups.
- Validated learning: Startups exist not just to make stuff, make money, or even serve customers. They exist to learn how to build a sustainable business. This learning can be validated scientifically by running frequent experiments that allow entrepreneurs to test each element of their vision.
- Build-Measure-Learn: The fundamental activity of a startup is to turn ideas into products, measure how customers respond, and then learn whether to pivot or persevere. All successful startup processes should be geared to accelerate that feedback loop.
- Innovation accounting: To improve entrepreneurial outcomes and hold innovators accountable, we need to focus on the boring stuff: how to measure progress, how to set up milestones, and how to prioritize work. This requires a new kind of accounting designed for startups—and the people who hold them accountable.

- The Build-Measure-Learn Feedback Loop

Throughout the process of driving, you always have a clear idea of where you're going. If you're commuting to work, you don't give up because there's a detour in the road or you made a wrong turn. You remain thoroughly focused on getting to your destination. Startups also have a true north, a destination in mind: creating a thriving and world-changing business. I call that a startup's vision.

To achieve that vision, startups employ a strategy, which includes a business model, a product road map, a point of view about partners and competitors, and ideas about who the customer will be. The product is the result of this strategy

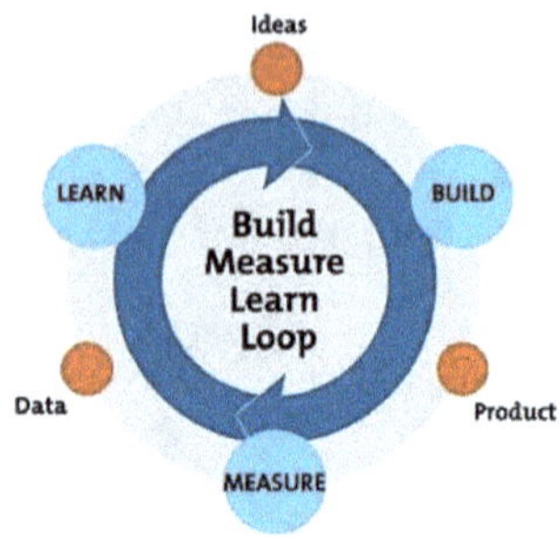

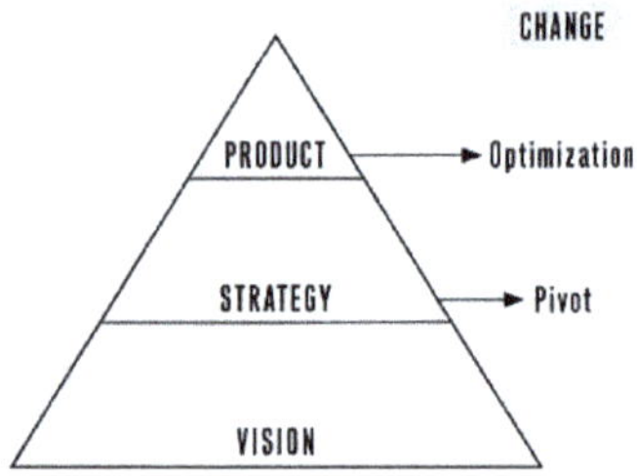

Products change constantly through the process of optimization, what I call tuning the engine. Less frequently, the strategy may have to change (called a pivot). However, the overarching vision rarely changes. Entrepreneurs are committed to seeing the startup through to that destination. Every setback is an opportunity for learning how to get where they want to go (see the previous chart).

In real life, a startup is a portfolio of activities. A lot is happening simultaneously: the engine is running, acquiring new customers, and serving existing ones; we are tuning, and trying to improve our product, marketing, and operations; and we are steering, deciding if and when to pivot. The challenge of entrepreneurship is to balance all these activities. Even the smallest startup faces the challenge of supporting existing customers while trying to innovate. Even the most established company faces the imperative to invest in innovation lest it become obsolete. As companies grow, what changes in the mix of these activities in the company's portfolio of work?

Business Model Canvas: is a set of nine focus areas used in assessing new ventures. It helps to systematically think through the business model and identify those areas needed to test the initial hypothesis. The canvas can be adjusted as a company grows. This approach is not new. IBM's Emerging Business Opportunity (*deployed a similar method in the 2000s*).

Each area has a unit linked to accomplishing milestones of validating or refuting this business design. The focus areas are Problem, Solution, Unique Value Proposition, Unfair Advantage, Customer Segments, Key Metrics, Channels, Cost Structure, and Revenue Streams. **The Lean Startup Canvas** (Below)

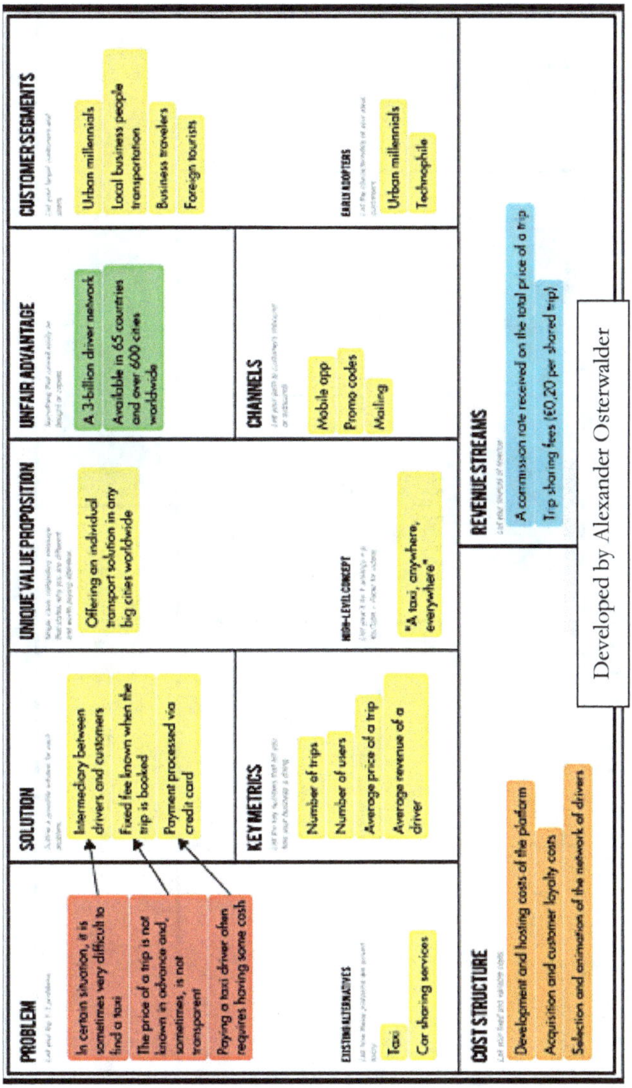

Example of **Startup Canvas** that become a giant Corporate Tech "Google" and disrupted the whole Ads industry.

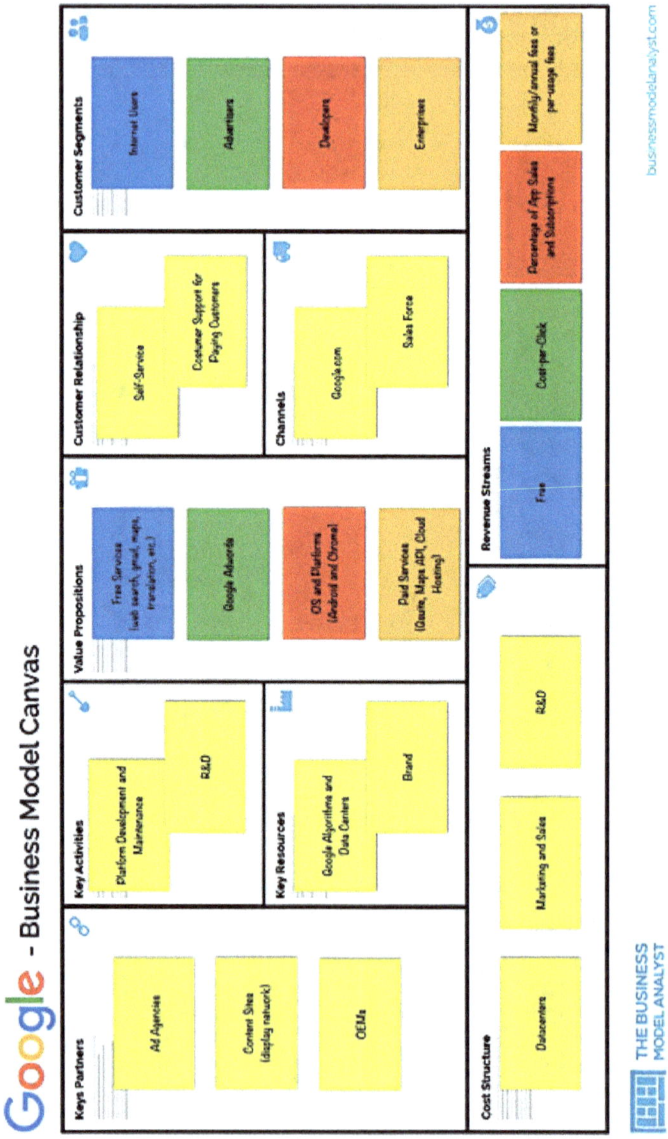

Innovation Emerging Practices:

The latest emerging innovation includes a wide range of breakthrough innovations from the founder of a startup that wants to build solar-powered mass transit pods suspended above traffic to a citizen scientist organizer furthering space exploration via crowdsourcing to a biotech engineer working with artists to explore future applications. There are many different ways creative-minded people can transform the world.

Nowadays, the differences between engineers, scientists, designers, and students are much fuzzier than they've ever been. So-called amateur thinkers and hackers can come up with transformational projects just as easily as seasoned technology entrepreneurs. At its best, technology can level the playing field, enabling anyone to manifest their big ideas into meaningful actions.

These creators all have one important thing in common: To use technology and creative thinking to make our lives better. Sometimes, coming up with new ways to improve the environment, make smarter use of existing resources or bring individuals together around a shared goal is enough on its own, but often these innovations can have an amplifying effect. They also teach us to celebrate our differences, push us towards more equitable access and inspire us to strive for a better tomorrow.

Innovators don't just focus on a single area of change, but instead, look more broadly at positive innovations that can remake what's possible. Any time we're asked to contemplate the new and the next, particularly around technology, there's always going to worry about unintended (or intended) consequences. That's why we're excited to highlight pioneers who endeavor to deliver proactive, additive value to our lives.

Sometimes they find ways to redistribute an existing resource, or even create one out of thin air. Other times, they make an existing process run more efficiently, or create an entirely new way of doing things. They've stopped asking "What is it?" or

"Why now?" and started doing and leading instead for a better tomorrow for all of us.

We tend to think of innovation as arising from a single brilliant thinker, but the truth is that it is drawn over time, involving the discovery and refinement of an engineering process or solution, new business model, or new material, leading to the gradual transformation of an industry or field. That's rarely achieved by one person or even within one organization, which is the opposite of how usually the media like to portray the most innovative leaders or organizations as the sole holders of our future well-being.

Enablement of the knowledge economy: On December 9th, 1968, a US-funded research project initiated a first stage of a knowledge economy, through a presentation by an engineer named Douglas Engelbart, that was so consequential that it is now called The Mother of All Demos. He was also awarded the National Medal of Technology, the U.S.'s highest technology award by President Bill Clinton.

Two of those in attendance, Bob Taylor and Alan Kay would go on to develop Engelbart's ideas into the Alto, the first truly personal computer, and expand to lay down the first pillars of the modern internet. Later, Steve Jobs would inspire by the Alto to create the Macintosh.

So, who deserves credit? Engelbart for coming up with the idea? Taylor and Kay for engineering solutions around it? Jobs for turning it all into a marketable product that created an impact on the world. Strong arguments can be made for each, as well as for many others not mentioned here. The truth is that there are many paths to innovation. Here are ten of them:

Innovation is Sequential not a Single Event: Alexander Fleming discovered penicillin in 1928, but it wasn't until 15 years later, in 1943, that the miracle drug came into widespread use. The reason that Fleming was unable to bring Penicillin to market was that, as a biologist, he lacked many of the requisite skills. It wasn't until a decade later that two chemists, Howard

Florey, and Ernst Boris Chain, picked up the problem and were able to synthesize penicillin. Even then, it took people with additional expertise in fermentation and manufacturing to turn it into the miracle cure we know today. Alan Turing came up with the idea of a universal computer in 1936, but it wasn't until 1946 that one was built, and not until the 1990s that computers began to impact productivity statistics.

Innovation Is Incremental Pivots: This isn't the exception, but the norm. Darwin's theory of natural selection borrowed ideas from Thomas Malthus, an economist, and Charles Lyell, a geologist. Watson and Crick's discovery of DNA was not achieved by simply plowing away at the lab, but by incorporating discoveries in biology, chemistry, and x-ray diffraction to inform their model building. Great innovation rarely occurs within one field of expertise but is almost invariably the product of synthesis across domains.
Innovation starts with The Right Questions: Too often, we treat innovation as a monolith, as if every problem was the same, but that's not the case. In laboratories and factory floors, universities and coffee shops, or even over a beer after work, people are talking about better ways to do things. There is no monopoly on creative thought.

How should we go about innovation? Should we hand it over to the guys with white lab coats? An external partner? A specialist in the field? Crowdsource it? What we need is a clear framework for defining the scope of each focus area.

Albert Einstein is often quoted as saying, "If I had 20 days to solve a problem, I would spend 19 days defining it." Therefore, the best way to start is by asking the right questions: (a) How well is the problem defined? and (b) How well is the domain defined? And (c) what we know and don't know? Once you've gathered inputs to those framing questions, you can start defining the problem using the innovation matrix.

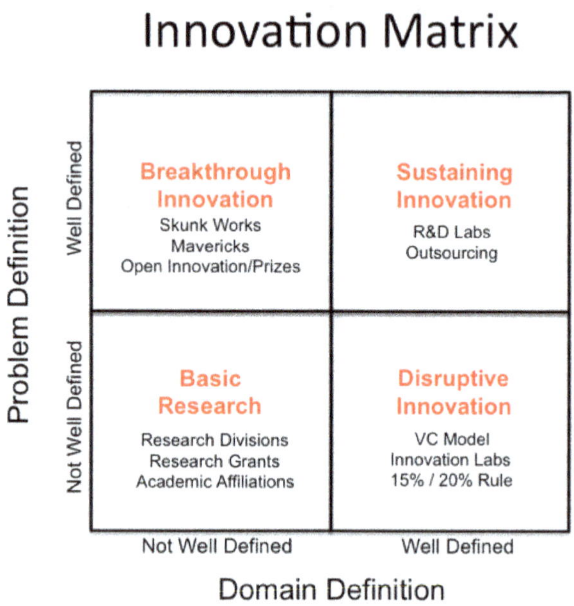

No one method can suffice. Look at any great innovator, whether it is Apple, Tesla, or Google, and you'll find a portfolio of strategies. So, the first step toward solving a difficult problem is asking the questions you need to define your approach. To paraphrase Voltaire, if you need to solve a problem, first define your terms.

There is no one size for Innovation: When most people think about innovation, they think about startups. And certainly, new firms like Uber, Airbnb, and Space X can transform markets. But others such as IBM, Procter and Gamble, and 3M have managed to stay on top for decades, even as competitors rise to challenge them and then, when technology and markets shift, disappear just as quickly into oblivion.

While it's true that small, agile firms can move fast, larger enterprises have the luxury of going slow. They have loyal customers and an abundance of resources. They can see past the next hot trend and invest for the long term. There's a big difference between hitting on the next big thing and developing it consistently, generation after generation.

Open Innovation Expands Your Capabilities: When Microsoft launched Kinect for the Xbox, it quickly became the hottest consumer device ever, selling 8 million units in just the first two months. Almost immediately, hackers began altering its capabilities to do things that Microsoft never intended. Yet instead of asking them to stop, it embraced the hackers, quickly releasing a software development kit to help them along.

Like Microsoft, many firms today are embracing open innovation to expand capabilities. Cisco outfoxed Lucent not by developing technology internally, but by smartly acquiring startups. Procter & Gamble has found great success with its Connect and Develop program and platforms like Innocentive allow firms to expose thorny problems to a more diverse skill set.

Disruptive Innovations need New Business Models: When Chester Carlson perfected his invention in 1938, he tried to market it to more than 20 companies but had no takers. It was simply far too expensive for the market. Finally, in 1946, Joe Wilson, President of the Haloid Company, came up with the idea of leasing the machines instead of selling them outright. The idea was a rousing success and in 1948 the firm changed its name to Xerox.

The tricky thing about disruptive innovations is that they rarely fit into existing business models and so the value they create isn't immediately clear. Kodak made money by selling film, so was slow to adopt the digital cameras that the company had itself invented.

Yahoo's business was focused on keeping users on its site, so passed on the chance to acquire Google. It's not just products that we have to innovate, but business models as well

The 360 Degree Innovation: Many people think of innovation as discarding the old to make room for the new, but as Bain &

Co. 's Chris Zook points out in *Profit from The Core*, smart companies realize that the bulk of their profits will come from current lines of business.

Take Google for example. Yes, it pursues radical innovation, like self-driving cars, at its Google X unit, but the continual improvement of its core search business is what made it the world's most valuable company. That's why Google, as well as many other innovative companies, follow the 360-degree rule as 70/20/10.

The premise of the rule is simple. Focus 70% of your resources on improving existing technology (i.e., search), 20% toward adjacent markets (i.e., Gmail, Google Drive, etc.), and 10% on completely new markets (i.e., self-driving cars).

Digitization Needs Platforms to Access Ecosystems: It's no accident that the people who would make the vision Engelbart presented at "The Mother of All Demos" a reality actually attended the event and knew Engelbart personally. In those days, it was difficult, if not impossible, to actively collaborate across time and space. Today, however, we can use platforms to access ecosystems of technology, talent, and information.

Take Apple's App Store. It is, of course, a highly effective way for Apple's network of customers to access functionality on their phones, but it also allows the firm to access the talents of literally millions of developers. It's hard to imagine any single enterprise, no matter how efficient or well-organized, pulling off that kind of scale. In a networked world, the surest path to success is not acquiring and controlling assets, but widening and deepening connections.

Collaboration is the New Competitive Advantage: When we look back to the great innovations of the past, it is hard not to wonder how they could've gone differently. What if chemists had picked up on Fleming's discovery of penicillin in weeks rather than years? How many lives could have been saved? Was there no one who could have helped develop Engelbart's vision of the personal computer outside of Northern California?

And now, the problems we seek to solve are significantly more complex than in earlier generations. That's one reason why the journal *Nature* recently noted that the average scientific paper today has four times as many authors as one did in 1950. At the same time, knowledge has been democratized. A teenager with a smartphone today has more access to information than a highly trained specialist a generation ago. That's why now collaboration itself is becoming a competitive advantage.

Take a slightly broader view and it becomes clear that innovation today goes far beyond research labs, Silicon Valley pitch meetings, and large corporate initiatives. We all have something to offer and can add to the world's knowledge in a way that may differ in degree, but not in kind, from the giants of the past. It's no secret: innovation is difficult for well-established companies. By and large, they are better executors than innovators, and most succeed less through game-changing creativity than by optimizing their existing businesses.

On-Demand Innovation: Was developed by OneTraction Ventures at their campus based in the heart of Silicon Valley and within Stanford Research Park. The model flips the high-risk narrative of venture capital that they must fund future unicorns with monopolistic potential within the target market to ensure large returns that cover their 90% failed investments, and rather start from market access custodians who are Global Fortune 500 companies that generated USD 30 Trillion in last year and map truly disruptive startup that can go to market with at the product or service level, get funded or become a distribution channel for their product or services.

These, reduce the failure risks by 90% and shorten time to market by the same ratio which extends innovation benefits to the whole society.

Lean and Open Innovation Cycle

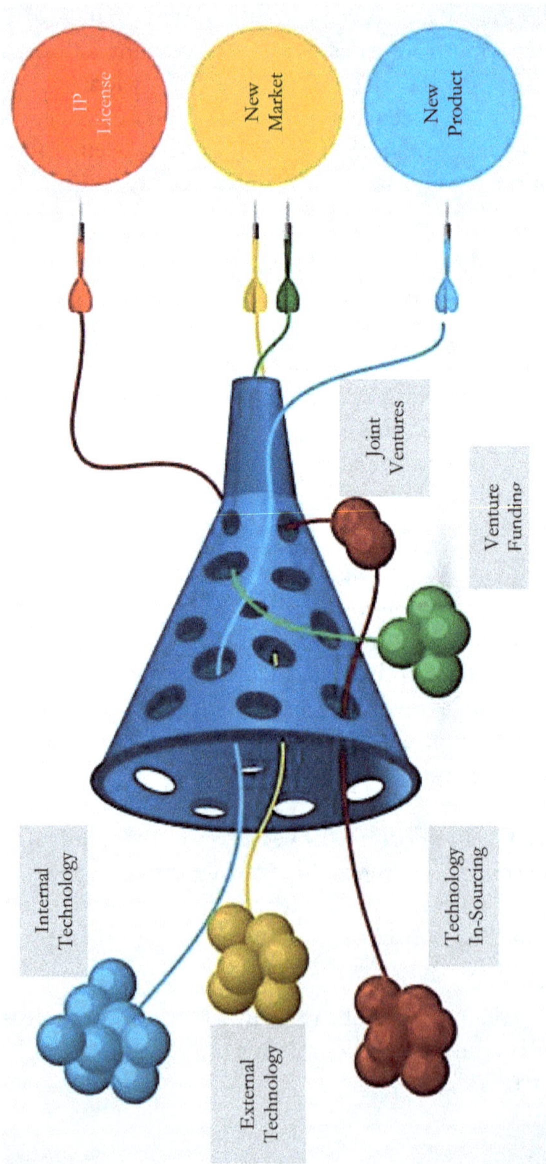

Markets Ripe for Disruption (Cash Cow) 2030:

Market	Size	Gaps	Target Area	Impact
Finance	$5T	Equal Access Pricing	Transparent Cost / Benefit	Equitable ESG
Media Digital Ads	$1,5T $0.4T	Alternate Facts/ Privacy/Related	Biased Addict Content Video Search/Email/	Fact Learning Positive
Mobility New/Used	$3T	Pollute Congest Parking	Clean Share vs Own-Ride usage	Cleaner
Travel	$3T	Pollution	Daily Travel	Cleaner
Shipping	$1,5T	Pollution Congestion	Localized Fresh Groceries	Cleaner
B2B Rental	$1,2T	Pollution Congestion	Local Hubs Telecommute	Cleaner
B2C Rental	$1,5T	% Occupied	Weekly and Monthly flexible	Cleaner
Agriculture	$10 T	Shipping Fast-food	Local Fresh/ Nutrition	Cleaner Healthy
Healthcare	$12T	Insurance / Cost/Quality	Preventive Telehealth NaturalMedicine	Healthy Cheaper
Government (Excl. ML)	$30T	Access Transparency Quality	Digital Uniform Warning/ Cyber	Clean Cheap Safer
Telecomm	$1,7T	Wi-Fi, Calls	Speed / Access / Cost / Battery	Clean Cheap Reliable
Industrial Construction Energy	$12T	Offline to Online	Sensors Clean Energy / Noise reduction	Cleaner / Safer / Cheaper

Experts excerpt from pew research on the evolution of technology by 2030.

Social media: Experts see a reckoning coming that will lead to large-scale changes. There will be changes in the overall environment of social media during the next decade. Including major revisions to their platforms. Possible break up of such firms, with the rise of new platforms designed to make their users' best interests paramount, including:

- Actions will be taken to better protect people's privacy
- Efforts will be made to identify and address misinformation
- Government policymaking will open to more citizen engagement, and public activism will grow

- Some innovations will help connect people and bring
- them together for a common purpose
- Innovations will address physical and mental health; major change is coming for the healthcare sector
- Artificial intelligence: will continue to improve and be applied to improve human lives online and offline
- Education systems will evolve in response to many multilayered societal changes
- Labor and jobs: Business practices, individuals' work lives, and the larger economy will substantially change
- Climate change and other environmental issues will inspire innovation out of necessity
- Regulation will play a key role in determining tech's effects

The internet has opened doors for people to learn of issues faced by others around the world or the corner. No longer restricted by proximity, people can provide emotional support, financial aid, political advocacy, and much more for others around the world without leaving their own homes.

Andrew Lippman, senior research scientist, and associate director at MIT's Media Lab, wrote, "There are social reforms that would be good, such as changing Section 230 of the Communications Act that relieves 'platform' companies of responsibility for what is done on those fora. While the law might have been a good idea when it was passed, it needs updating and better application.

If a company processes the information that is contributed or selectively distributes it, then they are not a simple platform, they are exerting editorial control. Also, some technologies can protect privacy and personal data if we choose to use them. We have not done so in the past, but one never knows. Working against this is the network effect – large companies such as Facebook have a potentially overwhelming advantage. Society may change its attitude toward that as well."

Jason Hong, a professor at the Human-Computer Interaction Institute at Carnegie Mellon University, said, "Healthcare is an area that will likely see many innovations. There are already multiple research prototypes underway looking at monitoring one's physical and mental health. Some of my colleagues (and myself as well) are also looking at social behaviors, and how those behaviors not only impact one's health but also how innovations spread through one's social network.

I'm highly optimistic on this front, given that the problems are there, the sensing technology is feasible, and the interventions should work (based on what has been done in the past using less sophisticated interventions or based on existing theory)."

Sam Lehman-Wilzig, a professor of communications at Bar-Ilan University specializing in Israeli politics and the impact of technological evolution, said, "The biggest advance will be the use of artificial intelligence to fight disinformation, deep fakes, and the like. There will be an AI 'arms' race between those spreading disinformation and those fighting/preventing it. Overall, I see the latter gaining the upper hand."

Faisal A. Nasr, an advocate, research scientist, futurist, and professor, wrote, "Modulating the power of large technology companies is inherent in the legislative and regulatory reform that could take place, possibly prodded on by emerging social and civic innovation.

Ethical advances in the use of algorithms can stand a chance through a reformed legal structure and global governance system to deter unethical practices. Improving the economic stability of the news media is a complex issue that involves the functioning and balance among three branches of government and the degree of power of the private sector, all critical issues which could enhance the trust in democratic institutions, lead to the creation of social media platforms and [strengthen] self-expression.

However, mitigating mental and emotional health problems tied to digital life is a monumental educational process and social and civic innovation can only have a very small impact."

As society shifts under the influence of technology, a number of the experts in this canvassing foresee education changing in response. Some expectations include a greater focus on science, technology, engineering, and math (STEM) subjects and a greater focus on digital literacy programs in the standard curriculum. Others believe that education systems will make greater shifts toward being digitally based.

Frank Feather, president of AI-Future, predicted, "Education systems will be reformed to include full orientation of the benefits and risks of digital technology applications in the curriculum. Simultaneously, education will increasingly be done remotely. Mass education is obsolete; individualized learning will evolve in all subjects. All students will become STEM-educated and will understand the positive benefits and negative harms of technology.

Technology will also decentralize the workplace. In society at large, online social networks will be the predominant form of interaction and creation of socio-political movements as needed."

Paola Ricaurte, a fellow at Harvard's Berkman Klein Center for Internet & Society, predicted, "There will be more labor demands from workers in the technology industry. Awareness of the environmental impact of technology will grow, and technology companies will be required to abandon programmed obsolescence."

Arthur Asa Berger, a professor emeritus of communications at San Francisco State University, responded, "Innovation is a two-edged sword: It can be used for negative purposes (new viruses, for example) or positive purposes (diagnose medical problems using smartphones).

The development of Twitter is now used as a propaganda tool by the president – a negative innovation as I see things. The internet can also be used to create flash mobs for protesters of the political order or champions of it. So, a good deal depends on the ingenuity of those using innovations for their own purposes."

Sharon Sputz, executive director of strategic programs at the Columbia University Data Science Institute, responded, "New laws and policies will be needed to protect citizens from the misuse of technology. One example is around ensuring the use of machine learning systems does not have a bias or unfair outcomes."

Jeremy Foote, a computational social scientist and professor at Northwestern University, responded, "So far, institutions of many different kinds have been fairly responsive and creative in dealing with troubling aspects of technology. Examples include journalists who have brought attention to [National Security Agency] abuses to institutional responses by Facebook and Twitter seeking to identify and reduce the influence of disinformation campaigns.

Our current responses are often blunt, like the GDPR, and have unintended consequences, but they are a signal of institutions that are willing and able to respond. Platforms and communities have also shown a surprising ability to police themselves. Tools (including automated tools) to moderate conversations are getting better and allowing for the reduction of some of the worst problems.

I would not be surprised to see the emergence of public institutions that are more technologically savvy, and which do things like identifying bias in algorithms or enforce technological transparency."

Christian Schoon, the external foresight consultant at Future Impacts, based in Germany, wrote, "In [the] future, a focus on the development of social and civic innovations is of great relevance because of changing circumstances in developing societies via disruptive trends like globalization, in-migration, expanding social networks in interrelation with AI development, the growing gap between poor and rich, discontinuous political power patterns in established democracies and the volatile economic systems which are moving a lot due to differing tax regulations of nations. Consider the interaction between social and technological innovations. Both go with each other. But we need to place more focus on local and global social innovation-management systems."

Tim Bray, a technology leader who has worked for Amazon, Google, and Sun Microsystems, wrote, "If we are to survive the incoming environmental devastation, we will be forced willy-nilly to bring all our human capabilities to bear on what amounts to a war footing.

Imminent existential threats tend to sweep mercenary self-interests aside and focus the mind on making the best use of the tools available to us. Among other things, the malignant technology choices that have helped get us into this mess should have become thoroughly discredited."

Daniel Estrada, a digital humanities and ethics lecturer at the New Jersey Institute of Technology, said, "A changing environment, in the form of mass migration, food and water shortages, and other health and governance emergencies, will impose a demand for social and civic change.

These emergencies will require people to organize networks of support online. We will see tools for collective action at both global and local scales; tools for sharing information and resources, and for fact-checking and rooting out malicious actors. We will also see increasing use of AI technologies, both as tools of oppression and as tools to resist digital oppression. The new laws banning facial-recognition technologies and requiring bot disclosure give some hints of the legal and political landscape to come."

Sasha Costanza-Chock, an associate professor of civic media at MIT, wrote, "On the bright side, there is a growing movement among technologists to rethink the ways we develop and deploy technology. Unfolding movements like #TechWontBuildIt are based on tech workers' desire to hold their companies accountable for harmful activities. There is increasing interest in how to co-design technologies together with marginalized communities, as reflected in the emergence of groups like the Design Justice Network.

Innovation Execution Pathways: if companies assimilate and apply these essentials—in their own way, following their particular context, capabilities, organizational culture, and appetite for risk—they will improve the likelihood that they, too, can rekindle the lost spark of innovation. In the digital age, the pace of change has gone into hyper-speed, so companies must get these strategic, creative, execution, and organizational factors right to innovate successfully.

Aspiring: President John F. Kennedy's bold aspiration, in 1962, to "go to the moon in this decade" motivated a nation to unprecedented levels of innovation. A far-reaching vision can be a compelling catalyst, provided it's realistic enough to stimulate action today.

But in a corporate setting, it helps to combine high-level aspirations with estimates of the value that innovation should generate to meet financial-growth objectives. Quantifying an "innovation target for growth," and making it an explicit part of future strategic plans, helps solidify the importance of and accountability for innovation.

The target value needs to be apportioned to relevant business "owners" and cascaded down to their organizations in the form of performance targets and timelines.

For example, a big Nordic agricultural cooperative was challenged by flat organic growth and directionless innovation. Top executives created an aspirational vision and strategic plan linked to financial targets: 6 percent growth in the core business and 2 percent growth in new organic ventures.

To encourage innovation projects, these quantitative targets were cascaded down to business units and, ultimately, to product groups. During the development of each innovation project, it had to show how it was helping to achieve the growth targets for its category and markets.

As a result, they went from 4 percent to 13 percent annual growth, underpinned by the successful launch of several new brands. Indeed, it became the market leader in pre-made food only four years after entry and created a new premium segment in this market.

Choosing: Fresh, creative insights are invaluable, but in our experience, many companies run into difficulty less from a scarcity of new ideas than from the struggle to determine *which* ideas to support and scale. At bigger companies, this can be particularly problematic during market discontinuities, when supporting the next wave of growth may seem too risky, at least until competitive dynamics force painful changes.

Most established companies err on the side of overloading their innovation pipelines with relatively safe, short-term, and incremental projects that have little chance of realizing their growth targets or staying within their risk parameters. Some spread themselves thinly across too many projects instead of focusing on those with the highest potential for success and resourcing them to win.

These tendencies get reinforced by a sluggish resource-reallocation process. Recent research shows that a company typically reallocates only a tiny fraction of its resources from year to year, thereby sentencing innovation to a stagnating march of incrementalism.

Discovering: Innovation also requires actionable and differentiated insights—the kind that excites customers and brings new categories and markets into being. How do companies develop them? A genius is always an appealing approach if you have or can get it. Fortunately, innovation yields other approaches besides exceptional creativity.

The rest of us can look for insights by methodically and systematically scrutinizing three areas: a *valuable problem to solve*, a *technology that enables a solution*, and a *business model that generates money from it*. You could argue that nearly every successful innovation occurs at the intersection of these three elements. Companies that effectively collect, synthesize, and "collide" them stand the highest probability of success. "If you get the sweet spot of what the customer is struggling with, and at the same time get a deeper knowledge of the new technologies coming along and find a mechanism for how these two things can come together, then you are going to get good returns,".

The insight-discovery process, which extends beyond a company's boundaries to include insight-generating partnerships, is the lifeblood of innovation.

Evolving: Business-model innovations—which change the economics of the value chain, diversify profit streams, and/or modify delivery models—have always been a vital part of a strong innovation portfolio.

As smartphones and mobile apps threaten to upend old-line industries, business-model innovation has become all the more urgent: established companies must reinvent their businesses before technology-driven upstarts do. Why, then, do most innovation systems so squarely emphasize new products? The reason, of course, is that most big companies are reluctant to risk tampering with their core business model until it's visibly under threat. At that point, they can only hope it's not too late.

Leading companies combat this troubling tendency in several ways. They up their game in market intelligence, the better to separate signal from noise. They establish funding vehicles for new businesses that don't fit into the current structure.

They constantly reevaluate their position in the value chain, carefully considering business models that might deliver value to priority groups of new customers.

They sponsor pilot projects and experiments away from the core business to help combat narrow conceptions of what they are and do. And they stress-test newly emerging value propositions and operating models against countermoves by competitors.

Amazon does a particularly strong job extending itself into new business models by addressing the emerging needs of its customers and suppliers. In fact, it has included many of its suppliers in its customer base by offering them an increasingly wide range of services, from hosted computing to warehouse management.

Another strong performer, the *Financial Times*, was already experimenting with its business model in response to the increasing digitalization of media when it launched an innovative subscription model, upending its relationship with advertisers and readers.

"We went against the received wisdom of popular strategies at the time," says Caspar de Bono, *FT* board member and managing director of B2B. "We were very deliberate in getting ahead of the emerging structural change, and the decisions turned out to be very successful." In print's heyday, 80 percent of the *FT*'s revenue came from print advertising. Now, more than half of it comes from content, and two-thirds of circulation comes from digital subscriptions.

Mobilizing: How do leading companies stimulate, encourage, support, and reward innovative behavior and thinking among the right groups of people? The best companies find ways to embed innovation into the fibers of their culture, from the core to the periphery.

The Discovery Group, for example, is upending the medical and life-insurance industries in its native South Africa and also has operations in the United Kingdom, the United States, and China, among other locations. Innovation is a standard measure in the company's semiannual divisional scorecards—a process that helps mobilize the organization and affects roughly 1,000 of the company's business leaders.

"They are all required to innovate every year," Discovery founder and CEO Adrian Gore says of the company's business leaders. "They have no choice."

Companies must help people to share ideas and knowledge freely, perhaps by locating teams working on different types of innovation in the same place, reviewing the structure of project teams to make sure they always have new blood, ensuring that lessons learned from success and failure are captured and assimilated, and recognizing innovation efforts even when they fall short of success.

Internal collaboration and experimentation can take years to establish, particularly in large, mature companies with strong cultures and ways of working that, in other respects, may have served them well. Some companies set up "innovation garages" where small groups can work on important projects unconstrained by the normal working environment while building new ways of working that can be scaled up and absorbed into the larger organization.

NASA, for example, has ten field centers. But the space agency relies on the Ames Research Center, in Silicon Valley, to maintain what its former director, Dr. Pete Worden, calls "the character of rebels" to function as "a laboratory that's part of a much larger organization."

Accelerating: Virulent antibodies undermine innovation at many large companies. Cautious governance processes make it easy for stifling bureaucracies in marketing, legal, IT, and other functions to find reasons to halt or slow approvals. Too often, companies simply get in the way of their own attempts to innovate.

A surprising number of impressive innovations from companies were actually the fruit of their mavericks, who succeeded in bypassing their early-approval processes. Clearly, there's a balance to be maintained: bureaucracy must be held in check, yet the rush to market should not undermine the cross-functional collaboration, continuous learning cycles, and clear decision pathways that help enable innovation.

Are managers with the right knowledge, skills, and experience making crucial decisions promptly, so that innovation continually moves through an organization in a way that creates and maintains competitive advantage, without exposing a company to unnecessary risk?

Companies also thrive by testing their promising ideas with customers early in the process, before internal forces impose modifications that blur the original value proposition. To end up with the innovation initially envisioned, it's necessary to knock down the barriers that stand between a great idea and the end user.

A well-connected manager must take charge of a project and be responsible for the budget, time to market, and key specifications—a person who can say yes rather than no. In addition, the project team needs to be cross-functional in reality, not just on paper.

This means locating its members in a single place and ensuring that they give the project a significant amount of their time (at least half) to support a culture that puts the innovation project's success above the success of each function.

Cross-functional collaboration can help ensure end-user involvement throughout the development process. At many companies, marketing's role is to champion the interests of end users as development teams evolve products and to help ensure that the final result is what everyone first envisioned. But this responsibility is honored more often in the breach than in the observance.

Consumers don't necessarily know what they want until it becomes available. This may be true, but customers can certainly say what they *don't* like. And the more quickly and frequently a project team gets—and uses—feedback, the more quickly it gets a great end result.

Scaling: Some ideas, such as luxury goods and many smartphone apps, are destined for niche markets. Others, like social networks, work on a global scale. Explicitly considering the appropriate magnitude and reach of a given idea is important to ensure that the right resources and risks are involved in pursuing it.

The seemingly safer option of scaling up over time can be a death sentence. Resources and capabilities must be marshaled to make sure a new product or service can be delivered quickly at the desired volume and quality.

Manufacturing facilities, suppliers, distributors, and others must be prepared to execute a rapid and full rollout.

For example, when TomTom launched its first touch-screen navigational device, in 2004, the product flew off the shelves. By 2006, TomTom's line of portable navigation devices reached sales of about 5 million units a year, and by 2008, yearly volume had jumped to more than 12 million. "That's faster market penetration than mobile phones" had, says Harold Goddijn, TomTom's CEO and co-founder.

Smart collaboration with external partners, though, goes beyond merely sourcing new ideas and insights; it can involve sharing costs and finding faster routes to market. Famously, the components of Apple's first iPod were developed almost entirely outside the company; by efficiently managing these external partnerships, Apple was able to move from an initial concept to a marketable product in only nine months.

NASA's Ames Research Center teams up not just with international partners—launching joint satellites with nations as diverse as Lithuania, Saudi Arabia, and Sweden—but also with emerging companies, such as SpaceX.

High-performing innovators work hard to develop the ecosystems that help deliver these benefits. Indeed, they strive to become partners of choice, increasing the likelihood that the best ideas and people will come their way. That requires a systematic approach. First, these companies find out which partners they are already working with; surprisingly few companies know this.

Then they decide which networks—say, four or five of them—they ideally need to support their innovation strategies. This step helps them to narrow and focus their collaboration efforts and to manage the flow of possibilities from outside the company. Strong innovators also regularly review their networks, extending and pruning them as appropriate and using sophisticated incentives and contractual structures to motivate high-performing business partners.

The word "innovative" has arguably lost its punch, right along with "disruptive", "awesome," and "amazing." Many times, tech startups and their founders get called out for hyping their products as innovative, when they're really just building apps that help you book a babysitter or nail appointment on the fly. And while these kinds of tech startups are doing great work — and making our lives more convenient in the process — they're not necessarily creating game-changing technology.

But then there are startups like Issinova.

The Italian engineering firm teamed up with Decathlon, an athletic equipment company, to use the blueprints of a snorkeling mask to make emergency respirators to serve patients during the coronavirus crisis. Together, the companies leveraged 3D printing to quickly help get the respirators to hospitals that needed them.

Though there's no governing body tasked with defining what constitutes "positive social impact," many in the impact innovation community use the United Nations' Sustainable Development Goals (SDGs) as a benchmark.

Takeaways: leading innovators must adhere to:

Getting Better at What You Do: Every year, Apple comes up with a new iPhone. That's not as exciting as it used to be, but it's still key to the company maintaining its competitive edge. Every model is a bit faster, more secure, and has new features that make it more capable. It's still an iPhone, but better.

Apply What You're Good At: Amazon started out selling books online. It then applied its approach to other categories, such as electronics and toys. That took enormous investments in technology, which it then used to create new businesses, such as Amazon Web Services (AWS), Kindle tablets, and its Echo line of smart speakers.

Scooting and Exploration are the most neglected. All too often, in our over-optimized business environment, any business opportunity that can't be immediately quantified is considered a non-starter. So, we fail to begin to explore new problems until their market value has been unlocked by someone else. By that point, we are already behind the curve. Make no mistake. The next big thing always starts out looking like nothing at all. Things that change the world always arrive out of context for the simple reason that the world hasn't changed yet. But if you do not explore, you will not discover. If you do not discover, you will not invent. And if you do not invent, you will be disrupted. It's just a matter of time.

Finding A Completely New Problem to Solve: Besides getting better at what you already do and applying things you already know to a different market or capability; you can also look for a new problem to solve. This is, of course, the most uncertain type of opportunity, because no one knows what a good solution will look like. To return to Moore's law example, everybody knows what a 20 percent performance improvement in computer chips looks like. Metrics for speed and power consumption have long been established, so there is little ambiguity around what would constitute success. Customers will instantly recognize the improvement as having a specific market value.

Emerging Deep Tech: On the other hand, no one knows the value of emerging operating technologies such as quantum computing, blockchain, artificial intelligence, or AR/VR stand-alone. It's a fundamentally new kind of technology that will solve new types of problems. So, customers will have to explore the technology and figure out how to use it to create better products and services.

These are the most impactful innovation projected to help shape and evolve the foundation of modern life during the next 20 years and drive the *4.0 innovation era*:

1. Nanotechnology
2. Quantum Computing
3. Blockchain
4. Artificial Intelligence
5. Driver Less Cars
6. Stem Cell Research
7. Gene Editing
8. Multi Use Space Rocket
9. Artificial Heart and Part

Framed Execution: a key input into your innovation is having a deep dive insight gathering "landscape scooting" of what's out there after you define your niche market or new market by peers or emerging leaders as follows:

Media Coverage	Expert Input	Customer Input
Industry Leader	Thought Leader	Top Peers Blog
Unicorn Startup	Academia Insight	Social Media
Contest Winner	Founder Interview	Product Survey
Peers Funding	Conference Talk	Industry Research
Peers M&A	Corporate Insight	10 Years CAGR

Filter the Noise: avoid getting influenced by popular faces "C Suite, Unicorn Fonder, and Top VC partner", instead bundle their inputs and extract the highest data point supporting your vision, while separating the executioners from the talking head.

Roadmap Convergence: align your innovation to either consumer-facing or deep tech which is the underlying of several industries then design your roadmap and stick to it. Examples of Consumer-facing is Robinhood, and Deep Tech is Twilio.

Case studies: on how leading companies in the solar panel become lagging in innovation, and how to learn from it:

America invented silicon solar cells in the 1950s. It spent more on solar R&D than any other country in the 1980s. It lost its technological advantage anyway. You wouldn't know it today, but the silicon photovoltaic solar cell—the standard, black-and-copper solar panel you can find on suburban rooftops and solar farms—was born and raised in America.

Technology was invented here. In 1954, three American engineers at Bell Labs discovered that electrons flow freely through silicon wafers when they are exposed to sunlight.

It was deployed here. In 1958, the U.S. The Navy bolted solar panels to Vanguard 1, the second American satellite in space. And for a time, it was even made here. In the 1960s and '70s, American companies dominated the global solar market and registered most solar patents. As late as 1978, American firms commanded 95 percent of the global solar market, according to one study.

The key phrase is "for a time." Solar panels aren't made in the United States anymore, even though the market for them is larger than ever. Starting in the 1980s, leadership in the industry passed to Japan, then to China. Today, only one of the world's 10 largest makers of solar cells is American. For the past decades, this kind of story of invention, globalization, and deindustrialization has been part of the background of the American economy. Lately, policy makers seem eager to do something about it. Last week, a robust and bipartisan majority in the Senate passed a bill aimed at preserving America's "technological competitiveness" against China. It will spend more than $100 billion on basic research and development over the next several years.

And as part of his infrastructure proposal, Joe Biden has asked Congress to authorize $35 billion for clean-energy R&D (Research and Development). Observers on the left have painted this figure as pitifully small, pointing out that it's about equal to what Americans spend on pet food every year.

The U.S. leads the world in R&D spending and has done so for decades, although China is in the No. 2 spot and gaining. R&D might seem like an unfathomably boring topic, akin to arguing about medical data or grant approvals, but it revolves around some of the most profound and unanswered questions of industrial civilization.

Why do some technologies get developed instead of others?

Why do some countries become richer faster than others? How can we materially improve people's lives as fast as possible, and can the government do anything to help? Above all, where does economic growth come from? This is what we're fighting about when we fight about R&D. And this is why I think the history of the solar industry is so important. (The following account is indebted to my reading of Max Jerneck, a researcher at the Stockholm School of Economics who documented a history of solar energy in U.S. and Japan.)

In the late 1970s, it was not obvious that the American solar industry was in danger. President Jimmy Carter and Congress had just established the Department of Energy, which promised to develop new energy technologies with the same seriousness that the U.S. devotes to developing new military technologies. Solar engineers saw a bright future. But then a series of changes racked the American economy.

The Federal Reserve jacked interest rates up to all-time highs, which made it harder for Americans to obtain car loans while strengthening the dollar against other currencies, which made it difficult for American exporters to sell goods abroad.

Presidents Carter and Ronald Reagan loosened rules against "corporate raiding," allowing Wall Street traders to force companies to close or spin off part of their business. After

1980, Reagan also weakened federal environmental rules while dismantling the new Department of Energy, removing support for alternative energy sources such as solar power.

American manufacturers had already been struggling to compete with imports from East Asia. Now they foundered. Start-ups shut down; experts left the industry. Corporate raiders forced oil companies, such as Exxon, to sell or close their small solar R&D divisions.

The United States, the country that once produced *all* the world's solar panels, saw its market share crash. In 1990, U.S. firms produced 32 percent of solar panels worldwide; by 2005, they made only nine percent.

Japan benefited from this sudden abdication. In the 1980s, Japanese, German, and Taiwanese firms bought the patents and divisions sold off by American firms. Whereas Japan had no solar industry to speak of in 1980, it was producing nearly half the world's solar panels by 2005.

This may seem like the kind of classic tale that Congress is hoping to prevent. Yet R&D had almost nothing to do with the collapse of the U.S. solar industry. From 1980 to 2001, the United States outspent Japan in solar R&D every year but one. Let me repeat: **The U.S. outspent Japan on R&D every year but one.** It lost the technological frontier anyway.

The American system, in the 1980s and today, is designed to produce basic science research with no immediate obvious application. In the U.S., in the early '80s, most solar companies were preparing for the predicted mass markets of the future: residential rooftops and grid-scale solar farms.

Both required solar panels to get significantly cheaper and more efficient than they were at the time: They required R&D, in other words. But Japan's industrial policy—as orchestrated by its powerful Ministry of International Trade and Industry—focused on finding commercial applications for technologies immediately.

It also provided consistent, supportive funding for companies that wanted to invest in finding applications. As such, Japanese companies were pressured to incorporate solar panels into products as soon as possible.

Within a few years, they had found solar panels' first major commercial application, putting them inside pocket calculators, wristwatches, and other consumer electronics. Because those devices didn't require much electricity, they were well served by solar panels *as they existed* in the 1980s, not as whatever an R&D study said they could notionally become in the future.

And Japan's willingness to ship fast and imperfectly eventually helped it develop utility-scale solar. As Japanese firms mass-produced more solar panels, they got better at it. They learned how to do it cheaply. This "learning by doing" eventually brought down the cost of solar cells more than America's theoretical R&D ever managed to. More recently, Chinese firms have emulated this technique to eat Japan's share of the global solar industry, Greg Nemet, a public-policy professor at the University of Wisconsin and the author of *How Solar Energy Became Cheap,* stated.

You have probably lived with a leaky faucet in your home at some point, a sink or shower in which you had to get the cold knob *just right* to shut off the flow of water. How did you learn to turn the knob in just the right way did you find and read a college textbook on Advanced Leaky-Faucet Studies, or did you just fiddle with the knob until you learned how to make it work?

Getting the faucet not to leak is an example of what anthropologists call *tacit knowledge,* information that is stored in human minds and difficult to explain. High technology requires much more tacit knowledge than the American system usually admits. The understanding of how to mass produce a car or solar panel is not stored in a book or patent filing; it exists in the brains and bodies of workers, foremen, and engineers on the line. That's why the *places* where engineers, designers, and workers come together whether in Detroit, Silicon Valley, or Shenzhen have always been the fount of progress.

The American R&D system is designed to fix an alleged failure of the free market that no corporation has the incentive to fund science for science's sake. To be sure, this approach has brought advances, especially in medicine:

The COVID-19 mRNA vaccines drew on years of thankless "pure" R&D. Yet, as the Niskanen Institute scholar Samuel Hammond writes, this distinction—between pure and applied science—is illusory. R&D is useful, but ultimately only *organizations deploying technology at a mass scale* can advance the technological frontier. We don't need the government to fund more science alone; we need the government to support a thriving industrial sector and incentivize companies to deploy new technology, as Japan's government does.

Government Enablement: The Biden administration seems mindful of some of the problems with investing only in "pure" R&D. The American Jobs Plan proposes spending $20 billion on new "regional innovation hubs" that will unite public and private investment to speed up the development of various energy technologies. It also aims to establish 10 new "pioneer facilities," large-scale demonstration projects that will work on some of the most challenging applied problems in decarbonizing, such as making zero-carbon steel and concrete. I think those are more promising than throwing more money at R&D per se.

Addressing climate change requires us to get R&D right. The United States is responsible for 11 percent of annual global greenhouse-gas emissions today. Its share has fallen since the 1990s and will keep dwindling. Yet it remains the world's R&D lab. One of the best ways that the U.S. can serve the world is to develop technologies *here* that make decarbonization cheap and easy, then export it.

Don't get entangled in science for science with its ego-centered dilemma that get you nowhere other than "if you cannot do, teach", instead be a laser focus on how to solve urgent customer needs as the ultimate goal "doers don't need to talk", think of fancy restaurant costing $500 per dinner that you leave "unsatisfied" or worst "hungry" vs a food track costing 2% with joy and uplifting spirit after a 30 min meal.

So inventing technology is not the end, what matters is who takes it to market and locks that market "i.e., Hand Calculator Solar Powered" by Japan.

Abolish all taxes for startups during their first five years, or until reaching $1m net profit, along with special banking working capital for startups at the profit stage of $100,000 or more

14 Future Emerging Technologies by BOA Research

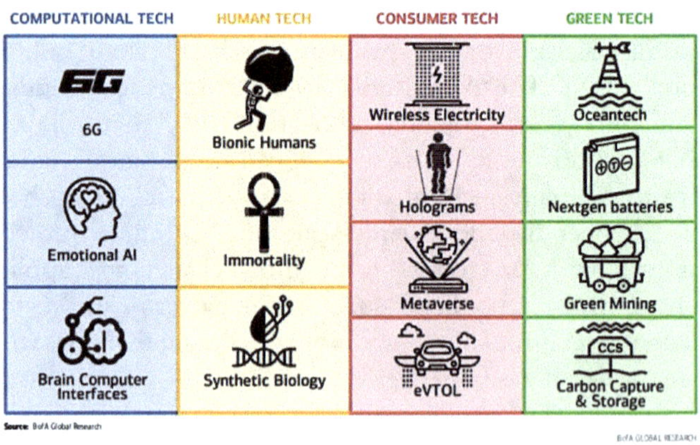

The emergence of Generative AI and Chat GPT

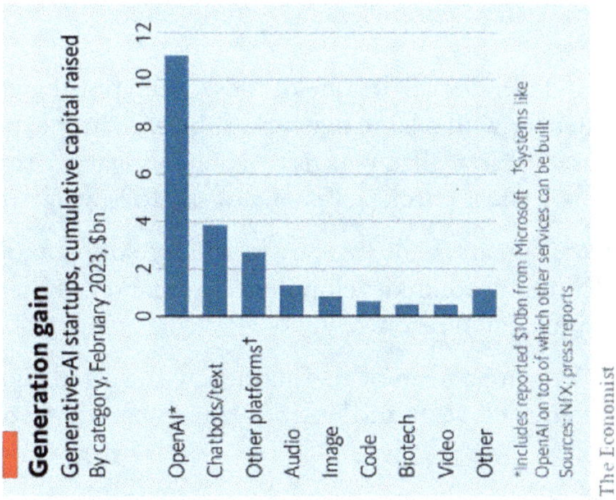

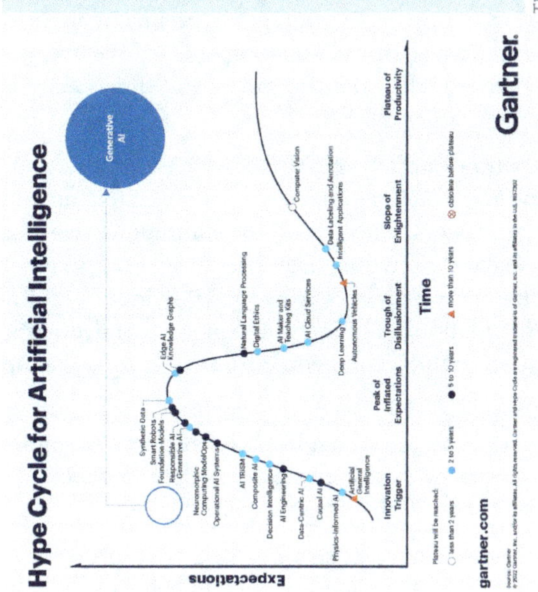

CHAPTER VIII
HOW TO LAUNCH

Startup Founder can be one of these, deep pocket, celebrity influencer with a large network, subject matter experts, or super users. Now that you have your innovation ready for launch, you must check as yes one of the following:

Corporate: You have all the buy-in of key sponsors and are ready for the product development and marketing stage with properly allocated resource

Startup: You are a team of co-founders with vested equity and committed for 4 years and ready to launch based on your area of focus

Solo-Founder: You have your pitch or built your prototype. Before launching or even getting a first investor, you must add before launch two co-founders and three board advisors within your target market.

Teams who can pitch and attract users, customers, investors, and new associates are critical vs passive or technical advisers. Prioritize talents with the best communication skills and target market network. The best way to find your initial founding team members is by word of mouth and personal recommendations. This can be done by connecting with old colleagues, friends, and people from your school alumni.

They should have these key qualities: flexibility, passion, trustworthiness, drive, and self-reliance. It is important to bring people who are flexible enough to take on diverse responsibilities until you can expand further.

When interviewing, pose questions that probe a person's drive and how well-suited they might be to your company's culture.

In addition, use hands-on simulations to get a sense of how the candidate will act in common work situations “self-reliant talented vs analysis paralysis analyst”.

The Startup Narrative: If your dream is to change the world or build "the next big thing and become a billionaire", you're in the wrong line of work. Here's the reality:

- Nothing in life will prepare you for entrepreneurship, besides experiencing startup from idea to IPO exit.
- If you're not obsessed with the problem you intend to solve and the solution you're building, you already lost.
- No one will, or can, tell you what to do or how to do it. Models, analysis, and patterns will only get you so far.
- If you can't talk to anyone and everyone about your venture, it won't get off the ground. "Stealth mode" is for well-funded serial entrepreneurs' not first-time founders.
- No one can change the world, but you can positively impact your community incrementally at the regional and maybe at the country level. Be open to, trust, and plan but leave room for serendipity.
- As Reid Hoffman, the former COO of PayPal and LinkedIn Founder, once said, "If you are not embarrassed by the first version of your product, you've launched too late." So, focus on early adaptors first.
- A startup is not a small business, but rather a small venture with the potential to take over the biggest corporations, think cat vs baby tiger who looks similar but grows differently at an exponential rate.
- Listen to advice with "grain of salt" from venture capital and influencer CEO, since they are managers of their agenda, not yours.

Some tips learned along the way as well as pitfalls to avoid:

Start as soon as possible: As soon as you have an idea in mind, check to see if anyone else has already done it. If you don't find anything like your idea, roll up your sleeves and get to work, but make sure your idea solves a real-world problem, or in other words, alleviates the user's pain. So, think big. If the idea is just one of a million things floating around in your target audience's mind, then it won't work.

Management and Startup Mismatch: As a society, we have a proven set of techniques for managing big companies and we know the best practices for building physical products. But when it comes to startups and innovation, we are still shooting in the dark. We are relying on vision, chasing the "great men" who can make magic happen, or trying to analyze our new products to death. These are new problems, born of the success of management in the twentieth century.

Be ready for both failure and success: It's natural to be worried that you won't succeed or that your idea isn't good enough. You're bound to hit some bumps along the way before you get to where you want to be. But sometimes doing something minor can get you big results. You just have to be ready to take that first step.

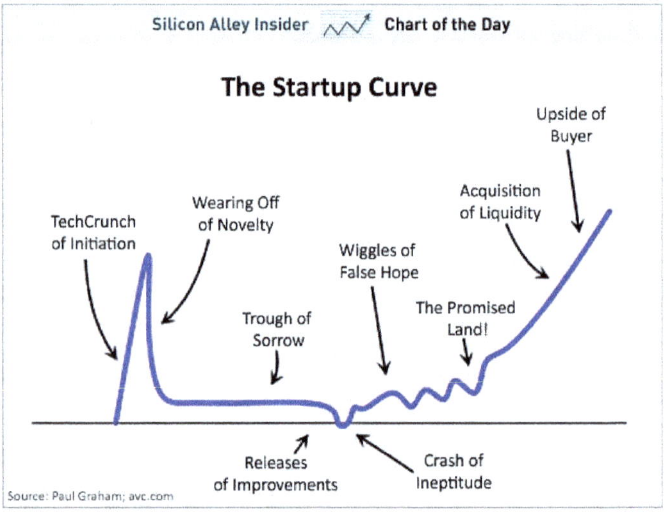

You must have the drive to run your startup for three years minimum "This is when the failure becomes success and success become failure" and expect to fail but will capitalize on earned expertise and industry network that will get you your next best job through acquihire or direct hire from any of your suppliers, distributor, investor or competitors.
Technical skill is important but can be alleviated by hiring your first CTO.

In a study of the undergraduate backgrounds of the S&P 500 CEOs, IBM researchers found that 33% of the S&P 500 CEOs' undergraduate degrees are in engineering and only 11% are in business administration.

- So, what if you are not a technical founder, engineer, or software programmer? Should you quit now because you're wasting your time?
- With the right mindset and skill set, non-technical founders can be equally successful founders and entrepreneurs as technical founders and entrepreneurs. It has been done before, plenty of times; and it can be done again.

Before You Launch Do's: You should consider your reasons besides money for launching a company in the first place, and plan to bootstrap for three years to ensure proper exit vs total failure.

The following items must be completed before Launch and in the order listed:

1. *Pitch:* Create a compelling elevator pitch, "My name is XYZ, and my innovation is a coffee cap that can hold hot coffee at a minimum of 120 degrees for a maximum of three hours".

   Test your pitch: with target users, customers, partners, and investors, and you shall have 2/3 positive feedback, otherwise stop here. Try Alexa Pitch Generator: Amazon Alexa synthetic pitch.

2. *Execution Plan:* Draft a fact-based plan for the following:
   - Innovation: Define it in 360 degrees, and if it is incremental or disruptive at both the transactional "product" and market level impacting the entire industry.
   - Product Roadmap: Detailed plan on how to build and scale your product or service from idea, through exit.
   - Team: How to build your unpaid team with equity, who are they, where are they, and how to get them on board and incentivize them, along with mapping each deliverable to each of them.
   - User: How to get them to try your offering, what value they get, and how to incentivize network effect referral
   - Customer: How to get them, what value they get, and how to create a network effect for scalable growth.
   - First Investor: It is you "*the founder*", so budget your time with a scale on a daily, weekly, and monthly basis that you allocate to this venture and how you can cover all startup costs along with maintaining your basic living expenses.
   - Funding: Define how to feed your bootstrapped engine from 360-degree angles, including how to drive your funding from all sources, including venture capital (i.e., co-founders, customers, suppliers, competitors, etc.)
   - First Hire: is you, plan when you can get paid a full-time salary by this venture with a transitional plan (i.e., start working on weekends unpaid for six months, then switch

to part-time paid for three months and full-time employee once you get your first $500k investment).

3. *Investors Package:* Must be completed but exclude your trade secret "making it impossible to copy by anyone".

    - Startup Funding Pitch Deck (Short 10 – 12 pages)
        - Market Opportunity
        - Problem and Solution
        - Market Size and Growth
        - Product or Service Offering
        - Use case and case studies.
        - Peers and Competitive Advantage
        - Traction and Growth Timeline
        - Leadership Team and Partners
        - Funding Need and Budget

    Examples of Prominent Unicorns Pitch at Slideshare.net: are Airbnb, Uber, and Mint. Example Template from top Venture Capital: https://www.sequoiacap.com/article/writing-a-business-plan/

4. *Name Your Company and Get Your Domain Name:* Pick a name for your company that is simple to spell and easy to remember. While sticking to as few syllables as possible can be challenging, putting restrictions on the length of your company's name can force you to be creative. If possible, stick to two syllables. Take a look at the names of the following companies with short names (remember legal entity name is less important than domain name): Google, Twitter, Zoom

5. Three Points to Consider when naming your company:
    - Memorable: Users need to remember the name to share it
    - Spellable: difficult spelling name led users to miss your site.
    - Engaging: can be tied to the act like Tweeting? Zooming?

Having a matching domain name is inconsequential, so worry more about a name that emphasizes what your company is and does and less about how well it corresponds with the actual name of your company.

Mint.com is quality, it's a place where money is made, it's short and spelled unambiguously. It's a very good brand name for what we're doing. We spent three months, hundreds of hours, and more money than I care to comment on for that domain - but it was worth it. Offhand, who do you trust investing.com or MoneyAnalyzr.com?

Below are some resources to help you name your company and secure your domain:

- Domain Registrar - a short list of major providers

Network Solution, Domain.com, GoDaddy.com, Google Domain, Web.com

- *Company Branding:* Your logo, like your startup's name, and slogan should be simple and memorable that resonate with your target audience while representing what you have to offer.

Unless you're a designer, don't create your startup's logo by yourself. Treat your logo with respect and employ a designer to craft the ideal logo for your company. While you may have to spend some money on this, having a professional-looking logo can separate you from the competition.

Be original! It's way too easy to become infatuated with the iconic logos of other companies, but keep in mind that your logo is what should help make you stand out from the crowd and not to blend in with the rest. Also, think about posterity; will your company's logo be remembered 5, 10, or 20 years from now?

If you need help creating imagery for your startup, here are some resources to get you started:
99Designs: marketplace for graphic design, including logo design, web design, and other design tasks.

Canva: makes design simple for beginning designers.

6. *Legal/Diligence Package:* Incorporate as C Corp in Delaware, submit patents as provisional, and make sure that your secret sauce "trade secrets" are never shared

with anyone, including co-founders or investors "except when a company is acquired and upon receipt of full payment". An example of a tech trade secret using the pitch above is "that material how the cap was made, along with chemical formulas and steps to produce it". In the Software case: it's usually the architecture and algorithm "share high level" but never a 100 % detailed blueprint. The key is: to protect your secret, never share it, NDA will not protect it.

7. *Manage Assets and Liabilities:* A great lawyer is a must but be upfront with him or her about your funding situation. When you're running low on capital, the last thing you need is legal invoices piling up. Most startup lawyers understand that funds are limited and are more than willing to work with you. They're taking a bet on you as much as investors are, so treat them well and they'll treat you even better.

If you do have some early funding, set apart 10% for legal fees and tell your lawyer that's the budget you're working with. They'll optimize their time for the best outcomes.

Don't let people scoff at your work to patent your ideas or tech. It's another legal cost but it's better to have the protection than not. Some investors don't care, and they'll still invest. Others do care and they may not invest because your IPs are not protected. Better to just handle it and cover your bases.

Startup Journey (Across Each Stage)

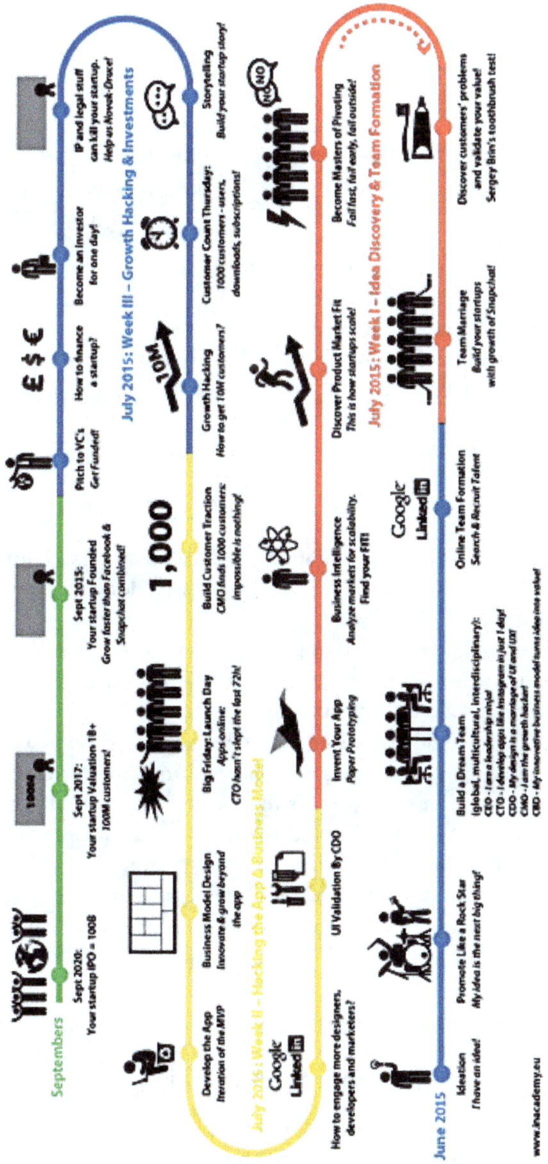

Source: European Innovation Academy

Product Design and User Experience: Analogy: picture UX design as a car where UI design is the driving dashboard console.

User interface (UI): design is the process designers use to build interfaces in software or computerized devices, focusing on looks or style. Designers aim to create interfaces that users find easy to use and pleasurable. UI design refers to graphical user interfaces and other forms e.g., voice-controlled.

UI are access points where users interact with product:

1. Graphical user interfaces (GUI): Users interact with visual representations on digital control panels.
2. Voice-controlled interfaces (VUI): Users interact with these through their voices. Most smart assistants e.g., Siri on iPhone and Alexa on Amazon are VUIs.
3. Gesture-based interfaces: Users engage with 3D design spaces through bodily motions: e.g., in virtual reality.

UI Design best practices:

- End Users care about usability and likeability. They don't care about your design, but rather to get tasks done with less effort.
- Your design should therefore be "invisible". Users shouldn't focus on it but on completing tasks: e.g., ordering pizza on Domino's Zero Click app.
- So, understand your users' contexts and task flows (which you can get from, e.g., your customer journey maps), to fine-tune the best, most intuitive UIs that deliver seamless experiences.
- UI should be enjoyable and frustration-free. When your design predicts users' needs, they can enjoy more personalized and immersive experiences. Delight them, and they'll be returning.
- Where appropriate, elements of gamification can make your design more fun. UIs should communicate brand values and reinforce users' trust.
- Good design is emotional design. Users associate good feelings with brands that speak to them at all levels and keep the magic of pleasurable, seamless experiences alive.

User Experience (UX): user experience (UX) design is the process design teams use to create products that provide meaningful and relevant experiences to users. This involves the design of the entire process of acquiring and integrating the product, including aspects of branding, design, usability, and function.

Products that provide great user experience (e.g., the iPhone or Google Search Home Page) are thus designed with not only the product's consumption or use in mind but also the entire process of acquiring, owning, and even troubleshooting it. Similarly, UX designers don't just focus on creating products that are usable; we concentrate on other aspects of the user experience, such as pleasure, efficiency, and fun, too.

Consequently, there is no single definition of a good user experience. Instead, a good user experience meets a particular user's needs in the specific context where he or she uses the product.

As a UX designer, you should consider the Why, What, and How of product use. The Why involves the users' motivations for adopting a product, whether they relate to a task they wish to perform with it or to values and views which users associate with the ownership and use of the product. What addresses the things people can do with a product's functionality. Finally, the How relates to the design of functionality in an accessible and aesthetically pleasant way.

UX designers start with the *Why* before determining the *What* and then, finally, the *How* to create products that users can form meaningful experiences with. In software designs, you will need to ensure the product's "substance" comes through an existing device and offers a seamless, fluid experience.

You Don't Need a Designer Early On: High-fidelity mockups are great, but until you get the product in consumers' hands, settle on basic sketches. Most developers can handle basic sketches and mockups, but if yours can't, just get someone to throw together the main screens so your developer has something to work with. These designs are guaranteed to change based on UI/UX and user feedback which means you can flush that money you spent on a designer down the toilet. Save the money and obsess about design later on.

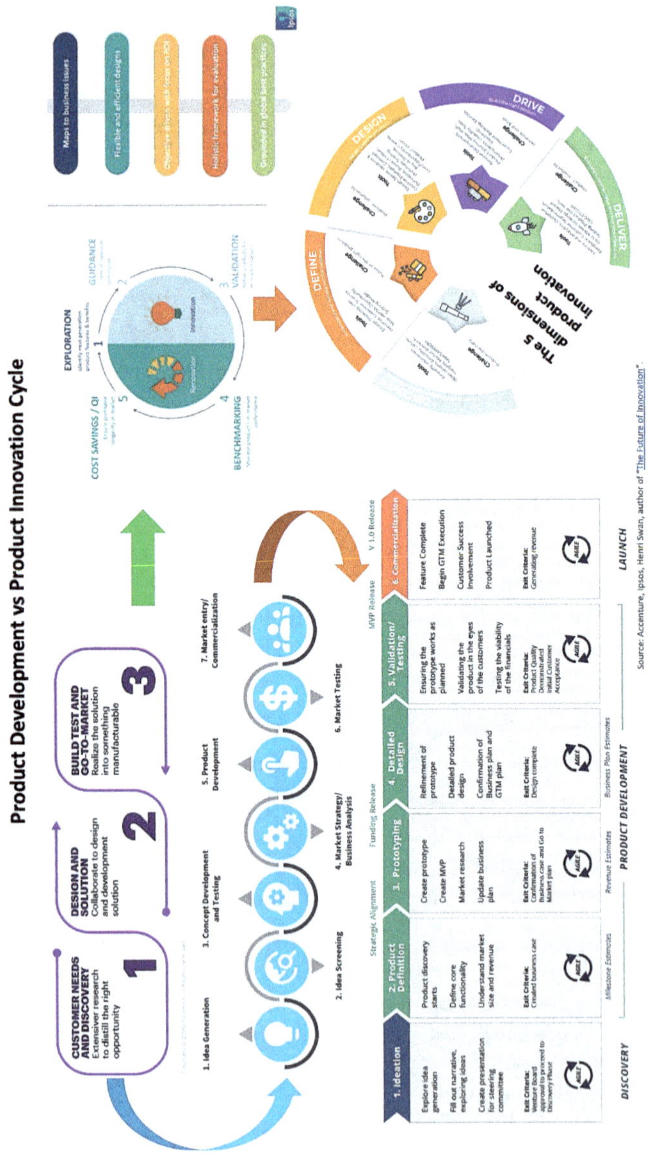
Product Development vs Product Innovation Cycle
CUSTOMER NEEDS AND DISCOVERY
Extensiver research to distill the right opportunity
1
DESIGN AND SOLUTION
Collaborate to design and development solution
2
BUILD TEST AND GO-TO-MARKET
Realize the solution into something manufacturable
3
1. Idea Generation
2. Idea Screening
3. Concept Development and Testing
4. Market Strategy/ Business Analysis
5. Product Development
6. Market Testing
7. Market entry/ Commercialization
Strategic Alignment
Funding Release
MVP Release
V 1.0 Release
1. Ideation
Explore idea generation
Fill out narrative, exploring ideas
Create presentation for steering committee
Exit Criteria: Venture Board approval to proceed to Discovery Phase
2. Product Definition
Product discovery starts
Define core functionality
Understand market size and revenue
Exit Criteria: Created business case
3. Prototyping
Create prototype
Create MVP
Market research
Update business plan
Exit Criteria: Confirmation of Business case and Go to Market plan
4. Detailed Design
Refinement of prototype
Detailed product design
Confirmation of Business plan and GTM plan
Exit Criteria: Design complete
5. Validation/ Testing
Ensuring the prototype works as planned
Validating the product in the eyes of the customers
Testing the viability of the financials
Exit Criteria: Product Quality Demonstrated Initial Customer Acceptance
6. Commercialization
Feature Complete
Begin GTM Execution
Customer Success Involvement
Product Launched
Exit Criteria: Generating revenue
AGILE
Milestone Estimates
Revenue Estimates
Business Plan Estimates
DISCOVERY
PRODUCT DEVELOPMENT
LAUNCH
EXPLORATION
GUIDANCE
VALIDATION
BENCHMARKING
COST SAVINGS / QI
Renovation
Innovation
Maps to business issues
Flexible and efficient designs
Objective driven with focus on ROI
Holistic framework for evaluation
Grounded in global best practices
Ipsos
DEFINE
DESIGN
DRIVE
DELIVER
The 5 dimensions of product innovation
Source: Accenture, Ipsos, Henri Swan, author of "The Future of Innovation".

Product Engineering and Development: Even though you have a great idea, however, there are always concerns about its performance in the market. Therefore, you are required to test your idea by conducting your own A/B testing. This will play an important role in providing you with first-hand information directly from real customers.

You cannot allocate most of your time to perfecting your business. It will modify and acclimatize as soon as you launch. Therefore, you are advised to just get it live and start obtaining feedback. Broadly speaking, the new product development process is the entire process of bringing a product to market, starting with recognizing a marketing opportunity and ending with a product launch. For some founders, that process may look like a haphazard "drunken walk," but others prefer a more structured approach. The key steps are:

Ideation: How do you even know whether an idea is worth pursuing in the first place? The fact is, if you start with that question, you'll never know the answer – because you'll kill every idea before it's even really an idea. Take your ideas to people whose opinions you value, who you know won't be "nice" because they're afraid to hurt your feelings. Ask them to use your idea for target practice. Don't be afraid to beat it up a little. Kick the tires, and see if it's road worthy. If it fails the test, then guess what? You've saved yourself a lot of wasted time and energy.

Architecture: start with a work breakdown structure that captures all deliverables with an order of priority mapped to the top three business goals "e.g., Users Sign up, Users Usage, Users conversion". Then draft both architectures, a business model canvas and technology architecture based on users' experiences flowchart "start to end point steps".

Engineering Architecture: Using the two architectures above, hire a savvy technical advisor to create this blueprint for your startup. It is a design process of defining a collection of hardware and software components and their interfaces to establish the framework for the development of a computer system. The key focus is scalability, availability, and security.

Wireframes Mockups: Provide detailed explanations and annotations for every aspect of your wireframe, especially if you are working with designers. Dummy boxes should also be filled with text, even if it's only placeholder text, as this will give you an idea of how much text should exist on your site. Create your website wireframes and mockups in high fidelity to better replicate the look, feel, and functionality you're striving for. If you need help bringing your vision to life, here are some wireframe and mockup tools that can get you started:

- Balsamiq: is a rapid low-fidelity UI wireframing tool that reproduces the experience of sketching on a notepad or whiteboard computer.
- Gliffy: Create professional flowcharts, wireframes, and UML diagrams.
- Lovely Charts: the free tool is built to create prototypes fast.
- NinjaMock: Everything from mobile app design to website design is possible with this free online web application.
- Mockflow: A simple website wireframe tool that lets you create blueprints, mockups of websites, and app wireframes in minutes.

Demo Development: start with a scalable stage by having On-Demand Cloud as the back end and everything else that map to your product or services, including payments.

- Alpha: This can be a landing page for sign-up or a basic app
- MVP: This is a minimum viable product with a user demo, it lacks many of the features that may prove essential later on. However, you must be able to measure its impact. For example, it is inadequate to build a prototype that is evaluated solely for internal quality by engineers and designers.
- Beta / Proof of Concept: we know who our customers are, we know with some certainty what set of features our version 1 will contain, and we think we know how our customers will use the product. We have market confirmation to back up our beliefs. We are looking for showstoppers and quick, easy opportunities for improvement. A beta can be described as a slightly buggy, firm but still tweakable feature set that a limited number of real (or potentially real) customers are using.
- Commercial: This is paid and scalable with full support

- Enterprise: the level where global users are by millions

Alpha: (Site, Landing Page, and Apps): Your startup's landing page should include your logo and a description that perfectly and clearly demonstrates what your offering is and what it does. Your landing page is also the ideal place to collect the email addresses of your potential users and keep them updated and increase customer retention.

Remember, it's perfectly acceptable to launch your landing page before your product is built, as long as you're upfront about the status of your product. However, be sure to include as much information about what you have to offer to increase customer anticipation for when you do release your product.

MVP (First Prototype): Your Minimum Viable Product (MVP) should not use the technology you wish to build. This is as much of a way to prove you can build a business as it is a proof of concept for the business itself. Hack together a basic website and grow traffic, sell the service, get your first 5 paying customers, produce a crappy product, and sell it. Sure, you'll want to build the tech to assist with growing the business, but those first customers and early wins prove there is a market for what you're selling, shows potential investors you have early traction, and can give you early revenue and a reason to bootstrap the business yourself.

Start with a Landing Page with pre-release sign-up targeting your network, then scale to prototype "Alpha " and gradually transition to public beta MVP. Don't wait until the product is completely ready before launch "stuck in gold plating". As soon as you have a minimum viable product (MVP), give real users the possibility to test it out in exchange for priceless feedback using informal or formal surveys.

This knowledge will allow you to make worthy last-minute changes to your product instead of spending more time on meaningless tweaks, only to go back to the drawing board once you go live. In reality, every successful product gets updated and improved all the time.

If someone notices a typo, a poorly designed button, or some other minor mistake, don't worry as it won't result in a disaster. What may seem like a problem to you may very well go unnoticed by real users? Product info and technical content are rewritten along with the growth of the product. For this reason, focus your efforts primarily on the user experience "Remember Google kept in Gmail 5 years in Beta".

Most entrepreneurs approach a question like this by building the product and then checking to see how customers react to it. I consider this to be exactly backward because it can lead to a lot of waste. First, if it turns out that we're building something nobody wants, the whole exercise will be an avoidable expense of time and money.

If customers won't sign up for the free trial, they'll never get to experience the amazing features that await them. Even if they do sign up, there are many other opportunities for waste. For example, how many features do we really need to include to appeal to early adopters? Every extra feature is a form of waste, and if we delay the test for these extra features, it comes with a tremendous potential cost in terms of learning and cycle time. The lesson of the MVP is that any additional work beyond what was required to start learning is waste, no matter how important it might have seemed at the time.

Video MVP: Drew Houston is the CEO of Dropbox, a Silicon Valley company that makes an extremely easy-to-use file-sharing tool. Install its application, and a Dropbox folder appears on your computer desktop. Anything you drag into that folder is uploaded automatically to the Dropbox service and then instantly replicated across all your computers and devices.

The founding team was made up of engineers, as the product demanded significant technical expertise to build. It required, for example, integration with a variety of computer platforms and operating systems.

Windows, Macintosh, iPhone, Android, and so on. Each of these implementations happens at a deep level of the system and requires specialized know-how to make the user experience exceptional. In fact, one of Dropbox's biggest competitive advantages is that the product works in such a seamless way that the competition struggles to emulate it.

In fact, none of them had ever worked in a marketing job. They had prominent venture capital backers and could have been expected to apply the standard engineering thinking to building the business: build it and they will come. But Dropbox did something different.

In parallel with their product development efforts, the founders wanted feedback from customers about what mattered to them. In particular, Dropbox needed to test its leap-of-faith question: if we can provide a superior customer experience, will people give our product a try? They believed rightly that file synchronization was a problem that most people didn't know they had. Once you experience the solution, you can't imagine how you ever lived without it.

Customers often don't know what they want, and they often had a hard time understanding Dropbox when the concept was explained. Houston learned this the hard way when he tried to raise venture capital. In meeting after meeting, investors would explain that this "market space" was crowded with existing products, none of them had made much money, and the problem wasn't a very important one.

Drew would ask: "Have you personally tried those other products?" When they would say yes, he'd ask: "Did they work seamlessly for you?" The answer was almost always no. Yet in meeting after meeting, the venture capitalists could not imagine a world in line with Drew's vision. Drew, in contrast, believed that if the software "just worked like magic," customers would flock to it.

The challenge was that it was impossible to demonstrate the working software in a prototype form. The product required that they overcome significant technical hurdles; it also had an online service component that required high reliability and availability. To avoid the risk of waking up after years of development with a product nobody wanted, Drew did something unexpectedly easy: he made a video.

Product and Services Map: Construct a product roadmap using the following method:

- On sticky notes, write down a series of features that you want your potential offering to have.
- Organize the features into logical groups, which may be in categories such as "Registration" or "Search."
- On a wall or other flat space, organize the sticky notes by placing the important features on top of less important features vertically within the group, and placing the more important group to the right of the less important groups.
- Batch items from top to bottom and from left to right into named releases, such as "MVP", "Beta", "Test", or "Version 1."

Demo Demonstration: you need to demo your innovation asap using the simplest and fastest tools possible, so you can get early feedback and reach the go no go decision before wasting any time or resources, some of the recommended approaches from simple to hard:

- Video Explainer, Landing page with survey inputs for pre-order
- Screenshot of mobile app and automated tasks
- 3D Screen Design of Hardware blueprint
- Scaled-down mobile or web app with limited functionality.
- Hardware demo "i.e., Drones, wearables, etc.".

The map below shows us the big picture of our product and allows us to modify our mindset. We are focused now on the overall vision and purpose behind the product and not solely on the particular features we need to deliver.

Then it is easier for us to answer the question: 'Why are we building it?', which is probably the most important question one can ask while creating products.

Product and Services Map

User Registration	Content Creation	Administration	Advertising	Social Media
Feature 1 (MVP)	Feature 1 (MVP)	Feature 1 (MVP)	Feature 1 (Beta)	Feature 1 (Beta)
Feature 2 (MVP)	Feature 2 (MVP)	Feature 2 (Beta)	Feature 2 (Beta)	Feature 2
Feature 3 (MVP)	Feature 3 (Beta)	Feature 3 (Beta)	Feature 3	Feature 3
Feature 4 (Beta)	Feature 4 (Beta)	Feature 4 (Beta)	Feature 4	Feature 4
Feature 5 (Beta)	Feature 5	Feature 5	Feature 5	Feature 5
Feature 6	Feature 6	Feature 6	Feature 6	

Lifecycle of Users Design and Product Development

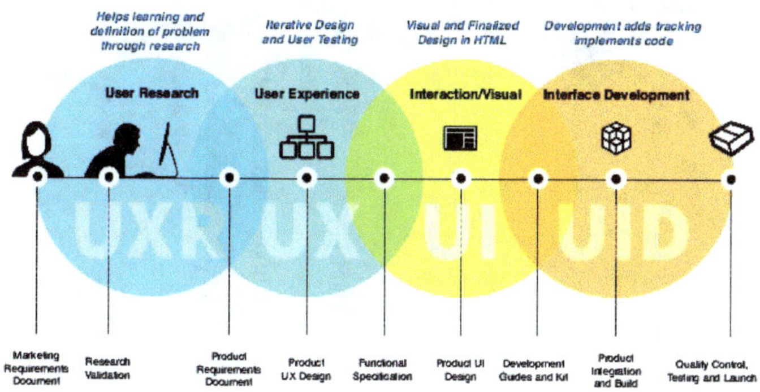

To apply a scientific method, we need to identify hypotheses to test.

Measuring MVP success for mobile app:

	E-commerce	2-sided market	SaaS	Mobile app	User-gen content	Media
Empathy	Interviews; qualitative results; quantitative scoring; surveys					
Stickiness	Loyalty, conversion	Inventory, listings	Engagement, churn	Downloads, churn, virality	Content, spam	Traffic, visits, returns
Virality	CAC, shares, reactivation	SEM, sharing	Inherent virality, CAC	WoM, app ratings, CAC	Invites, sharing	Content virality, SEM
	(Money from transactions)		(Money from active users)		(Money from ad clicks)	
Revenue	Transaction, CLV	Transactions, commission	Upselling, CAC, CLV	CLV, ARPDAU	Ads, donations	CPE, affiliate %, eyeballs
Scale	Affiliates, white-label	Other verticals	API, magic #, mktplace	Spinoffs, publishers	Analytics, user data	Syndication, licenses

The two most important assumptions are the value hypothesis and the growth hypothesis. These give rise to tuning variables that control a startup's engine of growth. Each iteration of a startup is an attempt to rev this engine to see if it will turn. Once it is running, the process repeats, shifting into higher and higher gears.

Once clear on these leap-of-faith assumptions, the first step is to enter the Build phase as quickly as possible with a minimum viable product (MVP). The MVP is that version of the product that enables a full turn of the Build-Measure-Learn loop with a minimum amount of effort and the least amount of development time. The minimum viable product lacks many features that may prove essential later on. However, in some ways, creating an MVP requires extra work: we must be able to measure its impact.

For example, it is inadequate to build a prototype that is evaluated solely for internal quality by engineers and designers. We also need to get it in front of potential customers to gauge their reactions. We may even need to try selling them the prototype, as we'll soon see.

When we enter the Measure phase, the biggest challenge will be determining whether the product development efforts are leading to real progress. Remember, if we're building something that nobody wants, it doesn't matter much if we're doing it on time and budget.

The method I recommend is called innovation accounting, a quantitative approach that allows us to see whether our engine-tuning efforts are bearing fruit. It also allows us to create learning milestones, which are an alternative to traditional business and product milestones.

Learning milestones are useful for entrepreneurs as a way of assessing their progress accurately and objectively; they are also invaluable to managers and investors who use them, without a dollar of marketing or advertising having been spent. In other words, Facebook also validated its growth hypothesis. These two hypotheses represent two of the most important leap-of-faith questions any new startup faces.

UX and Usability Testing: Conduct usability tests to get an in-depth view of how typical users interact with your product and/or site as this will inform you where exactly your users get lost, which features are most useful, etc. While there are numerous paid usability services, the do-it-yourself version is to bring in a test user (with a promise of free lunch, perhaps?) and simply watch them interact with your offering.

Customer feedback helps us understand the WHY behind what people are doing. Why are people using one feature three times as often as another? Why do most of your customers stop creating accounts on the last step? Or what causes customers to use your product less frequently?

For an example check out the following resources:

- Mailchimp.com: An email newsletter and landing page service provider featuring a drag-and-drop builder.
- Blogger.com: Your company blog should focus less on your offering and more on providing your audience with useful and insightful information which will generate more organic traffic towards your site. Be sure to optimize your blog for conversions and make it easy for your audience to sign up for more content or invest in your offering. All other features are just distractions.
- Survey: One of the most effective ways to determine what your customers want is to employ surveys. Remember, keep surveys short (5-10 questions) and only include questions that will generate the most useful answers.

Below are some tools to help you survey your potential customers and get the most reliable feedback:

- SurveyMonkey: This enables anyone to create professional online surveys quickly and easily.
- Key Survey: An enterprise-level application that enables users to collect, manage and leverage feedback within the customer base.
- SurveyGizmo: An easy-to-use survey software tool that allows you to easily create online surveys, quizzes, polls, and web forms.

Agile Development: Lean manufacturers discovered the benefits of small batches decades ago. In the post–World War II economy, Japanese carmakers such as Toyota could not compete with huge American factories that used the latest mass production techniques. Following the intuitively efficient way of building, mass-production factories-built cars by using ever-larger batch sizes. They would spend huge amounts of money buying machines that could produce car parts by amounts of money buying machines that could produce car parts by the tens, hundreds, or thousands. By keeping those machines running at peak speed, they could drive down the unit cost of each part and produce cars that were incredibly inexpensive so long as they were completely uniform.

The Japanese car market was far too small for companies such as Toyota to employ those economies of scale; thus, Japanese companies faced intense pressure from mass production. Also, in the war-ravaged Japanese economy, the capital was not available for massive investments in large machines.

It was against this backdrop that innovators such as Taiichi Ohno, Shigeo Shingo, and others found a way to succeed by using small batches. Instead of buying large, specialized machines that could produce thousands of parts at a time, Toyota used smaller general-purpose machines that could produce a wide variety of parts in small batches.

This required figuring out ways to reconfigure each machine rapidly to make the right part at the right time. By focusing on this "changeover time," Toyota was able to produce entire automobiles by using small batches throughout the process.

This rapid change in machines was no easy feat. As in any lean transformation, existing systems and tools often need to be reinvented to support working in smaller batches. Shigeo Shingo created the concept of SMED (Single-Minute Exchange of Die) in order to enable a smaller batch size of work in early Toyota factories.

He was so relentless in rethinking the way machines were operated that he was able to reduce changeover times that previously took hours to less than ten minutes. He did this, not by asking workers to work faster, but by reimagining and restructuring the work that needed to be done. Every investment in better tools and processes had a corresponding benefit in terms of shrinking the batch size of work.

Because of its smaller batch size, Toyota was able to produce a much greater diversity of products. It was no longer necessary that each product be the same to gain the economies of scale that powered mass production.

Thus, Toyota could serve its smaller, more fragmented markets and still compete with the mass producers. Over time, that capability allowed Toyota to move producers successfully into larger and larger markets until it became the world's largest automaker in 2008.

The biggest advantage of working in small batches is that quality problems can be identified much sooner. This is the origin of Toyota's famous hand-on cord, which allows any worker to ask for help as soon as they notice any problem, such as a defect in a physical part, stopping the entire production line if it cannot be corrected immediately.

This is another very counterintuitive practice. An assembly line works best when it is functioning smoothly, rolling car after car at the end of the line. The hand-on cord can interrupt this careful flow as the line is halted repeatedly. However, the benefits of halting and fixing problems faster outweigh this cost. This process of continuously driving out defects has been a win-win for Toyota and its customers. It is the root cause of Toyota's historic high-quality ratings and low costs.

Take a look at your cell phone. Odds are, it is not the very first version of its kind. Even innovative companies such as Apple produce a new version of their flagship phones about once a year. Bundled up in that product release are dozens of new features (at the release of iPhone 4, Apple boasted more than 1,500 changes).

Ironically, many high-tech products are manufactured in advanced facilities that follow the latest in lean thinking, including small batches and single-piece Flow. However, the process that is used to design the product is stuck in the era of mass production. Think of all the changes that are made to a product such as the iPhone; all 1,500 of them are released to customers in one giant batch.

Behind the scenes, in the development and design of the product itself, large batches are still the rule. The work that goes into the development of a new product proceeds on a virtual assembly line. Product managers figure out what features are likely to please customers; product designers then figure out how those features should look and feel.

These designs are passed to engineering, which builds something new or modifies an existing product and, once this is done, hands it to somebody responsible for verifying that the new product works the way the product managers and designers intended. For a product such as the iPhone, these internal handoffs may happen on a monthly or quarterly basis.

Instead of working in separate departments, engineers and designers would work together side by side on one feature at a time. Whenever that feature was ready to be tested with customers, time. Whenever that feature was ready to be tested with customers, they immediately would release a new version of the product, which would go live on our website for a relatively small number of people.

The team would be able immediately to assess the impact of their work, evaluate its effect on customers, and decide what to do next. For tiny changes, the whole process might be repeated several times per day. In fact, the best startup makes about fifty changes to its product (on average) every single day.

Just as with the Toyota Production System, the key to being able to operate this quickly is to check for defects immediately, thus preventing bigger problems later. For example, we had an extensive set of automated tests that assured that after every change our product still worked as designed.

Let's say an engineer accidentally removed an important feature, such as the checkout button on one of our e-commerce pages. Without this button, customers no longer could buy anything from us. It's as if our business instantly became a hobby. Analogously to the Toyota hand-on cord, we used an elaborate set of defense mechanisms that prevented engineers from accidentally breaking something important.

The essential lesson is not that everyone should be shipping fifty times per day but that by reducing batch size, we can get through the Build-Measure-Learn feedback loop more quickly than our competitors can. The ability to learn faster from customers is the essential competitive advantage that startups must possess as shown below.

THE PROJECT TIMELINE	
Design and engineering of the initial virtual prototype	1 day
Production and assembly of initial hard prototypes	3 days
Design iteration: two additional cycles	5 days
Initial production run and assembly of initial forty units	15 days

The Toyota Production System is probably the most advanced system of management in the world, but even more impressive is the fact that Toyota has built the most advanced learning organization in history. It has demonstrated an ability to unleash the creativity of its employees, achieve consistent growth, and produce innovative new products relentlessly over the course of nearly a century.

This is the kind of long-term success to which entrepreneurs should aspire. Although lean production techniques are powerful, they are only a manifestation of a high-functioning organization that is committed to achieving maximum performance by employing the right measures of progress over the long term.

The process is only the foundation upon which a great company culture can develop. But without this foundation, efforts to encourage learning, creativity, and innovation will fall.

Entrepreneurship is management. And yet, imagine a modern manager who is tasked with building a new product in the context of an established company. Imagine that she goes back to her company's chief financial officer (CFO) a year later and says, "We have failed to meet the growth targets we predicted. In fact, we have almost no new customers and no new revenue.

However, we have learned an incredible amount and are on the cusp of a breakthrough new line of business. All we need is another year." Most of the time, this would be the last report this intrapreneur would give her employer.

The reason is that in general management, a failure to deliver results is due to either a failure to plan adequately or a failure to execute properly. Both are significant lapses, yet new product development in our modern economy routinely requires exactly this kind of failure on the way to greatness.

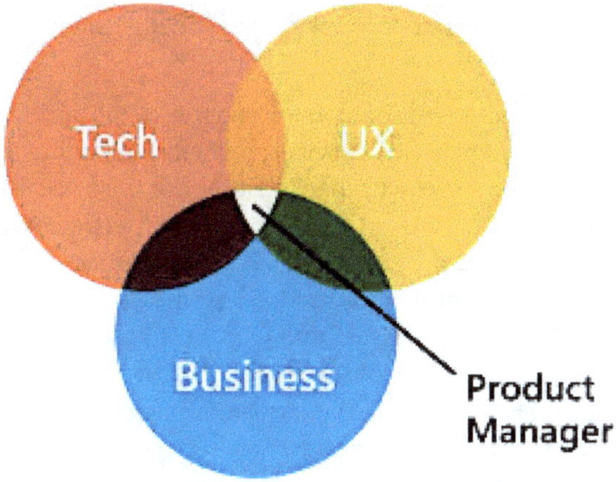

Product Marketing and Growth Scaling: A marketing strategy focuses on how a company can reach an identified market over time and deliver against its overall value proposition.

Product marketing: is the process of bringing a product to market. This includes deciding the product's positioning and messaging, launching the product, and ensuring salespeople and customers understand it. Product marketing aims to drive the demand and usage of the product and can include any of the following:

Route to Market (RTM): Route-to-market is a strategy that determines which distribution channels you use to deliver a product to your target customers. It's a strategy that companies use when they want to achieve a specific business objective or accelerate growth in a given market.

Time to Market: Time to market (TTM) is defined as the period from the conception of a new idea until it is released to the marketplace. Another definition: it is the time between when the team starts work and when the first unit is sold.

Go-To-Market: A go-to-market strategy focuses on how to bring new products or services to market; it is short-term and product-driven.

Growth Hacking: Traditional marketing is all about selling a company's products and services, growth hacking is a more holistic function. Growth hackers are not just focused on sales, they are focused on finding the most efficient way to grow a business at a minimum budget and broad tech tools. It is a subfield of marketing focused on the rapid growth of a company. It is referred to as both a process and a set of cross-disciplinary skills. The goal is to regularly conduct A/B testing that will lead to improving the customer journey and replicate and scale the ideas that work and modify or abandon the ones that don't before investing a lot of resources.

Pre-Launch Promo: Start with a landing page for pre-orders, similar to a kick-start campaign, and expand from there.

Consider prospects the same way you consider investors. A "No" just means "Not now". Establish a relationship with prospects before your product or service is ready. Like your user community, prospects should be throwing money at you by the time you're ready to monetize.

Target Market Survey: Ask at least one random person a question every day. Polling people can be an effective way to find unique markets, ways to phrase questions or hone your pitch. Use random interactions, networking events, and scheduled meetings to clarify a theory or question. You could even set it up formally. Each week pick a new question and attempt to collect 24+ responses from random people. Collect and assess the data. The next week, replicate with different questions.

Listen to Advice: Be good at taking everyone's advice but analyzing just how valuable it is. You'll find patterns in both good and bad advice and learn to recognize them easily. Learn to depict the motive behind each piece of advice, usually an investor or industry expert is driven by their ego and the lack of their inability to see the future, so don't assume because they succeeded in the past deal will make their advice accurate.

Pre-Launch Growth Hacking (Marketing with no Budget): target locals and social influencers to attend and shoot vertical videos at client demo events, edit their video in a post, and have them share the video via Instagram and Snapchat stories.

Here are the top questions I've asked at the end of meetings:

- May I add you to a list of individuals I keep updated with occasional emails? If I come across a founder looking for investors in your industry, may I make a connection?
- Do you happen to know any Angels or VCs that have an interest in my industry? Would any of your portfolio companies benefit from using my product or service?
- What are the biggest challenges you find founders come across in your industry focus? What are the biggest challenges you come across as an investor?
- Don't forget to offer something in return. Make it a mutually beneficial exchange and you'll be rewarded

Tracking early-stage KPI metrics with the rule of three

Business model			Bootstrap (size, growth%)	Angel/Pre-Seed (size, growth%)	Seed/Pre-A (size, growth%)	Typical industries	Typical companies
Subscription	B2C B2B	Freemium	- # communities reached - # potential core users talked to - core users overall feedback	- # DAU - free-to-paid users conversion rate - MRR	- MRR - free-to-paid users conversion rate - LTV/CAC	- SaaS - Cloud storage - Online media streaming	Heroku, Buffer, Dropbox, Spotify, LinkedIn
		Free-trial	- # communities reached - # potential core users talked to - core users overall feedback	- MRR - churn rate (-)	- MRR - LTV-to-CAC - payback period		Intercom, Zendesk, Netflix
	B2B	Enterprise	- # potential core users talked to - core users overall feedback	- annual bookings - MRR - professional service revenue	- annual bookings - MRR - payback period	- SaaS - Cloud storage	Salesforce, Oracle, Amazon AWS
Transactional	B2C	Direct	- # communities reached - # potential core users talked to - core users overall feedback	- revenue - conversion rate	- revenue - conversion rate - LTV-to-CAC	- Online retail	Bonobos
	C2C B2B	Intermediary, Peer-to-peer	- # communities reached - # potential core users talked to - core users overall feedback	- GMV/Rides booked/Loan volume - conversion rate	- GMV/Rides booked/Loan volume - conversion rate - LTV-to-CAC	- Online retail - Online lending - Travel/hospitality - Ride-hailing	Tokopedia, AirBnB, Booking, Grab, Alibaba, Lending Club
	B2B	Direct	- # potential core users talked to - core users overall feedback	- # New clients per-month - Total transaction/Delivery volume	- Total transaction/Delivery volume - LTV-to-CAC - payback period	- Logistic technology - Payment gateway	Ninja Van, Stripe

Product Pivot, Sales, and Market Fit:

Worry more about functionality and less about the appearance of your site. It's important to launch your site and product, even if they are still unrefined, as you need to start generating interest in your offering and keep potential users updated about the status of your company.

Collect feedback, analyze data, and refine your offering. This is an ongoing process, so the sooner you start improving your offering the better from Alpha "Internal" to Beta "invitation only" to Public Beta "commercial with limited scaling". This approach is called a pivot.

Lead generation: If you're launching without any outside investments, set a good chunk of the budget that you have aside for marketing and lead generation.
Start by researching the competition and learning from their experience. If you want to get a head start, use paid advertising. But don't forget to invest in long-term prospects like SEO and brand awareness.

Social proof and customer feedback are what people pay attention to the most, so make sure you have business accounts on LinkedIn, Twitter, Facebook, G2, Capterra, and Google My Business and that those accounts represent your business well.

Create content for blogs and join conference discussions within your industry to drive recognition and awareness of your innovation along with expanding your circle to the mover and shaker who can make your startup a viable venture "Product, Sales, and Investment influencers.

Pay utmost attention to what your customers want. You need to polish off every existing tool, but, at the same time, develop new ones based on customer feedback. This requires marketing campaigns and having a customer success team that takes care of every issue your users may have. Plus, you need people to constantly reach out to users to ask them to let the world know what they think of your product.

Customer Definition: start by finding the Customers Who Need Your Product, aspiring founders who think they've developed an amazing offering often believe that their products will sell themselves.

While there are occasional instances of unique apps, software, hardware, and services that were so valuable that they instantly made their founders famous, this is rarely the case. For the rest of us, we have to put in the work to determine just what kind of audience there is for the products we develop and hope that what we create will satisfy their needs.

And while finding our ideal customers is a time-consuming and arduous process, there's no denying that putting in the work will increase the chances of finding those who not only want your product but those who NEED it. Fortunately, we've put together a guide that lays out how you can ensure that your customers go crazy for your product.

Ideally, you should create your initial customer archetype before building a product. However, whether you're still validating your startup idea or you're working on your MVP (minimum viable product), it is still essential that you create your initial customer archetype, as it will help you guide the development of your final offering. Take the time to outline who you think your ideal customer is and remember to be as specific as possible.

Be VERY specific; making your ideal customer more real and relatable will only enable you to better understand the needs and wants of those who will invest in your product. Even giving them a name will help.

Founders should ask themselves the following questions about their target customers:

- What are their interests, aspirations, challenges, and problems?
- Who does the research?
- How do they make buying decisions?
- Who makes the buying decisions?

- What kind of content do they consume when exploring, considering, and making a purchase?

Limit the number of customer personas to reduce distractions, 3-5 is a good starting number. Regardless of how many you create, each one should consist of:

- Background (employment status, education, family information, etc.), demographics (gender, age, income, etc.)
- Needs (pain points, motivations), goals
- Objections (hurdles, obstacles), fears (competitive), Interests/Hobbies.

By the time you've clearly listed the pertinent details of your initial customer archetype, you should have a summary that looks something like this:
"Sam is a 32-year-old project manager at a mid-market bank who likes to read sci-fi novels."

Users and Customers: Potential users need to be updated. Sure, you may not have much to tell them, and some may not enjoy the teasers, but a prolonged absence will be worse than too much "hype". Don't let this fear stop you though. Spend an hour or two a month to engage with potential customers and you'll be rewarded once your product is available.

The individuals that are begging for early access are those early adopters that will evangelize your product or serve. Consider creating a real relationship with these people and tap into more than just their enthusiasm.

Position: It's not easy being number two. As a marketer, you have limited choices - you can pretend you're not defined by the market leader, or you can embrace your position and go directly after your nemesis.

What position do you want in the marketplace? This is a key part of the process which almost everyone skips over while designing their offering because it takes upfront planning and commitment to an approach using imperfect information on what is going to work.

Your very resistance to this process is just more confirmation of why most people don't even consider doing this, and therein lies the unique value of leveraging this process for your capital-raising efforts.

Focus: how a $5 disposable camera can take a better picture than a $20,000 camera if the expensive camera doesn't do one thing: focus. The point? You can beat your competition with a smaller staff, less financial resources, and less experience if you learn to focus.

Focus can be powerful, and this chapter is about focusing your positioning efforts on the most important area. Now that you have completed the previous chapter's analysis exercises, you are better informed about your marketplace and investors' needs. Why Niche?

If you already dominated a marketplace or raised $100M+ a year, you wouldn't be reading this book. If you are not already dominating, then you need to gain traction, a foothold, or some momentum as a first step to building confidence in the capital-raising process.

It is much easier to compete for a niche segment of the market rather than trying to be the best option for everyone in the marketplace. Typically, only the largest dominant players, long-time incumbent players, or very well-financed players can use a mass-market generic approach and make it profitable before running out of cash or patience on their path to profitability.

If you started a cereal business in 1920, you could get away with a generic approach, as the Kellogg Brothers did. At that time, the brothers who started Kellogg's cereals were only competing with oatmeal and grits.

Now if you walk down the cereal aisle at any major U.S. grocery store you will see over 100 options, and in the U.S. alone there are over 1,000 cereal options available.

You can't just offer cornflakes; you have to offer gluten-free, organic, fair trade, locally grown, Olympian-endorsed super flakes to appeal to niche demographics while also standing out from the noise.

Customers' Key Assumptions List: Once you have a basic understanding of who your target customer is, take the time to list out the key assumptions to help you tailor your offering to their needs.

While making assumptions often has a negative connotation, making careful, thoughtful assumptions about your product and customer base is an indispensable step when launching a startup because it enables founders to plan for "what if" scenarios.

Defining your key assumptions is an exercise that should require at least a few hours, so make sure you set aside enough time to thoroughly complete this task. Remember, the more detailed you are, the better your final product will be, so don't cheat!

We've included some of the most important points to keep in mind below. Basically, all you need to do is fill in the blanks based on data you've compiled on your initial customer target.

- I believe that my customers need to ________.
- This need can be fulfilled with ________.
- My initial customers will be ________.
- The primary value a customer wants to get out of my product/service is ________.
- My customer can also get these additional benefits: ________, ________, ________, etc.
- I will acquire the majority of my users/customers through the following channels: ________, ________, ________, etc.
- I will make money from/by ________.
- My main competitors are the following companies: ________, ________, ________, etc.
- My company will beat them in the market because of: ________, ________, ________, etc.
- My biggest product risk(s) is/are: ________, ________, ________, etc.

- We will address our risks through ________, ________, ________, etc.

Once you've completed the above statements, list out and prioritize what you think are the most important assumptions to address in the following format:

What assumptions does my company hold, that if proven wrong, could cause the company to fail?

1. ________
2. ________
3. ________

Test Your Target Customer: Now that you've drafted your initial customer archetype and created your key assumptions from that information, it's time to test your data. One of the best and most effective ways to test your data is through conducting extensive customer interviews.

After you've found people whom you think accurately represent your target market, set aside some time to interview them over the phone, through email, surveys, or in person.

Whichever method you choose, keep in mind that the questions you ask are what ultimately matter the most.

Here are some of the most important questions to consider when you set out to interview your potential customers:

Customer Segmentation:

- What do you do professionally?
- Who handles the process you're improving at your office?
- Tell me about your role at [company].
- How much time do you spend on [process you're improving]? [Specific questions related to your product/customer] – For example, "Do you have kids?"

Problem Discovery:

- What's the hardest part of your day?
- What product do you wish you had that doesn't exist yet?
- What tasks take up the most time in your day?

- What could be done to improve your experience with [process/role]?
- What's the hardest part about being a [demographic]?
- What are your biggest/most important professional and personal responsibilities/goals?

Problem Validation:

- Do you find it hard to [process/problem]?
- How important is [value you're delivering] to you?
- Tell me about the last time you [process you're improving].
- How motivated are you to solve/improve [problem/process]?
- If you had a solution to this problem, what would it mean to you/how would it affect you?

If you've followed the above steps, you should now have a wealth of information that you will use to update your initial customer archetype. To help guide you through this process, start by answering the questions below:

- What does your customer think about your product?
- How will your customer learn about your offering?
- Will your customer use your product?
- What motivates your customer to engage with your offering?
- When will your customer pay for the offering?
- What will be the prompt that encourages your customer to pay?
- How likely is your customer to tell others about your product?
- How soon is your customer likely to start using your product?
- What might prevent your customer from using your product?
- How much is your customer willing to pay for your product? To pay for expanded features.

Your customer archetype should be very detailed once you've updated it, perhaps several paragraphs or pages long, and it may even go through several more iterations until you have an incredibly detailed idea of who it is you're targeting.

If you notice any gaps that you think pertain to your offering, no matter how small those concerns may be, go back and conduct more research to fill in those blanks, even if it means doing more interviews.

Now that you know exactly who your customer is, what they want, and most importantly, what they need, it's time for you to go out and build something great.
Keep in mind, however, that knowing your customer is an iterative process, that while your current customers may love your product now, they may not be as excited about v2. As your company grows and your offering evolves, remember to always have your ear to the ground and your finger on the pulse of the people you build your product for.

Scaling: growth strategy consists of four steps:

Gather the data: To start, you must understand the characteristics of your best customers, which include:

The features they use, how often they open the app, the items they buy the most, their average order sizes, The time of day and days they shop, the acquisition sources (e.g., Google Ads, SEO, referral, The devices they use, Their demographics (age, income, and more), Their locations.

You must also understand the behaviors of customers who "churn," that is, those who stop using the product or decide against buying, which include:

The pages that have the highest exit rates

The bugs that prevent people from taking a particular action (sharing with a friend, making a purchase, etc.)

The actions they don't take that your best customers do

You also need to carry out interviews and surveys to get to know both your best customers along with those who have churned and understand the reasons behind their behaviors.

Test your scenario: The insights you get from your data will help you understand the way your users interact with your company. They will guide your future experiments. So, first, come up with A/B test ideas. These will be based on your data (both quantitative and qualitative) as well as on your intuition.

Remember, you want to find opportunities for improvement and, at the same time, come up with new original ideas related to the data you gathered.

As you come up with test ideas, make sure to write there:

1. Name
2. Description
3. Hypothesis
4. Metrics to be measured.

Prioritize: Your idea generation will likely result in more tests than you can run. That's why it's important to prioritize those that have the most potential for improvement at the lowest cost.

The idea's potential impact—the expected degree to which the ideas will improve the metric being focused on

The submitter's level of confidence in how effective it will be.

The ease of implementation—the time and resources needed to run the experiment.

1. *Run the experiments:* Once you've generated and prioritized your test ideas, you must create them and run them. When running tests, have two rules of the road:

Use a 99% statistical confidence level.

Control wins in a tie

Many of your experiments will help you improve the metrics previously defined, while many will fail in making a difference. What matters is that you continue testing and learning to see what works and what doesn't.

The following can be used to speed up the customer acquisition for a given product or service:

Selling: now that you have successfully proven your marketing campaign, you need to set a conversion framework to convert all the metrics generated above into revenues and profit:

1: Create a Sales Funnel: A sales funnel is an automated system that allows you to attract people to a page and convert them into potential customers.

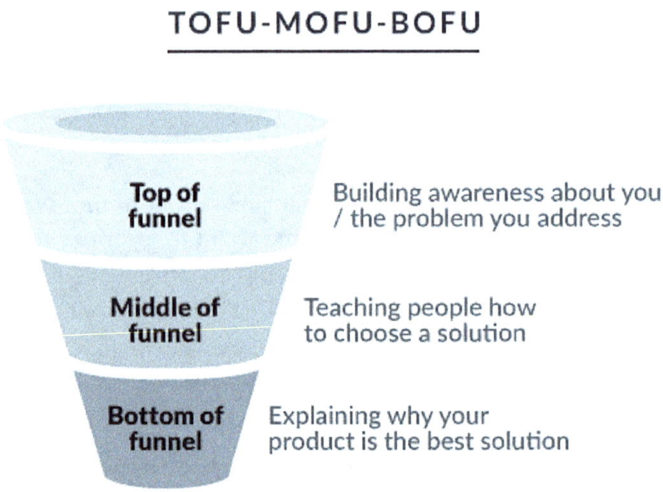

To start with a sales funnel, you need to identify your core offer—the product you want the prospect to buy.

Then, you need to create a compelling lead magnet to convert visitors into leads. This lead magnet should be a simplified version of the solution your main product offers.
To attract leads with your lead magnet, you need to create content that attracts ideal customers to it.

As you acquire leads, you need to continue delivering value. This can be done by sending three or four educational emails that amplify the concepts explained in your lead magnet and core offer. Finally, you need to make a sales pitch that shows your leads how your core offer will solve the exact problem you've been educating them on in your content, lead magnet, and previous emails.

2: Conversion Rate / Landing Page Optimization: Instead of focusing on attracting visitors into your sales funnel, you can optimize the existing traffic you get. That's what conversion rate optimization (CRO) is all about.

The conversion rate is the number of conversions (sales, signups, etc.) divided by traffic (the number of people who visited the sales page or signup page) and multiplied by 100. To improve your conversion rates, leverage the power of A/B testing. This requires you to create an exact copy of a given page, change one element of it, send traffic to it, and see the changes in each version.

For example, if we wanted to create an A/B test for this blog post to improve the reading time, we could change the blog post title. It may be that certain titles have a higher chance of making people want to read the entire piece and thus improving our business metrics.

To start optimizing your conversions, identify your biggest driver of sales. This could be a specific product or a specific page. Then, review the conversion rate data for that product or page.

Pick one variable to improve and create an A/B test. This could be the call to action, the timing of an email, the color of a CTA button, an image on the sales page, and much more. Finally, use the results to improve your metrics. Keep testing new variables and elements so you can increase the number of leads or customers.

3: Customer Success: Customer service "Success" is often seen as a secondary aspect of doing business. But more and more, people are starting to consider it as a key part of a purchase decision.

A recent study found that 86% of consumers are willing to pay more for a better customer experience. What's more, Bain & Company found that by increasing customer retention by 5%, a company can expect a 25% to_95% increase in profits.

If you focus on your customer service, you can easily acquire (thanks to the word-of-mouth from your current satisfied customers) and retain more customers without having to spend any more money on deploying expensive marketing tactics.

In order to use customer service as marketing, you need to start tracking your Net Promoter Score (NPS). This is a scale that goes from 0 (least satisfied) to 10 (most satisfied) based on the answer to the question: "How likely is it that you would recommend to a friend or colleague?" Based on the results from your NPS score, you need to work on integrating your customer service and marketing teams.

There's an almost symbiotic—yet often ignored—aspect of both teams. The customer service team can provide the marketing team with the latest complaints and ideas taken from conversations with customers, which marketers can use to improve their messaging. On the other hand, the marketing team can notify the customer service team about the latest promotions and offers, which the latter can then use in their conversations with customers.

Another important thing to consider is to create small ways to delight your customers. These ideas can be as simple as sending handwritten thank-you notes to customers and providing free gifts to those customers who are either loyal to the brand or who have had problems with it.

Finally, you can send special offers to your current customers, so they stay loyal to your company. This offer can include special coupons and discounts, unique deals, and new products that only loyal customers can find out about.

4: Affiliate or Referral Programs: The power of word-of-mouth is second to none in the marketing world. People who recommend your company to others are giving you free advertising. Not only that, but it works incredibly well.
A Nielsen study found that 92% of consumers believe recommendations from friends and family more than they do

from advertising. Both affiliate and referral programs are effective at tapping the power of word of mouth.

The former incentivizes people by giving them a commission from the sale of a given product, while the latter gives them more indirect benefits, such as discounts and free products. To use either affiliate program, you need to start by choosing a platform like Refersion, Referral Candy, or Ambassador, which allows you to implement a program in your company.

You then need to pick enticing rewards for your customers either a specific commission from the sale of your products or an incentive as a free product. With your program in place, you need to start promoting your program to your customers and/or influencers. If you have an existing customer base, invite them all to join the referral program. Otherwise, you can talk to influencers in your industry and partner with them to promote your referral or affiliate program.

As you promote your program, keep track of the main referrals or affiliate partners and maintain relationships with them. Their success is your success, so make sure to help them with the promotion of your program.

Content marketing: has been one of the key growth drivers for countless brands, and that includes us. Unfortunately, achieving the level of scale with content marketing can take a long time. And yes, that's something we've also had to struggle with. You can create the very best content, but it can take months, if not years, until you start to see the exponential growth you are looking for.

Search Engine Optimization (SEO): Stefan Debois, the founder, and CEO of Survey Anyplace, was able to create a large volume of links and rank for a lot of relevant, high-traffic keywords, getting a lot of organic traffic, by creating a glossary on his site. This glossary is similar to a Wikipedia entry page: it summarized a list of concepts in his industry so people could use it as a resource. People love evergreen resources like this, so it's no surprise so many people are linked to it.

The glossary he created included a list of words related to surveys and market research, the keyword focuses that define his company. Each item was about 300 to 500 words long. Out of the 36 glossary articles he created, he acquired an additional 8,000 monthly visitors to his site.

Landing Page	Acquisition		
	Sessions	% New Sessions	New Users
Organic Traffic	8,309 % of Total: 12.62% (65,816)	91.67% Avg for View: 76.48% (19.86%)	7,617 % of Total: 15.13% (50,337)
1. surveyanyplace.com/docs/closed-ended-question/	2,508 (30.18%)	93.18%	2,337 (30.68%)
2. surveyanyplace.com/docs/how-to-make-a-logo-with-transparent-background-using-gimp-or-photoshop/	1,411 (16.98%)	91.14%	1,286 (16.88%)
3. surveyanyplace.com/docs/double-barreled-question/	679 (8.17%)	96.02%	652 (8.56%)
4. surveyanyplace.com/docs/how-to-create-animated-background-in-photoshop/	481 (5.79%)	92.93%	447 (5.87%)
5. surveyanyplace.com/docs/forced-choice-scale/	421 (5.07%)	94.30%	397 (5.21%)
6. surveyanyplace.com/docs/numerical-scale/	399 (4.80%)	90.73%	362 (4.75%)
7. surveyanyplace.com/docs/rating-scale-questions/	323 (3.89%)	91.64%	296 (3.89%)
8. surveyanyplace.com/docs/leading-question/	264 (3.18%)	91.29%	241 (3.16%)
9. surveyanyplace.com/docs/rating-questions/	188 (2.26%)	93.62%	176 (2.31%)
10. surveyanyplace.com/docs/guttman-scale/	185 (2.23%)	88.11%	163 (2.14%)

Branding: One of the biggest challenges new startups face is the lack of brand awareness. A startup needs to develop a brand to cement its company in the minds of its customers.

But when you read about developing a brand, you usually find a list of tactics like billboards or TV advertising. These are effective, but they come at a steep cost that most young or bootstrapped startups can't afford.

Fortunately, there are ways to growth hack this and receive coverage in top sites like Techcrunch, Forbes, *Inc.*, Influencive, and *Entrepreneur* without spending a dollar. Here's how to do it:

Step 1: Start Networking: You want to be where your customers are. Join popular subreddits in your niche as well as Facebook groups, events, and blogs to start connecting with your customers.

Step 2: Define Your Narrative: A brand is much more than a logo or a tagline. It encompasses a narrative, a purpose, and a storyline that explains why the company came to be. In order to draw some attention to your brand, you need to have a great story.
Start by picking your favorite superhero and recalling their origin story. As you define your narrative, pitch it to a few friends before approaching your PR contacts. Find your lowest and highest points as a person or business and describe exactly how you got from a point of struggle to success.

Step 3: Create PR Strategy and Execute It: Make a list of sites where you'd like to be published. It can be *The New York Times* or a niche local blog. The point is that the people who read this outlet should be the same customers you'd like to work with. Don't expect to get your company published in any big outlet rather, focus on the story you have and the way the readers of that site would benefit from learning about it.

You want to start looking for people to pick—writers, editors, managers. Your pitch should mention your story and the readers of the site, so the person who receives the pitch gets interested in your story right away.

Step 4: Use Influencers: Leverage the power of influencers. See who are the top players on Twitter, Instagram, and Facebook groups. Use a search query like "top NICHE influencers" or "top NICHE Facebook groups" to find potential opportunities. You want to pitch them and make them share your story with their followers.

Once you collect around 10 influencers who are willing to share your storyline, create a content calendar with the captions you want them to use so they don't have to do any work.

Instagram: is one of the most powerful channels for new online businesses that want to connect with their potential customers and develop loyal followers. These are some proven Instagram growth hacks you can implement in your account to start generating followers, visitors, and leads:

1: Instagram Stories: Instagram Stories are one of the most popular features people use. The 24-hour snippets provide an intimate, behind-the-scenes look at your business through photos and videos.

Here are some creative ways you can leverage your stories in order to grow an engaged following:

- Ask for opinions with the "questions" sticker. These interactive stickers Instagram gives you work wonders to engage with your audience and get to know them.
- Ask your followers to submit their opinions on your latest product, questions they have about your business, or something else to get them to interact with your brand and to allow you to gain valuable user feedback.
- Use location tags and hashtags. Location tags and hashtags help users who don't follow you find out about your brand.

2: IGTV Channel: An IGTV channel allows you to have a chance to get featured prominently in the Explore tab, which in turn can allow you to reach more potential followers. IGTV videos aren't limited to 15 seconds like stories or to one minute like in your feed. Instead, IGTV videos can be up to one hour long. What's more, you can keep IGTV videos for as long as you want them there.

In order to get your latest videos, which can be about your brand, your products, or a specific topic that your followers are interested in, people must follow your account.
An IGTV channel can help you increase your following while boosting your brand's reach.

The Three Driving Engines of Growth: You know how important it is for startups to use the right kind of metrics—actionable metrics—to evaluate their progress. However, this leaves a large amount of variety in terms of which numbers one should measure.

In fact, one of the most expensive forms of potential waste for a startup is spending time arguing about how to prioritize new development once it has a product on the market.

At any time, the company could invest its energy in finding new customers, servicing existing customers better, improving overall quality, or driving down costs. In my experience, discussions about these kinds of priority decisions can consume a substantial fraction of the company's time.

Engines of growth are designed to give startups a relatively small set of metrics on which to focus their energies. "Startups don't starve; they drown." There are always a zillion new ideas about how to make the product better floating around, but the hard truth is that most of those ideas make a difference only at the margins.

They are mere optimizations. Startups have to focus on the big experiments that lead to validated learning. The engines of the growth framework help them stay focused on the metrics that matter.

The Sticky Engine: Two startups are using the exact same engine of growth despite being in very different industries. Both products are designed to attract and retain customers for the long term. The underlying mechanism of that retention is different in the two cases. For the collectible company, the idea is to become the number one shopping destination for fanatical collectors.

These are people who are constantly hunting for the latest items and the best deals. If the company's product works as designed, collectors who start using it will check constantly and repeatedly to see if new items are for sale as well as list their own items for sale or trade.

The startup database vendor relies on repeat usage for a very different reason. Database technology is used only as the foundation for a customer's own products, such as a website or a point-of-sale system.

Once you build a product on top of a particular database technology, it is extremely difficult to switch. In the Tech industry, such customers are said to be locked into the vendor they choose. For such a product to grow, it has to offer such a compelling new capability that customers are willing to risk being tied to a proprietary vendor for a potentially long time.

Thus, both businesses rely on having a high customer retention rate. They expect that once you start using their product, you will continue to do so. This is the same dynamic as a mobile telephone service provider: when a customer cancels his or her service, it generally means that he or she is extremely dissatisfied or is switching to a competitor's product.

This is in contrast to, say, groceries on a store aisle. In the grocery retail business, customer tastes fluctuate, and if a customer buys a Pepsi this week instead of Coke, it's not necessarily a big deal.

Therefore, companies using the sticky engine of growth track their attrition rate or churn rate very carefully. The churn rate is defined as the fraction of customers in any period who fail to remain engaged with the company's product.

The rules that govern the sticky engine of growth are pretty simple: if the rate of new customer acquisition exceeds the churn rate, the product will grow.

The speed of growth is determined by what I call the rate of compounding, which is simply the natural growth rate minus the churn rate. Like a bank account that earns compounding interest, having a high rate of compounding will lead to extremely rapid growth—without advertising, viral growth, or publicity stunts.

Unfortunately, both of these sticky startups were tracking their progress using generic indicators such as the total number of customers. Even the actionable metrics they were using, such as the activation rate and revenue per customer, weren't very helpful because, in the sticky engine of growth, these variables have little impact on growth. In the sticky engine of growth, they are better suited to testing the value hypothesis that was discussed previously.

One of the two startups started to model its customer behavior by using the sticky engine of growth as a template. The results were striking: a 61 percent retention rate and a 39 percent growth rate of new customers. In other words, its churn rate and new customer acquisition balanced each other almost perfectly, leading to a compounding growth rate of just 0.02 percent—almost zero.

This is typical for companies in an engagement business that are struggling to find growth. Unfortunately, this growth is being offset by an equivalent amount of churn. Once it is modeled this way, the good news should be apparent: there are plenty of new customers coming in the door. The way to find growth is to focus on existing customers for the product even more engaging to them.

For example, the company could focus on getting more and better listings. This would create an incentive for customers to check back often. Alternatively, the company could do something more direct such as messaging them about limited-time sales or special offers.

Either way, its focus needs to be on improving customer retention. This goes against the standard intuition that if a company lacks growth, it should invest more in sales and marketing. This counterintuitive result is hard to infer from standard vanity metrics.

The Viral Engine: social networks are examples of products for which customers do the lion's share of the marketing. Awareness of the product spreads rapidly from person to person similar to the way a virus becomes an epidemic. This is distinct from the simple word-of-mouth growth discussed above.

Instead, products that exhibit viral growth depend on person-to-person transmission as a necessary consequence of normal product use. Customers are not intentionally acting as evangelists; they are not necessarily trying to spread the word about the product. Growth happens automatically as a side effect of customers using the product.

For example, one of the most famous viral success stories was Hotmail's "Outlook Now". At first, growth was sluggish; and the team could not afford an extensive marketing campaign.

But everything changed when they made one small tweak to the product. They added to the bottom of every single e-mail the message "P.S. Get your free e-mail at Hotmail" along with a clickable link.

Within weeks, that small product change produced massive results. Within a few weeks, they signed up more than 1 million new customers. Five weeks later, they hit the 2 million marks. Eighteen months after launching the service, with 12 million subscribers, they sold the company to Microsoft for $400 million.

Like the other engines of growth, the viral engine is powered by a feedback loop that can be quantified. It is called the viral loop, and its speed is determined by a single mathematical term called the viral coefficient.

The higher this coefficient is, the faster the product will spread. The viral coefficient measures how many new customers will use a product as a consequence of each new customer who signs up.

Put another way, how many friends will each customer bring with him or her? Since each friend is also a new customer, he or she has an opportunity to recruit yet more friends.

For a product with a viral coefficient of 0.1, one in every ten customers will recruit one of his or her friends. This is not a sustainable loop. Imagine that one hundred customers sign up. They will cause ten friends to sign up. Those ten friends will cause one additional person to sign up, but there the loop will fizzle out.

By contrast, a viral loop with a coefficient that is greater than 1.0 will grow exponentially, because each person who signs up will bring, on average, more than one other person with him or her. To see these effects graphically, take a look at this chart:

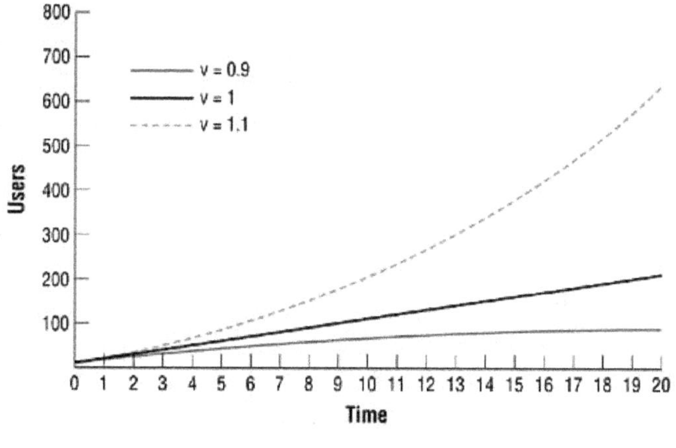

Companies that rely on the viral engine of growth must focus on increasing the viral coefficient more than anything else because even tiny changes in this number will cause dramatic changes in their prospects.

A consequence of this is that many viral products do not charge customers directly but rely on indirect sources of revenue such as advertising.

This is the case because viral products cannot afford to have any friction impede the process of signing customers up and recruiting their friends. This can make testing the value hypothesis for viral products, especially challenging.

The true test of the value hypothesis is always a voluntary exchange of value between customers and the startup that serves them. A lot of confusion stems from the fact that this exchange can be monetary, or nonmonetary, as in the case of Facebook.

In the viral engine of growth, the monetary exchange does not drive new growth; it is useful only as an indicator that customers value the product enough to pay for it.

If Facebook or Hotmail had started charging customers in their early days, it would have been foolish, as it would have impeded their ability to grow.

However, it is not true that customers do not give these companies something of value: by investing their time and attention in the product, they make the product valuable to advertisers. Companies that sell advertising serve two different groups of customers—consumers and advertisers—and exchange a different currency of value with each.

This is markedly different from companies that actively use the money to fuel their expansion, such as a retail chain that can grow as fast as it can fund the opening of new stores at suitable locations. These companies are using a different engine of growth altogether.

The Paid Engine: Imagine another pair of businesses. The first makes $1 for each customer it signs up; the second makes

$100,000 for each customer it signs up. To predict which company will grow faster, you need to know only one additional thing: how much it costs to sign up a new customer.

Imagine that the first company uses Google AdWords to and new customers online and pays an average of 80 cents each time a new customer join.

The second company sells heavy goods to large companies. Each sale requires a significant time investment from a salesperson and on-site sales engineering to help install the product; these hard costs total up to $80,000 per new customer. Both companies will grow at the same rate.

Each has the same proportion of revenue (20 percent) available to reinvest in new customer acquisition. If either company wants to increase its rate of growth, it can do so in one of two ways: increase the revenue from each customer or drive down the cost of acquiring a new customer.

Technical Caveat: Technically, more than one engine of growth can operate in a business at a time. For example, some products have extremely fast viral growth as well as extremely low customer churn rates. Also, there is no reason why a product cannot have both high margins and high retention.

However, in my experience, successful startups usually focus on just one engine of growth, specializing in everything that is required to make it work. Companies that attempt to build a dashboard that includes all three engines tend to cause a lot of confusion because the operations expertise required to model all these effects simultaneously is quite complicated.

Therefore, I strongly recommend that startups focus on one engine at a time.

Most entrepreneurs already have a strong leap-of-faith hypothesis about which engine is most likely to work. If they do not, time spent out of the building with customers will quickly suggest one that seems profitable. Only after pursuing one engine thoroughly should a startup consider a pivot to one of the others.

Product Market Fit: Product/market fit, is the degree to which a product satisfies a strong market demand. It has been identified as a first step to building a successful venture in which the company meets early adopters, gathers feedback, and gauges interest in its product(s).

The 40% rule: One metric for product/market fit is if at least 40% percent of surveyed customers indicate that they would be "very disappointed" if they no longer have access to a particular product or service. Alternatively, it could be measured by having at least 40% of surveyed customers consider the product or service as a "must-have".

Analytics metrics: There are five metrics any online business could measure to empirically verify if they achieved Product / Market fit. They are 1. Bounce Rate, 2. Time on Site, 3. Pages per Visit, 4. Returning Visitors, 5. Customer Lifetime Value.

Low bounce rates mean a visitor's expectation is being met. High Time on Site and Pages per Visit indicate that the experience of the user is satisfactory. High Returning Visitor reflects the lasting impact a product has on its customers, causing them to come back, and Customer Lifetime Value measures the profitability each customer brings to the company.

If these 5 metrics are above average and your 40% rule is met, you'll know you have a Product / Market Fit company.

Marc Andreessen, the legendary entrepreneur, and investor, coined the term product/market fit to describe the moment when a startup finally finds a widespread set of customers that resonate with its product:

In a great market—a market with lots of real potential customers—the market pulls products out of the startup. This is the story of search keyword advertising, Internet, and mobile apps.

Conversely, in a terrible market, you can have the best product in the world and a killer team, and it doesn't matter if you're going to fail. When you see a startup that has found a fit with a large market, it's exhilarating. It leaves no room for doubt. It is Ford's Model T "current Tesla". Facebook sweeping college campuses practically overnight.

For example, imagine two startups that are working diligently to tune the sticky engine of growth. One has a compounding rate of growth of 5 percent, and the other 10 percent. Which company is the better bet? On the surface, it may seem that the larger rate of growth is better, but what if each company's innovation accounting dashboard looks like the following chart?

COMPOUNDING GROWTH RATE	COMPANY A	COMPANY B
Six months ago,	0.1%	9.8%
Five months ago,	0.5%	9.6%
Four months ago,	2.0%	9.9%
Three months ago,	3.2%	9.8%
Two months ago,	4.5%	9.7%
One month ago,	5.0%	10.0%

Even with no insight into these two companies' gross numbers, we can tell that company A is making real progress whereas company B is stuck in the mud. This is true even though Company B is growing faster than Company A right now.

When Engines Run Out: Getting a startup's engine of growth up and running is hard enough, but the truth is that every engine of growth eventually runs out of gas. Every engine is tied to a given set of customers and their related habits, preferences, advertising channels, and interconnections. At some point, that set of customers will be exhausted. This may take a long time or a short time, depending on one's industry and timing.

We emphasized the importance of building the minimum viable product in such a way that it contains no additional features beyond what is required by early adopters. Following that strategy successfully will unlock an engine of growth that can reach that target audience. However, making the transition to mainstream customers will require tremendous additional work.

Once we have a product that is growing among early adopters, we could in theory stop work in product development entirely. The product would continue to grow until it reached the limits of that early market. Then growth would level off or even stop completely. The challenge comes from the fact that this slowdown might take months or even years to take place. Some unfortunate companies wind up following this strategy inadvertently. Because they are using vanity metrics and traditional accounting, they think they are making progress when they see their numbers growing.

They falsely believe they are making their product better when in fact they are having no impact on customer behavior. The growth is all coming from an engine of growth that is working—running efficiently to bring in new customers—not from improvements driven by product development. Thus, when the growth suddenly slows, it provokes a crisis.

This is the same problem as established company experience. Their past successes were built on a finely tuned engine of growth. If that engine runs its course and growth slows or stops, there can be a crisis if the company does not have new startups incubating within its ranks that can provide new sources of growth. Companies of any size can suffer from this perpetual affection. They need to manage a portfolio of activities, simultaneously tuning their engine of growth and developing new sources of growth for when that engine inevitably runs its course.

Startup Product Market Fit (PMF) Cycle

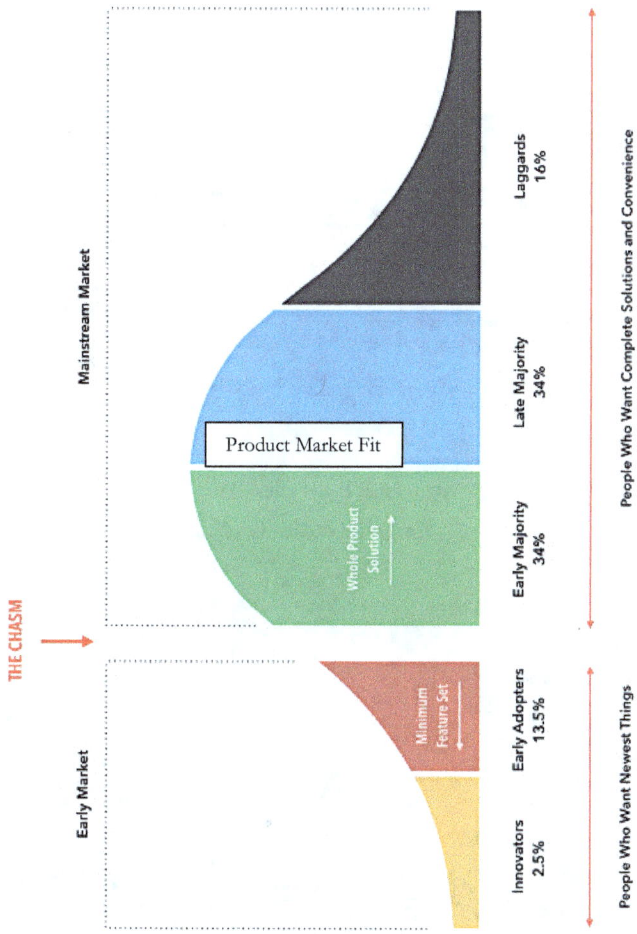

This why experienced founders do everything in their control to discover strong PMF, think of Uber; from the beginning, they had a clear PMF reaching revenues of $11M in first year, which allowed them to fundraise a ton of money. Along the way, they triggered all kinds of issues. Despite all that, the company has fundraised about $20B at a valuation of about $70B. That's the power of a strong PMF. On the other hand, you may run your business really well, with HR policies in place, a great sales model and team, a well-designed marketing plan, a top-tier team, and VCs onboard, and still shut down the company due to never finding PMF.

Consumer vs Enterprise Buying Cycle

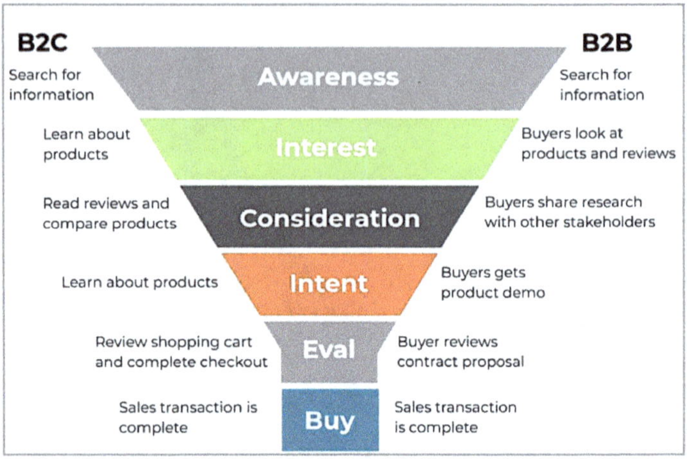

Inside sales team as customer success is the emerging trend replacing the traditional fields sales agent.

Enterprise Sales Cycle

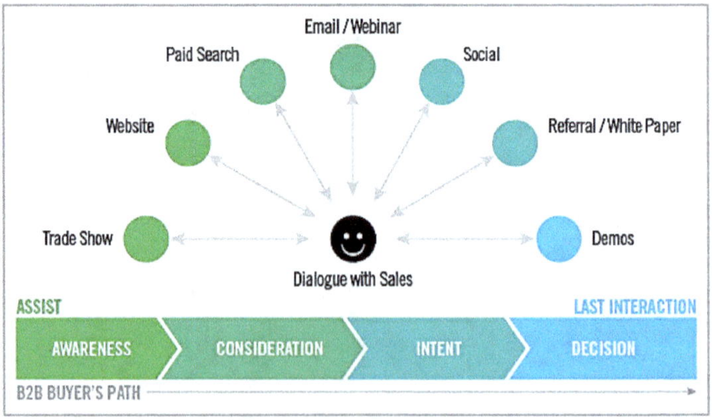

Generally speaking, B2B sales have a much higher average order value, which is one of the biggest attractions. Prospects often need to review product information and talk to several people before committing to a purchase.

The average sales closing cycle is 1 to 3 months for a first purchase, 6 months for multi-year deals, and 12 months plus for strategic deals. The fewer decision makers involved the faster the deal close.

After you Launch Don't:

It is important to differentiate between product/market fit and problem/solution fit when measuring a company's customer base. More specifically, when gauging a customer's desire, companies need to be sure they are measuring desire for the product or service—not just for a solution. Misinterpreting customers' desire for a solution as the desire for a company's product or service will end up being a false positive for product/market fit.

Product/market fit is not binary. For a fledgling startup, a *minimum* degree of product/market fit will not be adequate in order to achieve market traction and success. Rather, what is required is a high degree of product/market fit, or *extreme* product/market fit.

We routinely green-light new projects more on the basis of intuition than facts. As we've seen throughout this book, that is not the root cause of the problem. All innovation begins with a vision.

It's what happens next that is critical. As we've seen, too many innovation teams engage in success theater, selectively finding data that support their vision rather than exposing the elements of the vision to true experiments, or, even worse, staying in stealth mode to create a data-free zone for unlimited "experimentation" that is devoid of customer feedback or external accountability of any kind.

Anytime a team attempts to demonstrate cause and effect by placing highlights on a graph of gross metrics, it is engaging in pseudoscience. How do we know that the proposed cause and effect are true? Anytime a team attempts to justify its failures by resorting to learning as an excuse, it is engaged in pseudoscience as well.

If learning has taken place in one iteration cycle, let us demonstrate it by turning it into validated learning in the next cycle. Only by building a model of customer behavior and then showing our ability to use our product or service to change it over time can we establish real facts about the validity of our vision.

Can any of us imagine a modern knowledge-work manager with the same level of interest in the methods his or her employees use?

How much of our current innovation work is guided by catchphrases that lack a scientific foundation? With scientific learning as our yardstick, we can discover and eliminate the sources of waste that are plaguing entrepreneurship.

A comprehensive theory of entrepreneurship should address all the functions of an early-stage venture: vision and concept, product development, marketing, and sales, scaling up, partnerships and distribution, and structure and organizational design. It has to provide a method for measuring progress in the context of extreme uncertainty.

It can give entrepreneurs clear guidance on how to make the many trade-of decisions they face: whether and when to invest in the process; formulating, planning, and creating infrastructure; when to go it alone and when to partner; when to respond to feedback and when to stick with vision; and how and when to invest in scaling the business. Most of all, it must allow entrepreneurs to make testable predictions.

For example, consider the recommendation that you build cross-functional teams and hold them accountable to what we call learning milestones instead of organizing your company into strict functional departments (marketing, sales, information technology, human resources, etc.) that hold people accountable for performing well in their specialized areas.

The important feedback loop in an automobile is between the driver and the steering wheel. This feedback is so immediate and automatic that we often don't think about it, but it is steering that differentiates driving from most other forms of transportation. If you have a daily commute, you probably know the route so well that your hands seem to steer you there on their own accord. We can practically drive the route in our sleep. Yet if I asked you to close your eyes and write down exactly how to get to your office—not the street directions but every action you need to take, every push of hand on wheel and foot on pedals—you'd find it impossible.

The choreography of driving is incredibly complex when one slows down to think about it.

By contrast, a rocket ship requires just this kind of in-advance calibration. It must be launched with the most precise instructions on what to do: every thrust, every firing of a booster, and every change in direction. The tiniest error at the point of launch could yield catastrophic results thousands of miles later.

Unfortunately, too many startup business plans look more like they are planning to launch a rocket ship than drive a car. They are set up in such a way that even tiny errors in assumptions can lead to catastrophic outcomes.

A failed Startup among many forecasted significant customer adoption—in the millions—for one of its new products. Powered by a splashy launch, the company successfully executed its plan. Unfortunately, customers did not rock to the product in great numbers.

Even worse, the company had invested in massive infrastructure, hiring, and support to handle the influx of customers it expected. When the customers failed to materialize, the company had committed itself so completely that it could not adapt in time.

Building your Team: Hire Board Advisors (Strategy) with the goal to convert them to full-time co-founders if they deliver and commit to investing one year to cover their salary, for execution leads start with a developer and marketer, each must come from the target industry and can work in parallel without creating a conflict of interest, then convert gradually to paid P/T and F/T as you get funded.

Equity grants and co-founder's conversion must be tied to tangible quarterly deliverables and the option to terminate by founder "so you don't get stuck with fake cofounders", ideal equity per co-founder is 5% per 4 years vested yearly, plus own investments equity which must be restricted at all time.

A team must come from the target industry and add instant credibility.

After launching, you may face scalability issues. The number of users might grow faster than you can accommodate. If so, you might have to switch your technical team to a round-the-clock schedule just to keep up.

Of course, hiring experienced experts for core development tasks will give you a solid foundation for expansion and growth but this happens later on.

Instead, focus on hiring people who firmly believe in your vision and are committed to your short-term goals and culture. The team that can jump on the fast-moving train, take ownership of multi-hats initiates, and delivers with excellence and near total independence with zero analysis paralysis.

As the leader of the company, you need a very demanding eye for the product and aim to look at it as the end-user would. So, if something doesn't go according to plan, you should be the first to notice it. That way, you can fix any issue long before it becomes a problem for your customers.

You may think giving your team space to work, to be nimble and flexible, and solve big problems organically, is a great thing, but it's not early on. I left my team to their own devices for two solid weeks.

It was as much a test for them as it was for me. I wanted to know how effective they would be when left alone and whether *I* could even be hands-off for that period.

It wasn't worth it. Teams and team members need consistent check-ins, time frames, goals, and an understanding of your expectations. A light touch is sufficient, but don't leave them alone and expect miracles.

Bring smarter people to help: Protecting your equity is a fool's errand for a first-time founder or co-founder. Be open to opportunities as they come your way and understand that it's impossible to do it all on your own.

Be willing to build success *with* other people. Make sure that you bring the team from a larger market with fluent language within that market and a proven network, for example:

- North America: US (SF/SV, LA, NY) is ideal
- Europe: Germany, France, and Spain are ideal
- Asia: Japan, South Korea, and Singapore are ideal
- Africa: Algeria, Egypt, and South Africa are ideal
- Middle East: UAE, Israel, and Turkey are ideal
- South America: Argentina, Brazil, and Chile are ideal

When businesses succeed and everyone gets a nice slice of an exit, you'll be proud that you built something together and more likely to assist each other again in future ventures. Here are some thoughts regarding finding and setting up a great co-founder relationship.

- Know your strengths and weaknesses. I've tried starting a company with a close friend of mine that is far too similar in talent, knowledge, and demeanor. We figured out fast that founding a company together would be challenging and our friendship meant more than any potential business success. Be self-aware enough to know what value you add to the relationship and make sure any goal setting and measurement is based upon these strengths and the actual role you're playing in the partnership.

- Take your time. Talk at length before diving into a working relationship. Luckily when ending a contract with your prototype developer and design team will allow you to add a technical lead. You worked on the beta product together for six months and then started discussing whether coming on as the technical co-founder made sense.
- Formalize the co-founder agreement with goals, timelines, and clear roles but acknowledge that these will remain fluid as the relationship and business change over time.

The positive mindset with strong drive and talent: You must understand that the technical person needs you as much as you need them. But *what* do they need from you?

How do you start a tech startup without a tech skill set? Inspiration. You're the ideas founder; the person with all the answers because you can't sleep most nights due to your constantly racing mind on how to solve the next puzzle piece in your elaborate plan.

A person that can do that is not only invaluable but irreplaceable. It rubs off on people. You will create excitement with the people you talk to and interview and they will become incredibly loyal because they believe in you and your vision.

I honestly feel that a lot of people struggle to find a technical co-founder because they're not driven. They think they can put some initial thought into an idea, pass it to a tech guy, and poof, they have a product. Very few people can solve problems and think like a true visionary.

Your technical co-founder needs your ideas and thought process as much as you need them to help execute it. When you realize that and can portray that attitude, it will be a lot easier to find the right one. Creative ideas, contagious excitement, hustle, and vision are the "assets" a non-technical co-founder brings to the table.

Reading: "The average CEO is said to read 60+ books a year and makes 319x the income of the average worker who reads 1 book a year but finds the time to watch 700 YouTube videos a year."

Just as a programmer research new SDKs or a graphic designer watches tutorial, an entrepreneur reads business books, especially the stories of other entrepreneurs.

Writing: Ideas begin in your mind but will end there unless they are written down. Keep a business idea journal. Jot every idea down in a notebook app on your phone using Evernote or OneNote. You never know when the idea will resurface later in life. In today's digital age, writing is the number one way to build a community online.

An entrepreneur needs to bring to the table an audience, or the ability to grow an audience. This is something the technical person probably will not have or enjoy doing. Building an audience requires excellent communication skills and an entrepreneur who writes will have it. "If you are awake, and you're an entrepreneur, you should be writing. It's the single biggest skill I think you could develop into impactful innovation."

Networking: The strength of an entrepreneur is reflected in the strength of his/her network. While technical people can build or design on their own, an entrepreneur needs to find the right people. Often, an entrepreneur is the one that knits a project together; he finds the "right people to put in the right seat on the right bus."

As a non-technical founder, you may believe that it would be so much easier if you were able to build the product yourself. But there are plenty of non-technical entrepreneurs-now-billionaires who did not lift a finger to build.

Reid Hoffman, the co-founder of LinkedIn, studied philosophy but jumped into entrepreneurship to best influence the world. His net worth is estimated to be over $5 billion.

Richard Branson, serial entrepreneur, and founder of the Virgin brand had dyslexia and performed poorly academically. His first business venture was the high school music magazine *Student* which experienced overnight success. Branson lives on his island and is valued at over $5 billion.

Jack Ma grew up in China where, after college, he applied for and was rejected from 30 jobs including a Berger king, before becoming an English teacher. Then, after he was introduced to the internet on a trip to the United States in 1995, he went on to found Chinese e-commerce behemoth Alibaba with no technical or business skills, he says. Ma is worth $35 billion.

Xavier Nicolas: an autodidact serial entrepreneur on the internet, who launched at 19 and sold several of his startups to become the 12th largest fortune in France. He was named the most influential French tech entrepreneur in the world by Vanity Fair.

Whether you have a background in philosophy or media, it does not require a technical or academically prestigious background to be successful as an entrepreneur. Branson and Hoffman will be the first to tell you that people are the key to capitalizing on any opportunity.

Leverage your network: A good way to qualify an advisor, mentor, business associate, or even a friend is to ask for an introduction to someone in their network. If they successfully connect you, it's worth investing in the relationship. There are too many talking head and name-droppers in the world.

On the flip side, don't forget and be open to connecting people to your network! Do this without being asked and you'll be rewarded in the future.

Self-Motivate and drive your resourcefulness: The pit of sorrow most entrepreneurs will find themselves in can come at a cost. Disappointment, stress, sleepless nights, bad eating habits, the torment can seem to never end.

Elon Musk even compared entrepreneurship to "eating glass and walking on hot coals at the same time". This is the mental model I go through when I'm sitting in that pit:

- What specifically is still in my control?
- What would this look like if it was easy?
- What can I remove to reach the goal?

If you can't find a way forward after working through those three questions, then you're not being creative or resourceful enough.

"The more I feel backed into a corner, the more rewarding it is when I get myself out of it." - Steven Spielberg

Build credibility by asking: Come prepared with your #1 and #2 ask anyone you're pitching. It doesn't have to be for money.

Good businessmen and women know you asked them for a meeting to get something and great ones will simply cut to the chase and ask you at some point in the conversation (most likely before they waste time in a meeting).

Tell them straight up. Don't laugh if they laugh. Simply ask in the least number of words and wait. Be silent. Keep waiting. You don't need to fill the void with more talk.

Control your workday: Put away the screens by 8 p.m. If you didn't finish your work for that day, push it to tomorrow. If you're still on your phone, computer, or television that late, it's probably just bad entertainment. Put it away.

Find something not related to business, technology, startups, politics, etc.... to occupy your mind for at least an hour before going to bed. I've spent countless sleepless nights lying in bed worrying, strategizing, calculating, etc.... and it's going to take a toll.

Time off (Off the grid): Pause. Breathe. Relax. Save for immediate health or legal trouble, think through, or even forget altogether.

Realistic Timeline Projection: For your first year, triple your timeline projections. If your developer says 2 months, plan for 6. If your revenue forecasts say 6 months, anticipate 18. If you need 3 months to raise a round of funding, you actually need 9. You'll keep your sanity, impress customers & investors, and start at a manageable pace from which you can improve.

Corporate Team vs Startup Org Chart

CORPORATE

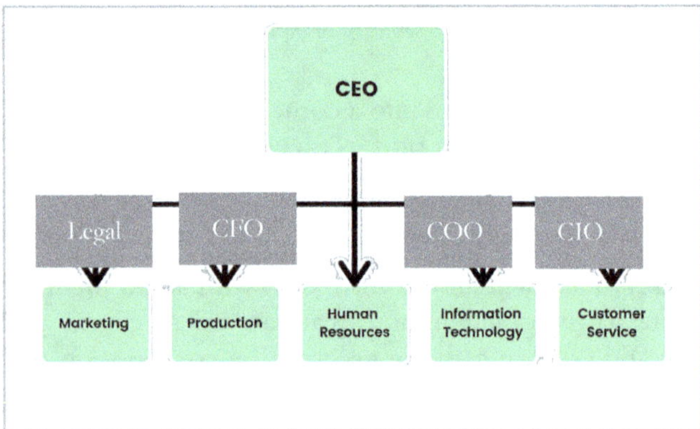

STARTUP

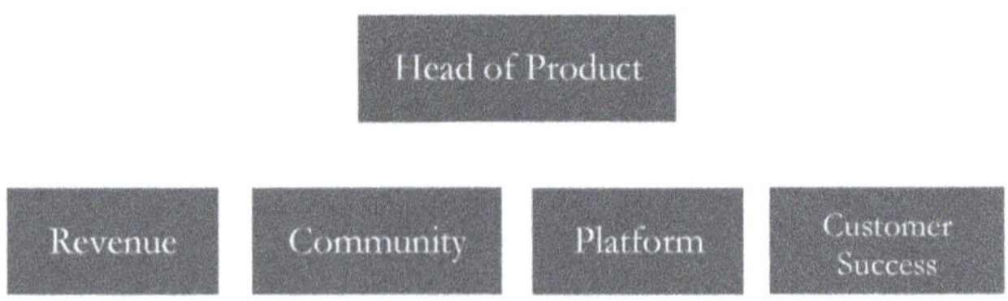

Note: The above startup roles, are the absolute minimum for the early stage, which are usually bundled under one hat "the founder", then gradually delegate to co-founders and new hires as you grow. Assign C suite as you grow based on performance, not seniority or equity ownership.

Takeaways: Be Laser Focus on Execution and crack out the 3 most important things on your to-do list as soon as possible in your day. You can then call it a productive day and consider anything over and above those 3 tasks as a distraction.

This requires you to be excruciatingly honest with yourself regarding what tasks help you reach your goals. You'll be surprised just how much time you're wasting on non-value work.

Execute what you say you will, but don't expect other people will until they've proved it. Establish yourself in other people's minds as someone that always does what he or she says they'll do. If the business fails, people will at least see you as someone who can execute and get it done.

Many entrepreneurs are attempting to build the next Google, yet when they try to apply the lessons of Google and other famous startup success stories, they quickly get confused. Is the lesson of Facebook that startups should not charge customers money in the early days?

Or is it that startups should never spend money on marketing? These questions cannot be answered in the abstract; Instead, startups need to conduct experiments that help determine what techniques will work in their unique circumstances.

For startups, the role of strategy is to help figure out the right questions to ask. Every business plan begins with a set of assumptions.

Large numbers of people already wanted access to the Internet. They knew what it was, and they could afford it, but they could not get access to it because the time it took to load images was too long.

When progressive image loading was introduced, it allowed people to get onto the World Wide Web and tell their friends about it. Thus, company X won market Y.

Similarly, there is already a large number of potential customers who want access to our products right now. They know they want it, they can afford it, but they cannot access it because the rendering is too slow.

When we debut our product with progressive rendering technology, they will flock to our software and tell their friends, and we will win market Y.

There are several things to notice in this revised statement. First, it's important to identify the facts clearly. Is it really true that progressive image loading caused the adoption of the World Wide Web, or was this just one factor among many?

More importantly, is it really true that there are large numbers of potential customers out there who want our solution right now? The earlier analogy was designed to convince stakeholders that a reasonable first step is to build the new startup's technology and see if customers will use it.

The restated approach should make clear that what is needed is to do some empirical testing first: let's make sure that there really are hungry customers out there eager to embrace our new technology.

Analogs and Antilogs:

There is nothing intrinsically wrong with basing strategy on comparisons to other companies and industries. In fact, that approach can help you discover assumptions that are not really leaps of faith.

Will explains the analog-antilog concept by using the iPod as an example. "If you were looking for analogs, you would have to look at the Walkman,". "It solved a critical question that Steve Jobs never had to ask himself: Will people listen to music in a public place using earphones?

We think of that as a nonsense question today, but it is fundamental. When Sony asked the question, they did not have the answer. Steve Jobs had [the answer] in the analog [version] Sony's Walkman was the analog. Jobs then had to face the fact that although people were willing to download music, they were not willing to pay for it. "Napster was an antilog".

That antilog had to lead him to address his business in a particular way. Out of these analogs and antilogs come a series of unique, unanswered questions. Those are leaps of faith that I, as an entrepreneur, am taking if I go through with this business venture.

They are going to make or break my business. In the iPod business, one of those leaps of faith was that people would pay for music. Of course, that leap of faith turned out to be correct.

Beyond "The Right Place at the Right Time"

There are many famous entrepreneurs who made millions because they seemed to be in the right place at the right time. However, for every successful entrepreneur who was in the right place at the right time, there are many more who were there, too, in that right place at the right time but still managed to fail.

Henry Ford was joined by nearly five hundred other entrepreneurs in the early twentieth century.

Plan to Fail: Have a detailed plan that captures the worst-case scenarios, on how to capture as much as possible of your invested principal, along with saving the face. Among viable options are selling your CRM accounts to your peers, partners, suppliers, or even a new startup just launched within your space and act as paid advisor while you find new jobs or even get hired by them. Make sure a PR exit is well-written and vetted by your legal team.

Why Startup Fails? So badly everywhere we look? The first problem is the allure of a good plan, a solid strategy, and thorough market research. In earlier eras, these things were indicators of likely success.

The overwhelming temptation is to apply them to startups too, but this doesn't work, because startups operate with too much uncertainty. Startups do not yet know who their customer is or what their product should be.

As the world becomes more uncertain, it gets harder and harder to predict the future. The old management methods are not up to the task. Planning and forecasting are only accurate when based on a long, stable operating history and a relatively static environment, Startups have neither.

The second problem is that after seeing traditional management fail to solve this problem, some entrepreneurs and investors have thrown up their hands and adopted the "Just Do It" school of startups.

This school believes that if management is the problem, chaos is the answer. Unfortunately, as I can attest firsthand, this doesn't work either.

It may seem counterintuitive to think that something as disruptive, innovative, and chaotic as a startup can be managed or, to be accurate, must be managed. Most people think of process and management as boring and dull, whereas startups are dynamic and exciting.

But what is actually exciting is to see startups succeed and change the world. The passion, energy, and vision that people bring to these new ventures are resources too precious to waste. We can and must do better.

Business Cycle and Tools Automation: Because small companies and startups don't have a huge budget and labor force to throw around, you should automate everything that can be automated. Instead of hiring a huge team of professionals to get each seemingly insignificant task done, you need to look for software solutions that can do all the heavy lifting for you and not break the bank. Along with making sure everything is a top-tier cloud "i.e., AWS, Microsoft, Google or IBM", secure and scalable.

Accelerator/Angel Investors: You do not need to join one, if you are driven, motivated, and well networked in your market, and getting $100k at 10% of your companies for a high valuation creates more constraints than benefits later on.

Venture Capital: avoid an early stage until you reach Series A, otherwise terms will be detrimental to your success.

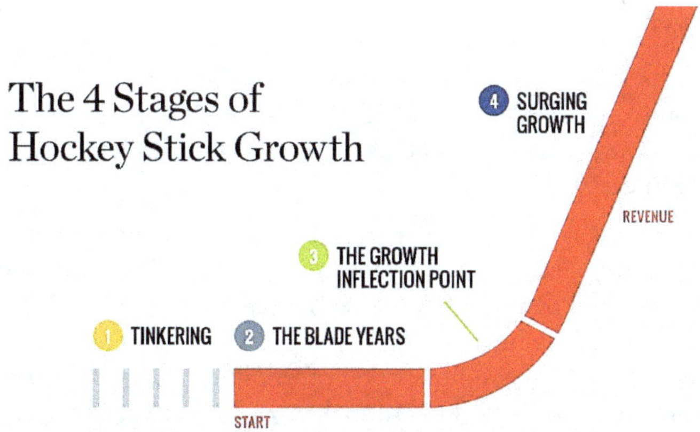

Best Options: use your corporate partners or customers for the seed round as the first round "$500k to $3m", supplemented with equity crowdfunding as series A, and only reach Venture Capital once you reached market fit with solid board members which gives you a huge leverage for fat series B or C round. This shall include Corporate V.C

Remember Startup Success relies on five pillars that require equal attention at all times: Product, Customer, Team, Profit, and Investors. As you grow, add Legal Liabilities and Risks.

CHAPTER IX
HOW TO FUND

Venture Capital Landscape: In the early days, entrepreneurs approached individuals, families, and privately owned companies with an interest in science and technology as the sole source of funding. Nowadays they turned to venture capitalists for early-stage investments.

In the early days, many venture capital firms were clustered around Stanford on sand hills road, where they had quick access to faculty members and students with ideas to commercialize.

Traditionally (V.C's), are perceived publicly as king makers, given their large funds' size which ranges from 100's to double-digit billions of dollars as a capacity to invest, masking the real role which is nothing more than an intermediary between the actual investors called limited partners who provide capital, and the deal makers or broker called venture capitalist. Additionally, most of the funds listed publicly are not actually available but rather on-call (fractionally wired on each approved investment that meets the limited partner criteria), which allows V.C. to earn 2% on fund managed plus 20% on positive exit after all fees are paid.

Given the generational demographic shift and global competition for innovators, new venture capital emerged located across the US and the globe, backed by wealthy families and global corporations that are both competing and taking large chunks of deals from Silicon Valley.

There are three types of venture capital, the globally prominent such as Sequoia, A16z, and so on with multibillion funds, the B type with 100+ million funds, and the micro with $1m to $50m+, almost all require intro by a third party and focus on potential unicorn investments "meaning new tech that open new market with high probability of monopoly" and unless you have strong growth don't waste your time on this channel. The second type is Corporate VC, backed by

Global Fortune 500 companies, among which are Softbank, Google Ventures, and so on. Their focus is on transformational innovation within their industry that can open new revenue streams, they are usually more flexible and can fund startups at better terms. The third is Family Office which invests on behalf of prominent name Tech founders, such as Iconiq Capital where they usually prefer to fund startups at series B and later.

Pre-Seed Funding: quantify your founder's sweat equity, which is unpaid labor and time, plus any monetary contribution, transferred to the company during your pre-launch. Sweat equity is rewarded in the form of sweat equity shares. These are shares given out by a company in exchange for labor and time rather than a monetary amount. Budget by converting weekly time used for startup effort as 2hr x 5 days = 10hr + 5 on weekend = 15 weekly hours x $200 "advisor rate", and repeat for "total number of co-founders" and budget this as $3000 x 4 weeks = $12k or $150k year + cloud & legal cost

Bootstrapping: One of the most common ways to get a business up and running is through "bootstrapping." Basically, you use your own funds to run your business. This money may come from personal savings, low or no interest credit cards, or lines of credit on your home. Knowing this will help you figure out the interest rate you will get on loans, which can give you access to affordable credit. The downside? If your business doesn't succeed, you may have a substantial amount of debt that you now need to manage.

Friends and Family: Borrowing money from friends and family is a classic way to start a business. While it may be harder to convince investors or banks of the quality of your idea, your family and friends often believe in your dream. They may be more willing to help fund your company. If you do go to friends and family for loans, it's a good idea to make sure that each of you gets sound legal advice, especially if you are taking the money as a loan. The downside? Borrowing money is a quick way to lose friends and sour family relationships. Be careful if you decide to proceed this way.

Angel Investor: An angel investor funds early-stage startup companies in exchange for equity ownership. Typically, angel investors contribute $25,000 to $100,000 to a company, but can go much higher. Raising funds through an angel investor always takes longer than you might expect — you need to find the right investor, prepare a pitch deck, negotiate investment terms, and more. Additionally, equity requirements may dissuade you from seeking angel funding:

"You could be giving away anywhere from 10 to more than 20 percent of your business,". On top of that, there's always the risk that your investors will decide that you are the business's greatest obstacle to success, and you could get fired from the company you created.

Incubator or Accelerator: Business accelerators and incubators have sprung up across the country, particularly near colleges with a strong business programs. These spaces are part communal workspace and part mentorship development centers. Young businesses can get a great start here while partnering with some amazing people.

Accelerator: supports growth-oriented startups through education, mentorship, and financing. Typically, accelerator programs are fixed-term, cohort-based programs that include investment opportunities, connections to high-value mentors, and educational programs, and culminate in a public pitch or demo day. While a handful of accelerators have been very successful in helping industry-leading startups — Airbnb, Stripe, Reddit, and Uber — achieve considerable traction, success isn't always guaranteed. The downside? They are often focused on tech-heavy businesses, so you might struggle to find one that works for your company.

Crowdfunding: If you have a sexy idea and you're great at social media, crowdfunding might be an option. When websites like Kickstarter and Indiegogo first started, there were several businesses that had great success pulling together funding through their reach. Crowdfunding is a method for raising capital through communities including customers or a collection of individual investors. Typically, crowdfunding campaigns are initiated through popular crowdfunding sites including Kickstarter, GoFundMe, Indiegogo, and others. Experts estimate that the crowdfunding industry will grow to over $300 billion by the year 2025. There are three types of crowdfunding including:

- Donation-Based Crowdfunding: There is no financial return to the investors or contributors. Typically, disaster relief efforts, charities, and nonprofits leverage the power of donation-based crowdfunding activities.
- Rewards-Based Crowdfunding: There is a "reward" in exchange for a financial contribution, typically in the form of a product or service. A rewards-based crowdfunding initiative is popular among early-stage startups eager to develop and market rapid prototypes.
- Equity-Based Crowdfunding: There is company ownership in exchange for a financial contribution. As equity owners, contributors receive a financial return on their investment and a share of the company's profits.

The downside? Lots of companies aim for crowdfunding, so you have to generate a lot of buzzes to make it through the overall signal noise. It's very possible to overextend yourself and frustrate backers, which can lead to a great deal of animosity before your company is even really off the ground.

Trade Equity or Services: Looking to get some web design done? See if you can barter with your neighbor who does some freelancing on the side. Perhaps you'll help with some marketing advice down the road. In virtually every city, there are communities of fledgling business who can work together. The downside? Trading services or equity can be an awful way to make a living, and so not everyone is willing to do it.

Small Business Loans: Small banks offer loans to small businesses, but historically are careful about giving money to small companies. It can be difficult to qualify. There are alternative lenders, however, who may be better equipped to help you. The downside? Some of those alternative lending companies are predatory. Make sure you know who you're borrowing from before you sign on the dotted line.

Small Business Grants: The Small Business Administration as well as other organizations sometimes offer grants to small businesses that are run by women, minorities, or veterans. If you fit into one of these categories, it's worth speaking to your local SBA chapter, or Chamber of Commerce, to see if there's local grant money that you may be able to apply for.

The downside? Check carefully to make sure you won't need to pay the money back or agree to certain conditions down the road. Not all grants have stipulations, but it's good to know what you're agreeing to before you accept the funds.

Startup Contests: Let's face it; unless you have an incredible idea and a strong business history, you're probably not going to make it onto Shark Tank. Many local COCs and SBAs have decided, however, to run local Shark Tank-style competitions. Since these are more locally focused, often requiring that a business operates in a particular area in order to enter, they may be less competitive.

They are also a great way to practice your pitch for other investors. Generally, you won't lose anything but time for trying. And even if you're not the number one choice, you may spread awareness of your business. The downside? You could invest a lot of time into your business plan and investor presentation, but not be chosen for one of the prizes.

Cash as Working Capital: this new emerging funding space allows startup with $50k+ monthly cash to borrow working capital each month and pay small fees without any equity or lengthy V.C negotiation, the most prominent leader is called Brex, among many others including some small bank and credit union, this is ideal for growth stage startup.

Keep Your Day Job: This is the suggestion no one likes: If you currently have a job that is meeting your expenses and letting you live a relatively comfortable lifestyle, don't be in such a hurry to quit your job and follow your business dreams. Spend some time getting the business off the ground and building through the early, difficult phases with the solidity of your 9-5 job paying your bills.

This lets you build your business with fewer compromises and lets you stay true to your vision without needing to give in to financial pressure. Ideally budget salary portion and revenue to gradually delegate tasks to outsourced partners, then gradually hire locally part time than full-time inc. you.

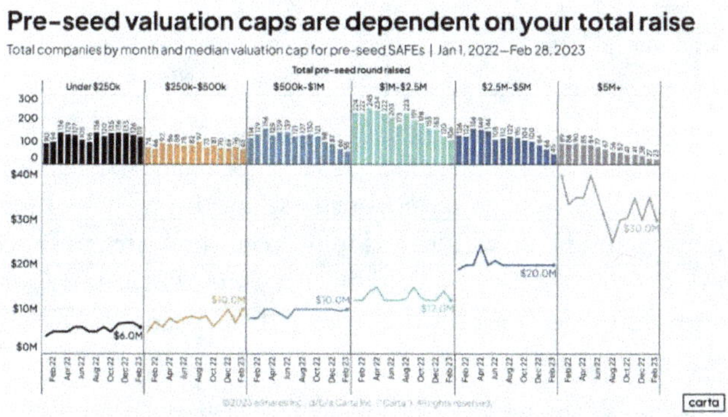

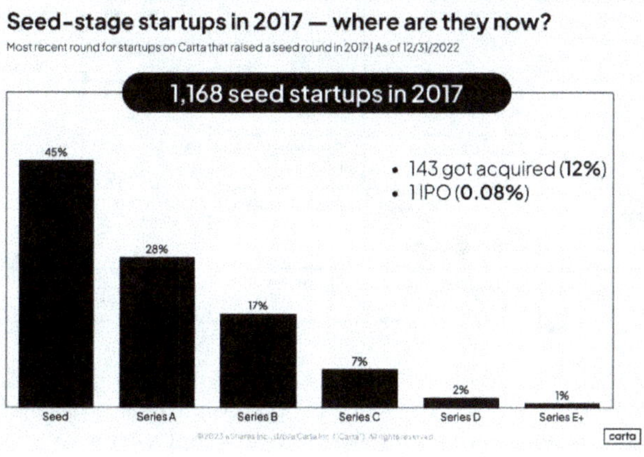

Startup Fundraising Roadmap: The best strategy is to skip angels and venture capital since they are not in the business of funding innovation, but mere speculators investing in potential unicorns which require extensive wasted time that you cannot afford. Focus on Product users as your main channel to grow and get funded "Top *VC will beg to fund you once you reach a market fit*"!

Matrix of Startup *Funding* Cycle by Stage "Optimal in Green"

Innovate	Funding	Build	Grow	Exit
Underserved Customers	Founder/ Cofounders	Landing Page	Network	IP License
Product Gap	Paying Customers	Web/Mobile	Group	Acquihire
Market Size	Advisors / Angel	Automated Support	Referrals	Acquired
Disruption	Corporate Partners	Scalable Back End	Channels Partners	Acquire or M&A
Chock Point Barrier	(Crowd/Financing /Customers)	Automated Transaction	Affiliates Network	SIPAC OTC/IPO

Since the Era of Ads-based business model with its built-in privacy liability is winding down, you shall structure your product or services to be paid by end users "customers" using the proven freemium model "free + paid premium" or "trial + scaled paid services".

Matrix of Startup *Investment* by Risk Level to Founder "High in Red"

Founders	Customers	Partners	Employee	Investors
Founder	Network	Suppliers	Employee	Venture Capital
Peers	Free Users	Services	Ex. Employees	Angel Investors
Friend	Users Upgrade	Strategic	New Employee	Corporate
Family	New Customers	Private Label	Contractor	(Crowd/Financing/ Customer)
Co-Founder	Referrals	Channels	Advisors	Public Listing

Founder shall avoid co-founders with equal vesting rights, new customers with high experience expectation, strategic partners that synch your resources during diligence, ex-employees with vested shares, along with venture capital preferred shares, liquidation right, double dipping exit premium, the option to add a new board or final say on exit, with corporate exclusivity and first right of refusal on exit.

Matrix of Startup *Acceleration* **by Optimal Exit to Founder** "High in Blue"

Product	Traction	Funding	Revenues	Scaling
Freelancers	PR Firms	Debt Financing	Channels	Private Label
Developers	Ads Agencies	Accelerators	OneTraction GTM	Distribution
Outsourcers	Marketer	OneTraction Incubator 5% for $250k Min. Note	eCommerce	Expansion
Cofounders	Growth Hackers	Customers / Partners	Sales Team	Acquisition
OneTraction Incubator Labs	Ads Campaign	Grant and Sponsors	Point of Sales	Acquired

As a Founder, you shall show that you are fully vested with the ability to execute prior to wasting any time on investors, this can be achieved by building a beta prototype or join OneTraction Incubator or any other labs that can match their offer, then add two co-founders to drive product and sales with 10% equity vested in 4 years against 1 year of their equal salary investment in the company.

Joining an accelerator purely for funding is not recommended, because only the fundable startup gets accepted in general "which cost you 10% of your company for $100k" at a high valuation that can prevent future investors from joining in, additionally plan to bootstrap during angel investors round, meaning no employee until you raise $1m "up to then, pay your team as a consultant based on completed deliverables like any other freelancer". Do not take any money from retail investors or less than $100k unless through a reputable crowdfunding platform.

Assessing your Fundability: It isn't hard to get an executive to talk at length about their own offering, their product, or their fund. We, as humans, love to talk about ourselves and we can expound endlessly on anything tied to our ego, such as a business we created, a product we are pitching, or what makes us remarkable.

It is much harder, though, to get an executive to really take a hard look in the mirror, to critically evaluate what he or she is selling, and to judge the actual value to an investor.

It usually requires you to get banged over the head with honest feedback from an investor, a friend, a spouse, or even the person you're chatting with on a flight before you actually internalize the criticism and do something about it.

But there are no second-place medals in capital raising and most of the time, there are no second chances either. So, take the time first to really analyze yourself and your firm instability.

1. Why does your firm exist and what is the compelling story behind it? 2. What is your unique ability, your #1 area of strength, and how does that relate to your firm's offering? 3. Based on what the competition is doing and what investors are wanting more of in your space, what are three obvious areas to focus on to differentiate yourself? 4. What is a positive quality that makes you completely different from the big competition? Customer Responsiveness? Business-minded? Pricing? Reliability? 5. What could you do as a startup which a large firm could never replicate due to its size and bureaucracy? 6. What are you passionate about? In what ways are you involved in your industry? What do you have fun doing which could naturally help produce new investor relationships from within your community or network?

7. Now that you have looked at the top 7-10 competitors in detail, what do their brands stand for vs. yours? What is the gap, the empty space, the high-end niche appeal that you could take to edge out the competition for the most prized turf? Is there a way to appeal to a top segment of their investors more than your competition by targeting this group and ignoring the rest?

"I would rather earn 1% off 100 people's efforts than 100% of my own efforts." - John D. Rockefeller

While completing your analysis, make sure and look deep into fee structures, levels of transparency, minimum investment requirements, conflicts of interest, and sharing profits with investors. Many investors are successful business professionals themselves and if you can come up with a proposal to these investors where they get far more transparency, risk less capital, or get early exit when the investment "wins," then you are more likely to win them over.

Everyone wants to feel like they got a good deal and if you are offering the same terms as your competition, or even worse than some, you are making the decision to decline very easy for your would-be investor. I hear too often from founders that they are leery of giving up too much equity or projecting too much performance upside, or too high a discount percentage to an investor. Be careful, but don't miss out. There are certainly investors that will try to gouge you, but if you're inflexible, then you won't have much room to negotiate the deal.

In capital raising, you are essentially making a sale, but you're starting typically with a massive disadvantage that others around you are already far better funded. So, they not only have more resources, but their track record is more validated and trusted, and they are seen as more promising in the marketplace.

You are asking them to be "first on the beach," meaning they may feel like they are taking a relatively big risk with the question of whether you will survive and make this into a real ongoing concern over time. This is exactly why you must use every strategy possible to increase your credibility, relevance, and effectiveness—so you are less likely to go out of business before raising the $5M, $25M, or $100M you need to make your operating startup viable.

Investor love funding a growing startup with a husky stick growth for their sales or user traction, but rarely fund startup to build their first products, or high salaries for the founding team, so don't budget your past corporate jobs in your startup pitch, this must be commensurate to your startup stage, i.e. Launch Stage CEO salary is $100-$120k, Series A – B, is $180k and C round with profit not loss can be around $250k a year.

Most investors prefer to join startup rounds that are already backed by the Sequoia Capital of the world, you spread your capital across treasuries, corporate bonds, large-cap stocks, etc. as suitable for the investor. After all, even if that hedge fund with $1 billion in assets under management (AUM) goes belly-up, you won't be the only one and no one can blame you for making the safe bet, right? *Why risk it*, your investor might be thinking. That is the logic you are up against, and you need to be prepared with a strong case for what makes your startup different, what the upside is, and why they should take a leap on a startup like yours that isn't off the ground.

In some cases, it is better to be open in your industry to partnerships, joint ventures, and channel distribution with others rather than treating everyone as competition. But there will inevitably be several counterparties that openly will dislike your positioning, question your credibility, or try to rain on your unique positioning parade.

There are a lot of really nice business leaders who enjoy a great reputation, and no one will say a bad word about them. But those typically aren't the same people dominating their industry. Listen to what is said by competitors of Goldman Sachs, Blackstone, Amazon, or similar peers.

Those negative stories in the news with anonymous sources are almost always a competitor looking to put a nice dent in the reputation of an industry leader. Would you rather be towering over your competition or get a Christmas card from all your rivals because you don't pose a threat to them at all?

Percent of Successful Fundraising by Stage (Venture Capital Association)

Startup Funding Cycle by Stage and Investors Type

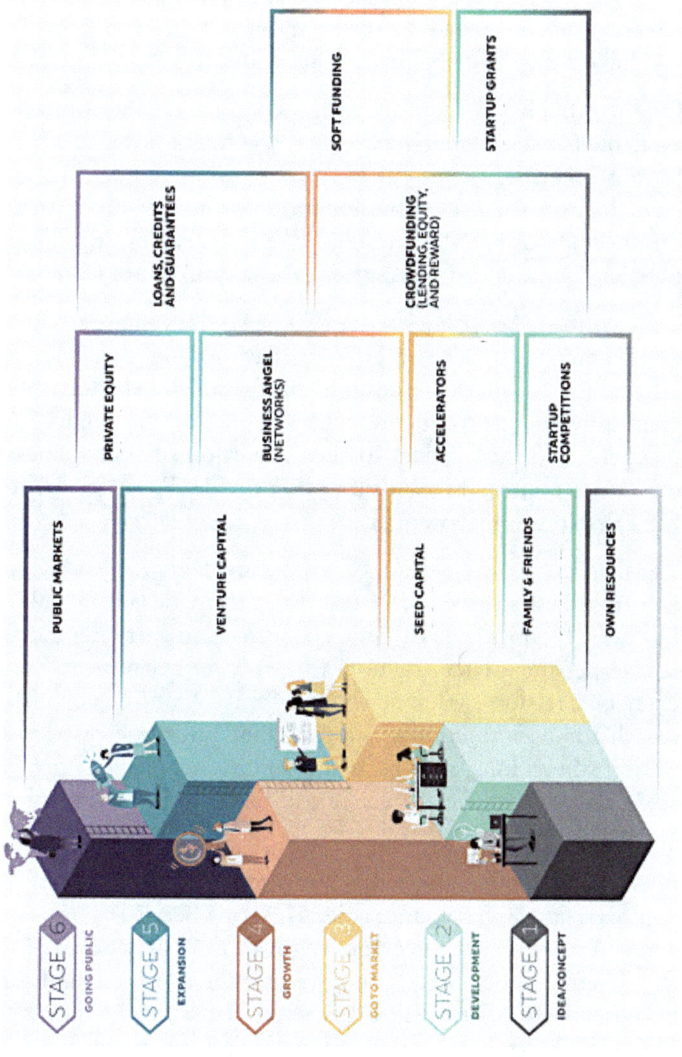

Fundraising Proven Method: One of the most frequent questions I get as a mentor to entrepreneurs is, "How do I find the money to start my business?" I always answer that there isn't any magic, and contrary to popular myth, nobody is waiting in the wings to throw money at you just because you have a new and exciting business idea.

On the other hand, there are many additional creative options available for starting a business that you might not find when buying a car, home, or other major consumer item. If you have the urge to be an entrepreneur, I encourage you to think seriously about each of these, before you zero in on one or two, and get totally discouraged if those don't work for you.

Of course, every alternative has advantages and disadvantages, so any given one may not be available or attractive to you. For example, professional investors put great priority on your previous experience in building a business, and they expect to own a portion of the business equity and control the funds they do provide. These are tough for a first-time entrepreneur.

Thus, it is always a question of what you qualify for, and what you are willing to give up, to turn your dream idea into a viable business. Despite the changing economic and entrepreneurial landscape, the advice for how to give your startup the best chance at raising capital stays consistent. Venture capitalists search for up-and-coming startups that offer one-of-a-kind value propositions, and have the strategy in place to grow, scale, and ultimately give a significant ROI to investors.

There has never been a better time to work on your startup's positioning if your long-term goal is to raise funds - whether you're raising a seed round, a Series A, or a Series B. A recent survey found that the average length of time between a seed round and a Series A is 22 months and the average length of time between a Series A and a Series B raise is 24 months. One thing's for sure: raising money is a long game. But by positioning your startup according to these tips, you're likely to find more success more quickly.

Pre-requisites: Prove That Your Company is "Disruptive" that big buzzword that can sometimes feel elusive and reserved for 'unicorns' like Airbnb or Uber. Simply, 'disruptive' refers to a company that is *innovative and groundbreaking*. In short, what are you doing that others cannot?

How are you changing your industry with your startup? this disruption is the key indicator of whether investors should invest.

Prove you are different with IP protection: "Focus your pitch and your value proposition on what everyone else is *not* doing,". How can you prove that your company will take over market share and cannibalize other companies in your industry?

"Investors want to make sure that they're investing in companies that are proprietary,".

Proprietary always wins. Go for legacy rather than money as you build your company. Focus your pitch on how you are different, rather than riding the cocktails of similar, successful companies. In this case, proving you're the black swan is an advantage - it's exactly what they're looking for.

Create A Wireframe Concept: Some tech companies have to wait to raise capital to actually build their product, which creates a chicken-and-egg scenario. What's far less expensive and important for a pitch is to create a wireframe concept for your app or technology, so you can actually show investors how it will work once it's developed.

It's second best to already have the tech developed but is non-negotiable if you don't. In addition to showing the wireframe, prove that you have the intellect and skill on your team to build what you're thinking of building.

This wireframe can also be functional - Shopify was created on the web application framework Ruby on Rails before it was built entirely, and actually enabled the founders to run the business for six years on their own before raising any money. Luckily, there are plenty of tech resources available to help you get started sooner rather than later.

Show You Can Bootstrap: One thing's for sure, investors don't like risk. They're great at disseminating which companies are more risk-averse than others, but the more you can help investors feel like it's a no-brainer to take a chance on you and your company the better. So, prove that you can bootstrap!

This proof may lean on past experiences that you or your founding team have had in previous companies, or on the work you've been able to do without cash so far. The more efficient you can be with funds; the more investors will view you as responsible.

Create a financial projection spreadsheet that shows how well you can bootstrap - which will likely depend on your connections and what you can do for free. For example, rather than allocating $20,000 to marketing in Q1, whom do you know in the publicity world? Who can you partner with for a sponsored Instagram post?

Michelle Phan, the founder of Ipsy, leveraged her eight million YouTube subscribers to get her business profitable ($150 million in revenue, to be specific) with a seed round alone before she went on to raise $100 million in a Series A. Bootstrapping is more than just financial savvy: it's proving the resources you have at your disposal to make your company work without flushing it with cash.

Every startup will have a different funding journey, but the more you can do on your own before you seek out investors, the better. Remember: investors want to jump on a rocket ship that already has enough fuel to break the earth's stratosphere.

They can get you to the moon and beyond with their investment, but you first have to prove you were heading there on your own.

Elevator Pitch Myth: the following are the top fallacy perpetuated by the Silicon Valley egocentric raiders:

- You must pitch and speak opulently to get funded.
- A perfect pitch guarantees access to V. C's funding
- You must be able to pitch fast like riding in an elevator.

What matters about pitching: focus on a uniform message using plain language by targeting users' referrals, customers acquisition, and early investors at once, using the following proven pitch:

1. Product (Performance): My name is ABC and founder of XYZ, our key innovation is a cup of coffee that keep any beverage hot at 120 degrees minimum for 3 hours.
2. Services (Pricing): Our innovation is Marketplace with a real-time engine that enables buyers to shop at the lowest prices, from the largest number of suppliers with the fastest shipping delivery; all with a guaranteed 90 days return policy.
3. Hybrid (Reliability): Our energy is supplied from 100% renewable sources, with an uptime guarantee 100% of the time with three-level backup capabilities.

Plan to Own Choke Points: **This** is a concept from Mastering the Rockefeller Habits. It is a strategic bottleneck or critical limited resource in your industry that if controlled would provide great leverage over your own ability to succeed and others as well. Think Uber, Google, Robinhood, Tesla, and Amazon.

Controlling a choke point should be something that makes progress and nets profits for you, while also providing opportunities to create another business within your business.

It's important to know what choke points you want to own within your own industry. Applying a choke point can be the turning point in your momentum at raising capital and getting deals. The example I like to use is of John D. Rockefeller. In his day, there were a lot of oil tycoons; just being an oil tycoon didn't differentiate him enough to become one of the wealthiest individuals on earth. No, one of Rockefeller's keys to becoming more than a tycoon, to becoming a legendary titan of industry, was identifying a choke point in his industry.

In short, Rockefeller found that the bottleneck was actually the oak barrels and being able to transport the oil. Rockefeller bought up oak barrel companies, bought up oak groves, and figured out how to dry the barrels.

By developing a more premium version of the oak barrels that delivered the oil, he was able to set the prices for his competitors and owned the choke point within his industry.

This led to him becoming the wealthiest person of his age and demonstrates just how powerful this strategy can be. Tech billionaire Peter Thiel claims in his book *Zero to One* that the whole goal in business is to monopolize a niche and be able to charge monopoly-like prices in it; this is exactly what Rockefeller did.

In fact, he was so successful at stomping out competition that several antitrust rules were developed as a direct result of Rockefeller's highly effective choke point strategies. The good news is that in small marketplaces, small geographies, and most areas of investment management, nobody is going to bring antitrust allegations against you for owning several choke points in your area until you reach a unicorn stage.

Get an A-Team: I have seen some startups raising capital succeed not because they spent money on placement agents and launched a massive fundraising campaign; rather they succeeded because they sought advice from a diverse and experienced group of industry professionals.

Building a board of advisors of 4-8 professionals with experience in running a similar industry startup with a successful exit, can make the difference between making it to the $1 million and $1 billion marks or staying off the radar of most investors forever.

Positioning: An example of the niche positioning approach is a client who for over a dozen years has been investing in your space and wants to showcase his expertise more so, by publishing a book on display and adding genuine value first before asking for a meeting or suggesting any actions be taken by an investor invite him/her to join as a board advisor.

He now will also have an oversized business card (his book) to hand out at every meeting he goes with you to which raises your startup credibility and separates you from the masses.

Strategic partners are "early adopters". There's nothing sweeter than finding a supplier, distributor, or especially a customer who stands to gain so much from your solution that they are willing and able to help foot the bill. This is a planning-for-success bonus play.

- The quality and reliability of your supply sources, whether for materials or software will be key to your success. Far better to create relationships and work out the kinks while your company is simple and small than to discover an issue when you're ready to scale.
- If your solution aligns with a B2B business problem that the market is clamoring to solve, there will be potential early adopters who could make a strategic investment if they think you have a chance at relieving their pain.
- Early adopters provide a unique and invaluable hands-on perspective of what's right and what needs to be changed to improve the value proposition of your solution to the markets you plan to serve. These companies will be less focused on final returns and more interested in getting your prototype to beta.
- Every startup has to sell its stuff. In-house sales teams are challenging to staff and a challenge to manage. Before you build a direct sales team into your business plan, explore other options online, manufacturers' reps, or companies in your industry that sell solutions that could be enhanced by yours.

7/70 Rule: at one-point Apple had a 7% market share yet 51% of the smartphone marketplace profits were generated for the year, and then grew to 13% market share and produced 81% of the profits in the industry. The point is not the exact percentage the point is to go after a valuable niche of the marketplace that plays off your DNA and passion and strengths so you can build up a defensive position within the most valuable subsegment of the marketplace possible.

Those who are passionate about their business offering will be relatively new to the capital raising process, or new to any offering in their industry and they try to skip the first. They try to rush through capital raising or their business model and they want to stand out so badly that they don't first move through immaturity to adolescence.

What happens, as a result, is that they are different in the marketplace, but in a bad or non-relevant way. They don't know the norms and best practices of the space and so don't know how to play off of the trends to be different in a way that not only stands out and is relevant, but in a way that really hits the investors between the eyes as the thing they have been looking for.

The point of bringing all of this up is that if you want to raise a lot of capital, you should build up a network of 4-7 peers who also are on this journey, share what you are working on, how you are getting it done, and hold each other accountable for progress.

Ideally, find someone who is a half-step ahead of you in the process so you can learn from what is working already for them and it will allow you to up your pace faster than just learning on your own.

There are around 3,000 billionaires and well over 60,000 cent millionaires globally, according to sources such as the *Financial Times* and *Bloomberg*. However, these numbers are under-reported due to lack of access to data as well as under-reporting by the families that have wealth spread across several family members or hold wealth in secret due to fear of media invasion of their personal lives, kidnapping/ransom, or being the target of potential government corruption or regulatory actions.

In other words, we do not know how many billionaires or centimillionaire families there are out there—we never will—but we do know that there are roughly 20 times as many cent-millionaires as there are billionaires.

Below is a chart showing recent figures of how many HNWI (High Net worth Individuals) there are and in what parts of the world these numbers are rising fastest, which, unsurprisingly, is Asia.

Mainstream media often talk about and sometimes vilify billionaires, Forbes magazine focuses primarily on the top 500. but most have never heard of centimillionaires as a term. In fact, this month, "billionaire" was searched for 49,500 times on Google, while "centimillionaire" was searched for just 320 times.

It is important to shine a light on this area so ideas can be cross-pollinated, evolved, and customized to this specific segment and its needs.

To show just how little this niche is talked about, there has never been a book written with the word "thousands-millionaire" in the title, most likely because it is thought of as too niche of a market to bother with.

As the number of billionaires grows, it is inevitable that more resources and statistics will emerge in this area and that more tools will be developed to help those with challenges and opportunities specific to this level.

My hope is to start that process, to provide dozens of tools that will genuinely be valuable and used by thousands of ultra-wealthy families globally.

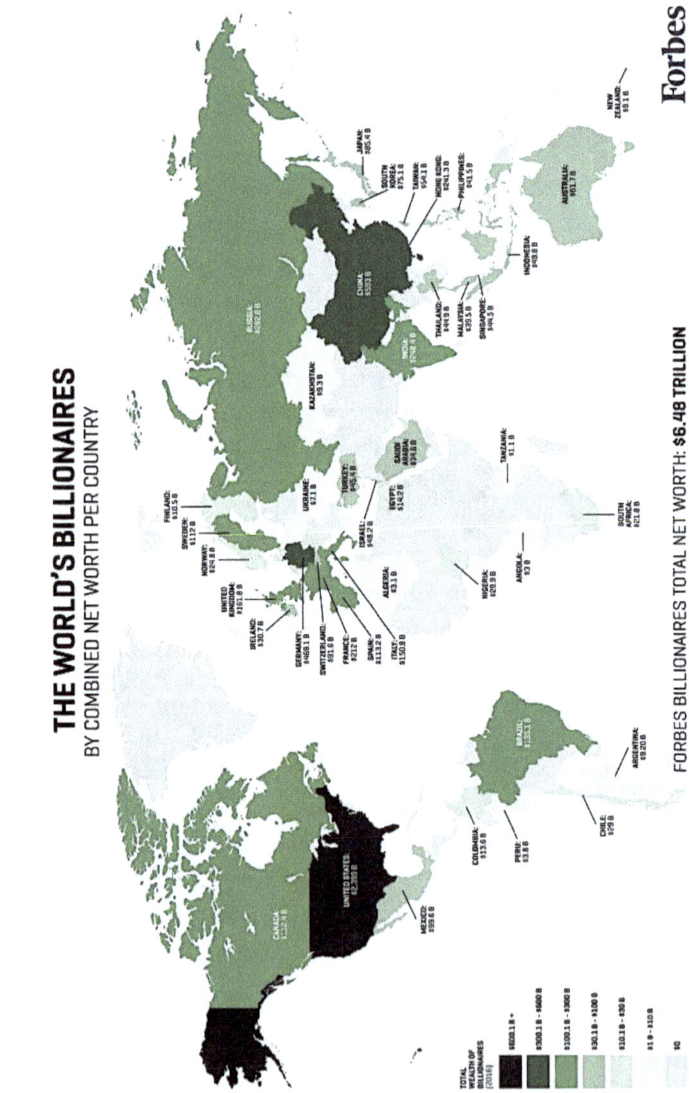
THE WORLD'S BILLIONAIRES
BY COMBINED NET WORTH PER COUNTRY
FORBES BILLIONAIRES TOTAL NET WORTH: $6.48 TRILLION

Investors Package: The following is a basic checklist of fundamental marketing:

1) Website: Formulating a comprehensive, yet well-designed website for your company will also give you a competitive edge. Depending on where you are based, your website may need to be password-protected. Those who want to be in front of the competition in this area would be wise to add video content, audio content, whitepapers, and articles that the team has written to show off your collective expertise and experience.

2) One-Pager or Tear-Sheet: This is the short, condensed overview of your startup at the 10,000-foot level. The purpose of this document is to grab the attention of your potential investor, draw them into your team and investment process, and make your plan clear in a minute or less. Literally, if it takes more than a minute to see what your strategy is and what your advantage is in the marketplace, you will lose the attention of many investors.

3) Pitch or "Deck": This is your standard PowerPoint presentation. Think long-term. Invest in creating a robust institutional-quality pitch the first time around and complete five drafts of it internally before showing it to a single investor. These typically run ten slides as a short version, backed with up to thirty slides for the diligence stage.

4) Master Due Diligence Questionnaire or DDQ: Most investors will require you to complete a due diligence form that is as short as five pages to as long as 50 pages or more, which will request details on your operations, investments, compensation structures, and team.

Most investors request similar types of information, so it is helpful to create a master document from which you can pull well-refined and compliance-approved answers. It is best if your answers cite sources and use graphs and charts that are accurate and refined to the point where they are concise yet robust enough to position your value offering in the marketplace.

The best strategy is to answer investor questions in as few words as possible while still being honest and forthcoming. The more words you add beyond what is required, the more opportunities you are giving an investor to decline your round based on some new information you are offering that wasn't even requested by the investor.

5) One-Pager FAQ and Answers: Investors often want you to participate in hour-long due diligence phone calls during which they will cover your pitch book or due diligence questionnaire. During these phone calls, some tough questions can come up which are unique to your plan, such as a key executive departing.

It is critical that you are able to answer these questions with some agility and precise figures, as well as a thought-through action plan of how you've learned from that experience and dealt with it to move forward. Investors always grow a little concerned when it takes more than a day to get a response to a yellow flag. Failure to anticipate an issue and then failing to communicate the explanation can turn a yellow flag into a red flag.

6) Newsletter: A rule of thumb in marketing is that every month you don't talk to a prospect, you lose 10% of your influence in that relationship. One way to keep your brand in front of potential and past investors is to send out a monthly or quarterly newsletter. This newsletter may cover your investment insights, the marketplace overall, or provide case studies of a few past investments you have made. These are most effective when they are just 1-3 pages long and when they are written with great care to add value to the receiver and not just simply pitch your offering.

Keeping your marketing materials updated is harder than it sounds, and it can create management and compliance headaches. To keep things straight, put one person in charge of keeping them fully updated and make sure there is an updated checklist that is referenced monthly to audit your own materials for performance figures, personnel change, or strategy adjustment updates.

Marketing Material: Here is a quick checklist of the required components of your marketing materials:

- Customize every piece of your marketing material to the exact investor that you have decided to focus on.
- Have a professionally designed logo and branded materials and do not use a pop-up $10 website that has a badge bragging about how cheap you were right on the website. Get a real website created—this is cheap in the scheme of things.
- Provide storytelling using pictures and videos and case studies and use persuasive writing best practices.
- Create a PowerPoint pitch book that is concise, yet captivating. Make each word and page count. One that is 20-80 pages long will usually not get read because everyone has lack of time.
- Ensure that the title at the top of each page grabs the reader, draws them in, and engages them on what is being presented with the large font as a point not articles.
- Make sure your complete contact details are included for easy follow-up in case the investor has an interest. This is basic but often left out.
- Include at least one video of your team, office, or the opportunity. This is the future of raising more capital in a busy world. People want to know what you are pitching and somehow see if they can trust you before meeting in person.
- Stress the importance and individual functions of your team, your experiences, and your pedigree. This should be the foundation upon which everything else is built.
- Include pictures of your entire team and your office. Pay to have these pictures taken by a professional photographer, this can be done for under $200. Ten years ago, you might have been excused for not having a professional headshot in your materials and on your website; today, it's almost unforgivable. No photos from a BBQ or cropped wedding photos; do it right once and have a professional photo for years.

Since many investors are being pitched constantly, it's important that you provide them with a clear picture of what you do and the benefits and risks of it. There was a study done that showed that 78% of institutional investors won't invest in something they do not understand.

If your investors don't understand your goals, how you get your returns, or how you manage risk, they are very unlikely to invest.

Having educational monthly newsletters and webinars in place that add knowledge to your industry is a great way to build a larger following. These newsletters and webinars could provide more information on how you handle the risks of your startup, and interviews with leading experts within your industry.

As more subscribers begin to follow the content you release, they will also share any insightful information you offer—which by word of mouth will get you more followers and more credibility. Twitter is best for this channel.

Key Goal Indicators (KGIs): The best tool for managing your executed goals is Key Goal Indicators. A KGI is a measure of a goal that needs to be completed, which must be compared to a Key Performance Indicator (KPI) as an action or activity which lets you know if work did get done, if that work is leading to results "add the percent of completion where 100% is success", and what the yield is on the time invested in that activity.

In capital raising, you will want to have different types of KGI/KPIs in a place assigned per team member, with some activity-based and some results-based. These will be the leading indicators as to whether you are raising capital effectively or at least on the right track to raise capital. Some potential capital raising KPIs could be:

1. Write One Article Per Week
2. Meet with 5 Investors Per Week in Person
3. Schedule and Complete 10 Conference Calls per Week
4. Speak at One Conference Per Month

5. Call 20 Investors Per Day
6. Meet with One Potential Connector or Networker Who Could Help in Raising More Capital Each Week

Each KPI must be measurable so you can say objectively if it was completed or not in the timeframe expected. Even if you are just managing yourself this can be helpful, with the goal being to set up realistic but challenging KPIs that will shape activities and make it more likely that capital will be raised.

Many times, there are unrealistic expectations about how quickly capital can be raised, so make sure if you have a business partner or others with these expectations that they are helping with the capital raising process, so they see how hard it is.

At the same time, you should share with them the KPIs and the results, so they know even if capital is not raised yet that you are taking consistent action every week and it isn't from lack of effort that the capital has yet to be raised.

Many co-founder partnerships fall apart because of pressure and expectations around capital-raising timelines. What KPIs for yourself and your team should you be setting up and tracking immediately?

Performance Dashboard: having a weekly dashboard. This dashboard includes the KPIs of team members, top goals, schedule, and the number one most important thing I must get done that day, week, and month. Supported with data on how our companies are performing financially—all on one page. It acts as a sort of cockpit as you pilot our business.

Systematically Raising Capital: One thing almost all investors have in common is that they want to work with credible professionals who are focused on their craft and take it seriously. Nobody will ever take you more seriously than you take yourself, and doing things sloppily, without care, and irregularly scares off investors very quickly.

In my experience, investors are looking for clues consciously or subconsciously that serve as evidence of a very long-term mindset or more of a short-term shortcut type bias. I have found there is one way of thinking that can help you raise more capital, improve your operations, and get access to more deal flow, and that is by creating operational systems and processes in your organization.

The whole idea here is to have one central document which lists out how processes will be managed and followed, where they will be stored and updated, and then to document your top five to ten operational processes.

These processes could be how you conduct due diligence on an investment, how you meet with investors and raise capital, how you hire someone new to your team, how you create new pieces of content to be reviewed and released, etc. In every business, some processes get repeated over and over again and there is a best way of completing them that should be documented and followed.

Almost nobody bothers to document their top ten processes that are critical to their operations and yet it costs nothing and can give you leverage, assurance of quality, and repeatability—things that everyone really does want.

This is another idea that is even more valuable because almost nobody does it; most people do not want to take one to two business days to get this in place.

Listening: If you go to the doctor and say that your leg hurts, the doctor will ask what part of your leg is hurting. If you say your knee hurts, he will ask what the pain feels like. He will ask about when it hurts and how long it has been hurting, etc.

In fact, he will spend most of the time simply asking you questions and narrowing down exactly what is bothering you. He is paid to listen to you and then typically spends just the last two minutes of the appointment prescribing the solution.

A similar approach needs to be taken when raising capital. When you sit down with an investor, you should spend the first 60-80% of the conversation asking questions, taking notes, and clarifying their background including past investment history and current challenges or problems.

You should confirm that you understand them completely before diving into your solution, which is the pitch you are trying. In addition to small talk and developing rapport with the investor, here are some additional questions to consider asking during meetings:

What are your last three investments or experiences in this area?

- Have you had positive experiences or challenges while investing in this space?
- How decisions to invest are made within your firm?
- What do you typically look for before investing capital?
- Where does your firm hope to be in 2-5 and 10 years in terms of your portfolio investment?
- Has the political or market (current event) affected your interest in X investment opportunities?
- What does your firm's due diligence process look like?
- What is typically the #1 roadblock in investing in something like our type of startup?

One trick that I have learned on asking great questions is to ask a question based on some detail you picked up in one of their responses. This way, your counterpart knows that you are listening, that you're interested in what they are saying, and that you can really dig into what you want to learn about most.

If you are passionate about what you are raising capital for, you believe in it and you could talk about it for a few hours to an investor. The problem is that the investor does not have a few hours—you have minutes or mere seconds to get their attention.

By asking questions first, you are accomplishing a few things at once. First, you are more likely to be "liked" by them and seen as someone on their side. Second, you are standing out from the crowd, appearing confident instead of looking like just another pushy salesperson.

Third, if you focus on just one investor type as I recommended, then over time you will really develop a clear picture of what the investor base overall is seeking through the "doctor approach." Fourth, you can boil down the 120 minutes of your longest pitch possible to the five minutes that truly matter.

Out of all the benefits of the investment that you are raising capital for, the investor will only care about one or two of them at most. If you got into a meeting or phone call pitching without asking questions, you will not know which two benefits those are or how to frame the application to their reality. Finally, this approach saves you time and allows you to efficiently meet with multiple investors in a day, rather than spending all your time working on a long pitch that won't resonate with every investor.

There are two more rules that I follow to ensure that I'm completely attuned to what my investors want. The first rule is that I simply repeat back to someone what they have said in a concise way in order to verify that I completely understand their point. The second strategy is to type up your notes from the meeting and create a "contact report" and email that documents it.

This is simply a concise summary of what was discussed and decided on at the meeting. Prospects appreciate being reminded of what was discussed, and once again it shows that you are taking a methodical and organized approach to meeting their needs.

Listening can really be a competitive advantage if you can use it to build the credibility and influence of a doctor, counterpunch with relevant proposals to investors you have listened to, and you will learn so much more from each interaction than you would by just spewing out pitches at every meeting you go to.

All of this becomes even more powerful when you consider that you are focused on just one type of investor avatar. Treating each prospect with respect and learning from each conversation will add up over time to becoming an absolute expert on what your targeted investor demographic wants and worries about every day.

The better you are at listening, the more influential you can be in raising your capital by leveraging the following:

- Commitment: It has been proven that we are all more influenced by those who show commitment and consistency.
- *Social Proof:* Scientific studies have also shown that when humans are unsure how to act or whom to trust, we look around to others for clues. We trust the decisions of the "herd" around us, so if a movie is liked by a lot of people or a book is a bestseller, it continues to do well in the marketplace as others have "endorsed" that commodity with their dollars spent.
- *Long-Term Cognitive Bias:* most people are naturally looking for shortcuts and fast ways of doing things, but credible professionals have focus, know their unique ability, and are focused on long-term success, the more you can show investors that you are serious about your venture, 100% both-feet-in committed to it, the better. It is better to own a choke point that makes you into an authority and re-invest heavily than take a quick payout in other words.
- *Scarcity:* It has been shown that those things in less volume are seen as more valuable. Gold is more valuable than aluminum and an alum of Harvard University is perceived as more valuable than someone who graduated from the thousands of public universities that are not nationally recognized. Everyone knows that this is true, but how do you use this to raise more capital? How can you be unique in your sandbox? How can you be the only investment or company that really gets your investor avatar and has every piece of your branding and messaging crafted just to reach them so that every message hits them right between their eyes? If you can combine a few benefits and positioning statements, you should be able to say, "We are the #1 __________ in the ______ market." It could be that you are #1 in any space, or you are #1 in a niche within

a niche in your industry but is important to either define what you are #1 at or decide on what you will work to become #1 at or you will always be laggard or average at best in the investor's eyes.

- *Addict Your Investors:* Virtually everyone becomes addicted to something at some point in their lives. Our brains are wired to reward positive experiences that benefit us while minimizing those things that create negative feelings. This reward center pathology is at the core of what creates patterns of use that are very reinforcing and can lead to positive or negative habits. This is because the brain can become conditioned to desire a certain behavior or substance to the point where the logical points of ceasing the activity are ignored. What does all of this have to do with Capital Raising? On top of the regular psychological benefits of making a good first impression, you should focus on over-delivering and making a powerful first impression in every way possible. You should do whatever is necessary to provide enormous value to the investor, listen to their needs, and connect in a real way during your first encounter.

Copywriting: Copywriting is the most undervalued and overlooked tool that a marketer or sales professional can develop. Many professionals value cold-calling skills, networking, branding, or public relations skills, but I think that copywriting skills are the most valuable. One quote that always comes to mind is: if you look at a one-dollar bill and a hundred-dollar bill, what's the difference? They're both green. They're both on the same-sized piece of paper. The difference is the message on the paper.

The words on the bills make one worth 100 times more than the other. If you translate that to the investment industry—what's the difference between your fund's marketing materials and the marketing materials of the leading startup unicorn in your space? The message on the paper.

Their message might be worth $100,000 every time they present it. Yours might be worth $1,000 every time you present it. Obviously, you cannot claim to have the highest pedigree team if you don't have it.

What you can do is write your fundraising marketing materials in the best light and ensure it is a clear and robust message. This can make a huge difference in your marketing plan. Some areas where you can embed improved copywriting include:

- Team bio
- Pitch deck
- Email subject lines
- Voicemails
- One-pager headline or description pieces
- Product Demo and Whitepaper

Negative Feedback: If you execute your investor funnel and after working on it for several months, you either get no feedback or get negative feedback, you will have to again analyze your market, get real feedback from real potential investors, and figure out where the gap was in your thinking and implementation.

You will also have to simply examine how broadly you are getting your thought leadership and resources seen and if you are following up enough with potential investors that you do attract.

Hiring Someone to Fundraise: you are looking to raise capital yourself, but it can be tempting to think if you just met that one person who could do this all for you or introduce a few investors that it may get the capital raised. While I am all for using connectors and well-networked people to distribute your content and keep you in mind for referrals of investors, you can't rely on someone else to get it done for you.

The most important reason why this is true is that they are not known in your sandbox by your investor avatar as being excellent in what they do. I have people who ask me all the time to introduce them to five to ten investors who could invest in what they do.

Technically I could, I would like to help, and I usually know relevant investors, but those investors don't know them—and the investors may not have a need right now. The power of building the investor funnel is that it gets potential investors to get to know you for your specific market and investment perspective.

That connection is critical and it's hard to establish that relationship and value exchange using an outsourced marketer. You need to use thought leadership and wave your flag of unique insight around so that people will come to you who are looking for your specific type of investment. Only you can wave your flag.

The Power of Follow-up: One statistic that always sticks in my mind is from a study that showed that 44% of all salespeople quit after one attempt, 24% quit after the second, 14% quit after the third, and 12% quit after the fourth call. This means that while 60% of all sales are made after the fourth call, over 94% of salespeople quit before the 5th call. Sure, some people stop following up because of very black-and-white "no's" or decline to learn more, but many times these days there is just so much noise in an investor's inbox or voicemail box that they don't know who is credible to meet with or more trust building is needed first.

So, learn to follow up on every communication, to drive further that relationship which may open unrelated channels such as new hire, customer, partner, and so on.

Use Fundraising Platform: The benefits stretch beyond strategy alignment. While letting retail investors and potential customers fund as low as $100 in the startup has potential financial benefits, additional support can be found in areas such as product development and promotion, and top crowdfunding platforms like Seed-Invest and Republic take a cut from your raised fund vs upfront fees.

"The beautiful thing is that if you do an equity crowdfunding campaign, you not only raise capital, but you also basically can market your product or service to hundreds of thousands of people and build an army of loyal brand followers,". "They will be your best customers and will spend more money." As you grow.

Target Investors and Relationship Building

Analyzing Potential Investors: Once you know whom you are competing against, you will have a better sense of the investors that you can conceivably target. The first thing to do is analyze target angel, V.C., and HNWI performance, team pedigree, and track record against their peers in the industry. This competitive analysis lets you focus more on ideal investors, and largely ignore all others.

I understood through my first phase of analysis, where I looked at the competition, that despite strong performance in some V.C. firms' funds, their track record was likely too mediocre for serious consideration from the top institutional investors. Part of that decision was informed by my competitive analysis, but another part came from my knowledge of the different investors in the industry and knowing what a credible lead was and what wasn't. That's why it's so important to do this analysis of your customers, too.

1. What potential investors are there to choose from for your specific investment type? 2. What is the most common investor for your offering? 3. What is the most profitable type of investor to serve that really would give you an audience? 4. Do you perceive any issues that most investors in your space complain about? 5. If you could get inside the minds of potential investors, what would be the ideal offering in your space? Investors love predictability and patterns. It's really the only thing they're looking for. They track it, measure it, and invest in it.

This is why a great way to establish an early pattern with potential and existing investors is with clear and consistent communication. The best way to do this is a monthly email that gives them a high-level summary of that month's wins, losses, revenue, customer pipeline, challenges, and next month's outlook. Some investors may ask for more info, most won't respond but simply read and stay abreast of your traction. Another piece of info to consider adding to that email each month is a 'Need's section. You may only value the capital infusion they provided, but your investors are worth MUCH more than that. Ask for strategic introductions, social shares of specific content, or even participation at meetings in which their insight, influence, or presence will be of value. They're not just there to write you a check.

The most used phrase in an investor's vocabulary is.

"Not now, but…"; …but keep me updated; …but contact me when you reach $1000,000/month in revenue.
…but get a lead investor and I'll jump in on this round.
…but when you're raising your Series A, give me a call.

This gives you permission to keep them on a list of investors you have established rapport with and can keep updated with a monthly or quarterly email.

Think of the long-term potential of this kind of list!

- 6 months down the road you find product market fit and they pull the investment trigger.
- 18 months down the road you're ready to raise a Series A round and all it takes is a few phone calls to the most enthusiastic on your list.
- 36 months down the road these guys are beating down your door to somehow get in before an IPO or acquisition.
- 5 years down the road you're raising a seed round for your next startup and without hesitation, the entire list takes your meeting, and they begin competing just to get in early.
- 10 years down the road you want to start your own venture fund or simply join one part-time. Each individual begs you to join their firm or throw money your way for your own fund.

Even if your company fails, you go further than most. You'll message these individuals, quickly explaining what you learned while building the team, product, and business model. These people are always looking to learn, so don't be embarrassed it was a failure. End your message with a note about planning to start something new in the near future and that you're hoping to stay in touch. This gives you 'permission' to pitch them again and again. By the time you look to retire, you'll look at this list and realize it's quite possibly one of the most valuable things you own.

Define Your Investor: Before you try to improve your capital-raising strategies, it's important to step back and consider what types of investors you are targeting. It is never a good idea to go after every type of investor because the returns or potential of an offer are so appealing.

Not every type of investor will agree with you, and you will want to maximize your time with those who are most likely to understand the investment and have a natural interest in it. This sounds obvious, but in practice, most people raising capital don't have a focus. They are going after several different types of investors at one time with an equal investment of energy and no customization of marketing materials for the group which is most likely to invest.

Are the investment objectives and criteria of an angel, V.C., and high net worth individual different than those of a sovereign wealth fund with $1 billion in assets under management? Yes. But even fairly successful capital raisers often make the mistake of not adjusting their presentation to account for different types of investors.

If you have no idea who you should be raising capital from, then you may want to see how your competition has raised capital in the past in order to pick up a few clues. Which types of investors have more easily taken meetings with your team?

If you find that you have two investor focuses, just pick one and provide the one you choose with 80-90% of your capital-raising efforts. The remaining 10-20% can be spent on the second alternative. Doing this, it'll allow you to meet with investors of just one type often enough to get to learn about their common needs, challenges, fears of investing in your offer, etc. Whether you are an early-stage startup seeking growth capital or an investor managing $100 million, it's instructive to see how many different types of investors are out there, and how you may need to adjust to serve different investors as you grow. If you have not raised any capital and you are starting from the bottom, then it is likely you will need to raise capital from friends and family, local HNW contacts, or HNW individuals who know your space well so that you don't have to teach them the ABCs of it.

Learning curves are expensive to bring people up when you are trying to raise capital because you are already trying to move them up the learning curve of your strategy and build their trust at the same time, and that is hard enough without having to teach them how the basics of your industry work.

There is a great learning effect when focusing on a single type of investor and their needs. If you reach out to just one type of investor, you will become extremely competent by meetings with these investors and listening to their questions, concerns, and feedback. You will get better at booking those meetings and setting yourself up for success when you get into the meeting. On the other hand, if you reach out to several types of investors while raising capital, you will learn more slowly due to your lack of focus and you will never gain the same level of expertise as you would by focusing more narrowly on one group.

Imagine you are hitting the road for your Series B round of financing and on Monday you're meeting with a hedge fund in Dallas, on Wednesday you're having dinner with a HNW individual in San Francisco, and Friday you are hosting a group of venture capitalists at your headquarters in Chicago. By failing to focus geographically or on an investor group, you are making your job that much harder.

How many connections in common will you have between these different investor groups? Not many, I'd venture. Are you confident that you understand the concerns, industry trends, pressures, and pain points of each of these different investors? I, and many other investors, can tell when a pitch has been carefully prepared with me (or at least my peer group) in mind, in stark comparison to when a pitch is obviously conceived for everyone and anyone.

Below is "*The Investor Pyramid*" which shows how the target investors change based on how large a fund is.

Investors by Stage or Amount (Avg. Check)

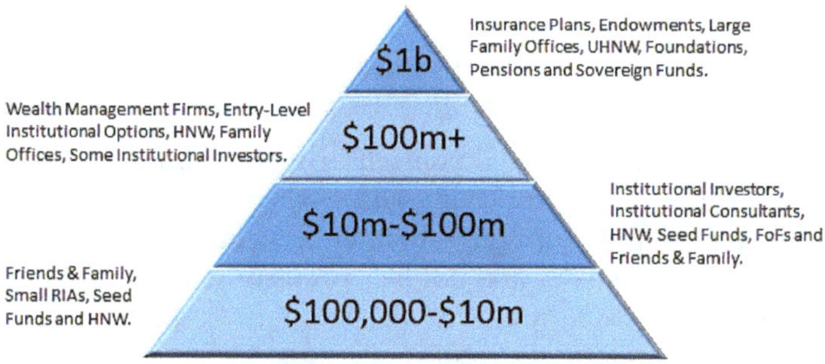

WHAT SHOULD BE ON YOUR PITCH DECK?

According to VCs or Successful Startups

Must-Have · Nice-To-Have

	500 Startups	Guy Kawasaki	Sequoia Capital	NextView Ventures	Crowdfunder	Airbnb Pitch Deck
Slides	11	10	11	15+	12	13
Executive Summary				Nice-To-Have		
Problem	Must-Have	Must-Have	Must-Have	Must-Have	Must-Have	Must-Have
Solution/Value Proposition	Must-Have	Must-Have	Must-Have	Must-Have	Must-Have	Must-Have
Market Validation/Why Now?			Nice-To-Have	Nice-To-Have	Nice-To-Have	Nice-To-Have
Product	Nice-To-Have		Nice-To-Have			Nice-To-Have
Market Size	Nice-To-Have		Nice-To-Have	Nice-To-Have		Nice-To-Have
Business Model	Must-Have	Must-Have	Must-Have	Must-Have	Must-Have	Must-Have
Underlying Magic	Nice-To-Have	Nice-To-Have		Nice-To-Have		
Competition	Must-Have	Must-Have	Must-Have	Must-Have	Must-Have	Must-Have
Competitive Advantage	Nice-To-Have					Nice-To-Have
Marketing Plan/GTM	Nice-To-Have			Nice-To-Have	Nice-To-Have	Nice-To-Have
Founding Team	Must-Have	Must-Have	Must-Have	Must-Have	Must-Have	Must-Have
Board/Advisors			Nice-To-Have	Nice-To-Have		
Traction/ Milestones	Nice-To-Have	Nice-To-Have		Nice-To-Have	Nice-To-Have	
Press/User Testimonials				Nice-To-Have		Nice-To-Have
Fundraising	Must-Have	Must-Have	Must-Have	Must-Have	Must-Have	Must-Have
Financials/Use of Funds		Nice-To-Have	Nice-To-Have	Nice-To-Have	Nice-To-Have	

Once you have chosen your investor focus, dedicate yourself to learning everything about them. For example, if you focus your capital raising efforts on HNW individuals who are serial entrepreneurs; you will want to attend their conferences, learn about their work schedules, and meet with enough of them that you learn about what their risk preferences are, etc.

You will want to embed yourself in their communities, see things from their perspective, and re-align all of your efforts to serve them. It's not only about understanding your client's needs; studying your investor helps you come across as more authentic, more in tune with their daily lives, and more like someone that they can relate to and trust with their money.

You need every strategy possible working for you so that you can raise capital consistently because it is very hard to succeed even if you're intelligent, hardworking, and focused.

While thinking over your investor consider:

What risks are your investors considering while reviewing your pitch? Why would they not invest? How educated are they about your industry and startup potential?

Think about the client's history and experiences. For example, let's say you're approaching a family office firm: you need to walk in their shoes and understand—have they been burned before by investing in a small startup? Will they have trouble explaining your strategy to their own LPs

Are they scared of your startup investment who have offices based out of their house or non-professionalized marketing materials or branding?

Are they scared to invest in teams that have few employees or no board of advisors?

Do they expect you to have certain types of audit firms or service providers?

You need to understand everything about that type of investor that you're focusing on. Then craft all of your marketing materials, everything you do, the types of emails you send, what clothes you wear, where your office is based, how often you call, and whether you request to meet in person. Everything in your business should be formed around those 1 or 2 investors that you've identified as your number one focus for capital raising.

You have to first conduct the analysis, then decide what sandbox you want to position yourself in, and after that, you can get more specific about the investor that fits your research findings and positioning.

It is great to have a unique proposition in the marketplace, but it shouldn't just be unique for your industry; it should be positioned in the marketplace to segment a valuable and explicitly targeted demographic—the precise type of investor you want to attract.

While it is common in the marketing world to talk about your client avatar or investor avatar, much of your competition that is raising capital has not thought this through and adapted every piece of their marketing materials

Avatar Exercise: If you haven't already defined it internally, it may help to write out your investor avatar on the few lines below as a starting point to have something to share with others on your team:

You can raise capital faster from local contacts than those who are halfway around the world. This is especially true since Investing is so much about trust and understanding that having an investor walk into your company office or meet with employees of a company several times over can't be replaced by a PowerPoint or a video conference.

Of course, travel and scheduling might require that you supplement your in-person experience, but a conference call is never as powerful as an in-person meeting and seeing first-hand how the technology works or picking up the product in your hands. For this reason, you may want to focus your capital raising on a handful of cities or just one or two that you can zero in on.

How to Generate More Investor Relationships Locally: To help those who do want to focus locally, I have provided the following strategies to generate more investor relationships every month.

Leverage Local Communities: One way to generate more investor relationships is to involve yourself in layers of social groups that are enjoyable and filled with high-net-worth individuals and potential investors. For example, one of the many startups I advised has a founder who lives on the island of Key Biscayne which you can't afford to live on if you are not HNW and he placed his office building directly above the most popular organic French café on the island. Most of his competitors would have chosen Miami Beach, downtown Miami, or Brickell Avenue, but after researching South Florida and talking to business owners and family offices. He found Key Biscayne to be the best location for building powerful relationships which makes it very easy for local HNWI to stop by, and he ultimately raised several rounds and now generating over $1m revenue per month and finally started to expand globally scattered team and office.

Google AdWords: One simple but powerful trick is to limit your advertising to areas where you are most likely to convert the prospects that you are targeting. If you are looking to find investors in high-tech and you have a whitepaper or article you want to get in front of people in your local community, you could find keywords they search for such as "high-tech investing" or "high-tech investments" and only target those.

A lot of businesses spend money on leads that aren't very valuable because they target the wrong demographic or the wrong location or use keywords that aren't a direct fit with the conversion goal. The campaign has to be carefully customized, budgeted, and geographically balanced while maintaining enough search volume for the term you select.

Use this method for goals like boosting users' sign up, sales, or white paper downloads by target investors, customers, and partners.

- *Keyword-Focused Content:* You can get local clients and attention by having focused related branding and content. For example, we wrote a whitepaper for NY Manhattan. It got over 30,000 views and went viral, and we received over 2,000 emails specifically from that whitepaper because it was highly focused on one geographical area. If you consistently produce valuable information on your niche area in your region, you will stand out and be known for it, and if it's great content, then they'll probably reach out to you for more information.
- Investor Databases: Essentially, the advice here is to know your position and your investor avatar and then find a strategy by which you find exact matches for your investor avatar leads or can create a database of prospects that likely would lead for you. Even if you only come up with a 30-name database or 200-name database, this could be useful to work with either invitation to meet in person when you are local to them or sending out educational content to them to see who raises their hand to learn more and engage on a deeper level. Some big names are Crunchbase, AngelList, and pitch book or deal book "The Funded is ideal to find the most active investor".
- Social Media: Leverage social media in many different ways, but since we are talking about local targeting, there are two strategies to use here. The first strategy is for Facebook. Although some mistakenly see Facebook as a trivial social network with the primary use being in keeping up with high school friends, this is the world's most powerful social network and users spend hours every day interacting with the website. As you can see below, Facebook has a very high usage rate—70%—and as you'll see next, their demographics are a good match.

Seven-in-ten Facebook users say they visit site daily

Among U.S. adults who say they use __, % who use that site ...

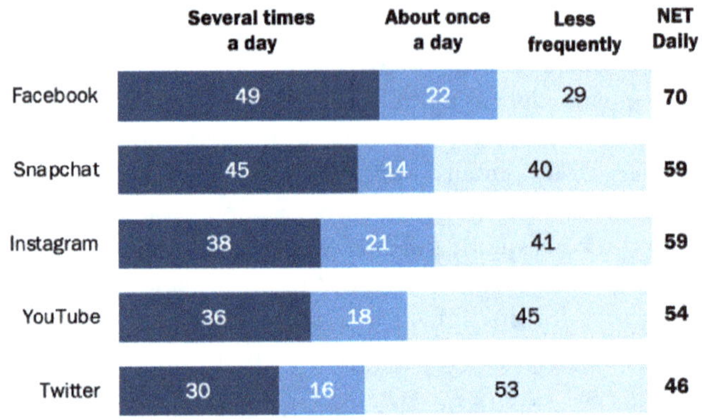

Note: Respondents who did not give an answer are not shown. "Less frequently" category includes users who visit these sites a few times a week, every few weeks or less often.
Source: Survey of U.S. adults conducted Jan. 25-Feb. 8, 2021.
"Social Media Use in 2021"

PEW RESEARCH CENTER

Why does that matter for your business? Because just like with Google Adwords, you can advertise on Facebook by restricting the geography to whom you are trying to reach and using other qualifying filters. To further target your spending, though, you can do two things that surprise people. One, you can upload a list of email addresses and Facebook will find those people on Facebook with those emails registered and you can target them.

These could be people that opted-in to learn more or that you met at an event perhaps, etc. Also, Facebook allows you to embed a single line of code on your website which allows you to embed a small image file in someone's browser when they visit your website so you can re-target them and advertise to them on Facebook.

If you are looking to tap into the affluent demographic, see the usage by users making $75,000 or more below.

Social Media Users by Demographic Group

Use of online platforms, apps varies – sometimes widely – by demographic group

% of U.S. adults in each demographic group who say they ever use ...

0% 20 40 60 80 100

	YouTube	Facebook	Instagram	Pinterest	LinkedIn	Snapchat	Twitter	WhatsApp	TikTok	Reddit	Nextdoor
Total	81	69	40	31	28	25	23	23	21	18	13
Men	82	61	36	16	31	22	25	26	17	23	10
Women	80	77	44	46	26	28	22	21	24	12	16
White	79	67	35	34	29	23	22	16	18	17	15
Black	84	74	49	35	27	26	29	23	30	17	10
Hispanic	85	72	52	18	19	31	23	46	31	14	8
Ages 18-29	95	70	71	32	30	65	42	24	48	36	5
30-49	91	77	48	34	36	24	27	30	22	22	17
50-64	83	73	29	38	33	12	18	23	14	10	16
65+	49	50	13	18	11	2	7	10	4	3	8
<$30K	75	70	35	21	12	25	12	23	22	10	6
$30K-$49,999	83	76	45	33	21	27	29	20	29	17	11
$50K-$74,999	79	61	39	29	21	29	22	19	20	20	12
$75K+	90	70	47	40	50	28	34	29	20	26	20
HS or less	70	64	30	22	10	21	14	20	21	9	4
Some college	86	71	44	36	28	32	26	16	24	20	12
College+	89	73	49	37	51	23	33	33	19	26	24
Urban	84	70	45	30	30	28	27	28	24	18	17
Suburban	81	70	41	32	33	25	23	23	20	21	14
Rural	74	67	25	34	15	18	18	9	16	10	2

Source: Pew Research Center

Social Media is important if you are highly geographically targeting the web traffic you get either naturally through people hearing about you locally, or if you are driving paid pay-per-click traffic locally via a Google AdWords campaign or something similar.

I would wager that most, if not all, of your targets, have a LinkedIn profile and you probably have experienced how that platform can help you enhance your professional standing, meet new clients, and grow your business.

Less likely is that you have spent significant advertising dollars with LinkedIn. Even less likely is that you have started a sizable Group on LinkedIn to build a lasting online network and interact with professionals in your niche.

Unlike Instagram or Snapchat, users are on LinkedIn for professional and business reasons, so your advertisement or brand presence is a natural fit with their engagement.

LinkedIn, which was acquired by Microsoft, has a big incentive to make sure you and your business are successful. In our experience, the platform can be very powerful AND there are many ways in which LinkedIn can and likely will improve the platform to make it even more powerful for entrepreneurs. LinkedIn collects huge amounts of data on its users which can be used by you to target investor leads more effectively than a purely social network.

Whether you are starting a LinkedIn Group or advertising to users on the site, it's a great way to build relationships and avoid wasting time on anyone who isn't your Investor Avatar.

The point with all of these local investor strategies is to be top of mind for your niche investor avatar. If you can deploy half or all of these strategies at once, then the benefits build on each other because people will start to see your brand in their email inbox, live at events, and through word of mouth or online, which adds up to your reputation locally.

Customer Relationship Management (CRM): Long term, it is important to have some sort of Customer Relationship Management (CRM) tool. If you are not familiar with the concept, a CRM tool is something that allows you to update a profile on a company or person so at every meeting you can record notes, contact details, and materials for reference later to help you keep hundreds or even thousands of relationships straight on who is who and what their preferences are.

This can help you sort investors out into A, B, and C quality leads, and make sure you don't waste time or insult investors by not taking good notes on their feedback from past meetings.

Yes, many people just use Excel to start out with, but eventually, you will want to graduate using something more sophisticated that can send out reminders of follow-up or easily track the bios and team members of a team faster and easier than you could on Excel. The trick is keeping the CRM updated and not having it be so powerful that it is overwhelming.

Once you find the momentum from implementing an investor funnel, working your positioning, and you see the results it can bring, once you feel that momentum you will not want to stop.

You will want to continue re-investing time and resources because you know what type of ROI it can produce.

Investor Funnel: An investor funnel is simply a series of intellectual property assets, forms of exposure, and relationship-building sources that all lead to more qualified inquiries to meet with you face-to-face or to invest in your company or investment offering.

The top of the funnel is the widest because that is where you have the most activity. For example, you may have press releases, the email list that you build up from aforementioned local investor lead generation strategies, your podcast, media appearances, published articles, and other content that you create to drive engagement with your prospects.

The next layer down could be your quarterly whitepapers, reports, or annual industry benchmark studies you conduct. These resources could be someone's first interaction with you, but likely this is a higher touch point with someone who has at least heard of your company before.

The third layer again is more qualified and has less volume to it. Resources could include: an event that you spoke at, a book that you write or very in-depth research coverage of a space.

The goal is to produce a resource that is so in-depth that only someone seriously researching the subject as a top priority would invest that amount of time and energy.

The fourth layer in the funnel would be those who want to see you speak live at an event, participate in your webinar, watch a recorded speech on YouTube, or otherwise take the time to engage with you specifically. Most people won't take the time to invest such energy into learning more about a subject, but if you can filter these prospects down to this layer of the funnel, that's a strong indication of interest—even if it is only 200-500 people a year.

That can lead to the next level, level five, which is in-person meetings and inquiry phone calls.

It's important to note that sometimes the funnel takes just a few weeks to complete, others will take years to get to the point where you are doing business together.

The prospects may read your articles for 5 years, then buy your book, and then invest while only talking to you on the phone, or they may move through your funnel any other number of ways including skipping it completely just because of your reputation as a leader in the space which has resulted from building the funnel.

No, you can technically raise capital without email, without a telephone, without any marketing materials—none of it is technically required. Certainly, you could keep raising capital the old-school way like almost everyone else.

I concede that you could obviously raise capital without writing any articles, a book, doing any press interviews, public speaking, etc., but it is also obvious that having those touch points with investors will make your capital raise easier. What I am trying to do in this book is to provide a unique approach, a way to attract investors instead of cold-calling or slowly networking your way into capital. Anyone who has cold-called hundreds of potential investors knows that it is a painful process in comparison to writing some content on your niche and becoming more of an expert in that niche naturally, which is not painful at all.

The last thing to note is that even if the investor you are meeting with didn't come to you through the funnel, you can use these intellectual properties and thought leadership assets to boost credibility instantly as you meet in person by handing them some of your work or use your book to "drip" on them for weeks after you meet to spur further follow-ups from your meeting.

In other words, there is no risk to building an investor funnel because you will gather market intelligence, grow your credibility with each person you meet, expand your network, and attract investors through the funnel naturally.

Public Relations: Once you speak to your legal counsel to check on exactly what you can say or not say to the press, utilize your knowledge to build interest in your fundraising:

1. Develop a list of ten to fifteen targeted publications in which you would like to appear. Identify the editor of financial columns in those publications and introduce yourself to them as a resource.

2. Speak at public events, conferences, networking events, where you will be heard not only by your peers but probably a few members of the press, as well.
3. Consider writing a book on your insights and experience. Many professionals in your industry are interviewed on TV after they have published a book on a specific topic within the industry, such as a trend, the economy, or quantitative trading. Yes, writing a book sounds extreme to many who are already working 80 hours a week. That is precisely why it would be so effective to consider doing so.
4. One of the most important things that get overlooked by small firms is the need to communicate with potential investors in many different forms. This means using the phone, email, physically mailed materials, and audio-visual versions of your content.
5. The benefits of this approach include higher credibility, as others can see that you are taking your business seriously; compensating for the fact that some of your investor lead lists may prefer email while others prefer printed materials, so you are covered by doing all mediums; and finally, those who want to consume your materials in every way possible and be able to share it easily with others in printed format can do so instantly inside of their office.

The intuitional firm do multi-million marketing because they know they need to and investors expect it, but many small firms don't. The smaller firms "including startup" send things via email to keep cost down or they don't bother to call because they feel it is lower pressure to just poke an investor via email and get lost in their inboxes.

How Investors Make Decisions: Typically, it is the founder and person with more technical, rather than marketing or sales expertise, who must take on the fundraising. These founders started their businesses to solve a problem for their clients, build creative products.

Whatever the reason, it is almost never related to selling and raising capital, but those are skills that these executives have to learn on the job—and quickly—if they are to survive.

Their #1 issue is "investor relationships or investor lead generation" and "getting our foot in the door." In other words, the big trend is that those who think they have something excellent to offer just can't attract investors, get meetings booked, and attract interest to their investment offering.

Capital Raising Critical Skills for Founders

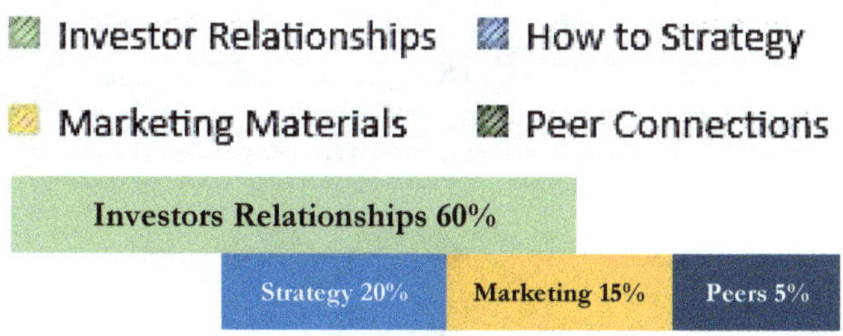

The bad news is that the startups that do know how to raise capital are also the ones that investors see as more credible. To make the capital raising process even more challenging, there are hundreds of additional reasons for why you may not close an investor.

The average investor won't do you any favors in understanding his objections, concerns, desires, or other factors influencing his decision.

You'll have to sift through the investor's responses and comments to find the reasons behind the decision.

You'll find below a diagram of some of the major determinants that go into whether someone invests or not.

This diagram cannot be detailed enough to show the top-25 factors, but if even one of these 7 basic factors is not aligned with the investor's preferences, you may be wasting both your time and their time.

This diagram shows just how hard capital raising is, as you could easily get all 7 of these top variables right and still not raise capital because of another factor such as timing, liquidity, or terms of the investment.

There are so many people competing for the attention of investors and so many ways that deal closings and capital raising can go south that you need to avoid the major mistakes that most capital raisers make while also employing every strategy you know to ensure your success.

The Seven Factors That Drive Investor Decision

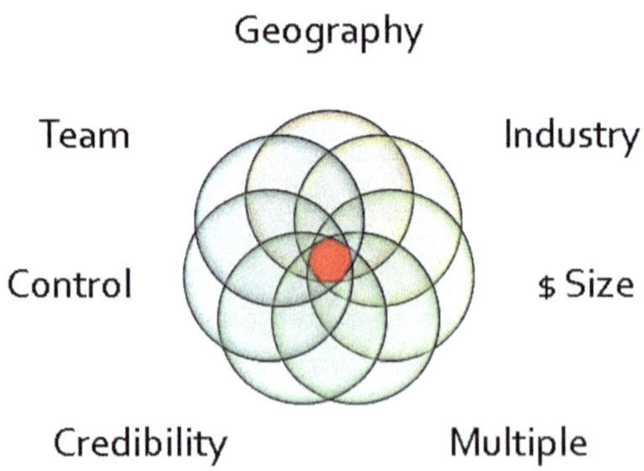

Startup Fundraising Roadmap

Step 1 (Analyze):

1. Your Competition Analysis
2. Target Market Analysis
3. What's Compelling about you

Step 2 (Position):

1. Describe your investor avatar
2. Define your competitive advantage
3. When the investor funnel become ready
4. What choke point can you defend
5. Who do you need to leverage or hire to help fundraise?
6. What is your key process that can be automated?

Step 3 (Architect):

1. Design your target investors' funnel
2. Define what strategy to execute
3. Prioritize your first target location

Step 4 (Asset):

1. List all your networks by type (School, Gym, Work)
2. List all other contributors' networks
3. Map the combined network and re-rank targets

Step 5 (Execute):

1. List pre-requisite marketing material
2. Define the top KGI (Key Goal Indicator)
3. Define the top KPI (Key Performance Indicator)

Step 6 (Iterate):

1. Speed of Implementation Metrics
2. Unique Ability of each contributor
3. Feedback capture and referral tracking

Step 7 (Legal):

1. Have Startup Lawyers ready to meet investors
2. Prepare what document to share and at what stage
3. Have investor's package and diligence ready to share

Fundraising Myths and Mistakes: To get out of the way some misconceptions and assumptions you may have about capital raising right away, below are some of the biggest myths and most expensive mistakes in capital raising. These misconceptions get repeated over and over again because a percentage of those raising capital have gotten lucky or had great market momentum behind them, so their tactics did not matter as much as they will in your case:

"You need to hire people who have a current network with real first level relationships in order to raise capital." This is the belief that all you need to do is find that one person who will do all the capital raising for you because they are so well connected. These people are extremely rare, and very expensive, and they are probably successful because they have invested in building their capital raising system and are therefore not available.

"If you build it, they will come". Also known as the "fund of dreams." This is simply believing that if you build a great product or an impressive investment track record, investors will find you and you don't need to work at raising capital. Even the founders of the legendary firm Blackstone Group had to pound the pavement in the early years, traveling from city to city to pitch investors to come aboard.

Not dedicating any resources to capital raising. This is the most obvious mistake that I see in the industry. Many fund managers will manage the portfolio full time, make 2-3 phone calls a week (or even per month), and then wonder why they have not raised more capital.

Performance does NOT market itself; pedigree does NOT swing all doors wide open. You need to have dedicated resources, an internal marketing person working at least 20 hours a week, and investor databases so you can spend your time calling on real prospects instead of always having to qualify them and have a growing internal CRM in place to track your investor relationships. Finally, never take money from family

or give away more than 30% equity at Series B (cumulative).

Completely miss the boat on authority positioning, educational forms of marketing, and improving their own pedigree standing in the industry. Many people are stuck in their old-school cold-call and networking strategies. Sure, this works some of the time, but most of us prefer to rely on a more sophisticated system that works all of the time and builds real relationships with investors.

A complete lack of capital raising training or marketing material. You do not have to pay to have your marketing staff trained, but at the very least you should document your own best practices, processes, and investor pipeline plans. In this way, your strategies and processes can be easily communicated to team members and board members and improved each quarter.

If you run an investment firm and you are running a model that requires capital raising, you should estimate that 20%-33% of the startup's energy and expenses may need to go towards raising capital.

You need to maximize outgoing phone calls and touches at all costs because it is purely a numbers game. This is one of the most time-consuming and painful myths to buy into. It's a brute-force mentality that doesn't build much momentum.

You have a 3-month capital-raising goal. This is unrealistic and the wrong mindset with which to go out of the gates. You need to plan, build relationships, educate potential clients, and design high-quality marketing strategies and materials for the long term. It takes time to raise lots of capital and usually the more valuable the investor, the longer the sales cycle. Don't try to cram everything into a 1-3-month capital raise.

Underestimating the value of being on a first-name basis with your investor relationships. Some professionals, especially those with technical backgrounds, think that marketing is a numbers game. Yes, you sometimes have to reach out to many to develop relationships with a few; but relationships are at the core of everything that gets done. As a sales expert says, "All things equal, people like to do business with friends. All things being unequal, people still like to do business with friends."

Spending $5,000 on graphic design and website design but $0 on hiring someone who is an expert at sales letter construction, copywriting, and creating taglines for your positioning in the marketplace. Many times, I see founders that spend their whole marketing budget on a fancy website, but they don't allocate any of that budget to the areas of marketing that actually bring money in the door.

The bad news is that there is no magic bullet to raising capital. There is no single strategy, no secret approach, and no special tactic that will change everything.

Most industries are so competitive when it comes to capital raising that even when you have the right team, remove the wrong actions, and pay attention to the top variables as to why investors could say no—you still need to work hard and use as many strategies as possible to make sure it goes well.

In the capital raising game, it is more brutal than in the Olympics: there's no reward for second place. Anything but a gold medal finish in capital raising means you lost the sale.

Startup Fundraising by Stage and Standard Rounds

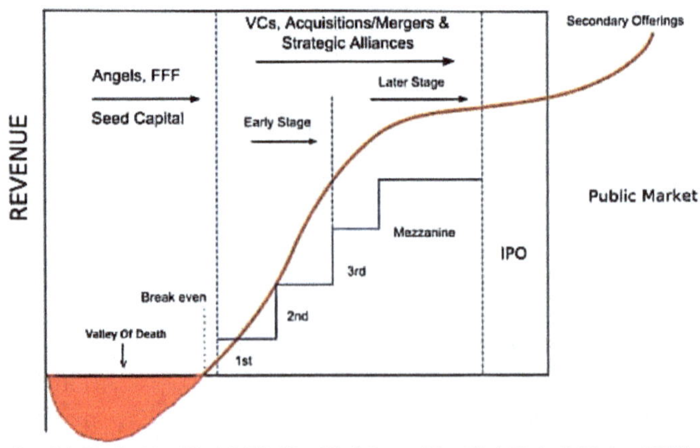

Seed | Early (A - B) | Mid (C - D) | Late (E – F) | Exit (M&A – IPO)

Legal & Compliance Foundation: Cover the key items that your startup needs to get right to succeed. This checklist was prepared for startups that plan to raise money from investors, but many of the items are applicable to any startup. Although failure is often celebrated in the startup world, legal failures are not.

Hire a business transaction lawyer: Read the lawyer's website bio and LinkedIn profile. You should quickly be able to figure out if the attorney is (1) local; (2) works with companies like yours (startups v. multinational corporations); (3) is licensed in your state; and (4) has the appropriate skill set for your startup's needs. Look for these practice areas/specialties:

1. "business law"
2. "corporate law"
3. "transactional"
4. "Fundraising"
5. "emerging growth"
6. "startups"
7. "venture capital"
8. "Securities"
9. "mergers and acquisitions"
10. "Intellectual property"
11. "Tax"

Do not hire attorneys with these practices:

1. "litigation"
2. "family law"
3. "Trust & estates"
4. "civil litigation"
5. "Labor & employment"
6. "data security & privacy"

Incorporation: Review all agreements with a former and current employer(s) (e.g., confidentiality, invention assignment, non-solicitation, non-compete).

- Conduct a basic trademark search on your company name.
- Form a Delaware C-Corporation (not an LLC)

    1. Authorize 10-15 million shares
    2. Issue 8-10 million shares to founders (a lesser amount if you plan to add more founders)
    3. Set the par value to $.00001 per share
    4. Use generally accepted incorporation forms prepared by startup lawyers (e.g., bylaws, stock restrictions agreements)

- File foreign qualifications in the states where a startup is doing business (e.g., California)
- Split equity decisively
- Founders pay cash and assign company-related IP for their shares
- Founder shares vest over time (e.g. 4 years with 1 year cliff)

    1. Founder vesting accelerates upon sale of the company
    2. Consider Class F Common Stock

- Founders file an 83(b) election within 30 days of receiving shares
- Founders sign Confidentiality & Invention Assignment agreements
- Setup founder-only board to start
- Board elects officers (President, Secretary, Treasurer)
- Prepare and issue electronic stock certificates (Carta)
- Secure a Federal Tax ID number (EIN) from the IRS
- Open a separate company bank account and keep personal and business finances separate
- Hire an accountant

Intellectual Property (IP): All founders, employees, and contractors sign Confidentiality & Invention Assignment agreements

- File trademark registrations for brand names
- File copyright registrations for works susceptible to copyright information
- Consult with a patent counsel (provisional patent applications can be a less expensive way to start the patent process)
- Understand the implications of using open-source software

Funding: Not DIY – securities laws in this area are complex and the penalties for noncompliance are severe

- Raise money from accredited investors with a $100K+ Check
- Do not pitch publicly (e.g., Twitter, website)
- Do pitch privately with 10-15 slides, not a full business plan (see Sequoia Capital business plan)
- Do not pay the finder's fees
- Consider convertible equity over convertible debt for seed financings.
- Understand 'high-resolution fundraising'
- Use generally accepted funding forms: Y Combinator's SAFE; 500 Startups' KISS, Series Seed, TechStars' Series AA
- Understand funding alternatives (equity, crowdfunding, Kickstarter, revenue financing)
- Use an investment term sheet to facilitate negotiations and investor coordination (i.e., WSGR or major law firm template) that has a strong footing in venture capital.
- Identify economic vs. control issues
- Build a model in Excel to understand the economics of the deal
- Be stingy with board seats understanding that the board can fire you the founders
- All directors/officers complete bad actor questionnaires
- File Form Ds with SEC and applicable state divisions of securities

Stock Options: Adopt a stock option plan upon equity financing, meaningful revenue, or other increase in valuation

- Allocate enough shares to the plan for the next 6-12 months
- Use market studies to determine how many option shares to grant (e.g., advisors 0.15%-0.5%)
- Set exercise price on option shares based on FMV (409a)
- Be intentional about whether you issue ISOs vs. NSOs
- Option shares should vest over time
- Carefully consider post-termination exercise periods

Human Resources: all advisors, employees, and contractors sign Confidentiality & Invention Assignment agreements

- All employees are due minimum wage (20% exception)
- Classify employees carefully
    1. Not everyone is a consultant
    2. Not everyone is exempt from overtime
    3. Unpaid interns (6-factor test)
- Define all employees "at will"
- Document employee misbehavior
- Consult with a lawyer on all terminations
- Use non-competes sparingly

Do make everyone sign the PIIA: All owners, founders, contractors, interns, and employees (aka anyone who does any work for the startup, especially creative and tech work) MUST sign a Proprietary Information and Inventions Assignment ("PIIA") agreement.

This agreement will assign all intellectual property ownership rights to the company, and not live with the individual who created the IP. If an independent contractor does not sign a PIIA agreement, the default rule is that the contractor owns all of the intellectual property that he/she creates. Make sure all workers sign this agreement before they start any work.

DON'T let any founders' stock vest immediately:

- The reality is that most startups or new businesses will say goodbye, adios, and au revoir to at least one of the initial founders. Your startup needs a plan for the beginning that clearly lays out the process for what happens when a founder leaves…or else it will be one big mess.
- No investor is going to give your startup money without IP assignments and vesting schedules (among other things).
- The point is you need "vesting schedules" for all founders/officers who have a piece of the equity pie. It is standard for startups to have their founders fully vest in four years, with 25% of the stock options vesting each year. Make sure your lawyer gets this right!

Suppliers Contracts: Good contracts are clear, precise, efficient, and do what they are intended to do

1. Be careful of creating contracts orally, via IM, or email
2. Always be due diligence ready

Class F Common Stock? What's one thing Google, Facebook, Snapchat, and Ford all have in common? At some point, they each implemented a dual-class stock structure that gave the founders super-sized control over the future direction of their respective companies.

Entrepreneurs who plan to raise capital from investors, but are concerned about maintaining control, might also consider implementing a dual-class stock structure. Currently, one of the most common dual-class stock structures is Class F Common Stock as developed by The Founders Institute in collaboration with Yokum Taku of Wilson Sonsini.

Under this structure, founders are issued Class F Stock that grants them the following special rights:

- Super-voting rights (10 votes per share instead of the standard 1 vote per share)
- Veto rights over certain key decisions (e.g., increasing the size of the board, selling the company)
- The right to elect a Class F director who has 2 votes instead of

While this sounds great for founders, there are some downsides that should also be considered:

- Implementing a dual-class stock structure will increase your legal costs at incorporation and when you raise money from investors.
- Despite the high-profile examples, implementing a dual-class stock structure is far from the norm. Consequently, potential investors may strongly (and reasonably) object to investing in a company with Class F Common Stock.

While Class F Stock is relatively easy to "turn off" in advance of investment financing, it shouldn't be adopted haphazardly. Before adopting a dual-class stock structure, make sure you consult with an attorney who can help you understand the pros and cons.

Exit: Be due diligence ready as time kills all deals (Expect 6 months to close):

- Negotiate all keys issues at the letters of intent / term sheet stage as leverage usually decreases over time
- Be very wary of no shop clauses > 60 days
- Build a model in Excel to understand the economics of the deal
- Structure the deal to optimize for tax (stock vs. asset sale)
- Clearly communicate priorities to lawyers so negotiations are focused on the issues that matter.

Takeaways: Plan to get funded regardless of what angel, venture capital or HNWI think of you, and the best approach is to follow the million small businesses that are launched every hour without relying on the venture capitalist and their never-ending rejection that erodes bold entrepreneurs, keep in mind that valuable investors hear dozens, hundreds, sometimes thousands of pitches a year.

Yes, some high net worth (HNW) investors that you know may only have a handful of opportunities shown to them in a given year, but the most active (and therefore most likely to seriously consider an attractive deal) see many more than your average HNW individual.

So, why not put a lot of work into making sure that these valuable investors see that you bring something unique and interesting to the table? While analyzing the competition and yourself, look for what could really make you stand out from the noise in the marketplace.

Provide something that is different in a way that matters to the investor. I have stopped many confident executives in their tracks with a simple question of, "What makes you unique?" Often, there is something that is truly unique about the business, or the individual, but they have failed to complete the basic analysis of their competitors, their clients, and their own startup offering.

There are three parts of the analysis: analyzing the competition, analyzing investor needs, and analyzing yourself.

Beyond the industry benchmarks, investors are evaluating you against your competition in countless other ways.

This is because investors have myriad opportunities to invest and, chances are, one of your competitors is meeting with one of your target investors this week (maybe even this minute) to make the case for why they deserve that investor's money more than you and others in your industry. So how do you compare with the competition? What separates you from the crowd? Why should a busy investor take a meeting with *you?*

This is where your analysis of the competition comes in handy. To begin with, you have to know what others are offering in your space. The following are angles to consider in your competitive analysis:

1. What are competitors offering?
2. How strong is their positioning?
3. How valuable is their offering?
4. How credible are they in reality?
5. Analyze their strengths, weaknesses, and stance in the marketplace.
6. What are the fund investment terms being offered?
7. How professional is their branding?
8. How do they develop relationships with investors, public appearances, word-of-mouth, billboards (for those that have registered to publicly solicit), and public relations?

How professional and credible is their branding and website presence? What investor set or subset are they appealing to and raising capital from most?

Execution: you must adhere to the following as a golden rule

Do's:

- Create 10x vote shares for founders and 1X for investor
- Include in pitch 10,000 feet view that cannot be copied
- Gat money from investors who can afford to lose.
- Get money from the one who can bring customers
- Prioritize investors coming from startup or corporate
- Ask investors why they want to invest & what they bring
- Use the same terms for all investors at the same round
- Set minimum and max subscription per round
- Take check between $50k and $500k for no board seat
- Add required conversion to equity for unpaid notes
- Share realistic projections compared to your peers
- Keep the number of investors in the cap table small
- Give board seat starting from Series A equity round
- Max equity given to investors cannot exceed 30% after series

B close

- Max equity allocated for C level is 5% vested in 4 years
- Max equity allocated for advisors is 0.5% per 4 years

Don't:

- Send full pitch prior to expressed interest in an initial email
- Solicit your direct competitor investor's "same stage"
- Careful when issuing preferred shares and liquidation preference to investors, especially double dipping "may wipe out your equity, will cover in the next chapter Exit"
- Add price match or current offer to first right of refusal
- Use NDA or investor pitch recipient to protect you
- Pay finder's fees as it is a deal breaker except broker for late-stage series and only when no investors are in sight
- Take any amount of money from any investor with cash
- Take money from anyone requiring a control board seat
- Befriend investors or buy them dinner prior to closing
- Chase celebrity investors since they add little to no value
- Take money from investors with legal litigation history
- Build debt that forces you to liquidate in 2 years or less
- Be all over news sharing your business model and IP
- Share your pitch with anyone online or permanently

Adhere to the following golden and proven simple rules:

1. The First and most important investor is you
2. The best money is from your paying customers
3. Investors are not there to validate your startup nor support you, they are after unleashing growth that can skyrocket their investments into 100s or 1000s multiple and nothing else.
4. Prioritize investors who are customers or partners
5. Talk to investors who invested in the last three month

Funding: Define a strong roadmap that works regardless of financial market state and investors' sentiments, by leveraging your bootstrapping stage "raise at best inflection point and only to reach next 24 months ARR growth at 25% Quarter over Quarter".

Market Fit: is not your MVP or first paying customers, rather it's the growth rate "when customers cannot get enough of your product or services, .i.e., > 25% growth WoW".
Instruments: carefully design your term sheet with your legal team that ensures deferred debt to equity "note that converts to equity in 24 months or upon next equity rounds".

Control: The key is to stay in control until your vision is executed and you cashed out "through IPO or M&A". Founder Shares with a 10X vote at Series A, Common share at Series B, and only consider preferred shares with "liquidation preference, Exclusivity and first right of refusal" at Series C.

Vesting must be 4 years on an annual basis for all co-founders and employees, add Board that you worked with at least for 1 year as Board Advisors with proven execution. Never give any investor more than 10% and ensure that by the time you close your Series B, all investors combined must not exceed 30% of ownership "to allow for further growth through your IPO". Additionally, you shall have the option to buy back any past investors at the board's discretion to weed out the one who may become a liability "i.e., their brand become damaged in media".

Growth: Use all cash from revenues and funding to expand your business equally not disproportionately, i.e., (Product Development 25%, Customer Success 10%, Marketing 10%, Sales 25%, IP 10%, Operation 20%). Avoid Press and PR until Series C or ready to exit. Adhere to the approved budget by the board and prioritize referrals that drive revenues, not users.

Team: It is critical to understand from day one that the best talents are not accessible, and you cannot afford them early on or at least until you reach stardom "Unicorn", instead build a strong culture that relays on soft benefits i.e., "telecommute, consensus-based" and referral, start with Board Advisors that fill the skill gaps, and only convert to employee founders and advisors that deliver hard metrics that propel your growth and nothing else.

Avoid interns and consultants, additionally connect compensation to measurable weekly performance and never sign a fixed-term employment contract even with your next CEO or key investors. Define a pool option that incentivizes your employee upon series A, and build an industry leader benefit package that goes beyond the top tech companies which may help you gain their talents "i.e., limit working hours to 8 per day and 40 per week, along mandatory 10 days' vacation every other quarter, cash bonus on completed goals on time, etc.

Avoid too young or too old near retirement founding teams, ideally (30-50 for cofounders, 40-60 for Board and 20-30 for staff), and make sure your team is gender and minority balanced (reflecting both your investors and customer-base).

Legal: Hire an attorney with strong investors relation and venture capital deal negotiation experience "ask for reference" from past founders with exit.

The attorney must be within your first target market and an expert in transactional corporate law, not litigation. Pay on a use basis not retainer and negotiate a rate based on your stage "i.e., Seed is $200 hr., Series B $500, etc.".

The best sources to find active investors globally:

- https://en.wikipedia.org/wiki/List_of_venture_capital_firms
- Pitchbook, Crunchbase, Angel List, The Funded, Techcrunch
- Top Universities Alumni Angel Groups
- National Venture Capital Association: https://nvca.org/

Global Universities (Most Active Angel Groups)

Stanford - Harvard - MIT - UC Berkeley - Cornell - Columbia UPenn - UChicago - Dartmouth - CalTech - NYU - INSEAD London Business School - HEC Paris – Waterloo - Singapore U

US Top Angel Groups for Seed Stage by CB Insights

Rank	Angel Group
1	Life Science Angels
2	Queen City Angels
3	Boston Harbor Angels
4	Atlanta Technology Angels
5	Tech Coast Angels
6	Band of Angels
7	Pasadena Angels
8	Upstate Carolina Angel Network
9	Launchpad Venture Group
10	Keiretsu Forum
11	Golden Seeds
12	Central Texas Angel Network
13	The Angels' Forum
14	Sand Hill Angels
15	New York Angels
16	TiE Angels
17	Desert Angels
18	Alliance of Angels
19	BlueTree Allied Angels
20	Arizona Technology Investor Forum

Startup Funding by Stages and Dollars (Seed to Pre-Exit)

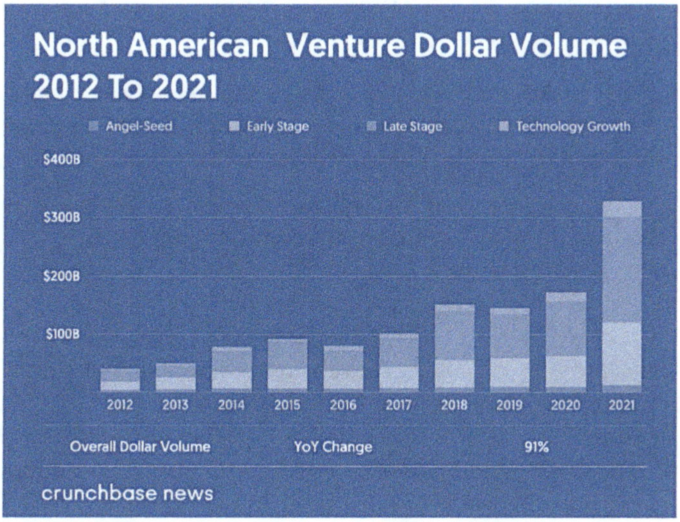

Top Corporate Venture Capital for any Stage

CHAPTER X
HOW TO EXIT

Startup Acquisition: The main exit strategy for startups is to sell to a bigger pool of investors "IPO" or large company for a profit. The same goes for investors.

The buyer takes over the startup using cash or stock as compensation, and key executives and employees from the startup often stay at the company for a period of time in order to be able to cash out and vest their stock.

Exits provide capital to startup investors, which can then return the money to their limited partners (in the case of Venture Capitalists) or to the investors themselves (in the case of angel investors). Startup acquisitions are much more frequent in the US than in Europe, but lately there's been a significant surge in the number of European and Asian acquisitions.

A different type of acquisition that is very common in Silicon Valley is **acquihires** (acquisition + hiring). In this case, the buyer is not so much interested in the product or services as it is in the team, the talent, where it's also important to have a development partner with a scalable team.

Acquihires often lead to the closure of the products and services that have been acquired and employees end up being transferred to build a company's own product or services who usually receive significant hiring premium bonuses.

Acquihires tend to happen at an earlier stage in comparison to late-stage startup acquisitions, which means that they often provide less capital to angels and Venture Capitalists.

Exit and IPO Strategy: there is a time for mature and late-stage technology startups where raising more capital from VCs or private equity firms is no longer an option. So, what comes next? An IPO.

IPO stands for 'initial public offering' and it basically means that a company starts floating on a stock market, selling a significant number of its shares in the process to institutional and non-institutional investors.

These large startups often called unicorns are the VC's dream, as they often provide multiples of 10 to 50 X on the initial investments as large lump sums of capital to all parts involved (founders, early employees, and investors). An interesting trend in the startup world when it comes to going public is that more and more companies are taking longer to IPO.

This is a consequence of the high amount of capital available in the startup market from Venture Capitalists, private equity firms and other investment institutions.

Mergers & Acquisitions: commonly known as M&As, these transactions usually imply a merger with a similar and larger company. This type of exit is often chosen by big companies that are looking for complementary offerings in the market, and buying a smaller startup is a better way to develop a product than creating it in-house.

Not selling a startup: In the same way that not every startup needs to raise money from VCs and business angels (bootstrapping is a viable alternative), not every startup needs to sell itself to a bigger company to provide a return to founders, employees, and investors.

Companies that are able to establish a solid business model and scale might choose to stay independent and reinvest the profits in the company. Part of those profits can also be distributed amongst investors as a dividend, providing liquidity to outside partners while avoiding the public markets and the obligations that come with it.

I'm not sure when I first knew the startup, I invested in last year was doomed. Maybe it was when they stopped fundraising efforts a month out from their goal, overly confident that one big investor was going to come through in the clutch. Maybe it was when they came to me for more money when that didn't work out. Or maybe it was because the founder left to go start a second company before the sale was complete.

Whatever the final straw was, no one was surprised to see the company eventually declare bankruptcy. While there's lots of advice out there on how investors can exit successfully, there's less for entrepreneurs in the trenches. That's a shame because how you exit as a first-time entrepreneur is going to define your career going forward, proving to onlookers that you can deliver (or, in a worst-case scenario, that you're a flake).

Having seen both frustrating losses and plenty of coveted 10-baggers (industry speaks for 10 times return on investment), I'd like to pass on a few key factors that can make for smoother exits for new entrepreneurs.

Know your exit options from day One: I know lots of first-time entrepreneurs who plunge into a business without ever giving a thought to how they'll get out of it. But this is actually important to do right from the outset, and to re-evaluate every six months or so. Your endgame influences how (and why) you build.

If you're seriously thinking about going public, for example, growth and user acquisition are going to be critical. Hoping to get acquired? You'll want to focus on building out a killer product that bigger competitors can't afford to snap up. And if you're planning to scale with venture capital, you'd better be ready to set aside the next three to seven years of your life to be head-down in the business.

Whichever route you go, it's all about the endgame right from the beginning. I saw how critical this can be with a startup I was involved with. Founder always looked at his options for exiting while building his business.

When the time came, he recognized that our main competitor was missing geographic coverage in our location and positioned the company to capture that market and accelerate an acquisition. From start to finish, the founder had exit options in mind, which made the final sale to one of the world's biggest tech platforms a seamless transition.

Up-level your board and exec team: One of the best ways to punch above your weight when it *does* come time to exit? Bring a ringer onto your board or executive team. Senior individuals with industry credibility and expertise can (literally, overnight) add multiples of value to your company.

Even if you don't necessarily have the resources to execute his/her vision right now, bringing in an industry leader shows you're serious and poised for growth. A junior company may not be able to bankroll and build a massive international customer base, for instance, but hiring an all-star CIO/business development adviser or executive creates a threat that they could.

And optics like these can make a huge difference in the size and number of offers at the time of exit. While it can be challenging for smaller companies to attract premier talent, I'm living proof that the right headhunter makes all the difference.

For example, I recently recruited an electric car legend to sit on the board of a company working to develop North American sources for cobalt, a key mineral in electric vehicle batteries. (The majority of cobalt today is mined in the violence-prone Democratic Republic of Congo, which makes it critical to find alternate sources.) Having an icon on their board helps distinguish them from competitors in a crowded space.

Always be building: It's a classic startup mistake: With a potential buyer on the horizon, a company will start cutting costs like crazy to look lean and efficient. They let money in the bank get dangerously low rather than securing more funding. They cut back on user acquisition to save funds.

They stop building and stretch to make ends meet, letting revenue growth slip. But cutting core competencies isn't fooling anyone: You might be making the bottom line look good, but your growth is suddenly in the tank. And that's often what determines the size and value of exit offers.

This is bad for business, generally speaking; even worse, it puts you in a very vulnerable position. (I've seen cases where investors will dangle an attractive offer, then withdraw it at the last hour once a startup has run out of money, forcing the founder to concede to far less favorable terms).

As a founder, you'll have the most offers and options if you can show growth with plenty of money in the till–just look at Uber's over-the-top valuation. The company is worth north of $70 billion today, despite losing $1 billion per quarter alone during their pre-IPO stage, precisely because of user and booking growth.

Know when to go: For founders, there are some clear signs that it's time to get out. First: are you "done," personally? If you're not feeling that passion anymore, it's time to bow out gracefully. And this doesn't always have to mean an exit: I saw how a former CEO of a health tech company successfully transitioned to an adviser and COO role when she needed to step back. By doing this, she increased the chance for success for the company and its stakeholders. More often than not, "sticking it out" as a founder culminates in a halfhearted fizzle out.

Other times, the industry itself is screaming at you to "get out." The clearest indicator here is a wave of consolidation: You generally don't want to be the only "little guy" left standing after the heavy hitters buy up all your competitors.

Not only will you have trouble finding a buyer, but you'll suddenly be up against much better-resourced adversaries.

And of course, there's the very best way to know it's time to go: Has someone offered you a ridiculously fat check? Admittedly, this doesn't happen often. But every once in a while, you get a WhatsApp scenario–where a bigger competitor is so scared of your product that they're willing to offer almost anything to mitigate that risk (like the $19 billion Facebook paid for WhatsApp back in 2014).

Don't do an exit off the side: A lot of entrepreneurs consider themselves to be lone wolves, but the worst thing you can do with an exit is trying to go it alone. Don't hole yourself up in a room and hammer out a contract: Get support from trusted people.

Your angel investors, the ones who believed in you from the start, are generally great people to turn to, as are fellow entrepreneurs who have been there before (in good times and not-so-good ones).

These are people who have your best interests (and those of your business) in mind. Note that this will NOT always be the case with your VCs, who, in many cases, need to be ruthless in pursuit of a quick return. It's not personal; it's simply the nature of their business.

Bringing in an adviser is a great way to get an outside perspective, or you can always ask your board of directors or investors to form a committee and pool their expertise.

Even then, exits aren't easy, and success is hardly a guarantee. But when you take the time to surround yourself with the right people, you'll always have the network behind you to build again.

The dream of a startup founder can often be summarized by the following well-intentioned, and mostly delusional, quote: *"We'll raise a few rounds and in a few years we'll IPO on Nasdaq."* But a more likely scenario looks something like this:

You invest a few years of hard work to build something of value. One day you receive an acquisition offer out of the blue. You're elated. And you're not prepared. You drop everything to focus on this opportunity. Exclusive due diligence starts.

Your company is a mess (IP, contracts, burn). Days become weeks; weeks become months. You've neglected business and fundraising. You're running out of money. M&A is now your one and only option. The buyer says they found a bunch of cockroaches in the walls and dropped the price. Now what? Sounds unlikely?

This is still a favorable situation: You had an offer! Think about how much time you invested in your various funding rounds. Have you spent even a fraction of that on understanding exit paths? If you'd rather not live in the situation described above, read along.

Exits matter because that's when you, your team, and your investors get paid. Oddly enough, and to use a chess metaphor, we hear a lot about the "opening game" (lean startup) and the "mid-game" (growth), but very little about this "end game."

As a result, founders miss opportunities or leave money on the table. You want the best possible exit. And fortune favors the prepared.

The E-word: A strange taboo: Investors live by exits, but many founders keep dreaming of uniformization and avoid the "E-word" until it's too late. Yet, 97 percent of exits were M&As. And most happened before Series B as shown below.

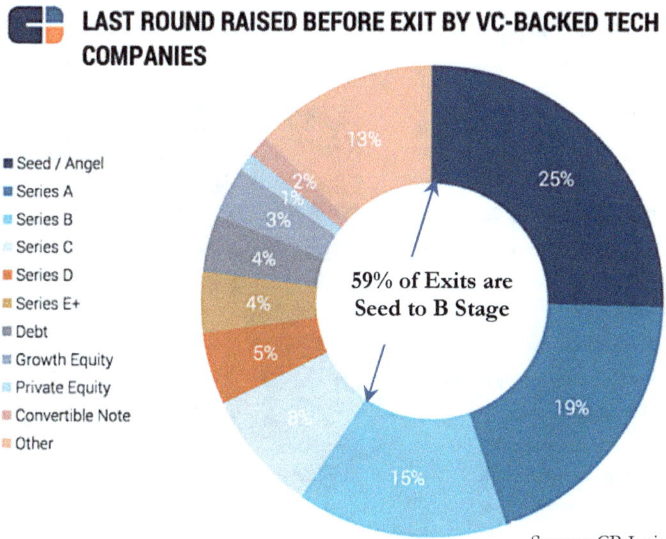

Source: CB Insights

The Rate of Successful M&A at Each Stage
(I.e., Series A 14% vs. Unicorn 1%) by CB Insights

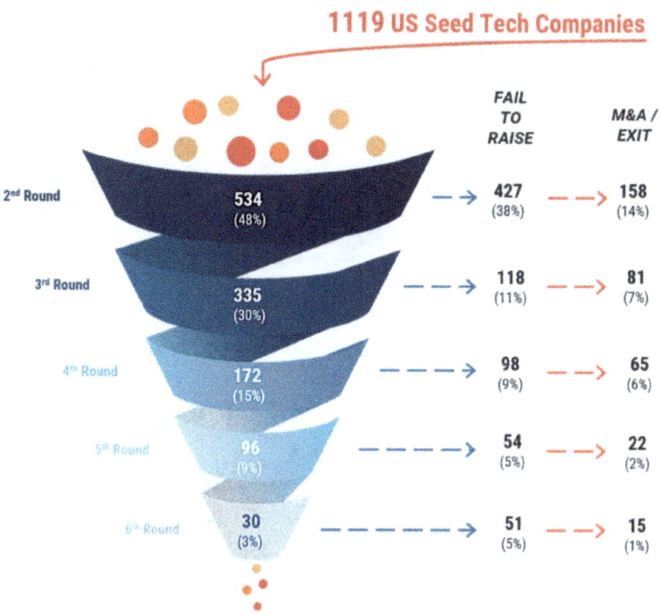

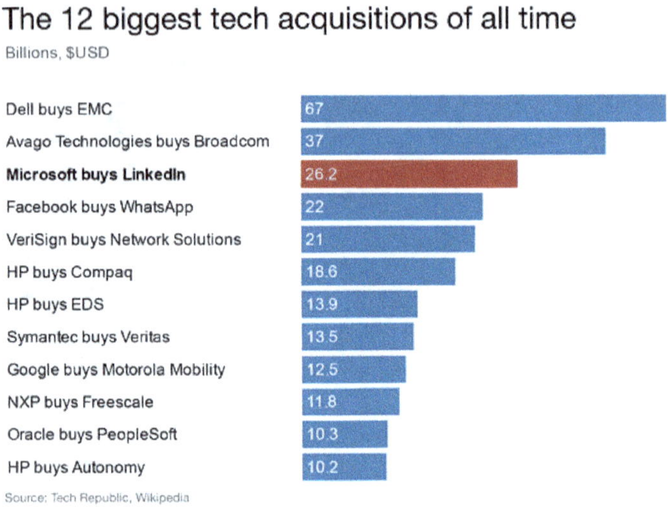

The Most Significant Consumer M&A

Exit Do's and Don'ts: "Founders must be aware of what contributes to an exit. This means understanding partnerships and how they are formed in the business space the entrepreneur is working in," said one Master Class participant. As founders, you build your product, your company, and your option. You need to understand the options open to your company and take steps to enable them.

The most likely one is an acquisition, but there are others like IPO (including small cap), RTO, SBO, LBO, Equity Crowdfunding, and even ICO. "Exit is not a goal, but as a CEO it is something you should think about as early in your cycle as possible while being business-focused," exits should always be on the chief executive's agenda, no matter how early in the process.

M&A is a by-product of a great business and targeted BD. IPOs are always an option once you've built significant cash flow forecasting. It's important to ask questions like: How many "strategic engagements" with potential buyers have you had this month? Is your message and value clear in their eyes? Have you considered an acquisition track in parallel to a fundraiser?

- **Equity crowdfunding** can help close some gaps at the seed stage.
- **Early IPOs** on smaller exchanges can be an option to raise over $10 million the robotics startup Balyo went public and raised €40 million on Euronext to get rid of a critical "right of first refusal" option held by one of its corporate investors.
- **Reverse mergers** can work: the medical exoskeleton company EKSO Bionics went public this way.

One thing is sure: The time to exit is *not* when you're running out of money.

Companies are bought, not sold: Unicorn or not, the most likely exit is an acquisition. As George Patterson, managing director at HSBC in New York said, "Good tech companies are bought, not sold. The question is thus: how to get bought?"

M&A Financing Alternatives (Shall Sell or Continue to Grow)

M&A		Capital Raise
Usually higher in M&A transaction due to takeover premium	**Valuation**	PE / Growth Equity firms are increasingly paying up for fast growth companies
Cleaner structure as shareholders typically get full liquidity	**Structure**	Will need to evaluate the impact of a new class of preferred shares on cap table
Will benefit from revenue and cost synergies, which are important if there is an earn-out	**Growth Opportunities**	Financial sponsor incentivized to grow the company by offering advice (operational, HR, sales & marketing, etc.) and capital for add-on acquisitions
Will typically receive 100% liquidity upfront	**Liquidity**	Could receive partial liquidity and get a "second bite of the apple"
Working for a large corporation during term of the employment agreement	**Personal**	Still have "fire in the belly" to take the company to the next level

Patterson says it's important to understand how mergers and acquisitions actually work; how to prepare a startup for an exit; and how to develop a "feel" for the market you're exiting through and into.

How M&A works: Hearing from Corp dev veterans from Cisco, Dassault, and IBM, a few key ideas emerged:

Motivations vary: It could be from low to high, or a mix:

1. Talent hire ($1 million/dev as a rule of thumb location matters)
2. Product gap
3. Revenue driver
4. Strategic threat (avoid or delay disruption)
5. Defensive move (can't afford competitor to own it)

How Acquirers Find You: Corporates find deals via the development of partnerships, investment (CVC), their business units, Corp dev research, media, and investor network. Asked about the best approach, Todd Neville, manager of Corporate Business Development and Strategy at IBM (who gave the most detailed description of the Corp dev process), said, "Do something cool to one of the IBM customers.

If they rave about even a POC, we're interested." In other words, business development is corporate development.

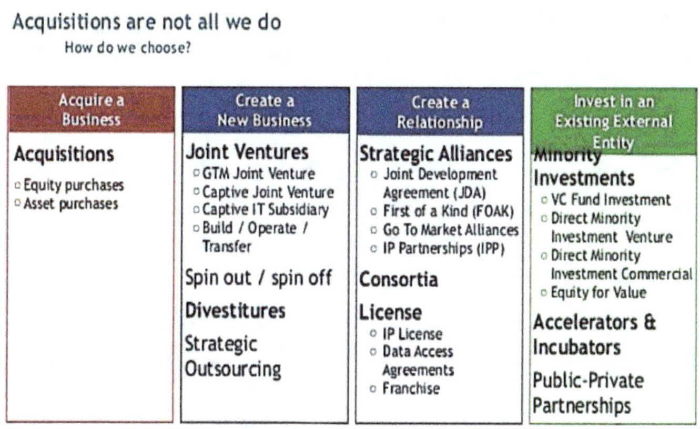

Get the house in order: Buyers typically want to know three things:

1. Is your IP really yours?
2. Is your team capable?
3. Will your customers stick around?

For IP, they will check your contracts (staff and contractors) and run some automated code analysis for proprietary code and open-source use. They will evaluate potential IP infringement. No point buying you if you end up costing more in lawsuits!

For your team skills: Sitting down with your engineers will tell them plenty enough without understanding the details of this or that algorithm. The last thing a corporate want is to be accused of stealing! Lawyers engaged early can help. The later the clean-up, the more costly and painful.

Develop a feel for your "market": Develop relationships and create champions within corporations. It will help promote your deal when the time comes and will let you keep your finger on the pulse of corporate strategy to time your moves.

Do you read the earning calls of Cisco or IBM (or others relevant to you)? This is where strategies are presented. Are your keywords coming up there or in their press releases? Chris Gilbert, former CEO of Ubiquisys (sold to Cisco for more than $300 million) was very deliberate in planning his exit. "Selling starts on day one and is a leadership-only function" work out who will be your buyer. Only the CEO can do this.

Constantly articulate why a company should buy you," Gilbert said. Bring clear messages into the acquiring company so they can be presented upwards: give them the presentation you would like them to show their boss!

When the time is right, force decisions through competition. If you know they have to buy you, your starting position is strong."

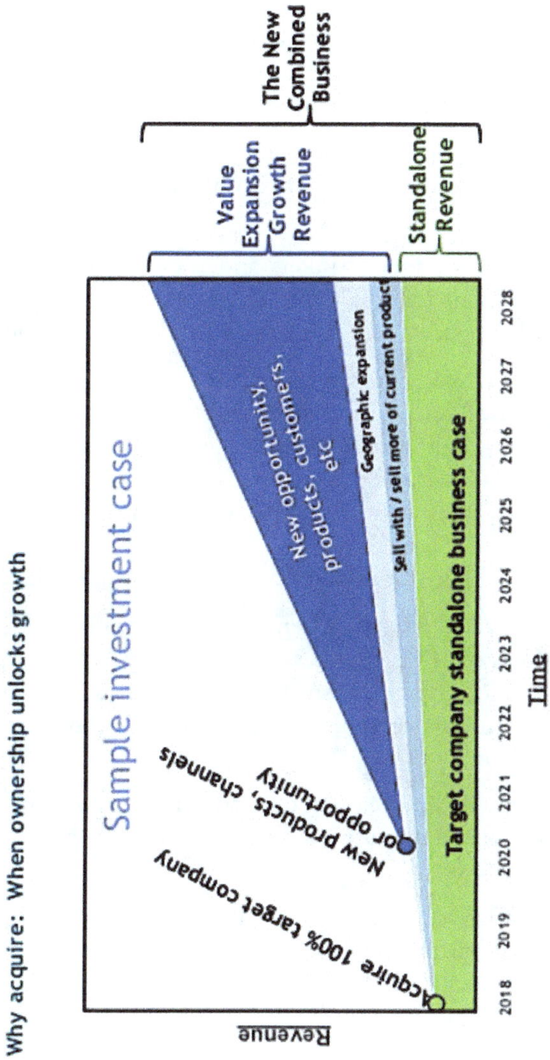

What IBM wants is a large "blue triangle" [7]

The dark art of price discovery: There are dozens of formulas (from DCF to comparables) to evaluate a deal which also means none is "correct." What matters is: How much would you sell for, and how much is the buyer ready to pay?

Gilbert, at Ubiquisys, described how close interactions with his banker helped drive the price up among the bidders assembled.

Just like buyers, we meet bankers and lawyers too rarely at startup events, but there is much to learn from them. They make deals happen, avoid value erosion, and optimize prices.

They often also make introductions before you engage them, to build goodwill and earn your business. And if you worry about fees, the right banker handsomely pays for itself by finding more bidders and playing "bad cop" for you, avoiding direct confrontation with your future employer.

Do you want a slice of the watermelon or the whole grape?

Final twist: Exits are not exits, when asked about what happens after an M&A or IPO, buyers said they generally hoped the founders would stay with them for many years. Often using re-vesting, earn-outs or shares of the acquiring company to incentivize them.

Neville, from IBM, mentioned a security company they acquired whose founder is now the head of one of the largest IBM divisions.

In the case of IPOs, supposedly the ultimate "exit," any block of shares sold by founders would face extreme scrutiny and might cause a price drop. So, who's excited about those deals? Investors (and not always).

Eventually, if the average age of a startup at exit is 8-10 years, the active-duty period of founders (if not replaced in the meantime) extends even more. Better love the problem you're solving, and your customers!

According to a Silicon Valley Bank survey, more than half of today's health and tech startups expect to exit via acquisition. All too many founders think their lofty dreams and cleverly worded pitch decks will carry them through to successful exits.

But acquisitions don't merely materialize; they require strategic planning and sustained effort over time, just like any other major company initiative.

Entrepreneurs need to consider early on which companies would be the best fit as potential acquirers, how acquisitions work in their industry sectors, and what they are aiming for in terms of valuation.

To position themselves for successful exits, entrepreneurs need to identify and, ideally, form partnerships with potential acquirers at the right stages in their development. And there are several factors to keep in mind about how to pinpoint the right time to sell.

Find your ideal buyer: I've met many entrepreneurs who think they are going to sell their company to Amazon or Google, but they have no clear idea of why those companies would be interested in buying them. Founders need to take a close look at companies that have been acquired by their targets and analyze why those transactions were successful.

In doing so, they'll notice a pattern: large companies like Google are often interested in acquiring startups that will either ***save them money or that have the potential to increase their revenue substantially.***

Amazon's purchase of Kiva Systems, a warehouse robotics company, for example, ultimately transformed the e-commerce giant's order fulfillment processes. Amazon bought Kiva for $775 million, and its technology has saved Amazon an estimated $2.5 billion in operating costs, according to Pitchbook.

If a company is building the right foundation for future acquisition, its founders and managers need to be clear about their value propositions and be able to articulate why their companies are a good fit with potential buyers.

Increase your company's exit price: Most entrepreneurs tend to focus on solving the problems that plague their customers and then build their companies around those solutions. For those hoping to exit via a successful acquisition, this strategy can be short-sighted. You're not selling your company to those customers. You're trying to sell your company to potential acquirers that share a similar customer base.

If you want to sell your company for a strong multiple, it's important to make sure your product serves the potential buyer's target customers. One goal is to save the acquiring company on their cost of customer acquisition essentially, the money they spend on marketing, sales, and other efforts necessary to attract new customers.

When Microsoft purchased the software development platform GitHub for $7.5 billion in stock, for example, Microsoft acquired not only a $200 million annual revenue stream; it also gained 27 million customers who were already using GitHub.

If a potential buyer showing interest in acquiring your company will save on customer acquisition, because you have created alignment between your product and the buyer's target customers, and your product or service has the potential to increase the buyer's revenue, then you've set the foundation for a profitable deal.

This ideal fit is known as attachment value and it can increase the sales price of your company significantly.

Know when to go: A startup's life cycle typically resembles a bell curve. Growth can be non-existent in the beginning, and then it slowly begins to escalate until it hits a peak.

That's usually around the time when a competitor comes along with a better product, the startup struggles to grow sustainably, or something else happens that causes a backslide.

Example of Startup Growth Bell Curve

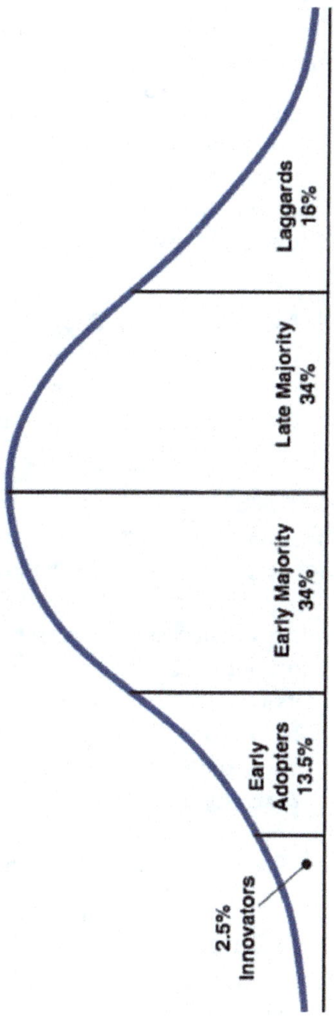

Ideally, buyers want to acquire a company at a lower point on the bell curve, when the startup still has significant room to grow.
They don't prefer to buy when it's reaching its peak, because that comes too late in the maturity cycle and they pay a significant premium. If you're the seller, you'd like to be acquired when things are going well so you can demand the best price for your company.

However, founders often wait too long, worrying they're going to leave money on the table. When that happens, they usually end up losing out. For example, Gilt Groupe, developer of the Gilt flash-sale site, was acquired by department store owner Hudson's Bay Company for $250 million.

At one time, Gilt had been valued at $1 billion, however, it was struggling to turn a profit, and it resorted to laying off nearly 50 people before being acquired by the retail giant. The founders held out for too long instead of selling the company at its peak.

Having this level of insight into your company's performance can help you determine how to approach potential buyers and put emotions aside to decide when it's the best time to make your exit.

- The vast majority of successful startup exits are not IPOs but rather acquisitions big or small, including acquihires.
- Big investments raise the bar for exits; founders should do a reality check before shooting for the stars.
- At times, an offer that feels disappointing may be your best bet. Any return on investment is better than none.

No one gets into the startup game with modest ambitions: founders and their financial backers always harbor dreams of outsized success.

The reality, however, is that entrepreneurial home runs are rare and happy outcomes often come in singles or doubles. To understand when to pursue those, you need to honestly assess your startup's potential and limitations and consider the life circumstances of all your stakeholders. While many founders may think that someday they'll ring the opening bell on a stock trading floor as their startup goes public, the reality is that most don't.

For example, 85 venture-backed companies went public, whereas 799, or nearly ten times as many, were acquired, according to the National Venture Capital Association. (The data, of course, doesn't begin to account for outright failures, which represent the vast majority of startup outcomes.)

Acquisitions big and small including acquihires can represent happy exits for any young company. Indeed, Silicon Valley Bank's latest survey of 1,400 startups shows that half expect to be acquired. As an entrepreneur, swinging for the fences makes sense. But as we recognize that often the wisest course may be single or double despite the professional investors pressing for the big score.

Don't get caught up in who had the latest giant exit on TechCrunch, says Ivan Gaviria, a lawyer at Gunderson Dettmer who has been advising startups for more than two decades. Consider your personal circumstances, Gaviria says, and those of your key employees.

Are there student loans to be repaid? Plans to start a family. Challenges making ends meet. Then factor in the odds against achieving the kind of success that puts a company's name in light.

Big financings only raise the bar: "I think sometimes people underestimate what it means to have five quality VCs that want to put twenty or thirty or forty million bucks into your company," Gaviria said. That kind of financing round, which implies a post-money valuation of between $100 million and $200 million, may seem like a victory in and of itself — until you realize that for your investors, it's just the opening gambit in a play for a 10x return. "Ask yourself," Gaviria says, "how many companies in your space have sold for a billion dollars?"

The answer, of course, is not many. So, as they weigh a big financing round, entrepreneurs need to be honest with themselves about how big they think they can get. Most startups, even those that are on a healthy trajectory, will run into limits on their growth potential that will force founders to grapple with whether to sell or go for it. "That's typically where that question comes into play," says Gaviria.

There's no definitive answer for when it's right to sell and when it's not. "If I knew, would I be selling my life in six-minute increments?" Gaviria jokes. Sometimes it's obvious.

If a struggling startup is presented with an acquisition offer, it'd be irresponsible to say no, even if it doesn't represent a win for investors. "The percentage [of success] drops precipitously for a company looking at a down round or any kind of big management change," Gaviria says. "That's just math." In other words, always remember that any deal is better than a strikeout.

But more often than not, things aren't so black and white. Gaviria says the decision of whether to be acquired can be both difficult and deeply personal. "If you're 23, 24, 25, you've probably got school loans," Gaviria says. "You probably don't have money in the bank. And here you've got an opportunity to sell the company in a transaction that might yield six, seven, eight, ten million bucks. That's super life-changing."

Pivot or Persevere till Closure:

The decision to pivot requires a clear-eyed and objective mindset. The telltale signs of the need to pivot are the decreasing effectiveness of product experiments and the general feeling that product development should be more productive.

Whenever you see those symptoms, consider a pivot.

The decision to pivot is emotionally charged for any startup and has to be addressed in a structured way. One way to mitigate this challenge is to schedule the meeting in advance.

I recommend that every startup have a regular "pivot or persevere" meeting. In my experience, less than a few weeks between meetings is too often and more than a few months is too infrequent. However, each startup needs to find its own pace.

Each pivot or perseverance meeting requires the participation of both the product development and business leadership teams. Add the perspectives of outside advisers who could help us see past our preconceptions and interpret data in new ways.

The product development team must bring a complete report of the results of its product optimization efforts over time (not just the past period) as well as a comparison of how those results stack up against expectations (again, over time). The business leadership should bring detailed accounts of their conversations with current and potential customers.

Failure to Pivot: The decision to pivot is so difficult that many companies fail to make it.

Unknowingly, most didn't know they had fallen into a classic startup trap. They had been so successful with their early efforts that they were ignoring the principles behind them. As a result, they missed the need to pivot even as it stared them in the face.

Pivots come in different types. The word pivot sometimes is used incorrectly as a synonym for change. A pivot is a special kind of change designed to test a new fundamental hypothesis about the product, business model, and engine of growth.

Zoom-in Pivot

In this case, what previously was considered a single feature in a product becomes the whole product. This is the type of pivot Votizen made when it pivoted away from a full social network and toward a simple voter contact product.

Zoom-out Pivot

In the reverse situation, sometimes a single feature is insufficient to support a whole product. In this type of pivot, what has been considered the whole product becomes a single feature of a much larger product.

Customer Segment Pivot

In this pivot, the company realizes that the product it is building solves a real problem for real customers but that they are not the type of customers it originally planned to serve. In other words, the product hypothesis is partially confirmed, solving the right problem, but for a different customer than originally anticipated.

Customer Need Pivot

As a result of getting to know customers extremely well, it sometimes becomes clear that the problem we're trying to solve for them is not very important. However, because of this customer intimacy, we often discover other related problems that are important and can be solved by our team.

In many cases, these related problems may require little more than repositioning the related problems may require little more than repositioning the existing product. In other cases, it may require a completely new product.

Platform Pivot

A platform pivot refers to a change from an application to a platform or vice versa. Most commonly, startups that aspire to create a new platform begin life by selling a single application, the so-called killer app, for their platform. Only later does the platform emerge as a vehicle for third parties to leverage as a way to create their own related products. However, this order is not always set-in-stone, and some companies have to execute this pivot multiple times.

Business Architecture Pivot

Companies generally follow one of two major business architectures: high margin, low volume (complex systems model) or low margin, high volume (volume operations model). The former commonly is associated with business to business (B2B) or enterprise sales cycles, and the latter with consumer products (there are notable exceptions).

In a business architecture pivot, a startup switches architecture. Some companies change from high margin too low volume by going mass market (e.g., Google's search "appliance"); others, originally designed for the mass market, turned out to require long and expensive sales cycles.

Value Capture Pivot

There are many ways to capture the value a company creates. These methods are referred to commonly as monetization or revenue models. These terms are much too limiting. Implicit in the idea of monetization is that it is a separate "feature" of a product that can be added or removed at will.

In reality, capturing value is an intrinsic part of the product hypothesis. Often, changes to the way a company captures value can have far-reaching consequences for the rest of the business, product, and marketing strategies.

The engine of Growth Pivot

As there are three primary engines of growth that power startups: the viral, sticky, and paid growth models. In this type of pivot, a company changes its growth strategy to seek faster or more profitable growth. Commonly but not always, the engine of growth also requires a change in the way value is captured.

Channel Pivot

In traditional sales terminology, the mechanism by which a company delivers its product to customers is called the sales channel or distribution channel. For example, consumer packaged goods are sold in grocery stores, cars are sold in dealerships, and much enterprise software is sold (with extensive customization) by consulting and professional services arms.

Often, the requirements of the channel determine the price, features, and competitive landscape of a product. A channel pivot is a recognition that the same basic solution could be delivered through a different channel with greater effectiveness. Whenever a company abandons a previously complex sales process to "sell direct" to its end users, a channel pivot is in progress.

It is precise because of its destructive effect on sales channels that the Internet has had such a disruptive influence in industries that previously required complex sales and distribution channels, such as newspaper, magazine, and book publishing.

Technology Pivot

Occasionally, a company discovers a way to achieve the same solution by using a completely different technology. Technology pivots are much more common in established businesses.

In other words, they are a sustaining innovation, an incremental improvement designed to appeal to and retain an existing customer base. Established companies excel at this kind of pivot because so much is not changing. The customer segment is the same, the problem is the same.

Exit Terms, Diligence and Data Room: The story is all too common in Silicon Valley. A high-profile startup sells for tens of millions or better. It's not the home run many were hoping for, but it appears to be a solid single or double.

And yet, after the dust settles, employees, and sometimes founders, find that their equity stakes in the company are essentially worthless. Investors, on the other hand, fare better, sometimes recouping their money or even pocketing a positive return. "That's how it works," says Tim Tuttle, founder, and former CEO of Mind Meld, a maker of conversational apps backed by artificial intelligence that was acquired by Cisco in 2017. "The people that give you money get paid back first."

The same dynamic, where investors take precedence over employees and founders, comes into play when a company is shuttered.

Welcome to the world of preferred stock. It is an essential part of venture deals in tech and beyond. And before issuing it, entrepreneurs must understand what it means, how it is structured, and how it behaves in different scenarios. VCs demand liquidation preferences to mitigate their risk Founders don't get preferred stock.

But it's nearly impossible to raise venture capital without issuing preferred stock, or preferred shares. In most cases, VCs today won't hand over a dime in exchange for common shares, the form of equity extended to founders and employees.

Preferred stock, unlike common stock, is exactly what the name implies. Its owners receive preferential treatment over other investors in specific situations. What exactly that means is negotiable, and it will end up in the fine print of your term sheet. It can involve a wide range of special rights. The most common and important is the liquidation preference.

If your company is a runaway hit, you'll likely never have to worry about liquidation preferences. But if your startup goes out of business or ends up selling for less than what it was once valued, liquidation preferences will come into play.

The liquidation preferences mitigate the risk investors face by ensuring they get paid first. The fine print will determine how much, if any, remains for you and your employees.

Fortunately, deal terms are increasingly standard. It's not as bad as it sounds. That's because deal terms have become increasingly standardized, says Ivan Gaviria, a partner at Gunderson Dettmer, a Silicon Valley law firm that has worked with startups for decades. And today's standards tend to favor founders.

"The leverage is with the entrepreneur," Gaviria says. "There's a ton of capital available and a lot of competition for deals."

Given those conditions, Gaviria says most venture capitalists will ask for and receive a liquidation preference called "1x, non-participating." Since liquidation preferences are expressed as a multiple of the initial investment, the 1x means they will receive a dollar back for every dollar invested, a full recouping of their money — as long as there's enough to cover this. Common shareholders will divvy up what's left. "The people that give you money get paid back first."

The term "nonparticipating" means that the investor has a choice. He or she can receive their original investment back or convert their preferred stock into common stock and share in the proceeds according to their equity ownership, whichever amount is greater.

While terms are becoming standardized, sometimes entrepreneurs get into trouble because they are fixated on maximizing their company's valuation in a given round. "I have seen companies raise money and negotiate for higher valuations and, in trade, they give up more favorable liquidation preferences," says David Van Horne, a partner at the law firm of Goodwin Procter. "More often than not, that ends up being a bad trade."

In later financing rounds, matters can become more complex and dangerous — especially if your company has struggled to hit milestones. In these situations, investors might ask for 2x or 3x liquidation preferences, meaning they would receive twice or three times their original investment before common shareholders are paid.

That all but guarantees that employees and founders won't ever see much for their equity unless they manage to turn the ship around. Investors might also ask for anti-dilution provisions. These are clauses designed to protect an investor's ownership percentage from being diluted in future funding rounds where the company issues new stock for a lower price.

If an investor has negotiated an anti-dilution clause, their stake in the company is maintained through formulas that turn each preferred share into more than one common share.

Exactly how much more depends on the situation and the method specified in the anti-dilution agreement.

Beware of 'double dipping': If a company lacks leverage, investors sensing big risks might even try to negotiate for "participating preferred shares," also known as the "double dip." Says Gaviria: "Preferred participating is the thing you want to be wary of."

During a liquidation event, an investor with participating preferred rights is first in line to recoup their initial investment. If any proceeds remain after that, the participating preferred investor will then pocket an additional share proportional to their percentage ownership stake in the company on a pro rata basis with common shareholders. (Pro-rata is a Latin term that means whatever is allocated will be distributed equally.) Hence, the double dip — preference and participation.

"If a company sells for $100 million," says Gaviria, "an investor with participating preferred shares might take their original $20 million investment off the top and then take 20% (their percentage share of the company) of the remaining $80 million such that commonly gets 80 cents on the dollar on the amount remaining after the preference."

In later rounds, common shareholders could end up with as little as 30 or 40 cents on the dollar, Gaviria adds. An example of preferred stock with and without liquidation: Say a company raises $500,000 in its seed round at a post-money valuation of $2.5 million, giving investors a 20% stake.

The chart below shows how much money investors receive if the company is sold for between $2 million and $6 million.

With non-participating preferred stock, investors get to choose the greater of:

a) exercising their liquidation preferences; or

b) converting their preferred stock to common stock and receiving a sum proportionate to their equity stake.

In the worst-case scenario for founders and employees ($2M exit with 2.0x liquidation), common stockholders with 80% ownership will receive $1 million — the same amount as preferred shareholders with a 20% stake.

Exit Value	Return based on ownership stake	Return based on 1x liquidation	Return based on 1.5x liquidation	Return based on 2x liquidation
$6 million	$1.2 million	$500,000	$750,000	$1 million
$4 million	$800,000	$500,000	$750,000	$1 million
$2 million	$400,000	$500,000	$750,000	$1 million

Giving up too much can hurt later: It's important to remember the terms of preferred shares are negotiated between founders and investors. Founders who agree to give up 3x preferred participating rights are typically desperate for money. In a bull market, such terms are very rare, said David Pakman, who founded one of the first cloud-music companies and is now a partner at venture capital firm Venrock. "The leverage is with the entrepreneur."

"If investor X asks for a bunch of things that are completely out of a market that no other investors are asking for," Pakman said, "then he or she is unlikely to get them unless the entrepreneur is having a super hard time raising funding."

Cash-strapped founders must make these decisions very carefully, as they could have dire consequences later, says MindMeld's Tuttle. Consider the following scenario, Tuttle says: You do a financing in desperation where you agree to a high liquidation preference, and shortly after, you get a modest acquisition offer.

While the deal would have been life-changing for founders and employees, due to the high liquidation preference, they don't see any upside. "At that moment it's very frustrating for founders," Tuttle says. "But the reason they're there is because they weren't able to convince investors to give them the money, they needed to get there without introducing these aggressive terms to offset the risk."

Diligence Checklist: Prior to an investment or sale transaction, prospective investors or acquirers will complete a comprehensive review of the target business and its records. A company's ability to quickly and completely respond to due diligence requests increases the likelihood that the deal at hand will close on favorable terms (or close at all). Prepare now for major transactions by maintaining the company records in the below due diligence checklist.

Corporate Records:

1. Certificate or Articles of Incorporation, including all amendments.
2. Bylaws, including all amendments.
3. Written consents of directors and stockholders.
4. Minutes of directors' and stockholders' meetings.

Securities:

1. A list of the company's stockholders and option holders (i.e., capitalization table).
2. Copies of options, warrants, or other agreements that provide for the purchase or acquisition of company securities.
3. Copies of all agreements relating to the company's past stock issuances and a summary of any related vesting schedules.
4. Copies of Form Ds, Blue Sky filings, and any other documents relating to compliance with applicable state and federal laws.
5. Any documents or agreements related to the sale or purchase of securities (e.g., investor rights agreements and voting agreements).

Agreements:

1. Any agreements or proposed transactions to which the company is a party that involves obligations of, or payments

to, the company.
2. Contracts with suppliers, distributors, customers, and manufacturers.
3. Property purchase, lease, or sublease agreements.
4. Documents relating to indebtedness for money borrowed, guaranties, leases, or any similar liabilities incurred by the company.
5. Mortgages, loans, or liens on the company's property or assets.
6. Loans or advances made by the company.
7. Any agreements, understandings, or proposed transactions between the company and any of its officers, directors, employees, or affiliates (e.g., employment agreements).
8. Copies of proprietary information and invention assignment agreements signed by all employees and contractors.
9. Employees' offer letters.
10. Consulting or independent contractor agreements.
11. A summary of insurance policies, or certificates of insurance, that the company holds or benefits from.
12. Employee benefit plans (e.g., stock option plans, pension plans, and insurance plans).
13. Acquisition agreements.
14. Confidentiality agreements.
15. Agreements with competitors, including non-compete NDAs.
16. Partnership, joint venture, association, and technical agreements
17. Any other agreement material to the company.

Intellectual Property

1. List of principal products (including products being developed) in each line of business, with short descriptions of the products, respective prices, and stages of development.
2. Company procedures for identifying, harvesting, and protecting inventions.

3. Licenses or agreements related to the company's or others' patent, copyright, trade secret, or other proprietary rights, proprietary information, or technology.
4. Issued patents, patent applications, and foreign patent filings.
5. All prior art patent searches, conclusions, reports, and opinions that the company possesses concerning the infringement of third-party patents by its products and the validity of such third-party patents.
6. Federal, state, and foreign trademark registrations and pending applications.
7. Documents relating to agreements dealing with trademarks.
8. Copyright registration records.
9. Restrictions on use of the copyrights or third-party ownership
10. Trade secrets, whether the company is licensor or licensee (e.g., license, secrecy, or non-analysis).
11. Agreements with the company's current and former employers relating to the use of the company's proprietary information.
12. Reseller agreements.

Litigation

1. Pending or threatening lawsuits, actions, or investigations.
2. Allegations of the company's infringement of the proprietary rights of others.
3. Settlement agreements.
4. Inquiries from federal, state, or other government officials (e.g., tax, environmental, occupational safety, and hazard).
5. Judgments or orders involving the company, its officers, or its directors.

Miscellaneous

1. Most recent financial statements.
2. List of officers and directors.

Startup Investments Performance: given the market opacity and the false presumption that startup investors are all tech savvy who can spot the perfect investments that makes them exponentially wealthy, along with having the equivalent of god's power that convert starving founders into king through venture capital large investment rounds which makes them unicorn and instant billionaires. The industry-wise ratio is (90% Loss, 5% Break-even, and 5% Multi X). Let's start with the facts by stage:

Angel Investments: Pre to Seed Round: $25k to $3m
Profile: Typical entrepreneur using exit cash to fund their investment

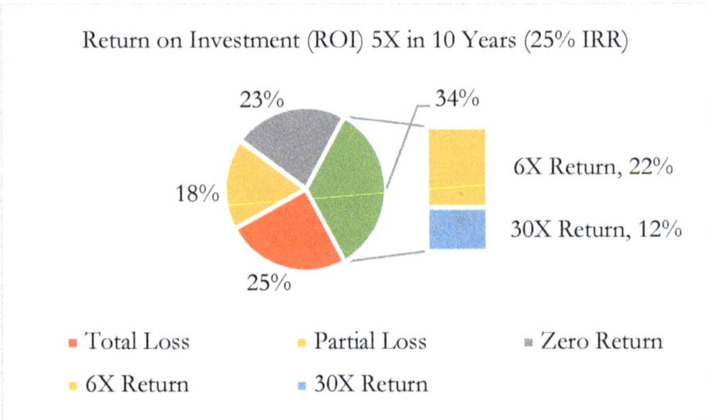

The Ewing Marion Kauffman Foundation published an extensive report that analyzes a combined portfolio of 117 angel investments made by four angel investors. The average investment size was approximately 85k. 68% of the investments resulted in a break-even or negative return. The total cash returned to the four investors from the portfolio was $51.1 million after 10 years, generating a 5X return on invested capital.

The authors divide the exited investments into 5 different categories based on the ROI multiple: As shown in the chart above, with the IRR at 25%. and the average time to exit is 4 years. A large, diversified angel portfolio should have a 100-startup portfolio at minimum to reach the above performance.

Venture Capital Investments: Series A to Exit Rounds

Profile: Most are brokers who invest on behalf of institutional investors called Limited partners and get an upfront fee of 2% with an upside on each positive exit capped at 20% in 10 years. Some are General Partners who invest up to 2% of each fund "usually founders with exit". *One of the biggest myths is that established mega funds are the only way to generate outperformance, but the facts speak by themselves:*

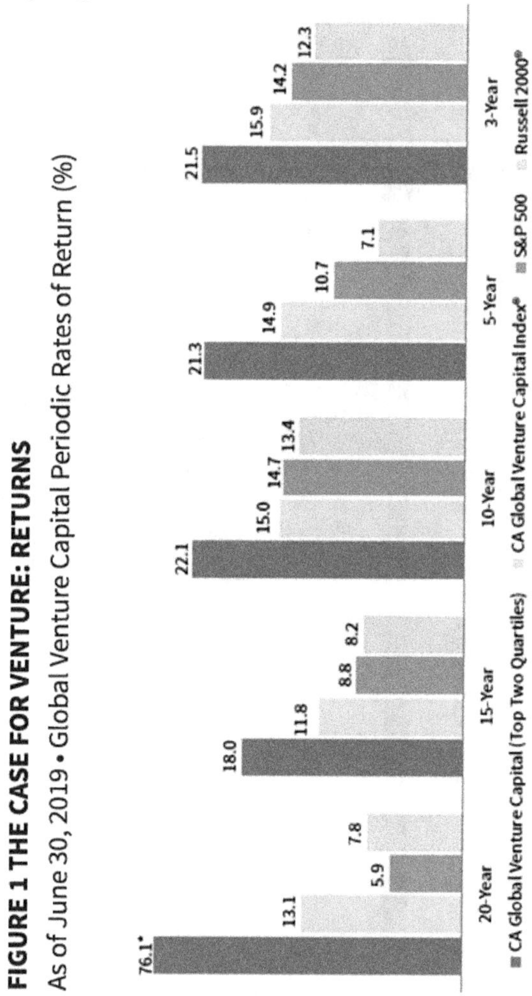

Source: Cambridge Associates

S&P500 matches or outperform Venture Capital within the 3-10-years benchmark.

New and Developing Funds outperform the established Venture Capital powerhouse IRR by holding top spots at 60% vs 40% to the old guard
Source: Cambridge Associates

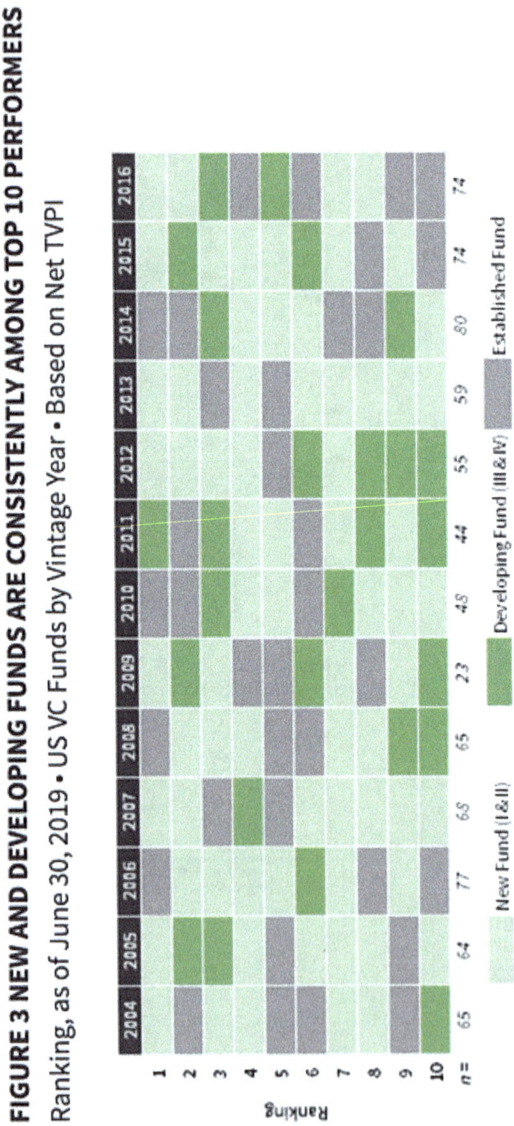

Average Startup valuation: at Seed Round is 7.5X, which multiplies by 3X at each next round, then abate to 2X post-Series C.

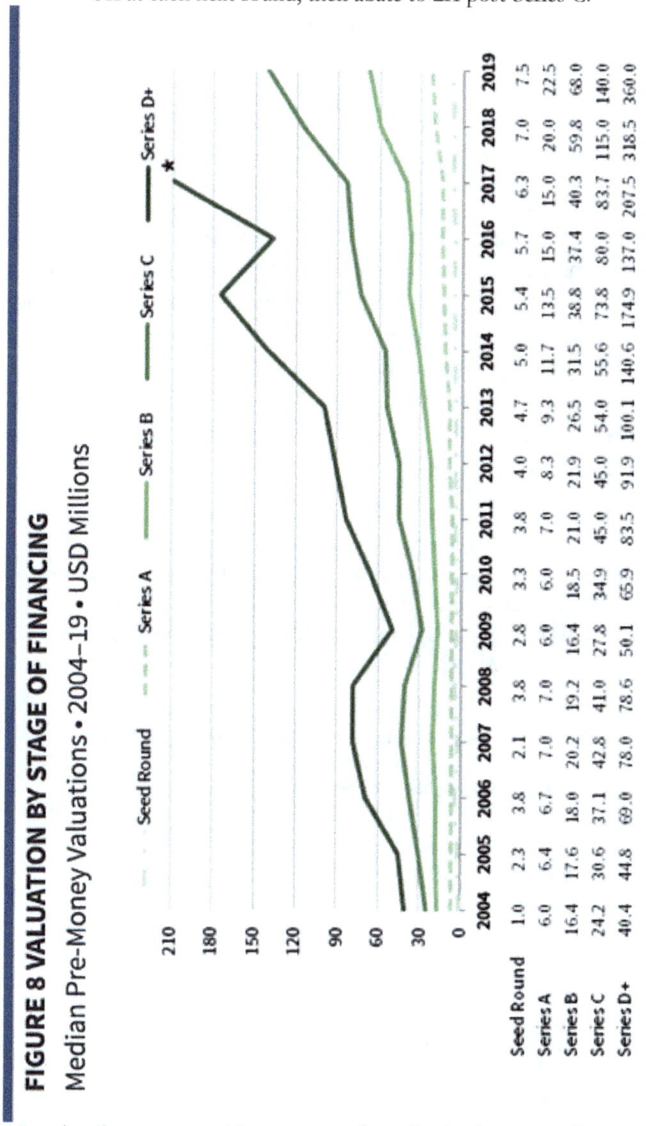

	2004	2005	2006	2007	2008	2009	2010	2011	2012	2013	2014	2015	2016	2017	2018	2019
Seed Round	1.0	2.3	3.8	2.1	3.8	2.8	3.3	3.8	4.0	4.7	5.0	5.4	5.7	6.3	7.0	7.5
Series A	6.0	6.4	6.7	7.0	7.0	6.0	6.0	7.0	8.3	9.3	11.7	13.5	15.0	15.0	20.0	22.5
Series B	16.4	17.6	18.0	20.2	19.2	16.4	18.5	21.0	21.9	26.5	31.5	38.8	37.4	40.3	59.8	68.0
Series C	24.2	30.6	37.1	42.8	41.0	27.8	34.9	45.0	45.0	54.0	55.6	73.8	80.0	83.7	115.0	140.0
Series D+	40.4	44.8	69.0	78.0	78.6	50.1	65.9	83.5	91.9	100.1	140.6	174.9	137.0	207.5	318.5	360.0

Exception for startups with revenue and profit who bootstrap for years or new startup with teams that had a billion exit, they raise from $100m Series A to $500m Series B (i.e., Nuvation S/A $275m, Better Place S/B $350m).

Corporate Venture Capital Investments: Series A to Exit Rounds

CVC is growing at a time when most corporate firms question the return on investment of their R&D departments, and wonder how much they should invest in research, as opposed to development. After decades of Development prevalence, Research seems to be needed again.

However, companies have no idea about the payback from their projects and therefore invest in a very discretionary and volatile manner, which is governed by economic conditions. CVC offers a welcome alternative option with clearer limits and greater efficiency. Some academic studies in the 1990s and the first wave of the corporate venture have shown that $1 invested in CVC pays back 3 to 4 times more than $1 invested in R&D, with cumulative investment in a startup at $120 Billion Globally.

There are close to 1,000 CVCs, the primary industries are IT, Healthcare, and Consumer. However, with the influx of CVC activity, we expect to see a growing number of industries represented. According to a study done by MIT, 74% of the interviewed CXO participants agree or strongly agree that the pandemic has acted as a catalyst for innovation within businesses.

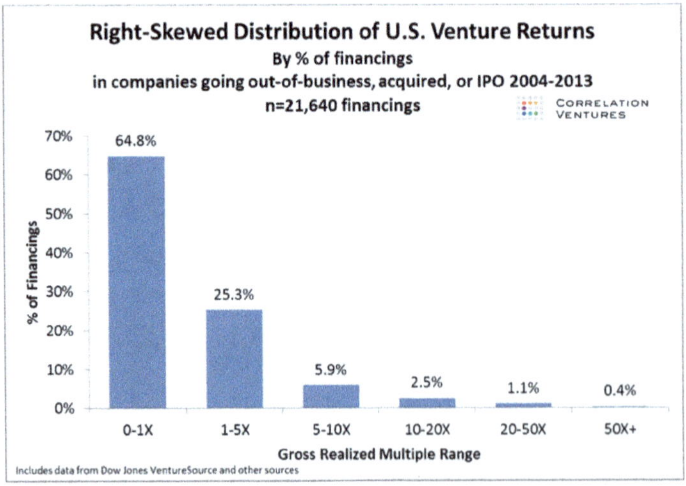

Startup Post Exit Listing – IPO

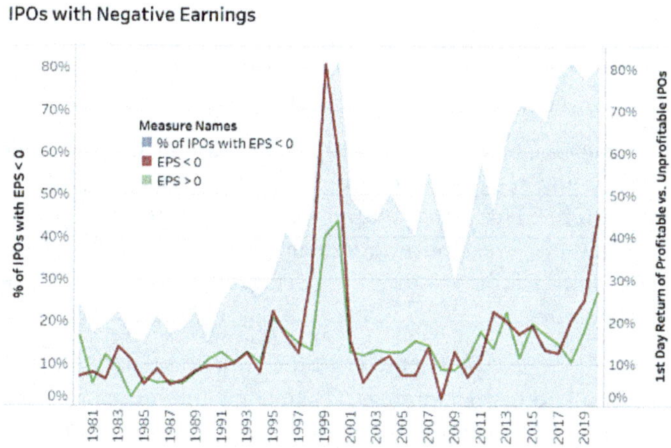

Source: NASDAQ

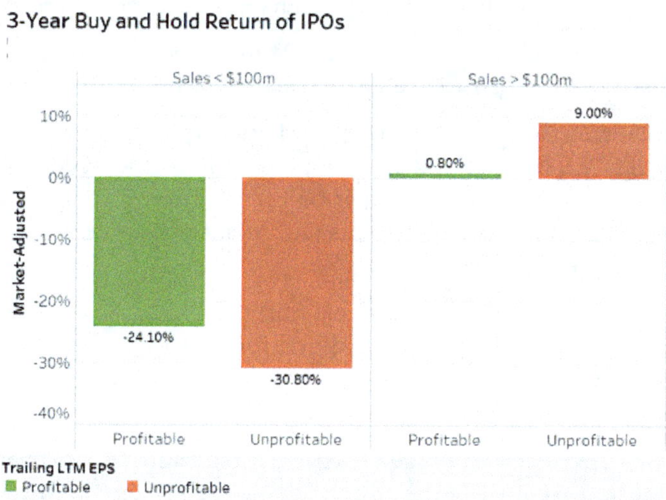

Source: NASDAQ

Takeaways: The end of the year is a great time to step back and take a bird's eye view of the business. Whether you are thinking of selling next year or in ten years.

The following should be reviewed on an annual basis and stored in one folder called by IB Data room:

Due Diligence Checklist: Get a sample (and simple) due diligence checklist and see how many of the items are readily available and current. This can save an enormous amount of time, especially if a great buyer suddenly shows up at your door. Work on it a little at a time (or delegate it) so that it is not overwhelming.

Vision/Strategy: When is the last time your company reviewed its vision and overall strategy? Take a few minutes and assess if these are still current and working. If not, make changes.

Culture: Step back and consider what the company culture is, and how that might be different from your goals. Use the time to reinforce positive culture and eliminate negative culture.

Dashboard KPIs: Be sure that Key Performance Indicators are kept current, organized, and in a state of improvement.

Financials: Every year, a business should try to improve the quality of its financial reporting as well as the speed of reporting. The year-end is a good time to remind your CPA to clean up income statements and balance sheet items that are no longer relevant.

If the company has only internal financials, have the CPA do a compilation. If compiled, move forward to reviewed or audited financials. If audited and you are considering a sale, get a sell-side quality earnings report.

If you have any one-time expenses, personal items, or other adjustments to EBITDA, check with your CPA and/or M&A advisor to see what is acceptable, and document those expenses.

Sales and Marketing: Step back and consider the company's overall sales and marketing strategy. Try something different, eliminate something that's not working. Be sure you can describe the strategy to an outsider.

Website, Social Media: If your website looks like it was made in 2010, it is time to invest in a new one. It is one of the things that most new customers and potential buyers will look at first, so make sure it looks professional, has accurate information, and works. If you have news, blogs, or social media posts, keep them as up to date as possible.

Ownership: This comes up in the due diligence checklist, so in case you skipped that, at least make sure your key ownership documents are available and up to date. For example, the operating agreement should be current, and any former founders (and ex-spouses) should be taken out. Check to make sure you have all current cap tables, vesting schedules with stock certificates.

Legal: Make sure all legal documents, such as customer contracts, supplier contracts, leases, maintenance agreements, NDAs, non-competes, IP, etc., are current and in an organized file.

Compliance: Taxes (Sales Taxes, State Taxes): This can be a major issue in due diligence, as regulations and taxes keep getting more complex. Have your CPA do a review of your policies, and if your CPA does not have much experience in interstate commerce, hire a consultant to review things.

Human Resources: Keep all policies and handbooks current. If the company does not use a PEO, consider making the change. If not using a payroll service, consider using one soon (if anything, to make sure that taxes and other matters are taken care of). Update your org chart.

M&A Advisor: Check in with an M&A advisor who you trust to discuss trends in the market, multiples, the pros and cons of your startup maintain a loop of potential leads, etc.

There are two important things you can do as a founder to mitigate the possible downside of preferred stock. The first is to hire a good advisor, someone with experience who knows the landscape and the players.

The second is to execute on your startup's plans, hit the key milestones and benchmarks and build a great product. If you do that, everything else falls in place. Gaviria says he often finds entrepreneurs too focused on deal terms and valuations.

His advice is to concentrate on building a great business. I tell them, 'Hey, let's focus on getting the investors to fall in love with your company, your team, you.'" he says.

Like with any negotiation, he adds, "most of this stuff is a leverage game."

BIBLIOGRAPHY – INDEX

Below are the various sources I have relied on, cited, referenced, or consulted during my research in writing this book, listed per first reference in this book with page number. This is not intended to be the most authoritative source since many insights have been acquired during my academic and professional endeavors.

1 - John F. Kennedy. 5 - Albert Einstein, Alfred Nobel, Antoine Saint-Exupery, Thomas Edison, Marie Claire, Henry Ford. 7 - Gates, Jobs and Bezos. 10 - Guinness book, Christian Church, To Explain the World by Steven Weinberg. 11 - Nikola Tesla, Ford, Global Positioning Satellite, Universal Computing Machine, Minitel, CSN, Motorola. 12 - Cloud Computing, Open Nebula NASA, VoIP Skype, Mobile Computing, Touch Screen, iPhone, Robotics, Human like Robot Android, IP, ID, Blockchain, Connection, Hi-Speed Internet, Wi-Fi, Hotspot, Bluetooth, Mac, Steve Job, C# Language, Anders Hejlsberg, 3G Mobile Network, NTT, IBM, Microsoft, America Online, Yahoo, Blackberry, Nokia, Olivetti, Philips, Panasonic, Sony. 13 - Leland Stanford, Wikipedia, Stanford University. U.S. Department of Defense, Frederick Terman, Stanford Research Park, Hewlett-Packard (HP), Google (Alphabet). Apple, Salesforce, Uber, Robinhood, Tesla.

14 - Brookings Institution, US Census Bureau. 15 - American Community Survey. FTC, William Shokley, Mohamed Atella, Licklider, Computer Science, Doug Engelbart, Computer Mouse, single-chip microprocessor, Kleiner Perkins, Sequoia, Frederick Terman, Fairchild Semiconductor; Intel Corporation, portable computer CPU (Central Processing Unit), Stanford Research Institute (now SRI International), ARPANET, Venture Capital investments. 16 - Oracle, Larry Ellison, Bob Miner, Ed Oates, Larry Page, Sergey Brin, Scott Hassan, Zoom, Eric Yuan, Cisco Webex, Covid-19, Image and Illustration Graphs: BW Research; U.S. Bureau of Labor Statistics; LinkedIn. 17 - Image and Illustration Graphs: California Department of Justice, Institute for Regional Studies, CBRE 2020 Scoring Tech Talent, Silicon Valley Institute for Regional Studies, US Department of Commerce. 18 - Image and Illustration Graphs: ACS, EPA. 19 – Image and Illustration Graphs: Silicon Valley Institute for Regional Studies, Crunchbase, Renaissance Capital. 20 - Christopher Columbus, Steven Shapin, Harvard University. 21 - theGlobe.com, Webvan, Amazon, iTunes, Ritmoteca, NASDAQ, CMGI, America Online, Time Warner, Yahoo!, Microsoft. 23 - UC Berkeley, Unix, Bell Laboratories, NOKIA. 24 - Yi Cui, Department of Materials Science and Engineering at Stanford University, National Science Foundation. 25 - Larry Page, Sergey Brin, University of California, Berkeley, UC San Francisco 27 - Image and Illustration Graphs: Total R&D Expenditure and Patents filed by Country by The Brookings Institute. 28 - Image and Illustration Graphs: Total Patents Grant by US Metro for Top Universities and Patents Lawsuits by owners that go to market vs speculators by The Brookings Institute. 29 - Sir Timothy Berners-Lee, CERN Genova. 31 - Image and Illustration Graphs: Social media Brand Usage by The Infinite Dial, Electric Vehicles on the road in the US & Battery pack price by Global X Research, Benchmark Mineral Intelligence, Edison Electric Institute and Bloomberg. 33 - Image and Illustration Graphs: Global Number of Connected Devices by Global X Research, Ericsson Mobility Report and Cisco. 34 - Image and Illustration Graphs: Edge Internet Growth by Chetan Sharma Consulting. Automated Mobility vs. Personal Sedan by Rocky Mountain Institute.

35 - Image and Illustration Graphs: Number of Industrial Robots Worldwide by Global X Research, Oxford Economics and International Federation of Robotics.

36 - Image and Illustration Graphs: E-Commerce Sales vs Retails by BigCommerce. 37 - CRISPR-Cas9, DNA. 38 - Image and Illustration Graphs: DNA Sequencing goes Mainstream by Illumina, Loihi, Intel Labs, Cornell University. 42 - Uber, Alibaba, Ries and Horhey candies, McDonald, and Frigidaire. 43 - Elon Musk, Jeff Bezos, Jack Ma, Pfizer, Charles Pfizer, Steve Jobs, Moderna, Noubar Afeyan. 45 - Xerox. 48 - Netflix, Blockbuster, U.S. mail. 56 - Compaq, DEC. 59 - Facebook. 65 - Barcelona Tech City - Spain, Historical Museum of Catalonia, Station F Paris - France, Xavier Neil. Miguel Vincente, Miquel Marti, The Volkswagen Group's SEAT Metropolis Lab, La Caixa Bank, Global Payments, Visa, Arval, and Samsung. 66 - Ubisoft, Airbnb, Line, L'Oréal, President Macron, Buenos Aires, Technological District - Argentina, Mauricio Macri, Norman Foster, Parque Patricios, Banco Ciudad. 67 - Telefónica, Deloitte, Accenture, Huawei, Tata consulting, Despegar.com, Mercadolibre.com, Metropolitan Design Center and Institute of Technology of Buenos Aires, *The Brooklyn Navy Yard,* US Federal Government, Steiner Studios, Situ Studio, Cooper Union, CUNY's Fierstein Graduate School of Cinema, USC. 68 - Adidas, Brooklyn Creative Farm, MakerLab, BMW, A/D/O, Claus Meyer, NOMA of Copenhagen, San Pelegrino, The Richemont Group (Cartier & Van Cleef & Arpels), Wylie Dufresne, CEA - France, Fraunhofer Society – Germany, Science and Technology Agency - Japan, Department of Health and Human Services - US. Brooklyn Grange, Thomson Reuters. 69 - Fortune 500, Kodak. 70 - Google x, Amazon Lab126, Kindle Chris Green, TechCrunch. Amazon Fire TVs and tablets and the Amazon Echo, Volkswagen Automotive Innovation Lab, or VAIL, the Center for Automotive Research at Stanford (a.k.a. CARS). 71 - Volkswagen Touareg, Xerox Parc: PARC (Palo Alto Research Center formerly Xerox PARC. 72 –GM, Walmart, State Grid, Exxon, GE, Citigroup, AT&T, Altria, Boeing, Walmart, State Grid, China NP, Sinopec, CVS, United Health, Toyota, Alphabet, Tencent, TSMC, Berkshire, Huawei, Roche, Johnson & Johnson, Aramco, Softbank, ICBA, CCB, ABOC, Samsung. 74 - StartX, University of California Berkeley, SkyDeck, Harvard Innovation Lab, Massachusetts Institute of Technology. 75 - Angel Pad, OneTraction, Founder Institute, Y Combinator, Techstars, 500 Startup, Mach49, Alchemist. 77 - Image and Illustration Graphs: Coworking vs. other remote work alternatives by buffer.com, Plug and Play, GSV Labs, Hanahaus, Galvanize, Bespoke, NextSpace, WeWork, Regis, CIC, HBR. 78 - Image and Illustration Graphs: The Average Cost of Coworking spaces by DeskMag with Coworking Growth. 82 - Senator Macro Rubio. 84 - 42 Silicon Valley. 85 – The Hitchhiker's Guide to the Galaxy by Douglas Adams. 86 - Stripe, Instacart, Apoorva Mehta, Databricks, Ali Ghodsi, Chris Britt, Michael Rubin, GoPuff, Yakir Gola, Max Lytvyn, Brex, Henrique Dubugras, Osman Kibar. 88 - University Research Park Facts, Battelle Study John Hennessy. 90 - University of California System, COSEPUP, Richard Zare, the Marguerite Blake Wilbur, Stanley Cohen, Herbert Boyer, DNA, Yamaha. Hewlett-Packard. 93 - Cornell Business and Technology Park, Cornell University, Michael Bloomberg. 94 - Stanford Research Park, Research Triangle Park (RTP), Duke University, North Carolina State University, University of North Carolina, SBIR, STTR, Sandia Science and Technology Park (SS&TP), Sandia National Laboratory, National Academy of Sciences. 95 - The University of New Mexico (UNM), NASA's Research Park, NASA Ames, Oak Ridge Science & Technology Park, Oak Ridge National Laboratory, the Livermore Valley Open Campus, Lawrence Livermore National Laboratory, the Sandia National Laboratories California. 96 - The Fraunhofer Institute. 97 - Research and Development Park - Florida Atlantic University. 98 - University of Arizona - Science and Technology Park, National Science Foundation. 100 - The Committee on Science Engineering Medicine and Public Policy "COSEPUP", US Department of

Energy. 101 - The Food and Drug Administration (FDA). 102 - Edward Penhoet, the President's Council of Advisors on Science and Technology (PCAST). 104 – Foxconn. 105 - Image and Illustration Graphs: Global Map of Top 60 Innovative Countries by Bloomberg. 106 - The Global Innovation Hubs Index (GIHI), the Center for Industrial Development and Environmental Governance at Tsinghua University in China, National Academy of Science, Catherine Mann, global chief economist at Citigroup Inc., Mckinsey Company Research, Harvard Business Review, BCG – Boston Consulting Group. 109 - U.S. News and World Report, Delece Smith-Barrow, Drexel University, University of Ann Arbor. 110 - Northeastern University, Georgia State University, University of Maryland, Arizona State – Tempe, Georgia Institute of Technology, Carnegie Mellon University, University of Baltimore Maryland, Purdue University West Lafayette, Elon University. 112 - Image and Illustration Graphs: Engineers as a Percentage of all occupations. Bureau of Labor Statistics, special tabulations of the Occupational Employment and Wage Statistics Survey. 113 – KPMG. 114 - The National Training Laboratories – Maine, retention rate. 115 – Nesta – UK's agency for innovation, Good and bad innovation report. 116 - European Commission, Erik Brynjolfsson, Andrew McAfee, faculty members at the MIT Sloan School of Management, the impact of technology on economies, Harvard Business Review, Amy Bernstein, Anand Raman. 117 - Ethan Zuckerman, the Center for Civic Media at the Massachusetts Institute of Technology, The Atlantic, The Internet's Original Sin, Tripod, The Office Cubicle by Bob Propst, Herman Miller. 118 - Image and Illustration Graphs: When Corporate Innovation Goes Bad by APQC and PDI (American Productivity and Quality Center, Product Development Institute, Delorean Motor Company (DMC). 119 - Airboard, Sony, iPad, Blackberry Storm, Verizon, Google Glass, Micah Altman, Center of Research in Equitable and Open Scholarship at MIT. 120 - Douglas Rushkoff, City University of New York, Paola Ricaurte, Harvard's Berkman Klein Center for Internet and Society, *Axel Bruns,* James Mickens. 121 - Peter Lunenfeld, University of California, Los Angeles. 122 - Oscar Gandy, a professor emeritus of communication at the University of Pennsylvania. 123 - Jonathan Grudin - Microsoft, Rebecca Theobald, the University of Colorado, Colorado Springs. 124 - Jonathan Morgan, Wikimedia Foundation, Mark Surman, Mozilla Foundation, Commons Group. 125 - Jeff Johnson, University of San Francisco, Sun Microsystems, Richard Sclove, YouTube, Snapchat, Bernie Hogan, Oxford Internet Institute. 126 - Ann Adams, Ioana Marinescu, University of Pennsylvania School of Social Policy and Practice, Melissa Michelson, Menlo College. 127 - Ethan Zuckerman. 128 - Mike Roberts, Internet Hall of Fame member and pioneer CEO of ICANN, Ben Shneiderman - founder of the Human Computer Interaction Lab at the University of Maryland. 129 - Image and Illustration Graphs: Global Internet Users with Impact of Tech by Young and Well, CRC. 134 - UN Sustainable Development. 141 - UN Global Compact, Millennium Development Goals (MDGs), Sustainable Development Goals (SDGs). 142 - Kofi Annan, The United Nations Convention, the Global Reporting Initiative (GRI), World Business Council for Sustainable Development (WBSCD). 143 - Maude Barlow, David Andrews, Peter Utting, UNRISD. 144 - Starbucks, L'Oréal, Bayer AG, Coca-Cola, 3M, Deloitte, Ban Ki-Moon. 145 – Robinhood, Fortune 500 companies, and the S&P 500. 146 – Image and Illustration Graphs: Impact Innovation on Business Profit and Performance by BCG, Accenture, GE, KPMG, Deloitte and Mckinsey, Our World in Data Graphs. 147 - World Trade Organization's (WTO) TRIPS. 149 - Santa Clara University School of Law. 153 - Glasgow Financial Alliance for Net Zero, GFANZ. 155 - MSCI, Moskowitz. 156 - Refinitiv, S&P Trucost, RobecoSam, Sustainalytics, ISS ESG, MSCI ESG, Vigeo Eiris, EcoVadis, Minerva Analytics. 158 – ERISA. 159

- Equator Principles Financial Institutions (EPFIs). 160 – the Latin American Quality Institute. 161 - ISO (International Organization for Standardization), London Stock Exchange and the Financial Reporting Commission, the Cadbury Commission, BCCI, Polly Peck. 162 – Robert Maxwell's Mirror Group, Francis Menassa (JAR Capital), Dow Jones Sustainability Index, the FTSE4Good Index, the London Stock Exchange and Financial Times, the MSCI ESG Indices, the GRESB benchmarks. 163 - Image and Illustration Graphs: ESG Criteria used by Sustainable Investors by US / SIF, UN Sustainability - Compact Goals. 164 - FlexJobs report, ADP Report. 170 – CBS, Design Thinking, Idea. 173 – Intuit, P&G, NASA, Kaggle. 178 - Image and Illustration Graphs: The Lean Startup Canvas - Developed by Alexander Osterwalder, Google Business Model Canvas by The Business Model Analyst. 180 – Douglas Engelbart, Bill Clinton, Bob Taylor, Alan Kay, Alto, Macintosh. Alexander Fleming, penicillin. 181 - Darwin's theory, Thomas Malthus, Charles Lyell, Watson and Crick's discovery of DNA. 182 - Airbnb, SpaceX, Procter and Gamble, 3M. 183 – Kodak, Chester Carlson, Joe Wilson - President of the Haloid Company. 184 - Bain & Co.'s Chris Zook in Profit from The Core. 187 – Disney, Comcast, News Corp, Renault, Honda, Vespa. 188 - Andrew Lippman, MIT's Media Lab, Jason Hong. 189 – Sam Lehman-Wilzig, Bar-Ilan University, Faisal A. Nasr. 190 - Frank Feather, AI-Future, Paola Ricaurte, Harvard's Berkman Klein Center for Internet & Society, Arthur Asa Berger, San Francisco State University. 191 – Sharon Sputz, Columbia University Data Science Institute, Jeremy Foote, Northwestern University, National Security Agency, GDPR, Christian Schoon, Future Impacts. 192 - Tim Bray, Daniel Estrada, New Jersey Institute of Technology, Sasha Costanza-Chock. 193 - John F. Kennedy. 196 - Financial Times, Caspar de Bono, Discovery, Adrian Gore. 197 - Pete Worden. 199 – Harold Goddijn, TomTom. 203 - Bell Labs, Twitter, Twilio. 205 – Max Jerneck, the Stockholm School of Economics, Jimmy Carter, Ronald Reagan. 207 – Greg Nemet, the University of Wisconsin. 208 - the Niskanen Institute, Samuel Hammond. 211 – Reid Hoffman, PayPal, Linkedin, Bank of America Research Graphs 212 – Image and Illustration Graphs: Startup Story in the european innovation academy. 216 - GoDaddy.com, Google Domain, Web.com. 217 – Image and Illustration Graphs: The Startup Curve by Paul Graham and AVC. 225 – Drew Houston is the CEO of Dropbox. 232 - Shigeo Shingo. 251 - Bain & Company. 253 - Stefan Debois. 264 – Instagram, Marc Andreessen. 282 - Sequoia, A16z. 283 - Softbank, Google Ventures, Iconiq Capital. 293 - Venture Capital Association. 301 – Image and Illustration Graphs: The World's Billionaires by Forbes. 324 – Image and Illustration Graphs: Facebook Users by Pew Research Center. 325 - Image and Illustration Graphs: Use of Online Platforms by Pew Research Center. 333 – Startup Fundraising Worksheet by Founder Institute. 341 - Yokum Taku of Wilson Sonsini. 348 – Top Angels Group and Venture Capital Partners by CB Insights. 349 – Top Unicorn Investors, Corporate Ventures and Bloggers by CB Insights. 357 – Image and Illustration Graphs: Last Rounds before exit by CB Insights with largest tech exits. 358 – Top Consumer and Medical Devices Tech Acquisitions by CB Insights. 359 – M&A vs Financing Alternatives by Sparring Partners. 362 - Chris Gilbert, former CEO of Ubiquisys (Cisco). 368 – Silicon Valley Bank, Pitchbook, Techcrunch, Ivan Gaviria of Gunderson Dettmer. 378 - David Pakman of Venrock. 382 – Angels Investments Performance by The Ewing Marion Kauffman Foundation. 383 – Venture Capital Investments Performance by Cambridge Associates. 384 – Fund and Valuation Performance by Cambridge Associates. 385 – Dow Jones Ventures Sources. 386 – Startup Post Exit Listing – IPO by FacSet and Nasdaq. 387 – Post IPO Performance by FactSet and Nasdaq - Ipsos - Carta.

Disclosure

The contents of this book, including any reference, quote, or assessment presented herein do provide accurate and authoritative insights within the subject matter covered but do not constitute investment advice or legal recommendation. As such, this book does not contain all information that a prospective investor may desire in evaluating an investment strategy or individual investment.

Each investor must rely on his or her own examination of an investment strategy or individual investment, including the merits and risks involved in making an investment decision. Prior to making an investment decision, a prospective investor should consult his or her own legal counsel, accountants, and other professional advisors to evaluate the merits of an investment strategy or individual investment. Additionally, any discussion of the past performance of any investment strategy or individual investment should not be relied on as a guarantee of future performance, and no warranty of future performance is intended or implied.

The author and its publisher are not liable to you or a third party for any indirect, consequential, exemplary, incidental, special, or punitive damages arising from your use of this book, and all contents are presented as is without warranty of any kind either express or implied.

ABOUT THE AUTHOR

This book was initiated during Henri's one of many across northern America road trips while venturing into a remote part that is strikingly reminiscent of outer space, and much less as another state, country, or even continent. The colossal gaps of disconnect between east, west, and Middle of nowhere, led Henri to make it his mission to write every insight he has in a way that enables anyone located anywhere to innovate and fund their ventures.

Henri Swan is a firm believer that "Knowledge Without Action Worth Nothing" and each "Story has Three Sides – Yours, Theirs and the Truth", this is why he spend years crafting this book to share first-rate knowledge and expertise along know-how with do-how accumulated over 20 years of being a partner, friend, and neighbor in "Silicon Valley, San Francisco" and Cambridge, MA to Tech Billionaires, Investors, and Founders, along prominent Subject-matter-experts, Professors, Investors, and thoughts leaders from Stanford, MIT, Harvard, USC, UC system, NYU, and Columbia University to list few.

While being a leader at various tier-one organizations, including Stanford, Accenture, and Google, he advised many Startups and Unicorns backed by Sequoia, Andreessen, Softbank, Google Ventures, and many others through their IPO or M&A exit; he executed the entire Innovation Cycle "idea through exit" ranging from $1m to over $10 Billion Innovation Initiatives at Fortune 500 companies. He is the inventor of the On-Demand Innovation Ventures Standard which is the prerequisite foundation of Impact Investing.

As a developer, technologist, investor, and venture capital insider, his Insights capture the collective intelligence of Silicon Valley's broad ecosystem, where he attended, sponsored, and spoke at over 1,000 Tech Conferences, including Startup Pitch or Demo Day at top accelerators and incubators, along top 100 thought leaders in tech and venture capital space, encompassing emerging deep tech domains, across industries, including Digital, Enterprise, Consumer, FinTech, Media, Cybersecurity, Health, BioTech, CleanTech, EdTech, AgroTech, FoodTech, Mobility, SpaceTech, Hardware, 4D, AR-VR, Shipping and Smart Manufacturing.

CLOSING REMARKS

For most people, Innovation is a word with a broad definition and the false narrative that, "To Innovate you must be in Silicon Valley and backed *(blessed by)* top Venture Capital to be worthy of Innovation".

Perpetuated by the intertwined commercial media and Silicon Valley elites to maintain the cycle of having global startups compete for few available funding, often bundled with dictated and unfavorable terms *(marketed as the industry standard)*.

This book is about reversing that, by leveling the playing ground to enable anyone anywhere to innovate, as long you are driven, flexible, and can adapt to the fast-moving environment of innovation and venture investing.

This book shall be your standard execution roadmap and regularly consulted reference manual as you evolve during your innovation journey, regardless of your role as a founder, investor, or corporate manager.

www.ingramcontent.com/pod-product-compliance
Lightning Source LLC
LaVergne TN
LVHW052025200926
848481LV00005B/1592